Residential
Interior Design

Residential Interior Design

A Guide to Planning Spaces

MAUREEN MITTON, CID, NCIDQ
COURTNEY NYSTUEN, AIA EMERITUS

With CAD Illustrations by Melissa Brewer, Shelley Pecha, and Jamey Bowe

THIRD EDITION

WILEY

Contents

Acknowledgments

Having worked in the design portion of the construction industry for many years, I am well aware of the collaborative nature of the industry. Throughout the duration of every project (from conception to occupancy), everyone needs to rely on the competence of those whose work precedes one's own. Short of that, it all starts to fall apart.

Another component of a successful project is an owner/client who clearly communicates his or her needs, collaborates on a vision of what could be, and is willing to take some calculated risks. I have had some outstanding clients over the years; I will not compromise their privacy by listing names, but those clients all have my ongoing respect and gratitude.

As this new edition goes to press, I am again reminded of the importance of collaboration. As you, the user of this book, look ahead to your career, my hope is that you will find and be able to work with good collaborators.

And there are those rare collaborators who go above and beyond. When I became disabled in the last few weeks prior to the deadline for the completion of this edition, it was my longtime colleague, collaborator, and coauthor who stepped and said, in essence, "you concentrate on getting well and I'll finish it up." We both knew that was going to be no small feat. One does not find that breed of collaborator on every corner.

Thank you, Maureen Mitton.

Courtney W. Nystuen

From the beginning it was important to me to work on this project with Courtney. He taught this subject matter (and much more) for years and educated so many design students during his academic tenure; I simply had to find a way to keep him connected with students. He has also kept a full range of professional architectural projects going throughout his academic career and into his alleged retirement.

Courtney's ability to consider the information and content most useful to students and present it in an approachable manner made this book happen. Working with Courtney has been delightful. How he puts up with me will forever remain a mystery.

Melissa Brewer did excellent, meticulous CAD work on the first edition of this book. Shelley Pecha stepped in to do new CAD and Revit drawing revisions for the second edition as well as for this edition. As always, Shelley's speedy and organized response and work are much appreciated! Thanks to Jamey Bowe of River Valley Architects for his work on some of the CAD illustrations in Chapter 8.

Thank you to Seth Schwartz and Melinda Noack at Wiley for their help and patience.

My family, as usual, paid the price on this project. Thank you all for putting up with my months of work on this project. Finally, I have to say thank you to Courtney Nystuen, one of my favorite people, for making this book a reality. I only hope that we have moved beyond "nice try" into "almost excellent" territory.

Maureen Mitton

Residential
Interior Design

CHAPTER 1

Introduction

Every cubic inch of space is a miracle.

Walt Whitman, *Leaves of Grass*, "Miracles"

WHAT THIS BOOK IS ABOUT

This book is meant to serve as a primer on space planning for rooms and spaces in a home. Related information regarding codes, mechanical and electrical systems, and a variety of additional factors that impact each type of room or space is also provided. In addition, this book includes information about accessible design in each chapter in order to provide a cohesive view of residential accessibility. This new edition includes updated 2015 International Residential Code information and additional updates.

Intended as a reference for use in the design process, this book can aid in teaching and understanding the planning of residential spaces. Most chapters follow a similar format, starting with an overview of the particular room or space and related issues of accessibility, followed by information about room-specific furnishings and appliances. Chapters continue with information about sizes and clearances, organizational flow, related codes and constraints, and issues regarding electrical, mechanical, plumbing, and basic lighting.

This book is meant to aid students and designers in understanding the amount of space that is minimally necessary in order for rooms to function usefully. Examples of larger spaces are also given, but at its heart, this book is intended to show students how to use space wisely and make good use of space throughout the dwelling. With clear knowledge about minimums, designers and students of design can learn when it is appropriate to exceed such standards for a variety of reasons that reflect specific project criteria based on client needs, budget, site, and other constraints.

This book is intended as an introduction to the topics covered with the aim of familiarizing the reader with the basic concepts so that he or she might move forward in design education or on to additional research in certain areas. To that end, an annotated references section is provided at the end of each chapter. Thinking of the information provided in each chapter as basic building blocks that allow for the discovery of the issues involved is a helpful approach in using this book (Figure 1-1).

There is much that goes into the design of a dwelling that is not covered in this book; our intent is to focus on the use and

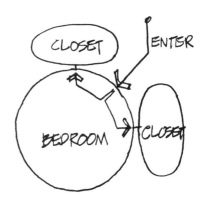

Figure 1-1 This book covers the design of houses using a basic room-by-room approach.

design of individual rooms (again, a building-block approach) so that the reader will have the core information required to understand the design of these individual spaces. This basic informational approach may bring up questions about the role of the interior designer versus the role of the architect. Clearly, the design of the totality of the structure is the role of the architect (or engineer); however, in many cases, the interior designer is taking an increasingly larger role in the design of rooms and spaces.

Interior designers engaged in renovation work can take a lead role in the design of the interior architecture of a space, with a significant hand in the design of a room or many rooms. This is in contrast to notions of the interior designer as the person in charge of materials and furnishings selections only.

The authors believe that interior designers and design students must be well versed in the aspects of residential design covered in this book. For example, readers will note that the detailed kitchen and bathroom information contained in this book is applicable to remodeling as well as to new construction.

AN OVERVIEW: QUALITY AND QUANTITY

Readers may note that, throughout this book, the authors mention the evolution of the use of rooms, room sizes, and the growth of the overall size of the American home. It's worth noting that the authors have a bias toward careful consideration of the *quality* of design rather than the *quantity* of space in a given home. We hope to make clear that the successful design of space requires careful consideration of the real needs of clients measured against budgetary, code, climate, and site restrictions—all of which require careful development of a project program prior to the beginning of the actual design of the project.

The last hundred years have brought dramatic changes related to the public perception of the design, furnishing, and size of the American house. According to the National Association of Home Builders (NAHB), the "typical" American house built in 1900 was between 700 and 1200 square feet (65 and 111 m²), with two or three bedrooms and one or no bathrooms. The average home built in 1950 was 983 square feet (91 m²), with 66 percent of homes containing two bedrooms or fewer. These earlier homes are quite a contrast to the 2736-square-foot (245-m²) average found in new single-family homes completed in the first quarter of 2015 (Figure 1-2).

The authors argue that a larger house is not necessarily a better house and that designing a house that works well on a functional level is more important than mere size in creating a useful and pleasant environment. Additionally, large single-family homes are currently out of the financial reach of many citizens, driving many into the rental market. Furthermore, such large single-family homes are seen by some as wasteful in a time when issues of sustainability are increasingly engaging many across the globe.

Consideration of housing size and use of related resources is not unique to this publication. Architect Sarah Susanka's book *The Not So Big House* has proven very popular, helped many people consider quality over quantity of space, and had an impact on the design of many homes (1998). *A Pattern Language*, by Christopher Alexander and colleagues, an earlier book considered seminal by many, has at its core the notion that spaces should be designed for the way people really live and that good design can be accessible for all (1977).

The notion of seeking quality of design rather than quantity of space is shared by many, and yet larger and larger houses continue to be built to house very small family groups. This dichotomy suggests that two opposing popular views of space exist. Although the architect Philip Johnson was once quoted as saying "architecture is the art of wasting space," clearly that was a bit tongue-in-cheek, and we concur more with Walt Whitman's notion that "every cubic inch of space is a miracle"—or should be.

Tiny Houses

While the average home in the United States has reached a new high in terms of square footage, the "tiny house" movement is gaining momentum. Roots of this approach can be found in the work of Jay Shafer, author of *The Small House Book*. Marianne Cusato, designer of the Katrina Cottages, has also been instrumental in igniting this movement. Cusato's Katrina Cottages were 308 square feet (28.6 m²) and designed as an alternative to the FEMA trailers used to house people who had lost their homes in Hurricane Katrina. The financial crisis of 2007–08, the limited affordability of housing, and a growing interest in sustainability and energy efficiency have combined to create a wave of interest in micro-homes.

Current building and zoning codes can create obstacles to inhabiting these micro-homes. Most building codes require a residence to meet minimum square footage requirements, but micro-homes are often well under this size. Placing the structure on wheels allows the home to meet the legal definition of a recreational vehicle or camper. However, many communities have zoning regulations or laws prohibiting long-term occupation of campers on residential lots. Additionally, some RV parks do not welcome tiny homes. Currently there is an absence of clear legal status of these tiny homes, or legal limitations on their use. Given the growing interest in the concept and issues with affordability and efficiency of traditional homes, the legal landscape may change to become more accepting of this type of dwelling.

The remainder of this chapter covers issues that relate to housing and serve as an introduction to the concepts that are covered in each chapter. In addition, basic interior design graphics are covered as an introduction to chapter illustrations.

HUMAN BEHAVIOR AND HOUSING

Environmental designers—including interior designers—benefit from gaining an understanding of human behavior as it relates to privacy, territoriality, and other issues connected to

1950	1970	1990	2007	2015
983 SQ. FT. (91 m²)	1,500 SQ. FT. (139 m²)	2,080 SQ. FT. (193 m²)	2,521 SQ. FT. (234 m²)	2,736 SQ. FT. (254m²)

Figure 1-2 The average new home in the United States has grown in size over time—despite the fact that family size has grown smaller. However, larger is not necessarily better, and well-planned spaces need not be excessively large. Given land and construction costs, as well as environmental concerns, smaller houses may be a necessity in the future. Numbers for square footage shown do not include garage spaces.

the built environment studied. Privacy can be defined as the ability to control our interactions with others.

According to Jon Lang, "The ability of the layout of the environment to afford privacy through territorial control is important because it allows the fulfillment of some basic human needs" (1987). Lang goes on to say that the single-family detached home "provides a clear hierarchy of territories from public to private."

Lang also states that "differences in the need for privacy are partially attributable to social group attitudes." He continues, "Norms of privacy for any group represent adaptation to what they can afford within the socioeconomic system of which they are a part." From Lang's comments, we can learn that the need for privacy is consistent but that privacy norms vary based on culture and socioeconomic status.

The notion of territory is closely linked to privacy in terms of human behavior. There is a range of theoretical work concerning the exact name and number of territories within the home. One, developed by Clare Cooper, describes the house as divided into two components: the intimate interior and the public exterior (1967). Interestingly, Cooper (now Cooper Marcus) later wrote *House as a Mirror of Self: Exploring the Deeper Meaning of Home* (1995), which traces the psychology of the relationship we have with the physical environment of our homes, and in which she refers to work being done by Rachel Sebba and Arza Churchman in studying territories within the home. Sebba and Churchman have identified areas within the home as those used by the whole family, those belonging to a subgroup (such as siblings or parents), and those belonging to an individual, such as a bedroom, a portion of a room, or a bed (1986). Figures 1-3a and 1-3b illustrate various theoretical approaches to territory and privacy.

The term *defensible space* was coined by Oscar Newman in relation to his study of neighborhood safety and refers to "a range of mechanisms—real and symbolic barriers . . . that combine to bring an environment under the control of its residents." Defensible space, as described by Newman, includes *public, semipublic, semiprivate,* and *private territories* (1972). Newman's work includes studies of various forms of housing (single-family attached, detached, high-rise, etc.) and the influence of the building type and design on territoriality and safety.

While there is variety based on housing type, Newman defines public spaces as streets, sidewalks, and those areas near or adjacent to the dwelling not possessed by any individual. Semipublic spaces include those areas that may be publicly owned but are cared for by homeowners, such as planted parkways adjacent to sidewalks. Semiprivate spaces can include yards or spaces owned in association. (Some theoreticians include porches and foyers in this category.) Private territory is the interior of a home, fenced areas within a yard, or the interior of a student's dorm room. Private interiors are seen as distinct from private exteriors in Newman's work. In addition, Newman pointed to the need for some type of buffer between the public world and private interior.

In the years since Newman's original work defining defensible space and related territories, his theories have come under some criticism; however, his work continues to have implications for planners, architects, and interior designers because taking these concepts into account in designing homes can help to create spaces in which residents feel safe and have genuine control over their immediate environment. See Figures 1-3a and 1-3b.

In *A Pattern Language,* Christopher Alexander and his colleagues describe territories as falling along an *intimacy gradient,* which is a sequence of spaces within the building containing public, semipublic, and private areas. The bedroom and bathroom are the most private, and the porch or entrance space the most public. Alexander writes, "Unless the spaces in a building

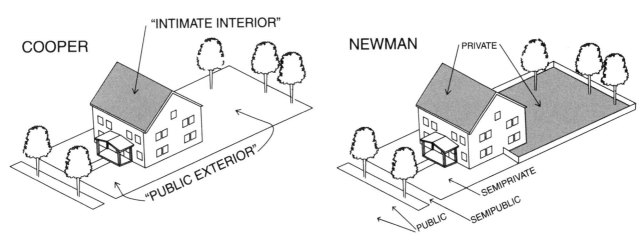

Figure 1-3a An illustration of territories as identified by theoreticians. Cooper identifies a public exterior and an intimate interior. Newman identifies public territories, which are not possessed or claimed; semipublic territories such as sidewalks, which are not owned but are seen as being possessed nonetheless; semiprivate territories, which are shared by owners or seen as being under surveillance by neighbors, such as front yards or shared swimming pools; and private territories, such as the private interior of a house or a fenced-in backyard.

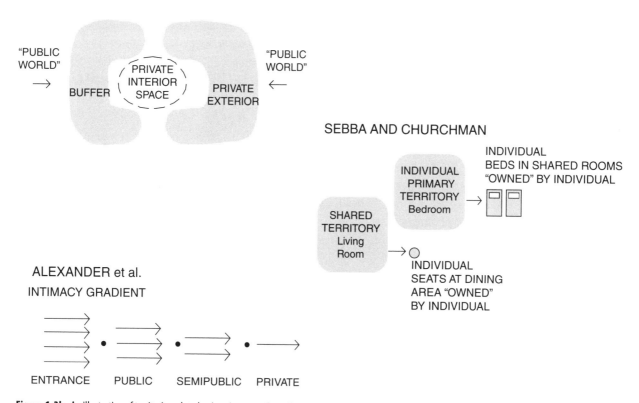

NEWMAN

"PUBLIC WORLD" → BUFFER PRIVATE INTERIOR SPACE PRIVATE EXTERIOR ← "PUBLIC WORLD"

SEBBA AND CHURCHMAN

SHARED TERRITORY Living Room

INDIVIDUAL PRIMARY TERRITORY Bedroom

→ INDIVIDUAL BEDS IN SHARED ROOMS "OWNED" BY INDIVIDUAL

→ INDIVIDUAL SEATS AT DINING AREA "OWNED" BY INDIVIDUAL

ALEXANDER et al.
INTIMACY GRADIENT

ENTRANCE   PUBLIC   SEMIPUBLIC   PRIVATE

Figure 1-3b An illustration of territories related to interior space. Oscar Newman described the need for some type of buffer between the public world and private interior territories. Sebba and Churchman describe areas within a home that are used by all as "shared territory," with limited privacy; "individual primary territories" are those seen as belonging to individuals, such as a bedroom, which becomes the private sanctuary of the individual. Alexander et al. describe an intimacy gradient, with the most public spaces related to the entrance leading to a sequence of increasingly private spaces.

are arranged in a sequence which corresponds to their degrees of privateness, the visits made by strangers, friends, guests, clients, family will always be a little awkward." The intimacy gradient is shown in Figure 1-3b. Chapter 2 provides additional information about public and private spaces as they relate to entry spaces.

Personal space is a term introduced by Robert Sommer in the 1960s. According to Sommer, "personal space refers to an area with an invisible boundary surrounding the person's body into which intruders may not come" (1969). See Figure 1-4a.

A similar-sounding term, *personal distance*, expresses a different concept and comes from work done by Edward Hall, an anthropologist who coined the term *proxemics*—for the "interrelated observations and theories of man's use of space as a specialized elaboration of culture" (1966). Hall identified four distinct body distances or boundaries that people will maintain in varying social situations: *intimate* (0 to 18 inches [0 to 0.5 m]), *personal-casual* (1½ to 4 feet [0.5 to 1.2 m]), *social-consultative* (4 to 12 feet [1.2 to 3.7 m]), and *public* (12 feet [3.7 m] and beyond). Each of the four types of boundaries has a close phase and a far phase, as shown in Figure 1-4b. Hall found that while actual spatial boundaries vary based on cultural differences, the concepts of intimate, personal, social, and public distances are consistent cross-culturally.

Figure 1-4a Sommer's personal space, which "refers to an area with an invisible boundary surrounding the person's body into which intruders may not come."

Hall's term *personal distance* refers to the distance maintained between friends and family members for discussion and interaction, whereas Sommer's term *personal space* refers to the invisible, territorial boundary around each person. Similarly, Hall's *intimate space* is a "bubble" of space around a person that can be entered only by intimates, whereas *social-consultative spaces* are those in which people feel comfortable engaging in routine social interaction for business or in conversation with strangers. *Public space* is that where there is little interaction and people are generally comfortable ignoring one another; this distance also allows one to flee when danger is sensed.

Considering Hall's spatial boundaries can be useful for designers in planning living spaces. For example, most casual social interaction takes place within personal distances. Later portions of this book focus on specific room-related dimensional information for encouraging interaction and creating privacy. It is also worth noting that in designing public and commercial spaces that encourage interaction and help users attain privacy, the designer will find it helpful to reference the work of social scientists such as Hall, Newman, Lang, and others. For those seeking additional information about environmental psychology and the related work of other social scientists, the references at the end of this chapter include related bibliographic information.

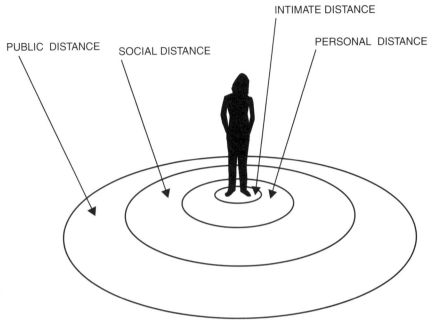

Figure 1-4b Hall's personal boundaries or body distances. Hall identified four distinct body distances or boundaries that people will maintain in varying social situations:

Intimate: 0 to 18 inches (0 to 0.5 m); *close phase* 0 to 6 inches (0 to 0.2 m), *far phase* 6 to 18 inches (0.2 to 0.5 m)
Personal-casual: 1½ to 4 feet (0.5 to 1.2 m); *close phase* 1½ to 2½ feet (0.5 to 0.8 m), *far phase* 2½ to 4 feet (0.8 to 1.2 m)
Social-consultative: 4 to 12 feet (1.2 to 3.7 m); *close phase* 4 to 7 feet (1.2 to 2.1 m), *far phase* 7 to 12 feet (2.1 to 3.7 m)
Public: 12 feet and beyond (3.7 m and beyond); *close phase* 12 to 25 feet (3.7 to 7.6 m), *far phase* 25 feet (7.6 m) and beyond

AN OVERVIEW OF CHAPTER TOPICS

Generally, the remainder of this first chapter is organized in a manner that is similar to most of the following chapters covering individual rooms and spaces. This chapter serves as an introduction to the definitions, concepts, and organizing principles that will be used throughout this book. Topics are as follows:

Accessibility, universal design, and visitability

Sustainability (also listed in relationship to specific items as necessary and not covered in detail in rooms that do not present specific challenges)

Ergonomics and required clearances

Organizational flow

Related codes and constraints

Electrical and mechanical

Lighting (while lighting is clearly part of the electrical system, it is separated here for purposes of organization)

INTRODUCTION TO ACCESSIBILITY NOTES

Throughout this book, content related to accessible design is treated visually similarly to this section in order to make it easy to reference.

ACCESSIBILITY, UNIVERSAL DESIGN, VISITABILITY, AND USABLITY

The terms *accessible design* and *universal design* are used interchangeably by some; however, for the purposes of this book they are considered distinct. The nuances involved are discussed below.

The term *accessible* was initially used to describe environments that do not present physical barriers for people with physical limitations, such as wheelchair users. The University of Washington defines accessible design as

a design process in which the needs of people with disabilities are specifically considered. Accessibility sometimes refers to the characteristic that products, services, and facilities can be independently used by people with a variety of disabilities.

According to Dr. Edward Steinfeld of the Center for Inclusive Design and Environmental Access (IDEA Center):

> Accessible design allows people with disabilities to demonstrate that they have capabilities—to work, manage a household, marry and raise children [—that] they can play a vital role in the community (1996).

Generally, the design of private, single-family homes is not mandated by any current accessibility regulations except as noted later in this chapter. However, many homeowners seek residences that are accessible, either because they plan to "age in place" in the home (defined as growing older in one's home without having to relocate) or because they or a family member have current needs that warrant the design of accessible spaces. These two distinct scenarios present two distinct design criteria.

In cases where current physical or other limitations create the need for accessible spaces, the design should address the specific needs of the owner or family member. For example, designing a home for a specific person who uses a wheelchair requires meeting a set of appropriate criteria and guidelines, whereas designing a home for a person with a vision impairment requires considering a different set of standards and guidelines.

In contrast, designing a home for aging in place or for general accessibility requires making design decisions based on basic accessibility standards and guidelines. These are presented throughout this book as part of the body of each chapter, set apart and identified as an Accesiblity Note (as this section is set apart). Incorporating accessibility information for each area is intended to provide readers with a comprehensive view of accessible design. Information about regulations and standards for accessibility is provided in the "Related Codes and Constraints" section of this chapter.

In cases where a home is intended to be wheelchair accessible, adequate clearance space must be provided for the chair as the user accesses items for daily activities; in addition, appropriate circulation space and turning space must be provided. See Figures 2-14b and 2-14c for specific information about wheelchair-accessible circulation and clearance requirements. Additional detailed information is provided in each room-based chapter within these Accessibility Note sections.

The concept of universal design grew, in part, out of the accessible design movement, but it is not synonymous with accessibility. Ron Mace, an architect, product designer, and educator, is credited with coining the term;

he also established what is now the Center for Universal Design at North Carolina State University. According to the IDEA Center (SUNY at Buffalo), universal design can be defined as

> an approach to the design of all products and environments to be as usable as possible by as many people as possible regardless of age, ability or situation [and that] results in better design and avoids the stigmatizing quality of accessible features that have been added on late in the design process or after it is complete.

Additional insight is provided by the Center for Universal Design at North Carolina State University:

> The intent of universal design is to simplify life for everyone by making products, communications, and the built environment more usable by as many people as possible at little or no extra cost. Universal design benefits people of all ages and abilities.

An example of universal design are lever door handles, which work well for people with limited hand strength but also work well for as many other people as possible. The lever design does not limit use but extends it to the greatest possible number of people.

One approach to universal design in the home is to provide *adaptable* elements designed to offer greater flexibility for a range of occupants. For example, counters can be made so that they are adjustable to adapt for users of varying heights (including those using seats and wheelchairs). Adaptable cabinets can be designed with fronts and bases that can be removed to create a clear area underneath for use by someone in a wheelchair. Illustrations of both of these examples can be found in Chapter 4.

Some common features to include to create a home that incorporates universal design principles are as follows: no stairs (at the entry or within the home); wide doorways to allow for wheelchairs and general ease of movement; wide hallways for wheelchairs and ease of movement; extra floor space, especially in areas such as bathrooms and kitchens and around closets and utility areas, allowing for wheelchair use as well as extra space for movement. Following the specific requirements for space for wheelchair movement included in the accessibility section of each chapter can aid in the creation of a home that meets universal design principles because it is usable by a wide range of people.

Visitability is a concept that shares some commonalities with universal design concepts; it refers to creating homes that can be visited or accessed by people with physical disabilities and is sometimes called basic home access or inclusive home design. Visitable residences must meet three important criteria:

■ At least one zero-step entrance approached by an accessible route on a firm surface no steeper than 1:12, proceeding from a driveway or public sidewalk.

■ Wide passage doors: all main-floor interior doors, including the bathroom, must provide 32 inches (813 mm) of clear passage space.

■ At least a half bath/powder room on the main floor (a full bath on the main floor is ideal).

Eleanor Smith is a founder of Concrete Change, a group that advocates to have visitability ordinances federally mandated or adopted by various jurisdictions. To date, a number of jurisdictions, including Austin, Texas; Vancouver, British Columbia; and Pima County, Arizona, have adopted visitability ordinances. Other jurisdictions have adopted visitability ordinances for residences built using city funds. (It is worth noting, however, that Pima County and Austin allow 32-inch [813-mm] doors, providing only 30 inches [762 mm] of clear space.) While visitability is a distinct concept, its principles also can be seen as universal design because visitable spaces are intended to be used by more people than standard private housing, making them meet the definition of being "as usable as possible by as many people as possible regardless of age, ability, or situation."

Of the three criteria for visitability, the most difficult to achieve nationally is the zero-step entrance requirement. This could prove problematic in parts of the country where basements are commonplace. Typically, the main floor of a house with a basement is 18 to 20 inches (457 to 508 mm) above ground level, which could require a significant ramp for a zero-step entry. In some cases, through careful building placement and site grading, the driveway and sidewalk to the entrance can be designed with a slope of not more than 1:12 for a zero-step entry. However, recent surveys of potential homeowners and architects have shown significant interest in accessibility, and using the criteria for visitablity is a helpful first step in creating a more accessible home for both homeowner and visitors.

Usablity is a word that has meanings related to accessibility. The International Organization for Standardization (ISO) has defined usability as

> the extent to which a product can be used by specified users to achieve specified goals with effectiveness, efficiency and satisfaction in a specified context of use.

Usability, also called usable design, can be tested and measured. While most often used in relation to describing electronics and communication, usability testing can be employed to test a range of products and environments. Although usablity shares goals with accessibility and universal design, usability studies do not necessarily include testing of people with a range of abilities and are not necessarily conducted for the purpose of achieving universal design. According to the University of Washington's DO-IT website (2013), if "designers apply universal design principles, with a special focus on accessibility for people with disabilities, and if usability experts routinely include people with a variety of disabilities in usability tests, more products will be accessible to and usable by everyone."

Table 1-1 Differences among Accessibility, Universal Design, Visitabiliy, and Usabillity

Term	Definition	Comment
Accessibility	The extent to which design specifically considers the needs of people with disabilities. Accessibility sometimes refers to the characteristic that products, services, and facilities can be independently used by people with a variety of disabilities.	Accessible and universal design both address the needs of users beyond those considered "average" or "typical."
Universal design	The design of all products and environments to be as usable as possible by as many people as possible regardless of age, ability, or situation.	Accessible and universal design both address the needs of users beyond those considered "average" or "typical."
Visitability	The extent to which new homes are designed so that they can be visited or accessed by people with physical disabilities.	Visitable homes incorporate concepts of universal design in that they can be used by a wider range of people than standard housing.
Usability	The extent to which products are easy and efficient to use.	While concerned with creating efficiency and ease of use, usability testing may not consider accessibility or the universal design of products because it may be focused on one specific type of user.

Introduction to Sustainability Notes

Throughout this book, content related to sustainability is treated visually similarly to this, in order to make it easy to reference. This section provides an overview, including background and historical information related to sustainability.

According to Alice Rawsthorn (2010),

> While most designers would agree that sustainability is important, they're very likely to disagree about everything else to do with it. What exactly is sustainable design? What constitutes success? And failure? On what criteria? Different designers may well give very different answers to all of those questions, and more.

As the previous quote indicates, perhaps more than any current area of design, definitions of sustainable design and green design seem to cause confusion, consternation, contradiction, and a search for clear answers. One way to understand issues of sustainability is to clearly define some commonly used terms and to outline areas of agreement and disagreement.

According to Louise Jones, writing in *Environmentally Responsible Design* (2008), "*sustainable design* suggests a macro perspective on environmental responsibility—protection of the health of and welfare of *global ecosystems*," whereas "*green design* suggests a micro perspective," related to protection of health and welfare of the people in the "built environment." And, according to Jones, *environmentally responsible design* (ERD) is "a combination of green and sustainable design."

Francis Ching (2008), an architect, educator, and author of seminal design books, has defined *sustainability* as "a whole-systems approach to development that encompasses the notion of green building but also addresses broader social, ethical and economic issues, as well as the community context of buildings."

Both Ching and Jones trace the roots of definitions of sustainable design and development to the 1987 United Nations World Commission on Environment and Development. The commission, also known as the Brundtland Commission after Gro Harlem Brundtland, its chairman, defined *sustainable development* as follows:

> Development that meets the needs of the present without compromising the ability of future generations to meet their own needs. It contains within it two key concepts:
>
> the concept of "needs," in particular the essential needs of the world's poor, to which overriding priority should be given
>
> the idea of limitations imposed by the state of technology and social organization on the environment's ability to meet present and future needs

Internationally, in 1990 England established the Building Research Establishment Environmental Assessment Method (BREEAM), the first environmental assessment tool to be used internationally. The tool was created to be used in analysis of new and existing buildings in terms of review and improvement of office buildings. BREEAM has been used as a model for systems developed in other countries. In addition, several European countries have joined efforts to define methodology for life-cycle analysis of buildings.

The World Green Building Council (WorldGBC) is a network of international green building councils that seeks "to promote local green building actions and address global issues such as climate change."

In seeking out helpful definitions, it is worth noting that the U.S. Environmental Protection Agency (EPA, 2010) has defined *green building* as

> The practice of creating structures and using processes that are environmentally responsible and resource-efficient throughout a building's life-cycle from siting to design, construction, operation, maintenance, renovation and deconstruction. . . . Green building is also known as a sustainable or high performance building.

The EPA (2010) also indicates that

> Green buildings are designed to reduce the overall impact of the environment on human health and the natural environment by:
>
> Efficiently using energy, water, and other resources
>
> Protecting occupant health and improving employee productivity
>
> Reducing waste, pollution and environmental degradation

According to the EPA, important developments in the United States related to green building history include those listed in Table 1-2.

The EPA has also identified the items covered in Table 1-3 as impacts of the built environment.

As one evaluates products and design solutions, it is worth measuring their impact as indicated in Table 1-3. This means not only assessing initial product sourcing or production but also considering how the demolition (deconstruction) may impact the environment.

Reviewing history and defining terms related to sustainability can provide a context and a framework for understanding this rather complex aspect of current design practice. Based on the definitions found in the preceding paragraphs, for the remainder of this book, we will use the following definitions.

Defining Sustainability

Sustainability can be seen as a "whole-systems approach to development that encompasses the notion of green building but also addresses broader social, ethical and economic issues." (Ching, 2008)

Table 1-2 Recent Green Building History in the United States

Historical Development	Year
American Institute of Architects (AIA) formed the Committee on the Environment (COTE).	1989
Environmental Resource Guide published by AIA, funded by EPA.	1992
EPA and the U.S. Department of Energy launched the Energy Star program.	1992
Executive Order 13123: Greening the Government through Efficient Energy Management.	1992
First local green building program introduced in Austin, Texas.	1992
U.S. Green Building Council (USGBC) founded.	1993
USGBC started Leadership in Energy and Environmental Design (LEED version 1.0 pilot program).	1998
First commercial-scale net-zero building project completed at Oberlin College, in Ohio.	2000
Energy Policy Act: includes building standards for federal buildings.	2005
The Energy Independence and Security Act of 2007.	2007
EPA adopted a new Green Building Strategy guide for EPA buildings.	2008
The International Code Council began development of the International Green Construction Code (IGCC), a model code jointly sponsored by AIA, ASTM International, ASHRAE, and IES.	2009
American Institute of Architects (AIA) created the 2030 Commitment, asking organizations to pledge to advance the goal of carbon-neutral buildings by 2030.	2009
2010 California Green Building Standards Code released (updated in 2013).	2010
ASHRAE (American Society of Heating Refrigerating and Air-Conditioning Engineers) released Standard 189.1: Standard for the Design of High-Performance Green Buildings. Initial draft created in 2007.	2010
The International Code Council (ICC) released the 2012 International Green Construction Code (IgCC), a model code jointly sponsored by AIA, ASTM International, ASHRAE, and IES. An updated version was approved in 2015.	2012
USGBC: Leadership in Energy and Environmental Design, LEED version approved.	2015

Table 1-3 Environmental Impacts of the Built Environment According to the EPA

Aspects of Built Environment	Consumption	Environmental Effects	Ultimate Effects
Siting (building site) Design Construction Operation Maintenance Renovation Deconstruction	Energy Water Materials Natural resources	Waste Air pollution Water pollution Indoor pollution Heat islands Storm-water runoff Noise	Harm to human health Environmental degradation Loss of resources

Green building (or green design) is the design of buildings that are efficient in the use of resources, limit the impact of building on the environment, and incorporate sustainable materials in their construction—all of which make green building part of sustainable development.

Green building standards programs include those certified by LEED, those required by the International Green Construction Code (IgCC); a variety of product standards and certification programs, including McDonough Braungart Design Chemistry (MBDC); and local, tribal, and state codes and building legislation (including CALGreen).

The U.S. Green Building Council's (USGBC) Leadership in Energy and Environmental Design (LEED) green building certification system is a set of green construction standards for certification that are widely recognized in the United States. In addition to setting standards that result in a building's receiving LEED certification, USGBC also grants LEED professional credentials for design and construction professionals. (This is done in conjunction with the Green Building Credential Institute [GBCI].) Additional detailed information about LEED building rating systems can be found in Appendix A.

The International Green Construction Code (IgCC) is a model code developed by the American Institute of Architects, ASTM International, and others in keeping with the American Institute of Architects 2030 Carbon Neutrality Goal. Additional information about the IgCC can be found in Appendix A.

The California Green Building Code includes *mandatory provisions for residential* and nonresidential buildings as well as voluntary standards for both residential and non-residential buildings. Residential mandatory requirements include planning/design; water efficiency/conservation; material and resource efficiency; building maintenance and operation; environmental quality, a section containing detailed requirements for sealants, coatings (including paint), carpet (and carpet cushion), and other interior finishes and materials; interior moisture control; environmental comfort; interior air quality; and exhaust.

In some cases, states and cities have LEED-based regulations that govern new projects, while in other cases, states and cities offer incentives for green building and energy efficiency. The State of Minnesota Sustainable Building Guidelines (known as B3 Guidelines) require compliance on projects receiving state funding and can be used voluntarily on other projects.

Another approach to sustainability is known as MBDC and is based on the framework developed by William McDonough and Michael Braungart and described in their book *Cradle to Cradle: Remaking the Way We Make Things*. As indicated on the MBDC website, this framework "moves beyond the traditional goal of reducing the negative impacts of commerce ('eco-efficiency'), to a new paradigm of increasing its positive impacts ('eco-effectiveness')." This approach addresses the use of energy, water, and social responsibility; MBDC sets criteria for C2C certification of products, produces case studies, and consults with a wide range of clients.

In addition to LEED, IGCC, and MBDC, there are a number of programs that provide certification and standards for green products and materials; some of these are listed in Appendix A. Such standards are one way for designers to seek out products that meet some of the criteria set by the EPA, as follows:

Green buildings may incorporate *sustainable* materials in their construction (e.g., *reused, recycled-content,* or made from *renewable resources*); create *healthy indoor environments* with *minimal pollutants* (e.g., reduced product emissions); and/or feature landscaping that *reduces water usage* (e.g., by using native plants that survive without extra watering).

Using some type of rating or certification system, in combination with weighing what is called for in the preceding quote, can provide a method for designers to determine whether a product is, in fact, green. Measuring products against such criteria is helpful because *greenwashing,* which is defined as making misleading statements about products or practices relative to issues of sustainability, is an ongoing problem.

Another important approach to analyzing sustainability is known as *life-cycle assessment* (LCA), which is a process that involves reviewing the total impact of a product's environmental cost over the *lifetime* of the product or building. According to the EPA, LCA "is unique because it encompasses all processes and environmental releases beginning with the extraction of raw materials and the production of energy used to create the product through the use and final disposition of the product. When deciding between two or more alternatives LCA can help decision-makers compare all major environmental impacts caused by products, processes or services."

A life-cycle assessment is an evaluation of the environmental consequences associated with a product or process. According to ISO 14040.2, "The assessment is a systematic set of procedures for compiling and examining the *inputs* and *outputs* of materials and energy and the associated impacts directly attributable to the functioning of a product or service system throughout its life cycle." The term *life cycle* refers to the activities occurring in the course of the product's life span, including use of raw materials and their acquisition, production, shipping, installation, maintenance, and disposal. By evaluating all phases of a product's life span, this assessment can aid in avoiding shifting environmental impact to the future or to future generations.

Issues mentioned thus far regarding sustainability are not specific to the design of houses but rather are intended to provide clarity and background. Some programs specific to the design and construction of homes are listed in Table 1-4.

While there are not currently many *mandatory* green codes regulating private residential design, residences should not be overlooked in terms of environmental impact or indoor air quality. According to the Consumer Reports website Greener Choices, "using green building

Table 1-4 Sustainable, Green, and Energy-Efficient Programs for Homes*

Title	Agency/Sponsor	Description
Built Green	Washington State and participating counties and master building organizations	Voluntary green building certification program.
California Green Building Standards Code, known as CALGreen Code	California Building Standards Commission	Mandatory state green building standards code (the first state-mandated code in the nation). Regulates the design and construction of buildings, including residences, and includes additional voluntary guidelines.
Green Star Home Certification	Alliance for Environmental Sustainability and Minnesota GreenStar	A voluntary residential building standards program that provides third-party rating and certification of new and remodeled homes.
LEED for Homes	U.S. Green Building Council	Designed to be efficient in energy, water, land use, materials, and indoor air quality. Voluntary rating system that promotes the design and construction of high-performance green homes.
REGREEN	American Society of Interior Designers and U.S. Green Building Council	Voluntary guidelines for sustainable residential remodeling/improvement projects. Provides strategies based on project scope, as well as an educational certificate program.
Energy Star Home Program	Federal government (EPA) and partner organizations	Voluntary energy efficiency program. Includes Energy Star rating system and labels for products and homes.
U.S. Department of Energy, Building America Program	U.S. Department of Energy (DOE) in partnership with industry	Voluntary program seeking to reduce home energy use by 30 to 90 percent and improve indoor air quality.
NAHB Model Green Building Guidelines/Certification	National Association of Home Builders (in conjunction with green building professionals)	Resource for builders to build houses that conserve resources, including energy, and have improved indoor air quality.
American Lung Association Health House Program	American Lung Association	Homes are built to be mold, radon, and allergy resistant as well as energy efficient.

* There are additional state and local voluntary programs, but those listed have the most in-depth documentation available.
Also: A number of Native American communities have adopted green building codes that include regulation of residences. These include the Kayenta Township (Navajo Nation) Building Codes, the Pinoleville Pomo Nation Tribal Building Code, and the Confederated Tribes of the Grand Ronde Community of Oregon Tribal Community Code Ordinance.

materials can help to address" a range of health and environmental concerns such as indoor air pollution, which the EPA ranks "among the top five environmental risks to public health. In particular, studies have found levels of certain pollutants, from products such as paints and wood preservatives, to be up to 10 times higher inside homes than outside."

Consumption and Environmental Impacts

Additional statistics indicate the following:

■ In the United States, the buildings sector accounted for about 41 percent of primary energy consumption in 2010. (U.S. Buildings Energy Data Book)

■ According to the EPA (2009), of the total energy consumption in an average household,

50 percent goes to space heating

27 percent runs appliances

19 percent heats water

4 percent goes to air-conditioning.

■ Buildings in the United States contribute

38.9 percent of the nation's total carbon dioxide emissions, including 20.8 percent from the residential sector. A leaky faucet wastes many gallons of water in a short period of time. A leaky toilet can waste 200 gallons (750 L) per day. (EPA 2009)

■ Sources of indoor air pollution may include "combustion sources; building materials and furnishings; household cleaning, maintenance, personal care, or hobby products; central heating and cooling systems and humidification devices; and outdoor sources such as radon, pesticides, and outdoor air pollution." (EPA 2009)

■ According to the EPA (2015), the average American family of four uses more than 400 gallons (1514 L) of water per day at home.

■ The EPA (2014) indicates that by 2015, consumer electronics and small appliances will be responsible for almost 30 percent of all household electricity use. In 2020, the average home is expected to be 5 percent larger and will rely on even more products powered by electricity.

■ Homes built between 2000 and 2005 used 14 percent less energy per square foot than homes built in the 1980s and 40 percent less energy per square foot than homes built before 1950. However, larger home sizes have offset these efficiency improvements. (U.S. Buildings Energy Data Book)

■ Space heating and cooling—which combined account for 54 percent of site energy consumption and 43 percent of primary energy consumption—drive residential energy demand. (U.S. Buildings Energy Data Book)

Construction of new homes creates waste, with the NAHB estimating that the average single-family house built in the United States generates between 7000 and 12,000 pounds (3200 to 5400 kg) of construction waste. Millions of homes are built each year, so clearly removal, recycling, and reusing construction waste should be considered in seeking green design solutions. And given the statistics indicated here, life-cycle assessments of materials and construction processes are worth pursuing relative to residential design. Further information about resources for assessing sustainable materials can be found in Appendices A and B.

Net Zero Energy Buildings (*NZEBs*) are seen as a solution to growing energy costs, energy consumption, and climate change. Lacy Johnson wrote in *Scientific American*, "By the purest definition, a net-zero building produces all the renewable energy it needs on site, drawing no more power from the grid than it gives back." Each NZEB building design uses some mix of renewable energy and architectural design features (strategic use of site and window placement, tight insulation, etc.) to achieve net zero energy use. Generally, these buildings are connected to the power grid, but they produce at least as much energy as they use over the course of a year.

A Note on Dimensions

Throughout this book, dimensions are given in imperial units such as feet and inches, with metric (International System of Units, or SI) equivalencies listed, typically in millimeters. In most illustrations, imperial measurements are listed above or preceding the metric measurements. Millimeters are typically listed followed by "mm." In the text, millimeters are most often given in parentheses following the imperial dimensions. One exception to the use of millimeters in this book is the use of centimeters (with numbers followed by the letters "cm") for furniture dimensions, which is in keeping with the common practice of many manufacturers. When information is given regarding square footage, it is typically followed by an equivalency in square meters, which is within parentheses followed by "m²."

Ergonomics and Required Clearances

The field of study known as *anthropometrics* provides detailed information about the dimensions and functional capacity of the human body. According to authors Julius Panero and Martin Zelnik, anthropometry is "the science dealing specifically with the measurement of the human body to determine differences in individuals, groups, etc." (1979). *Ergonomics* is the application of human-factors data, including anthropometric data, to design. Specific ergonomic information and information related to clearance space required for furniture, fixtures, and equipment is included in each chapter.

Chapter 2 is devoted to circulation space; the focus of that chapter is movement from room to room. The discussion of room-specific circulation is covered within each chapter.

The introductory discussion of proxemics earlier in this chapter described Edward Hall's finding that human spatial boundaries vary from one culture to another; readers should note that the clearances and ergonomic information provided throughout this book represent North American norms rather than reflecting a worldview. This is particularly true of dining and leisure spaces.

Many chapters also provide furniture and appliance sizes; these, too, are based on items currently available in North America.

Organizational Flow

The authors use the term *organizational flow* to refer to the use of activity areas or elements within a room in relationship to *traffic flow* or *circulation*. For example, in designing a kitchen, the designer must consider the various activity areas (such as cooking, cleanup, and preparation) and the ease of their use, as well as circulation within the room and to other areas within the residence. Each room in a home serves a distinct purpose, and the design of the room must support that purpose in order for the room to function well.

When considering organizational flow, the designer must review the range of uses of the room and make design decisions that support those purposes. For example, bedrooms are used for sleeping but also have other uses, such as clothing storage (in closets and dressers); the flow of the room should support both sleeping and accessing stored items as well as additional activities that occur within the room, such as watching television or working on a computer. Such issues of organizational flow are discussed in detail in the various chapters of this book.

Related Codes and Constraints

Building codes, zoning regulations, and fire, health, and safety codes all influence the design of buildings and their interior elements and provide constraints to the overall design. A basic understanding of the codes and regulations that affect residential design is required as projects are undertaken.

Building codes generally govern the construction of buildings based on the type of occupancy intended for the building. This means that residences are generally regulated by standards different from those regulating public spaces, and public spaces are regulated in varying ways based on intended use. Building codes are adopted by cities, states, and/or municipalities and, in rural areas, often by county agencies. In some cases, states adopt a statewide residential building code; however, codes adopted within states often can vary. Additionally, states and municipalities can add local requirements or amendments to generally adopted model codes to allow for incorporation of regional variation or geographic factors.

Prior to 2000, three model codes were widely used throughout the United States: the Uniform Building Code (UBC), the Building Officials and Code Administrators (BOCA) National Building Code (NBC), and the Standard Code. In 2000, various code entities came together to form the International Code Council (ICC) and to develop the International Building Code (IBC), which was written to serve as a consolidated model code for commercial and public buildings. Many states and municipalities have adopted the IBC, although it is not currently as consistently adopted as the name implies. Many code jurisdictions have intentions of adopting the IBC in the future, however.

ICC also publishes related codes, including the International Residential Code (IRC)—which is used in the regulation of one- and two-family homes—the International Mechanical Code, and the International Plumbing Code. See the "Electrical and Mechanical" section of this chapter for related information about electrical code requirements called for by the IRC, Section

E. The IRC does not cover multifamily dwellings, dormitories, apartments, nursing homes, or assisted-living facilities; these are covered by the IBC.

Throughout this book, the International Residential Code (2015 edition) is the code that is referenced. Referencing this single code is useful for purposes of clarity; however, not all locales or code jurisdictions have currently adopted this code, and this code does not regulate multifamily housing. Therefore, prior to beginning any project, the designer must research local codes and all related regulations.

Zoning regulations control building size, height, location, setbacks, and use. These regulations are adopted by local municipalities and vary greatly throughout the United States. In some areas, there are very strict zoning codes that control many facets of a building's design; in others, there are few zoning restrictions. As with the building code, zoning regulations should be researched prior to beginning the design of any project.

Additional codes and regulations that govern the design of buildings include energy codes and fire and flammability standards. There are additional standards developed by testing agencies that are incorporated into model codes and federal regulations. Such testing agencies include the American National Standards Institute (ANSI) and ASTM International (formerly the American Society for Testing and Materials).

Sustainability Note

As stated earlier in this chapter, there are some specific state codes and guidelines related to sustainability, including the California Green Building Standards Code, as well as energy codes such as California's Title 24. In addition, many municipalities and cities have energy and water conservation codes and guidelines. Therefore, a full review of local restrictions is recommended for all projects.

ACCESSIBILITY NOTE

Federal regulations that govern the design of multifamily dwellings include the Fair Housing Amendments Act of 1988 (FHAA), a civil rights law requiring that privately and publicly funded multifamily dwellings (units on the first floor and all units in buildings with elevators) provide limited accessibility. In addition, the Uniform Federal Accessibility Standards (UFAS) require a percentage of units within federally funded multifamily dwellings to be accessible.

Early residential accessibility standards were published in 1980 in the ANSI A117.1 standards, which included bathroom and kitchen accessibility standards. The most current version, ANSI A117.1-2003, which was approved in 2003, provides standards for two types of accessible units: Type A and Type B. In brief, Type A units (Section 1003) are

fully accessible, while Type B units (Section 1004) provide limited accessibility.

Type B units are consistent with FHAA requirements, while Type A units are consistent with UFAS. A review of Type A and Type B standards will show that Type B standards are less strict; however, Type B standards are more broadly applied. ANSI A117.1-2003 also sets standards for accessible communications features for dwelling and sleeping units (Section 1005).

Information about kitchen and bath layouts that meet ANSI standards for Type A and B units can be found in Appendix D.

The Americans with Disabilities Act (ADA) is also civil rights legislation that includes federal accessibility design standards and guidelines. The ADA requires that *public* buildings (including those owned privately) be designed so that they accommodate people with disabilities. ADA guidelines share many similarities with ANSI standards. While the ADA has significant implications for the interior design of public places and should be understood by the practicing designer, it does not directly impact the design of single-family homes—except in a small portion of housing built with public funding.

ACCESSIBILITY NOTE

SWITCHING FOR WHEELCHAIR USERS

The standard placement of outlets (12 inches [305 mm] off the floor) is rather low for wheelchair and other users. For these users, outlets are best placed between 15 and 17 inches (381 and 432 mm) off the floor, and wall switches should be placed no higher than 48 inches (1219 mm) off the floor, as shown in Figure 1-6. The IDEA Center states that "wall outlets should be located no lower than 15 inches (381 mm) from the floor" and controls "that will be used frequently should be within the 24–48 inch (610–1219 mm) 'comfort range.'" Such controls include thermostats and alarm systems. It is worth noting that placing controls in this comfort range and locating receptacles between 15 and 17 inches (381 and 432 mm) above the floor meets universal design criteria and adds no extra expense, making it worth considering on many projects.

More about the International Residential Code

As stated previously, the IRC regulates one- and two-family residences and is therefore referenced in this book. In order to understand more about codes as they relate to each room within a house, it is worthwhile to cover some key concepts in advance.

For example, the IRC defines habitable space as "a space in a building for living, sleeping, eating or cooking," which means that the rooms within a home in which those activities are conducted must follow the guidelines as required throughout the code for habitable spaces. Note that the IRC does not include bathrooms, toilet rooms, closets, halls, and storage or utility spaces in the list of "habitable spaces"; therefore, those follow different guidelines.

In addition, the following sections specify other requirements.

Section R303 of the IRC covers light, ventilation, and heating:

It requires that all habitable rooms shall have a certain quantity of glazing areas (also known as windows) of "not less than 8 percent of the floor area." This means that the aggregate size and number of windows in rooms is controlled by the floor area and required by the IRC.

Natural ventilation is to be provided through windows, doors, louvers, or other approved openings, with a required minimum openable area to the outdoors of not less than 4 percent of the floor area.

Section R304 of the IRC covers minimum room areas:

Each habitable room in every dwelling unit shall have a gross floor area not less than 70 square feet (6.5 m²) and a minimum dimension not less than 7 feet (2134 mm).

Section R305 of the IRC covers ceiling height:

"Habitable space, hallways and portions of basements containing these spaces shall have a ceiling height of not less than 7 feet (2134 mm)." Minimum listed ceiling height for toilets, bathrooms, and laundry rooms is 6 feet, 8 inches (2032 mm), with exceptions for beams and girders in basements, where 6 feet, 4 inches (1930 mm) is allowed.

Not more than 50 percent of the required floor area of a room or space is permitted to have a sloped ceiling less than 7 feet (2134 mm) in height, with no portion of the required floor area less than 5 feet (1524 mm) in height (see Figure 1-5).

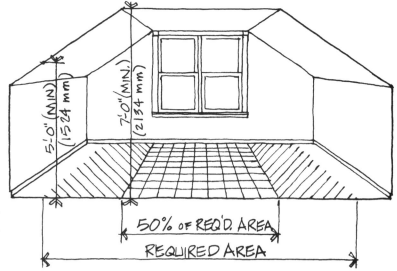

Figure 1-5 IRC required floor area in sloped ceiling situations: The IRC calls for habitable rooms to have a ceiling height of "not less than 7 feet (2134 mm)." It also states that no more than 50 percent of the required floor area of spaces may have sloped ceilings less than 7 feet (2134 mm) in height and requires that no portion of the required floor area be less than 5 feet (1524 mm) in height.

Section R331 of the IRC covers automatic fire sprinkler systems:

New residential town houses and one- and two-family dwellings shall have fire sprinkler systems. The authors of this book do not, at the time of this writing, know how widely this requirement will be applied.

The code issues mentioned to this point relate to single-family homes, which are governed by the IRC.

Electrical and Mechanical

Electrical and mechanical issues are covered in each chapter as they relate to individual rooms and spaces. With that said, there are some general rules for locating electrical switches and convenience outlets, with typical exceptions being in kitchens, bathrooms, and utility spaces. In most other locations, the on/off switches for overhead or general lights are best located close to the room entry door on the latch side of the doorway when possible. In larger rooms with more than one entrance, a second on/off switch can be employed in another convenient location; this is called a three-way switch. Where a number of light fixtures are used for general lighting, a single switch can be used to control several fixtures and outlets.

The IRC (Section E3903.2) requires that "at least one wall-switch-controlled lighting outlet shall be installed in every habitable room and bathroom." One exception to this requirement is "in other than kitchens and bathrooms, one or more receptacles controlled by a wall switch shall be considered equivalent to the required lighting outlet." The IRC (Section E3903.3) requires additional locations for a wall-switch-controlled lighting outlet in hallways, stairways, and attached and detached garages with electric power. This section of the code also requires that a wall-switch-controlled lighting outlet be installed on the exterior of egress doors with grade-level access.

The on/off switch should be mounted 44 to 48 inches (1118 to 1219 mm) off the floor. Because there are two receptacles, typical household electrical outlets are referred to as duplex outlets or duplex receptacles. These outlets are commonly placed about 12 inches (305 mm) off the floor, as shown in Figure 1-6.

A general rule of thumb for electrical outlet placement is one duplex receptacle per 12 feet (3658 mm) of wall space in order to avoid the use of extension cords. (Standard appliance cords are often 6 feet [1829 mm] long.) Following such rules can be a good starting point; however, the placement of outlets must be considered in relation to the design and layout of the room. It is important to consider the various possibilities for furniture placement so that the outlets can be designed in a way that is useful for a variety of scenarios. The IRC (Section E3901.2.1) requires that in most rooms receptacles be installed so that no point measured along the floor line is more than 6 feet (1289 mm) from a receptacle.

The term *mechanical* is an umbrella term used to describe the heating, ventilation, air-conditioning (known together as HVAC), and plumbing elements of a building. With very few exceptions, all residences in the United States are required by code to be heated; for example, the IRC calls for heating to a minimum of 68°F (20°C) when the winter temperature is below 60°F (15.5°C). Cooling may not be required by code, but in many parts of the country, most people consider it necessary.

The most common solution for providing heat is a furnace that burns a fossil fuel (such as natural gas, liquid propane, or heating oil) and less commonly wood, charcoal, or, coal. Alternatively, some furnaces derive heat from electric resistance coils or a heat pump. In almost all cases, the furnace uses a fan that moves air, via ducts, to the various rooms where heat is required. This type of system can be equipped to clean, with

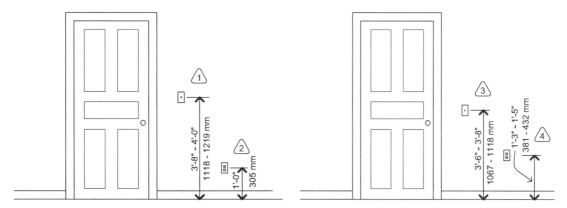

Figure 1-6 Switching and outlet locations for standing adult and seated (wheelchair) users

1. Standard switch placement is convenient to the latch side of the door and centered at 4 feet (1219 mm) above the floor.
2. Standard wall outlet placement is one outlet for each 12 lineal feet (3658 mm) of wall in general living spaces. Actual locations in individual rooms will vary based on room design and possible furniture arrangement.
3. For wheelchair users, switches are best located centered 3 feet, 6 inches to 3 feet, 8 inches (1067 to 118 mm) above the floor and never higher than 4 feet (1219 mm) above the floor.
4. For wheelchair users, wall outlets are best placed 1 foot, 3 inches to 1 foot, 5 inches (381 to 432 mm) above the floor and never lower than 1 foot, 3 inches (381 mm) above the floor.

with the use of filters; humidify; and, with the addition of a compressor or condensing unit, to cool the air, which in the process dehumidifies the air.

Other heating systems are available, such as a boiler that heats water in tandem with a pump that moves the heated water to a baseboard convector unit; a similar result can be achieved with electric resistance baseboard units. Hot water can also be delivered to radiant heating pipes located in the floors of a residence, with similar results achieved with resistance heating in the floors. None of these methods accomplish the cooling, cleaning, and dehumidifying that forced-air systems allow; these must be achieved through the use of separate equipment.

Air-to-air heat pumps are commonly used in temperate climates; these remove heat from the inside air in warm weather and work in reverse to provide heat to the interior during colder weather. In these systems, air is delivered much like the forced-air systems described previously.

Increasingly, consumers are seeking alternative sources for heating and cooling homes. Geothermal heat pumps use the relatively constant temperature of the soil, the groundwater, or surface water as a heat source for a heat pump that can provide heating and cooling. These systems use tubing submerged in the soil or a nearby lake or pond. Many consumers find the initial higher cost of geothermal heat pumps offset by energy savings and special tax incentive programs.

For many years, solar energy has been used to heat homes, and advocates see it as providing sustainability, energy independence, and cost reduction. Recent years have seen a significant increase in solar energy capacity, with 36 percent of all new electric capacity in the United States in 2014 coming from solar sources, according to the Solar Energy Industry Association (2015).

A great deal of information is available on designing solar heating and geothermal heating and cooling systems. These areas are clearly not the purview of this book, but designers are encouraged to seek additional information about these systems.

While interior designers are not responsible for the design of heating, ventilation, and air-conditioning systems, they should understand the various types of systems and their impact on the design of interior spaces. For example, knowing that hot water heat may require the use of baseboard convector units and that the location of such units will have a direct impact on the design and layout of interior spaces is useful.

Forced-air systems require the use of return-air grilles and supply-air registers/diffusers. These are available in a range of styles and in types such as baseboard, wall, floor, and ceiling units. Location of these items has an impact on the layout of a room and the level of comfort found there; for example, a favorite seating location that receives a constant blast of air will not remain a favorite for long. In addition, the visual qualities of grilles, diffusers, and registers should be in keeping with the overall design intent of the project—a Victorian-style grille placed within a mid-century modern interior may look ridiculous. Placement of grilles, diffusers, and registers in relationship to trim and architectural details is also worth careful consideration.

Lighting

Information about lighting specific rooms and spaces is provided in this book as a means of acquainting students with basic concepts related to planning and design. In no way is the information provided intended to be a significant source of a student's lighting design education. Instead, the information offered is introductory in nature and related to the overall design of rooms and spaces. So that the student can understand and work with the information provided in each chapter, an overview of terminology and basic lighting concepts is provided here. The references at the end of this chapter include lighting design publications helpful for more in-depth study.

Types of Lighting

Types of lighting discussed for various rooms include ambient, accent, task, and decorative lighting. See Figure 1-7.

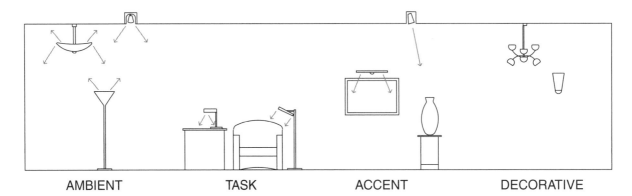

AMBIENT   TASK   ACCENT   DECORATIVE

Figure 1-7 Types of lighting include the following: Ambient light is general illumination that provides a uniform light level. Task lighting aids in performing work such as reading or preparing food. Accent lighting functions to illuminate objects or special features. Decorative lighting tends to draw attention to itself in the form of a decorative element such as a chandelier or wall sconce (decorative elements can add to a room's ambient lighting).

Ambient Light

Ambient light provides general illumination that renders a uniform light level throughout the area or room.

According to Randall Whitehead (2004), in residences "the best ambient light comes from sources that bounce illumination off the ceiling and walls." This is known as indirect lighting, which means that light arrives at a given surface after being reflected from one or more surfaces. This tends to cause less glare than downlights.

Downlights are defined as lighting sources that direct light downward. Whitehead adds that dark ceilings make this type of lighting ineffective.

There are also a number of direct-light sources that provide ambient lighting.

Accent Lighting (Also Referred to as Focal Lighting)

Aceent lighting illuminates features, objects, and/or specific areas. This type of lighting accents items or creates focal points and can add a level of interest to the general or ambient lighting.

Well-planned accent lighting puts the focus on the desired objects rather than on the light source or fixture.

Generally, using only accent lighting in a room without giving thought to ambient lighting creates clusters of darkness within rooms.

Task Lighting

As the name indicates, task lighting has a job to do—it aids in performing work and specific tasks.

In residences, many of these tasks are performed at table or counter height, requiring that the work surface be illuminated.

Considering the types of tasks performed and the body positions required to complete them helps the designer make choices about task lighting. For example, at kitchen counters and worktables, light coming directly from the ceiling is blocked by the human body or head, creating shadows on the work surface rather than illumination.

Decorative Lighting

Decorative lighting is ornamental in nature and provides interest based on its design and material qualities.

Unlike accent lighting, decorative lighting functions to show itself off and make a visual statement.

Decorative lighting can be used to accent elements and spaces or to add interest to ambient lighting, yet its function is typically secondary to the visual impact of the light source itself.

More Lighting Basics

Basic lighting design requires an understanding of glare, which the Lighting Research Center at Rensselaer Polytechnic University defines as "loss of visibility and/or the sensation of discomfort associated with bright light within the field of view." There are two types of glare: direct glare, which results from bright light in the field of view, and reflected glare, which results from reflections in the field of view (including surfaces and reading material). Locating light sources out of the line of vision or shielding them in some manner can prevent direct glare. Reflected glare can be minimized by using less reflective surfaces and placing the light source so that it is not directly above but rather at an angle to the surface and/or viewer.

Luminaire is a term used to describe the complete lighting unit, consisting of the following components:

1. A lamp or lamps (the general public calls these lightbulbs)
2. The parts (housing) necessary to distribute the light, position and protect the lamps, and connect the unit to the power supply

Light fixtures are luminaires that are permanently affixed to the architecture of the building. Portable luminaires are, as the name implies, easily moved; these include what the general public calls table lamps, desk lamps, floor lamps, and so on. A range of luminaires and fixtures may be used to create ambient, accent, task, and decorative light; some of these are shown in Figure 1-8. Recessed luminaires are illustrated in Figure 1-9.

Daylight is a term that correctly refers to what most people call natural light; it is light produced by solar radiation and includes direct sunlight as well as reflected light. The term *daylighting* refers to the process of designing buildings to utilize daylight. True daylighting requires careful consideration of the totality of the architecture of the building, so that the orientation of the building to the site, the location and size of building openings, and adequate shading devices are incorporated into the building design. Daylighting is a useful component of sustainable design because it does not require electricity and when done properly can also save energy on building cooling. Currently, daylighting is a strategy employed more commonly for public buildings than for private homes.

Regardless of how well daylighting is incorporated into a building design, electric light (referred to by the general public as artificial light) is required when it becomes dark outside. The appearance of electric light is rated by the color rendering index (CRI), which, according to the Lighting Research Center at Rensselaer Polytechnic University, is

> a technique for describing the effect of a light source
> on the color appearance of objects being illuminated,
> with a CRI of 100 representing the reference condition (and thus the maximum CRI possible). In general,
> a lower CRI indicates that some colors may appear
> unnatural when illuminated by the lamp.

PORTABLE

PENDANT MOUNTED

SURFACE MOUNTED

TRACK MOUNTED

RECESSED AND SEMIRECESSED

ARCHITECTURAL

Figure 1-8 *Luminaire* is a term used to describe a complete lighting unit. Luminaires may be portable, pendant mounted (also known as suspended), surface mounted on walls or ceilings (decorative luminaires mounted on walls are often called sconces), or track mounted (the track can be mounted on the ceiling or suspended and can include track heads or pendants). Other options include recessed and semirecessed fixtures as well as other architectural lighting options (lighting permanently affixed to the architecture of the building), such as cove and valance lighting. More information on recessed luminaires can be found in Figure 1-9.

For residences, a CRI of 80 to 89 provides color rendering where color quality is important in residential applications, such as spaces where the visual quality of colors, materials, finishes, artwork, and accessories are an important part of the experience of the room. In some cases, such as utility and storage spaces, a CRI lower than 80 is acceptable.

Another measure of color appearance, called color temperature or correlated color temperature (CCT), "describes the color appearance of the actual light produced in terms of its warmth or coolness," according to the Lighting Research Center. Color temperature is measured using the *Kelvin (K)* temperature scale, with lower temperatures (3000 K and lower) used to describe a warm source and higher temperatures (4000 K and above) used to describe a cool source. Typical incandescent lamps and warm fluorescent lamps are lower than 4000 K.

Lumen is a term used to describe the level of light (or brightness) gained from a lamp; it is a technical term measuring the luminous flux. Increasingly, a consideration of lumens produced is replacing a consideration of wattage; watts measure the energy consumed rather than the light produced. In the United States, packaging for lamps generally includes a lighting facts label that states the lumens produced as well as an estimated life of the lamp and the watts used.

RECESSED DOWNLIGHTS

RECESSED WALL WASH

ADJUSTABLE RECESSED

RECESSED TROFFERS

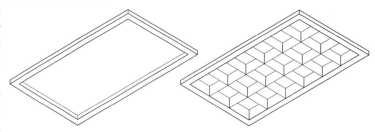

Figure 1-9 Recessed luminaires include recessed downlights (used for ambient lighting) and recessed adjustable downlights (also used for ambient lighting). Recessed wall washers direct light down at an angle and can be used for accent lighting. Recessed troffers are square or rectangular luminaires that house fluorescent lamps. These are available with diffusers or with louvers. Those with diffusers are used to provide ambient light, whereas louvers can direct light for tasks such as computer work. Surface-mounted versions with diffusers are used more commonly in residential settings.

According to the California Lighting Technology Center, in lighting terminology the term *efficacy* "refers to the ratio of luminous output produced by a light source to power consumed by that source (lm/W)."

Efficacy = Lumens/Watts

Varying light sources provide different levels of efficacy; "for example, a 75 W A19 incandescent lamp, a 16 W A19 CFL lamp, and a 15 W A19 LED lamp use different amounts of power to produce the same amount of light (approximately 1100 lumens). Each type of lamp has a different rated efficacy." It is important to consider the lumens produced (and therefore the efficacy) as well as initial costs and overall lamp life when purchasing lamps.

Designers must understand the roles of lamps in lighting design (remember, these are called lightbulbs by the general public). Lamps are most often discussed as being divided into categories as follows: *incandescent, fluorescent, light-emitting diode (LED)*, and *high-intensity discharge*. Within each category there is variety in how the lamps look and perform and the quality of light produced.

Incandescent lamps create light as electricity flows through a filament, heating it and making it glow. Incandescent lamps are popular because of the color quality of light that they create (remember the CRI and CCT). However, they use a great deal of energy to produce limited light and are therefore quite inefficient. Only 10 to 15 percent of the energy that goes into the filament is emitted as light; the remainder is generated as heat.

Incandescent lamps come in a range of shapes and sizes, with a letter designating shape and a number indicating the maximum diameter of the lamp (in eighths of an inch). For example, for a common A19 household lamp, the *A* refers to a standard bulb shape (*A* for "arbitrary"), and the *19* stands for 19 eighths of an inch, or 2⅜ inches. Figure 1-10 illustrates the shapes of other incandescent lamps. Other terms referred to in lamp names have to do with the glass used in the lamp, such as clear or frosted types.

There are also reduced-wattage incandescent lamps, which are shaped similarly to other incandescent types but use a different gas inside the lamp that allows different wattages or, in some cases, a longer lamp life. As standard incandescent lamps are being phased out, more energy-efficient incandescent lamps are under development. (See "Phasing Out Standard Incandescent Lamps.")

Halogen lamps (also called tungsten-halogen) are another type of incandescent lamp, in which the filament is inside a halogen-filled capsule. The use of halogen gas allows lamps of a similar wattage to produce more light, making these lamps more energy efficient than standard incandescent varieties. Halogen lamps can become quite hot, requiring special care or lamp protection. Dimming these lamps changes the color dramatically and can shorten lamp life. Xenon lamps are similar to halogen but use only xenon gas (and electricity). Xenon lamps are brighter than halogen. They also burn cooler and last

longer. Currently, xenon lamps for residential use are most commonly miniature types, often with pin or wedge bases, or those used in strip fixtures or puck fixtures.

Specialized incandescent reflector lamps have reflective coatings that create a directional light source and are available in a range of beam spreads from spot to flood. PAR lamps (for parabolic aluminized reflector), R lamps (for common reflector), and ER lamps (for ellipsoidal reflector) are all incandescent reflector types.

Incandescent lamps are also available in low-voltage versions, which require transformers to change the primary power (120 volts) to the required low voltage (often 12 volts). This type includes MR16 (the *MR* is for mirrored reflector; the *16* is for 16 eighths of an inch, or 2 inches) and PAR 36 lamps, which are often used for accent or display lighting. Figure 1-10 shows some halogen lamps.

Phasing Out Standard Incandescent Lamps

With the Energy Independence and Security Act of 2007, the United States legislated a gradual phaseout of incandescent lamps. This act required that as of 2014 the United States no longer manufacture or import standard tungsten-filament 40- and 60-watt lamps; however, existing lamps could be sold until supplies ran out. Rather than being a complete ban, however, this legislation requires only that many of the standard A-style lamps in inefficient wattages be phased out; more efficient incandescent lamps will continue to be available. Options for replacing high-wattage incandescent lamps include halogen, LEDs, and compact fluorescent (CFL).

Fluorescent lamps are coated glass tubes filled with gas; light is produced when the gas reacts with electrical energy, producing ultraviolet light, which in turn is absorbed by the coating and produces visible light. Fluorescent lamps require ballasts within the luminaire or lamp. These provide the starting voltage and control the current when in use. Compared to standard incandescent lamps, fluorescent lamps produce minimal heat and are more energy efficient. Lamp color, such as "cool white" or "warm white," is created by the chemicals (called phosphors) used to coat the lamps and is controlled by the manufacturer.

A range of fluorescent lamp shapes and types are available, including straight tubular (or linear), U-shaped, twin-tube, and circular (properly called circline) lamps. In addition, there are *compact fluorescent lamps* (CFLs), which, as the name implies, are smaller in size (allowing them to fit in smaller locations). CFLs require the use of a ballast, which may be integral to the lamp or may be part of a separate module that can be replaced separately, and are available in single, double, U-shaped, and

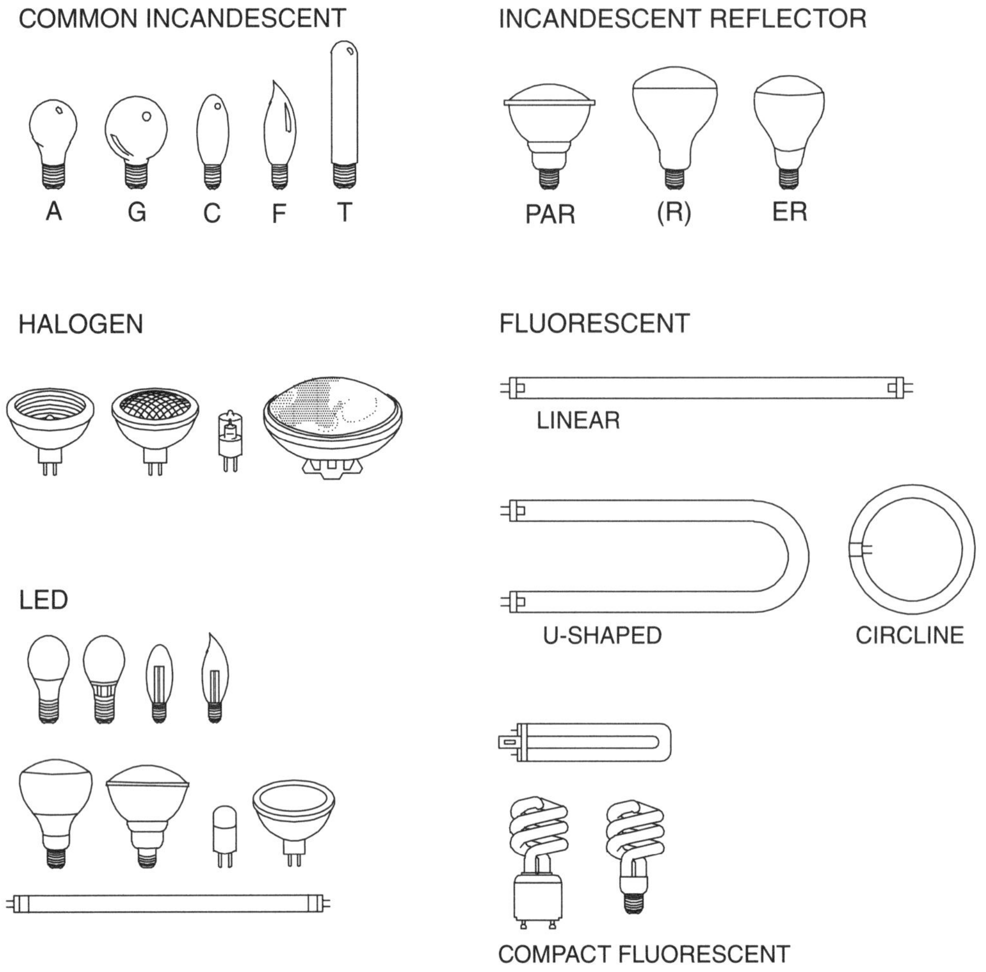

COMMON INCANDESCENT

A   G   C   F   T

INCANDESCENT REFLECTOR

PAR   (R)   ER

HALOGEN

FLUORESCENT

LINEAR

U-SHAPED   CIRCLINE

LED

COMPACT FLUORESCENT

Figure 1-10 Lamps are divided into broad categories: incandescent, fluorescent, light-emitting diode (LED), and high-intensity discharge (not shown). Incandescent lamps come in a range of shapes and sizes, with a letter designation referring to shape (as shown) and a number indicating the maximum diameter of the lamp (in eighths of an inch). Halogen (and xenon) lamps are another type of incandescent lamp. PAR, R, and ER lamps are incandescent reflector lamps that create directional beams. A range of fluorescent lamp shapes and types are available, including straight tubular (or linear), U-shaped, twin-tube, and circular (properly called circline) lamps. In addition, there are compact fluorescent lamps (CFLs), which may have a single, double, or U-shaped tube as well as spiral types with an adapter or with an integral adapter for use in an incandescent lampholder. These have become much more common in residential use in recent years because of their energy efficiency and lamp life. Light-emitting diodes (LEDs), also known as solid-state lighting, are rapidly evolving for residential use (See "Phasing Out Standard Incandescent Lamps"). Note that LEDs are available in a range of lamp shapes and base types that are intended to look similar to incandescent and fluorescent lamps. They can mimic other types of lighting and are also used in strip and rope lighting.

spiral tube types and with an adapter for use in incandescent lampholders. Residential use of CFLs has grown rapidly because of their energy efficiency and long lamp life. Figure 1-10 includes illustrations of some fluorescent lamps.

Light-emitting diodes (LEDs), also known as solid-state lighting, are rapidly evolving for residential use. LEDs use solid-state technology to generate light, making them more like electronic equipment than incandescent lamps. LEDs are long lasting and extremely energy efficient. While LEDs continue to improve in terms of light quality and may represent the future of lighting, they do have some limitations, particularly related to the highly directional nature of the light they generate. The directional light generated by most LEDs is ideal for spotlights and some

task lighting but can fail to fill larger spaces and may only light the top half of some fixtures. Several manufacturers have developed lamps that address this light dispersal problem, creating more flexibility in the use of LEDs. Options should continue to improve in the future as an interest in saving energy has caused some incandescent lamps to be phased out. (See "Phasing Out Standard Incandescent Lamps.")

Another type of lamp, known as high-intensity discharge (HID), uses a current and gas or vapor under high pressure to produce light. HID lamps also require a ballast. While highly energy efficient, they are not widely used in residential interiors except for applications where lights are left on for extended periods of time, such as for security or in multifamily stairway applications.

It is worth noting that references to bulb shape are different from those used to describe the lamp base; for example, the screw base seen on standard lamps is referred to as a standard base or an Edison base (after Thomas Edison). Lamp bases come in a range of sizes and types and are referred to by name. For example, a standard A lamp with a screw-in base is referred to as a standard base, whereas a smaller, flame-tip-shaped lamp (for use in a chandelier, for example) may have a medium or candelabra base. Also, compact fluorescent lamps are widely available with an integral ballast and a standard screw-in base for use in a standard socket.

Controls for lighting include switches, dimmers, timers, sensors, central controls, and motion detectors. This large family of controls can be divided into two categories: manual controls and automatic controls. Note that for effective use, dimmers require the use of dimmable lamps and often CFLs and LEDs require compatible dimmers (consult the manufacturer's list for dimmer and lamp compatibility).

Commonly used manual controls include switches and dimmers, with switches used to turn lamps on and off and dimmers used to control the light output of some lamps. Timers are automatic controls that are intended to control lamps based on a designated time period. Controls vary a great deal in complexity and cost, with the more advanced and costly options used in some cases as part of a complete home security system.

VISUAL THINKING AND BASIC DESIGN GRAPHICS

This section is meant as an introduction to basic design graphics and the types of visual thinking required in the design and construction of buildings. To introduce readers to the various types, design graphics are covered in two ways in this book: first, in general terms with simple introductory graphics in this chapter, and second, in relationship to a specific sample project with more detailed drawings and graphics in Chapter 8.

A range of types of drawings, sketches, and diagrams are used in the design of buildings and spaces within buildings and are used to explore and refine ideas and information as the design process takes place. Each type of drawing has a specific role or roles in the design process.

Writing in *Interior Design Illustrated,* Francis Ching identifies three basic stages in the design process: *analysis, synthesis,* and *evaluation.* According to Ching, analysis involves *defining and understanding the problem,* synthesis involves the *formulation of possible solutions,* and evaluation involves a *critical review of the strengths and weaknesses of the proposed solutions* and alternatives.

To these three stages, Ching adds *design development,* a generally accepted phase of architectural and interiors practice, which is the portion of the process when the design is fully refined, detailed, and ready for incorporation into construction drawings and documents.

In the early stages of the process, diagrams are used to bring quantitative and qualitative information together with visual information so that the designer can understand and synthesize it more easily. One type of diagram, commonly used as designers begin the preliminary design of residential projects, is known as the *bubble diagram.*

Bubble diagrams serve to visually represent project adjacency requirements and can also represent very rough proportional information. For example, client requirements for an addition that includes a painting studio, with a small bathroom, that is attached to the house through a gallery-like space with a separate entrance could be represented with a bubble diagram in which the bubbles represent not only room locations and adjacencies but also rough proportional information. See Figure 1-11a.

Generally, designers create *many* bubble diagrams as a means of generating multiple ideas. Later, the diagrams are reviewed and evaluated. They may be shown to the client for input and evaluation. On some occasions, another round of diagrams is generated, while in other instances the designer begins more refined project planning based on a successful diagram or a series of diagrams.

Other diagrams and images may be employed as well, including sketches and doodles drawn by the designer to represent some visual imagery suggested in programming or client interviews. Figure 1-11b is a massing sketch of the painting studio that is shown in Figure 1-11a.

It is worth noting that sketches such as the one shown in Figure 1-11b, perspective drawings, and three-dimensional models are used throughout the design process in order to help the designer visualize and refine the design and communicate the design (or design options) to clients and other interested parties. Such drawings and models are incredibly

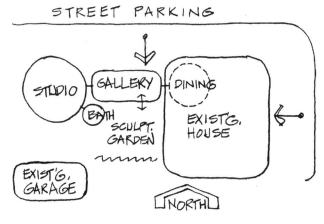

Figure 1-11a A bubble diagram representing client requirements for an addition including a painting studio and a small bathroom. The addition must be attached through a gallery-like space with a separate entrance. The bubbles represent not only room locations and adjacencies but also rough proportional information.

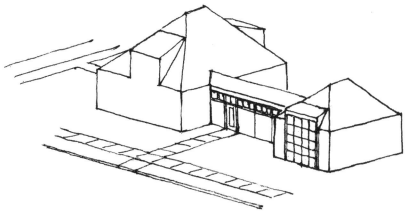

Figure 1-11b A preliminary sketch for the project represented in Figure 1-11a.

important to the overall success of any design project. They are not covered in this book because they fall outside its scope, but they should be seen as integral to the design process and used for every project.

Orthographic Projections

More refined project planning and design, which takes place as the designer moves through the design process, requires very specific drawings known as *orthographic projections,* which include plans, elevations, and sections. These drawings are created by projecting visual information onto an imaginary plane known as the picture plane. This direct projection of an object's dimensions allows for orthographic projections to retain the true shape and proportion, making these drawings accurate and precise and allowing them to be scaled to exact measurements.

Orthographic projection creates fragmentary views of an object, resulting in the need for multiple drawings. This means that, because of their fragmentary nature, orthographic projections become parts of a system and are dependent on one another. By their nature, orthographic projections appear flat and lack the three-dimensional quality of perspective drawings.

One way to visualize orthographic projection is to imagine a small building (in this case a writer's studio) enclosed in a transparent box. Each transparent plane of the enclosing box serves as the picture plane for that face of the object as the drawings are created.

The view through the top plane of the enclosing box is called a *plan* (in this case a roof plan). In a plan view, only those elements seen when looking directly down at the object through the picture plane are drawn, as shown in Figure 1-12a. The views through the picture planes that form the sides of the enclosing box are called *elevations.* Exterior elevations depict only what is visible when viewed directly through the picture plane on that side or portion of the building (Figure 1-12a).

A *section* portrays a view of the object or building with a vertical or horizontal plane sliced through it and removed. One way of understanding section views is to imagine that a very sharp plane has been inserted into the object or building, cutting neatly into it and revealing the structure and complexity of the object's form. Most building sections are drawn as though the picture plane has been inserted into the building vertically, neatly exposing structural elements and interior details, as shown in Figure 1-12b.

Floor plans are drawn as though a horizontal cut has been made in the building (typically 3 feet, 6 inches to 5 feet, 6 inches [1067 mm to 1676 mm] above the floor), as shown in Figure 1-12b. Cutting into the building at this location exposes the thickness of walls and other structural elements and shows windows, doors, and sometimes floor finishes and furnishings—all of which are located below the location of the cut.

One way to understand the creation of *interior elevations* is to picture yourself inside the room you are drawing. Imagine standing inside a room facing one wall directly, with a large sheet of glass (the picture plane) inserted between you and the wall. The interior elevation can then be created by outlining (projecting onto the picture plane) the significant features of the wall, as shown in Figure 1-12c. Each wall of the room can be drawn in elevation by means of projecting what is visible as you face that wall directly.

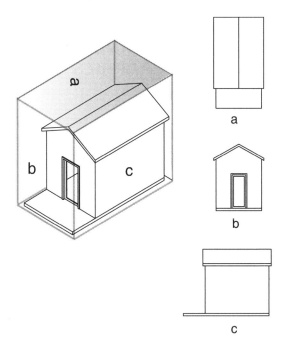

Figure 1-12a Orthographic projection drawings are drawn as though seen through a clear glass box, in which each plane of the box serves as a picture plane for each drawing. Item "a" represents a roof plan, drawn as though traced directly from above using the top plane (shaded for view "a") of the enclosing box as the picture plane. Item "b" represents the front elevation (front picture plane), drawn as though traced directly using the side (front) plane of the enclosing box as the picture plane. Item "c" represents a side elevation, drawn as though traced directly using the side plane of the enclosing box as the picture plane.

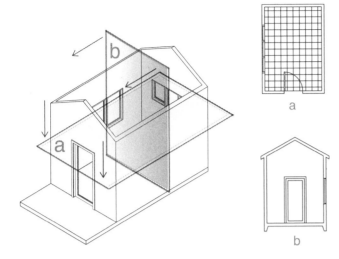

reflected ceiling plan is drawn as though a giant mirror were on the floor, reflecting the elements located on the ceiling. The use of reflective imagery allows for the ceiling plan to have exactly the same orientation as the floor plan.

Orthographic projection drawings are clearly an abstraction of reality and use specific conventions to delineate space and materials. Unlike some other types of drawings, orthographic projection drawings require adherence to conventions, proportional scale, and accuracy of line; these design drawings are highly standardized so that they carry universal meaning. Therefore, items such as walls, doors, windows, property boundaries, references to other drawings, and other items are represented by very specific graphic symbols or combinations of lines. Figure 1-13 illustrates some graphic notation used in these types of drawings, such as wall lines and door and window symbols.

Figure 1-12b Some orthographic projection drawings are sectional views drawn as though the picture plane slices through the building, exposing the structure. Item "a" is a floor plan drawn as though the picture plane has made a horizontal slice. Item "b" illustrates a building section drawn as though the picture plane has been inserted vertically, exposing the building's structure.

Reflected ceiling plans are specialized drawings used in interior design (more often for commercial projects than for residential projects). Reflected ceiling plans communicate important information about the design of the ceiling, such as height and materials, layout, and locations of fixtures. A

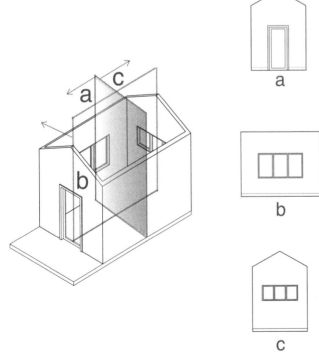

Figure 1-12c An interior elevation is drawn as though the picture plane has been inserted inside the building or room, exposing the interior architecture and details. Only interior elements are included in these drawings, as opposed to building sections, which expose structural elements. Note that the picture plane used for "a" and "c" views is shaded for clarity.

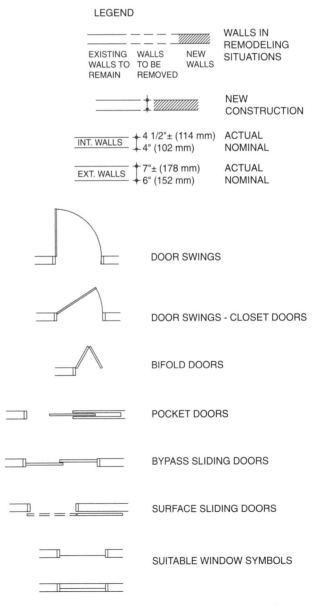

Figure 1-13 Common graphic notation used in orthographic projection drawings. These are standard drawing conventions used to show the items indicated.

Figure 1-14a illustrates graphic symbols used for notes and references, and Figure 1-14b shows graphic symbols used for electrical and lighting. These are standard drawing conventions used to show the items indicated. Figure 1-15 shows additional graphics used to describe construction materials.

In addition to graphic conventions and symbols, design drawings often contain written notes. Over the years, certain abbreviations have become commonplace for use in design practice. Use of abbreviations can save time in drawing production and space on the actual drawings; however, such use also requires that standard abbreviations be used—as opposed to some creative use of letters that may have no meaning to the reader. A partial list of common abbreviations is given in Table 1-5.

GRAPHIC SYMBOLS

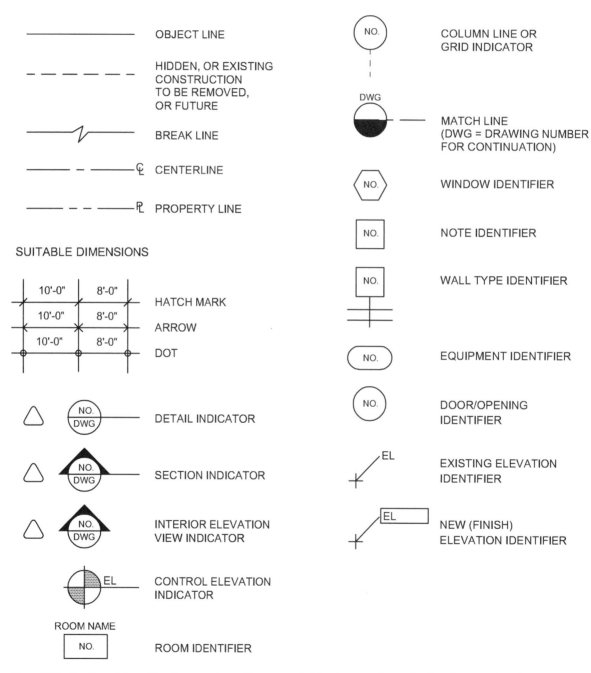

Figure 1-14a Graphic symbols used for references and notes. These are standard drawing conventions used to show the items indicated. Note that these symbols include a number on top of another number. The number on top refers to the individual drawing number; the lower number refers to the sheet where the individual drawing may be found.

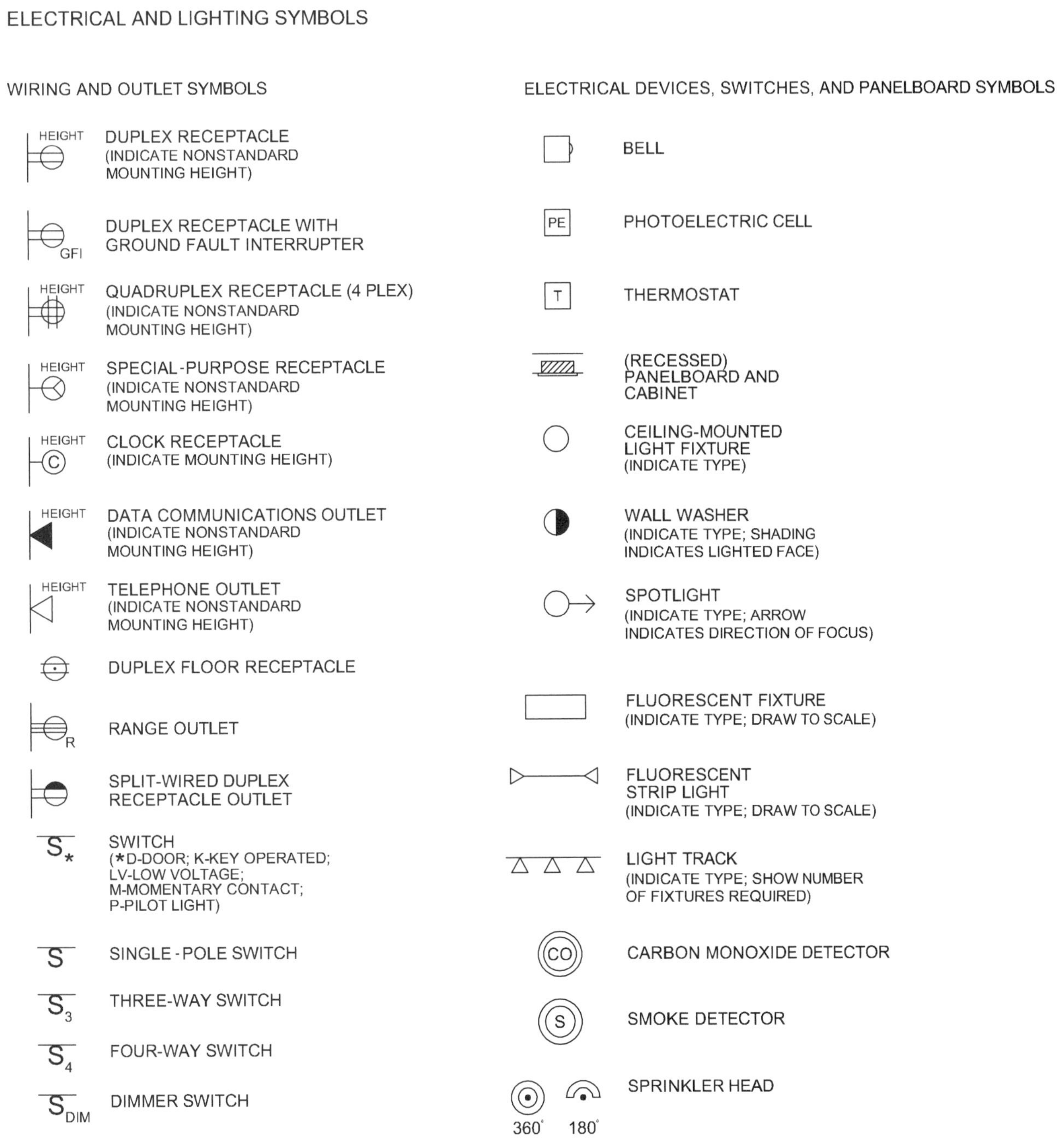

ELECTRICAL AND LIGHTING SYMBOLS

WIRING AND OUTLET SYMBOLS

HEIGHT	DUPLEX RECEPTACLE (INDICATE NONSTANDARD MOUNTING HEIGHT)
GFI	DUPLEX RECEPTACLE WITH GROUND FAULT INTERRUPTER
HEIGHT	QUADRUPLEX RECEPTACLE (4 PLEX) (INDICATE NONSTANDARD MOUNTING HEIGHT)
HEIGHT	SPECIAL-PURPOSE RECEPTACLE (INDICATE NONSTANDARD MOUNTING HEIGHT)
HEIGHT	CLOCK RECEPTACLE (INDICATE MOUNTING HEIGHT)
HEIGHT	DATA COMMUNICATIONS OUTLET (INDICATE NONSTANDARD MOUNTING HEIGHT)
HEIGHT	TELEPHONE OUTLET (INDICATE NONSTANDARD MOUNTING HEIGHT)
	DUPLEX FLOOR RECEPTACLE
R	RANGE OUTLET
	SPLIT-WIRED DUPLEX RECEPTACLE OUTLET
S*	SWITCH (*D-DOOR; K-KEY OPERATED; LV-LOW VOLTAGE; M-MOMENTARY CONTACT; P-PILOT LIGHT)
S	SINGLE-POLE SWITCH
S₃	THREE-WAY SWITCH
S₄	FOUR-WAY SWITCH
S DIM	DIMMER SWITCH

ELECTRICAL DEVICES, SWITCHES, AND PANELBOARD SYMBOLS

	BELL
PE	PHOTOELECTRIC CELL
T	THERMOSTAT
	(RECESSED) PANELBOARD AND CABINET
	CEILING-MOUNTED LIGHT FIXTURE (INDICATE TYPE)
	WALL WASHER (INDICATE TYPE; SHADING INDICATES LIGHTED FACE)
	SPOTLIGHT (INDICATE TYPE; ARROW INDICATES DIRECTION OF FOCUS)
	FLUORESCENT FIXTURE (INDICATE TYPE; DRAW TO SCALE)
	FLUORESCENT STRIP LIGHT (INDICATE TYPE; DRAW TO SCALE)
	LIGHT TRACK (INDICATE TYPE; SHOW NUMBER OF FIXTURES REQUIRED)
CO	CARBON MONOXIDE DETECTOR
S	SMOKE DETECTOR
360° 180°	SPRINKLER HEAD

Figure 1-14b Graphic symbols used for electrical and lighting. These are standard drawing conventions used to show the items indicated.

ARCHITECTURAL MATERIAL SYMBOLS

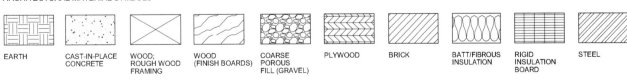

EARTH   CAST-IN-PLACE CONCRETE   WOOD; ROUGH WOOD FRAMING   WOOD (FINISH BOARDS)   COARSE POROUS FILL (GRAVEL)   PLYWOOD   BRICK   BATT/FIBROUS INSULATION   RIGID INSULATION BOARD   STEEL

Figure 1-15 Common graphic symbols used to indicate construction materials. These are standard drawing conventions used to show the items indicated.

Table 1-5 Common Abbreviations Used in Construction Notes and Drawings and in Portions of This Book

Abbreviation	Term
ADJ.	Adjacent or adjustable
A.F.F.	Above finished floor
BLDG.	Building
B.M.	Benchmark
BR.	Brick
BRG.	Bearing
CER.	Ceramic
CFL	Compact Fluorescent Lamp
C.M.U.	Concrete masonry unit
CONC.	Concrete
CONTR.	Contractor
D.	Dryer
DBL.	Double
DET.	Detail
DIA.	Diameter
DN.	Down
DW.	Dishwasher
ELECT.	Electrical
EXIST.	Existing
EXT.	Exterior
FDN.	Foundation
FIN.	Finished
FL.	Floor
FLUOR.	Fluorescent
FTG.	Footing
G.C.	General Contractor
G.F.I.	Ground fault interrupter
GL.	Glass
GYP. BD.	Gypsum board
HC.	Handicap accessible
HT.	Height

Abbreviation	Term
HTG.	Heating
KIT.	Kitchen
LAV.	Lavatory
LED	Light-Emitting Diode
CL ℄	Line of center
MAS.	Masonry
MAX.	Maximum
MECH.	Mechanical
MIN.	Minimum
M.O.	Masonry opening
MTD.	Mounted
N.I.C.	Not in contract
O.C.	On center
OH.	Overhead
OPG.	Opening
PL.	Plate
P.LAM.	Plastic laminate
PLAST.	Plastic or plaster
R.	Riser
RAD.	Radius
REF.	Refrigerator
RM.	Room
R.O.	Rough opening
SQ. FT.	Square foot/feet
T.	Tile
TOIL.	Toilet
TR.	Tread
TYP.	Typical
U.G.	Underground
V.	Vinyl
W.	Washer

Additional detailed examples of design drawings and graphics can be found in Chapter 8.

REFERENCES

Contains both works cited and recommended reading, with occasional annotation.

Alexander, Christopher, et al. 1977. *A Pattern Language*. New York: Oxford University Press. A seminal work and part of a series that is based on the notion that people can design and build their own structures. Urban planning, the design of dwellings, and details and ornament are covered. Spatial hierarchy, issues related to privacy, and the design of spaces that take advantage of daylight are all described and illustrated. The quotations in this chapter can be found on page 127.

Building Design and Construction Magazine. 2003. "The White Paper on Sustainability: A Report on the Green Building Movement." This is an excellent primer on sustainability. It contains historical information as well as information about LEED, although LEED has changed since the original publication of this paper.

Built Green Washington. 2015. "Welcome to Built Green Washington!" http://www.builtgreenwashington.org.

California Lighting Technology Center, UC Davis. 2010. "Residential Lighting: A Guide to Meeting or Exceeding California's 2013 Building Energy Efficiency Standards." http://cltc.ucdavis.edu/sites/default/files/files/publication/2013-title-24-residential-lighting-guide-jan15.pdf.

Ching, Francis. 1983. *Home Renovation*. New York: Van Nostrand Reinhold. A good general guide to residential design as it relates to renovation. Out of print but available from used booksellers.

———. 2004. *Interior Design Illustrated*. 2nd ed. Hoboken, NJ: John Wiley & Sons.

———. 2008. *Building Construction Illustrated*. 4th ed. Hoboken, NJ: John Wiley & Sons.

Concrete Change. 2015. "Concrete Change: Every New Home Visitable." http://concretechange.org.

Cooper, Clare. 1967. "The Fenced Back Yard—Unfenced Front Yard—Enclosed Porch." *Journal of Housing*. For additional information, see the notes under Jon Lang below.

———. 1974. "The House as a Symbol of the Self." In *Designing for Human Behavior*, edited by J. Lang, C. Burnette, W. Moleski, and D. Vachon. Stroudsburg, PA: Dowden, Hutchinson & Ross.

Cooper Marcus, Clare. 1995. *House as a Mirror of Self: Exploring the Deeper Meaning of Home*. Berkeley, CA: Conari Press.

Dietz, Robert. 2015. "New Single-Family Home Size Increases Start of 2015." *Eye on Housing*, May 19. http://eyeonhousing.org/2015/05/new-single-family-home-size-increases-at-the-start-of-2015/

EPA (U.S. Environmental Protection Agency). 2009. "Buildings and Their Impact on the Environment: A Statistical Survey."

———. 2010. "Green Building, Basic Information." http://www.epa.gov/greenbuilding/pubs/whybuild.htm.

———. 2014. "Climate Change: What You Can Do: At Home." http://www.epa.gov/climatechange/wycd/home.html.

———. 2015. "Water Sense: An EPA Partnership Program." http://www.epa.gov/watersense/our_water/water_use_today.html.

Ervin, Mike. 2010. "Visitability: A Concrete (and Brick and Wood) Change."NPR.http://www.npr.org/news/specials/housingfirst/whoneeds/visitability.html. Part of an interesting series on National Public Radio titled *Housing First: A Special Report* that details housing needs of various groups within the United States.

Hall, Edward. 1966. *The Hidden Dimension*. New York: Doubleday. While this book is often quoted, it is rarely read, but it should be by more designers and educators. Although some current theorists disagree with Hall, this pivotal book has many concepts worth considering.

International Code Council. n.d. "International Green Construction Code." http://www.iccsafe.org/cs/igcc/pages/default.aspx.

———. 2015. "2015 International Residential Code for One- and Two-Family Dwellings." Country Club Hills, IL: International Code Council.

International Organization for Standardization. 1998. ISO 9241-11. Ergonomic Requirements for Office Work with Visual Display Terminals (VDTs) — Part 11: Guidance on usability.

———. 2006. ISO 14040. Environmental Management: Life Cycle Assessment Principles and Framework.

Johnson, Lacey. 2012. "Net-Zero Energy Buildings Take Hold in U.S." *Scientific American*. http://www.scientificamerican.com/article/net-zero-energy-buildings-in-us.

Jones, Louise. 2008. *Environmentally Responsible Design*. Hoboken, NJ: John Wiley & Sons. The quotation can be found on page 3.

Lang, Jon. 1987. *Creating Architectural Theory: The Role of the Behavioral Sciences in Environmental Design*. New York: Van Nostrand Reinhold. An excellent overview covering exactly what the subtitle implies: a description of the work of psychologists, anthropologists, sociologists, and others as it relates to the built environment. The discussion of interior and exterior territories from early work by Clare Cooper Marcus comes from Chapter 14, which covers privacy and territoriality in detail. This title is currently out of print but is available from used booksellers.

"MBDC: Cradle to Cradle Design." http://www.mbdc.com.

National Association of Home Builders. 2006. "Facts, Figures, and Trends." http://www.soflo.fau.edu/report/NAHBhousingfactsMarch2006.pdf. This publication is the source for the historical home-size data prior to 2007 described in this chapter.

———. 2010. "Home Size Continues to Decline; Buyers Increasingly Opt for Single Story Homes." http://www.nahb.org/news_details.aspx?newsID510898.

Newman, Oscar. 1972. *Defensible Space: Crime Prevention through Urban Design*. New York: Macmillan.

———. 1976. *Design Guidelines for Creating Defensible Space*. National Institute of Law Enforcement and Criminal Justice. Washington, DC: U.S. Government Printing Office.

———. 1995. "Defensible Space." *Journal of the American Planning Association* 61 (2): 149.

Panero, Julius, and Martin Zelnik. 1979. *Human Dimension and Interior Space*. New York: Whitney. A quintessential guide to human dimensions.

Preiser, Wolfgang, and Elaine Ostroff, eds. 2001. *Universal Design Handbook*. New York: McGraw-Hill. A huge compilation of articles, presentations, and research papers; international in scope, with contributions from leaders in the movement.

Rawsthorn, Alice. 2010. "Debating Sustainability." *New York Times,* January 31.

Rensselaer University Lighting Research Center. 2006. "Web Glossary." http://www.lrc.rpi.edu/programs/nlpip/glossary.asp.

Russel, Leslie, and Kathryn Conway. 1993. *The Lighting Pattern Book for Homes*. Troy, NY: Rensselaer Polytechnic Institute. This publication provides excellent information about luminaires, lamps, color quality, and efficacy and includes a useful glossary of lighting terms with a clear focus on energy efficiency. Published by Rensselaer's Lighting Research Center, an entity with a helpful lighting research website at www.lrc.rpi.edu/index.asp.

Sebba, Rachel, and Arza Churchman. 1986. "The Uniqueness of the Home." *Architecture and Behaviour* 3 (1): 7–24.

Shafer, Jay. 2012. *The Small House Book*. Cotati, CA: Four Lights Tiny House Company.

Solar Energy Industry Association. 2015. "*Solar Industry Data.*" http://www.seia.org/research-resources/solar-industry-data.

Sommer, Robert. 1969. *Personal Space: The Behavioral Basis of Design*. Englewood Cliffs, NJ: Prentice Hall.

Steinfeld, Edward. 1996. "A Primer on Accessible Design." v. 1.0. Buffalo, NY: Center for Inclusive Design and Environmental Access, SUNY–Buffalo. A little pamphlet full of helpful information that can serve as an introduction to accessible design.

Susanka, Sarah. 1998. *The Not So Big House: A Blueprint for the Way We Really Live*. Newtown, CT: Taunton Press. This book started a bit of a revolution as a practical guide to thinking about how people really live.

Thompson, Boyce. 2009. "New-Home Shoppers Could Power Economic Recovery: 2009 BUILDER/American LIVES New-Home Shopper Survey Sheds New Light on Perceptions about the Home." *Builder Magazine.* http://www.builderonline .com/research/new-home-shoppers-could-power-economic-recovery.aspx?page51.

University of Washington, The Faculty Room. 2013. "What Is the Difference Between Accessible, Usable, and Universal Design?" http://www.washington.edu/doit/Faculty/articles ?337. This site is a resource for University of Washington faculty and contains clear and concise descriptions of universal and accessible design.

U.S. Energy Department. 2015. "Lumens and the Lighting Label." http://energy.gov/energysaver/articles/lumens-and-lighting-facts-label.

U.S. Energy Information Administration. 2013. "Newer U.S. Homes Are 30% Larger but Consume about as Much Energy as Older Homes." http://www.eia.gov/todayinenergy/detail.cfm?id=9951&src=%E2%80%B9%20Consumption%20%20%20%20%20%20Residential%20Energy%20Consumption%20Survey%20(RECS)-f2.

Whitehead, Randall. 2004. *Residential Lighting: A Practical Guide*. Hoboken, NJ: John Wiley & Sons. An easy-to-follow lighting primer that describes using "layered" lighting in residences.

Whitman, Walt. 2005. *Leaves of Grass*. New York: Oxford University Press.

Winter, Steven. "Net Zero Energy Buildings". *Whole Building Design Guide*. 2014. https://www.wbdg.org/resources/netzeroenergybuildings.php.

World Commission on Environment and Development. 1987. "Our Common Future." Chapter 2: Towards Sustainable Development. Document A/42/427. http://www.un-documents.net/ocf-02.htm#I.

World Green Building Council. 2015. "About WorldGBC." http://worldgbc.org/index.php?cID=220. The quotation given is from the organization's website (listed above).

Entrances and Circulation Spaces

INTRODUCTION

Circulation refers to the areas provided for horizontal and vertical movement within and along spaces. Providing adequate space for movement is essential and requires careful consideration of ergonomics, scale, and organizational flow. In addition to allowing for physical movement, circulation spaces provide for psychological transition from one type of space to another and/or from one territory to the next. The way we move from one place to another colors our experience of that place and therefore is a significant contributing factor to the quality of designed environments.

Much has been written about the significance of the main entry in residential design in terms of providing a symbolic transition space between public and private domains. Writing in *A Philosophy of Interior Design*, Stanley Abercrombie states, "In our own culture, rather than plunge directly into the heart of an interior, into its living room full of conversation . . . we prefer some transitional area." He also writes that entrances are "a physical transition point, obviously, and also a mental one, the entrant bringing into the interior memories of the exterior." In this discussion, Abercrombie is pointing out the role the entry plays symbolically, as well as how important the design of the space is in terms of articulation of the entry area relative to the architectural form of the building.

The seminal book *A Pattern Language* by Christopher Alexander et al. explores entrances and circulation space in detail.

Several of the patterns relate directly to building entry. For example, Pattern 112 describes the need for a graceful transition between the street and the inside and reads in part:

> The experience of entering a building influences the way you feel inside the building. If the transition is too abrupt there is no feeling of arrival, and the inside of the building fails to be an inner sanctum.

Also, in discussing entry area design, the authors of *A Pattern Language* continue with the description of a space that allows people "to settle down completely into the more intimate spirit appropriate to a house."

Clearly, the placement, location, and physical qualities of entry areas can provide not only an aesthetic experience—an adequate, safe passage area—but also a psychological barrier or symbolic transition between the outside world and the inner sanctum of a home. As stated in Chapter 1, there are zones of intimacy related to public and private territories within the home, and the entry area is the key buffer zone between the most public portions of a home and the more private areas, as shown in Figure 2-1.

An understanding of issues of privacy and territoriality can shape the design of the building entrance or entrances; however, additional cultural, geographic, and site-related issues impact the design and location of residential entrances. For example, in some locales, entering through the rear or back door of the house is common; neighbors and guests come to the back door to enter the house rather than approaching the front. This is particularly true when the building has an alley serving the rear portion of the house. In cases where the homeowners wish to receive guests only through the front, the design of the house can enforce such an entrance by screening auxiliary entrances (as shown in the diagram in Figure 2-2).

In climates with extreme weather, a mudroom is often necessary for family members and in some cases for guests,

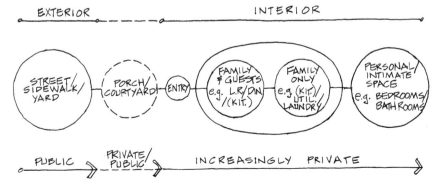

Figure 2-1 Bubble diagram illustrating public and private realms, with the entry area serving as a transition between the two realms.

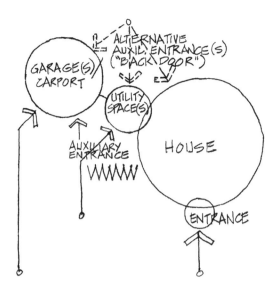

Figure 2-2 Bubble diagram illustrating main and auxiliary entry areas.

and use of this room should be considered as entrances and secondary entrances are designed. Mudrooms seem to be gaining popularity in places without extreme weather as well in that they can provide an excellent utility entrance and transition space with storage and room for outer clothes, sporting equipment, and, in some cases, charging stations for electronic devices. Increasingly, a "drop-zone," where items such as mail and electronic devices are "dropped" upon arrival, is included in mudrooms and other areas of the home.

In some cases, homeowners enter houses through the garage. In such instances, a mudroom, buffer, or transition area can be created between the garage and other rooms of the house. This can be done with a room or series of rooms that serve utility purposes, as shown in Figure 2-2. At minimum, locating a coat closet and/or additional storage in such rooms proves helpful as a place to shed outer clothes, shoes, bags, and so on, and aids in the transition from public to private space or from "messy" to "tidy," depending on the situation. Additional information on mudrooms and related rooms can be found in Chapter 7.

FOYER AND ENTRY AREAS

When planning the primary entrance to a residence, one must carefully consider and balance the exterior and interior design of such spaces. An entryway or foyer may be created in a number of ways, as indicated in Figure 2-3. It may be created through an indentation or a projection from the facade. An indentation has the distinct advantage of being kept a bit out of the weather with less heat loss from wind. Creating a useful roof or overhang at the entry is quite advantageous, as it allows the homeowner to stand protected from precipitation as he or she searches for keys and other items.

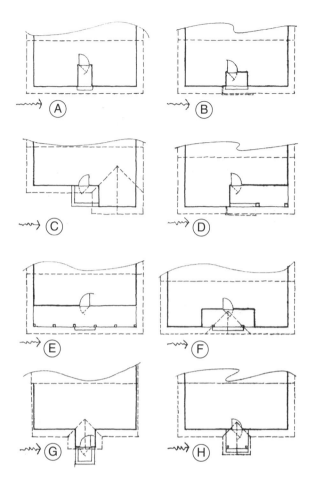

Figure 2-3 Entryways may be created with an indentation or projection from the facade of the building. An entryway that protects the entrant from rain, snow, and high winds is ideal. In colder climates, vulnerability to periodic ice formation on walking surfaces (from dripping roofs) is a constant threat. In such regions, storm doors are necessary and subject to being a high-wind hazard if no protection is built in. Prevailing winds vary by region but should always be considered—they are indicated in these illustrations as left to right. The following pairs of entrance designs present a problematic version side by side with an improved design and related notes.

A. **Problematic:** Avoid recessed entrances that are narrow and deep; water, melting snow, and ice need to be diverted from the entrance walkway.

B. **Better:** An entry recess should be wider than deep, as shown. Water from the roof is diverted in this example with a gutter and downspout.

C. **Problematic:** Avoid inside corner entrances where sloped roof junctures collect rain or melting ice/snow on the front stoop. (In harsh climates, that water will often refreeze on the stoop walking surface.) The storm door swing orientation leads to increased risk of being "wind whipped."

D. **Better:** A well-protected entrance with deep sheltered porch roof. Water from the roof is diverted in this case with a gutter and downspout.

E. **Problematic:** An open porch with entrance door provides good shelter from above but not from the wind; the door swing is not well oriented relative to prevailing wind direction.

F. **Better:** A modest-sized, recessed porch provides good shelter from rain/snow and prevailing winds. Rain and melting snow/ice diversion is necessary. (In this case, the roof configuration diverts the water.)

G. **Problematic:** Projecting entrances that do little other than catch maximum wind should be avoided. This roof configuration diverts water from the front stoop but does little to protect the entrants and the door from the elements. In addition, the front stoop is too small and is hazardous.

H. **Better:** A projecting and protective, column-supported roof over the front stoop provides good water diversion and protection from the elements; this does little for wind protection, but the storm door swing does not catch prevailing winds.

Figure 2-4 Examples in which the door scale, design, and detail reflect the building style or architectural details.

Foyer or entryway size will vary greatly, but an entrance generally should be at least as wide as it is deep and, when possible, wider than deep to allow for movement, storage, and general transition space. When possible, entrances should be sheltered from above and be located so that they are sheltered from the prevailing winds. Entrances that project from the face of the residence are more vulnerable to wind than other entrance configurations (see Figure 2-3).

The primary entrance door can create a sense of place within the residence. It can convey meaning related to the overall exterior/interior design and to the building's inhabitants. This relationship may be connected to the building stylistically, meaning that the style of the door selected works within the building's design context.

The physical qualities of the door are worthy of careful consideration. Decisions about whether the door is solid or has some degree of glazing (windows), and the door's relative size, width, and adjoining elements such as sidelights or transom must be made and will contribute to the overall design of the exterior and interior and to the overall design integrity of the project, as illustrated in Figure 2-4. Storm doors, which are most often necessary in harsh climates, will cover the entry door and alter its visual qualities, as will most screen doors.

The entry door should not appear as an afterthought or detract from the building's character. It should be easy to identify as the primary entrance and be reasonably easy to open and to move through. More information on door types and styles can be found in Chapter 9.

In terms of interior considerations, the entry has a number of functions and should be reviewed on a variety of levels. The entry can serve to set a visual direction for the rest of the residence, meaning that it can create an aesthetic that is well matched to the rest of the home. In terms of interior volume,

foyer/entry areas may be open to great heights, making use of openings within a second or even third story. Or, in contrast, the entry may have very low ceilings, which could set the stage for the transition to an adjacent high, open space, creating an air of suspense or visual variety.

The location of the foyer/entry area must allow it to function as a transition space from outside to inside and typically is seen as having direct adjacencies to the most public parts of the home (living or great room, for example), coat closet, a guest restroom, stair to other levels, guest room or office, and so on. Figures 2-5 to 2-10 illustrate possible adjacencies for a foyer/entryway. In extreme climates, a small vestibule known as an air lock can be placed between the exterior door and the foyer to serve as buffer between the outside and inside air temperatures.

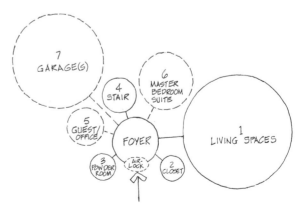

Figure 2-5 Access from foyer with ranking of priority of access to functional areas (these may or may not exist on the same level). In extreme climates, an air lock can serve as a buffer between outside and inside air temperatures. Note: for the purposes of the building code (IRC), spaces 1, 5 and 6 would all be classified as "habitable space."

Figure 2-6 Entrance area/foyer example: from a 1230-square-foot (114-m²) story-and-a-half house with a basement.

A. Foyer (44 square feet [4 m²]); 3.5 percent of total finished space in house; with a 3-foot (914-mm) entrance door.

B. This is a "mini air lock" for harsh climates; unheated or tempered (heated); space enough for one person to stand and close storm door prior to opening the entry door.

C. Down; 3 risers at 5 inches (127 mm) with a railing.

D. A ramp with railing; 1:8 slope would require assistance for many wheelchair users. The length of this ramp would be 9 feet (2743 mm) minimum.

E. Roof edge; gutter and downspout are recommended in this case at sidewalk and ramp areas.

F. A half bathroom for guests, which, with door (H) closed, can serve as a second toilet/sink facility for master bedroom. This space could be redesigned with a pocket door so that it would be considered visitable.

G. To mudroom and garage.

H. 3-foot (914-mm) pocket door for privacy and noise control.

I. Desk, mail, and charging area; this area is a place for recharging electronic items, sorting mail, and conducting household business. This type of area is also referred to as a drop-zone.

J. In-home office/studio at stair landing level.

K. 3-foot (914-mm) pocket door at landing level creates

> Visual separation from unfinished basement.
> Thermal separation from unheated basement.
> Sound/noise separation.

L. Built-in dining room cabinets (42 inches [1067 mm] high) also function as a stair railing/guard/barrier.

M. Stairs, 3 feet, 4 inches (1066 mm) wide: down to an unfinished basement and up to an unfinished attic/future bedrooms.

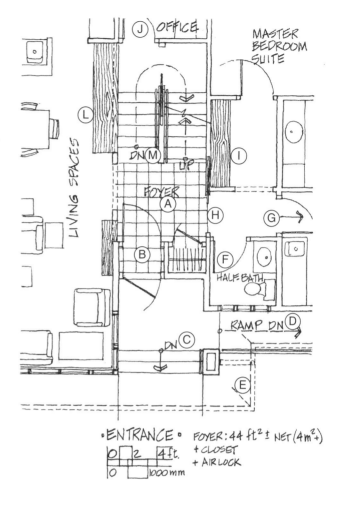

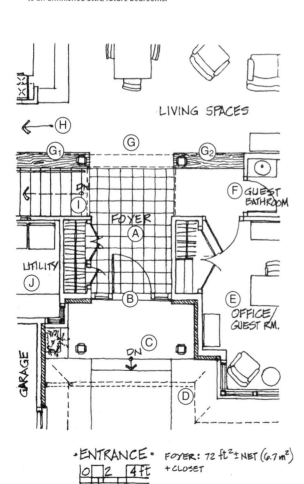

Figure 2-7 Entrance area/foyer example: from a 1900-square-foot (176.5-m²) one-story house with a partially finished basement.

A. Foyer (72 square feet [6.7 m²]); 3.8 percent of initially finished space in house. 3-foot, 4-inch (1016-mm) entrance door.

B. Insulated entrance door with sidelights; absence of storm door would increase heat loss in severe climates and requires that adequate roof protection be provided.

C. Entrance porch (stoop) of 50 square feet (15.2 m²); a minimum of two risers at 7½ inches (190.5 mm) required for this house with a basement and structural wood floor.

D. Roof edge with a rain gutter or deflector above sidewalk.

E. Room can function as an office and/or a guest bedroom (with different furnishings).

F. A guest bathroom, which in this case is more than the common guest half bath in that it contains a tub/shower.

G. Framed view through dining room to a private backyard.
G₁ and G₂. Built-in book shelves (3 feet [914 mm] high) also function as a stair railing/guard and/or circulation barrier.

H. Circulation to the remainder of first floor—master bedroom suite, utility/mudroom, garage (and auxiliary exit/entrance through garage).

I. Stair, 4 feet (1219 mm) wide, down to the future finished space in the lower level. The stair is wider than minimum to enhance the experience of entry to the lower level; door at bottom of stairs at the lower level serves as thermal and noise control.

J. Utility/mudroom accessible from garage entrance.

Figure 2-8 Entrance area/foyer example: from a 2380-square-foot (221-m²) one-story home with unfinished basement.

A. Foyer (60 square feet [5.6 m²]); 2.5 percent of initially finished space. However, because the foyer space is open to other areas, it has a feeling of spaciousness.
B. 3-foot (914-mm) insulated entrance door with sidelights. Although well protected because the area is recessed and has a roof overhang, the lack of a storm door could be problematic in severe climates.
C. Two steps down; each riser is 7½ inches (190.5 mm).
D. Roof edge.
E. Office, which could be converted for bedroom use.
F. Full bath (for use by guests). The space can be considered visitable due to the 3-foot (914-mm) bathroom door, if there is a zero-step entry provided at another location.
G. 3-foot (914-mm) pocket door allows acoustic isolation and provides privacy for guests.
H. This living room provides impressive views out the back that are visible from the foyer.
I. Open hallway leads to remainder of house (kitchen, master bedroom, utility/mud-room, stair to basement, etc.).
J. Dining room with vaulted ceiling and window with view of street.

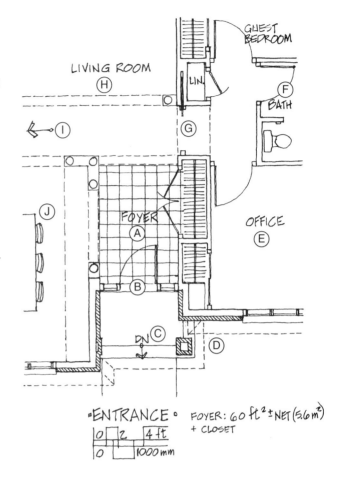

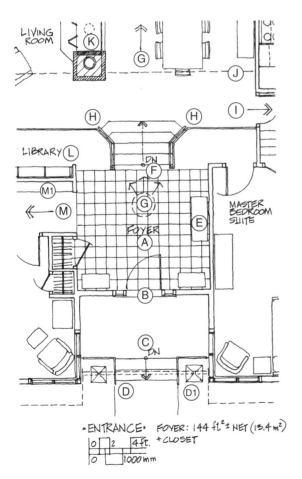

Figure 2-9 Entrance area/foyer example: from a 2300-square-foot (213.7-m²) (gross) one-story home with a loft and 700-square-foot (65-m²) finished "walk-out" basement. This house was designed so that it would cascade down to a lake and take advantage of views from each level.

A. Foyer (144 square feet [13.4 m²]); 4.8 percent of total finished space in the house.
B. A 3-foot, 4-inch (1016-mm) insulated door with sidelights. This is well protected due to the fact that the area is recessed and has a 7-foot (2133-mm) overhang, but could be problematic in northern climates without a storm door.
C. Porch with railings and steps; each of 3 risers is 5¾ inches (146 mm), down to grade.
D. Line of overhang; a roof gutter is required at step area, in this case with a chain downspout anchored to splash blocks (D₁).
E. Desk for mail and other elements used in entry/exit transition.
F. Stairs down; 5 risers at 6 inches (152.4 mm), with treads at 12 inches (304.8 mm).
G. View and access through lower level to a lower deck with lake views and access.
H. Open railing.
I. To lower level and rear entrance.
J. Clerestory windows at dashed line.
K. Wood-burning fireplace with an operable glass door on one side and fixed glass on the other side.
L. A wall of bookshelves (with a ladder used to access high shelves).
M. Hallway to office, guest bedroom, and bathroom; this hallway serves as a gallery for artwork (M₁). The bathroom can also serve as powder room.

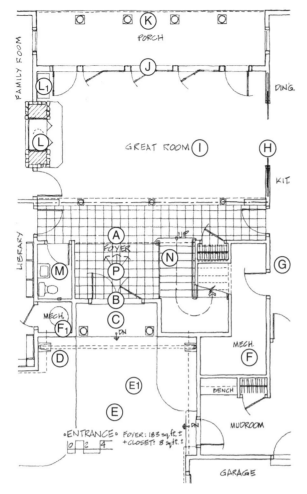

Figure 2-10 Entrance area/foyer example: from a 4250-square-foot (395-m²) two-story home with no basement. With no basement, a zero-step entry is possible, allowing for a visitable first floor.

A. Foyer (183 square feet [17 m²]); 4.3 percent of total (gross) finished space in the house.
B. A pair of 3-foot (914-mm) insulated entrance doors. Although well protected because the area is recessed and has a roof overhang, the lack of storm doors would be a heat loss problem in severe climates.
C. A porch with one step, a 6-inch (152-mm) riser, down to brick pavers at grade.
D. Roof edge with gutter, downspout, and splash blocks.
E. Brick paver sidewalk and driveway: sloped (E₁) to allow elimination of step.
F. Mechanical space required on first and/or second floor in absence of basement. Odd-shaped spaces can be used; however, a location that is central with the possibility of outside air intake can be advantageous.
   F₁. Water heater location for upstairs master bath.
G. Visitable bathroom and utility spaces (laundry, cleaning products, desk, mail, and charging station, etc.) accessible from this hallway.
H. A pair of 4-foot (1219-mm) pocket doors.
I. Great room with high ceiling (19 feet [5791 mm]).
J. French doors (5-foot [1524-mm] pairs and 3-foot [914-mm] singles at ends).
K. Porch with roof and columns (colonnade).
L. Wood-burning fireplace with an operable glass door on one side and fixed glass on the other side; wood storage bin at L₁.
M. Half bath or powder room for guests (narrow door creates a nonvisitable bath here. See G).
N. Stair up to balcony/ bridge overlooking great room and part of foyer; access to bedrooms.
O. All doors, except closet doors, are 3 feet (914 mm) except as noted.
P. This is the initial view granted as one enters the home, with views of the great room, porch, patio, lawn, and lake beyond.

VERTICAL MOVEMENT

Movement within a structure such as a residence can be horizontal (hallways/corridors), entirely vertical (elevators, firehouse pole), mostly vertical (ladders and circular stairs), or a combination (most stairs). Any of these can become strong design elements, facilitating the drama of movement.

Much like the building entrance, the stairs should be one of the first things to be considered, and their design and related relationships should remain a priority throughout the entire design process. This is due to the fact that stairs take up a significant amount of space; they dictate flow and need careful consideration from the beginning. The interior designer should be comfortable in manipulating stairs as easily as any other space. In order to gain such a comfort level, an understanding of the variations of vertical movement is required. Toward that end, an overview of the various means of vertical movement follows.

Forms of vertical circulation vary from fully upright ladders (at 90 degrees) to gently sloping ramps at 4 degrees, as shown in Figures 2-11a to 2-11c and 2-12. Each form of vertical movement has advantages and disadvantages related to use of space and ease of use, with some types clearly most useful in a residential setting, as described in the following paragraphs as well as in the captions to Figures 2-11a to 2-11c and 2-12.

Elevators and spiral stairs and ladders require the smallest footprint and generally involve little or no horizontal movement while making the vertical transition from level to level; the traveler moves up to the destination level, directly above or below where he or she started. Stairs and ramps can move the traveler a goodly distance horizontally (e.g., one can start the trip from floor to floor on one side of the house and wind up on the other). The use of a switchback stair or ramp (also known as scissor stairs) more closely emulates a spiral stair, because the traveler winds up on the destination floor approximately above or below where he or she started.

Generally speaking, ramps are seldom used in the interiors of a residence except for small vertical changes or in those cases where the design of the house is centered on movement (e.g., a linear house that "cascades" down a hillside, with the ramp becoming the spine of the house). Ramps consume significant space and are therefore largely relegated to the exterior, where there is more space.

An understanding of the various terms related to stair design and construction is necessary, as these terms are very specific and have significant design implications. Stair *treads* are the horizontal upper surfaces where the foot is placed, while *risers* are the vertical (or near vertical) face of a step/stair. The edge of a stair tread that extends over the riser is referred to as the *nosing* or *nose*. The nosing is often rounded, which makes it less likely to cause feet to catch and decreases the risk of tripping, and is more comfortable when in contact with the body. The sum of all treads is referred to as the total *run* of the stair,

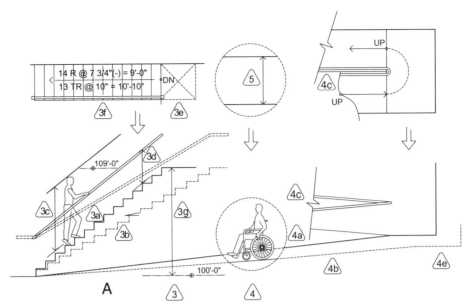

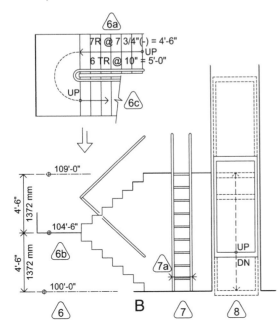

Figure 2-11a Graphic depiction of a wide range of possibilities for vertical movement. All examples are shown with a 9-foot (2743-mm) floor-to-floor height, although a wide range of floor-to-floor heights is possible. Those shown are residential examples, with two exceptions: public building requirements (per ADA Standards) for a stair and a ramp, to show their more restrictive requirements. Shown here and in Figures 2-11b and 2-11c are ranges of configurations required for functions that involve vertical and/or horizontal movement. For additional code information, see the "Related Codes and Constraints" section of this chapter.

AU: OK?

3. Straight-run stairs: maximum horizontal movement of all the stairs shown.
   3a. Profile shown is at a maximum slope for a residential stair (IRC): 7¾-inch (197-mm) risers; 10-inch (254-mm) treads (37-plus degrees).
   3b. Profile shown (with dotted line) is at maximum slope for stair that is accessible to the general public. 7-inch (178-mm) risers; 11-inch (279-mm) treads; (32 degrees) as required by the ADA and the International Building Code (IBC).
   3c. Required headroom (stair and landings). 6 feet, 8 inches (2032 mm), measured from the plane of the nosings.
   3d. Required handrail(s). 34- to 38-inch (864- to 965-mm) height (vertically from nose); 35 inches (889 mm) is shown.
   3e. Required landing (top and bottom). 36 by 36 inches (914 by 914 mm) minimum.
   3f. Always one fewer tread than riser in any given set of slopes.
   3g. IRC code maximum dimension between floors or landings is 12 feet, 3 inches (3734 mm).

4. Ramps.
   4a. Residential. Profile shown is maximum slope for residential use: 1:8 slope (7-plus degrees) (12.5 percent); This slope will require assistance for many wheelchair users. Ramps serving a required egress door must meet the 1:12 requirement (see 4b) unless approved by exception of local building officials. In all cases, a landing of 36 by 36 inches (914 by 914 mm) is required at top, bottom, and where ramp changes directions (IRC, Section R311.8.2).
   4b. Public. 1:12 slope is the maximum slope mandated by ADA; together with the required handrails and landing, intended for independent (unassisted) use by most wheelchair users.
   4c. Required handrails similar to stairs; no open sides.
   4e. Maximum ramp length (between landings). 30 feet (9144 mm) per ADA.

5. Hallways: 36-inch (914-mm) minimum width; no legal maximums.

Figure 2-11b Graphic depiction of a wide range of possibilities for vertical movement. All examples are shown with a 9-foot (2743-mm) floor-to-floor height, although a wide range of floor-to-floor heights is possible.

6. U stairs, also called scissor or switchback stairs.
   6a. Profile shown is at maximum slope (per IRC); thus, each run: 7 risers @ 7¾ inches (196.85 mm) = 4 feet, 6 inches (1.37 m) total rise to landing; 6 treads @ 10 inches = 5 feet (1.52 m) run.
   6b. The landing splits the 9-foot (2.74-m) floor-to-floor height exactly in half (not a requirement); the landing should occur at a point where both runs of the stair will have identical individual riser dimensions to ensure a safe, constant user (step) pace.
   6c. The break line is a drafting convention used to break the "up" run at a point that maximizes clarity and relates to horizontal cut of plan view.

7. Vertical ladder is not a code legal stair in residential use. These require descending backward (facing the ladder). Rungs 12 inches (305 mm) O.C., width 18 inches (457 mm). 7a results in the smallest footprint necessary to go from floor to floor (with the exception of a firefighter's pole). Rungs and side rails used for handgrip. 24-inch (610-mm) width required if confined by side walls.

8. Elevators. An increasingly common mode of residential floor-to-floor travel for those who have trouble negotiating stairs (including, but not limited to, wheelchair users). A modest footprint of 16 to 24 square feet (1.49 to 2.23 m²) is required for the clear inside hoistway in residential applications (check manufacturer's exact requirements).

Figure 2-11c Graphic depiction of a wide range of possibilities for vertical movement. All examples are shown with a 9-foot (2743-mm) floor-to-floor height, although a wide range of floor-to-floor heights is possible.

1. Ship's ladders. Not a legal required egress stair from habitable space in most codes; the IRC and some local codes may allow use for access to and egress from attics and/or limited-size open lofts. The angle (slope) of a ship's ladder can vary a great deal: 50 to 75 degrees (see Figure 2-12); the example shown is approximately 65 degrees; 9½ inches (241 mm) (–) R (riser) and 5 inches (127 mm) (+) TR (tread); required width of ladder between handrails is 20 inches minimum (508 mm). Hand rail required at 30 to 34 inches (762 to 864 mm) above tread.
2. Spiral stairs. The steepest of the legal residential stairs (covered in IRC Section R311.7.10.1): risers can be as much as 9½ inches (241 mm); 9 inches (229 mm) is shown. The minimum width is 26 inches (660 mm). The number of risers must be sufficient (and each of sufficient height) to create adequate headroom (6 feet, 6 inches minimum [1982 mm]) (see 2b) within three-fourths of a circle, so the user does not hit his or her head on the landing above (which almost always occupies one-fourth of the full circle; see 2a). The footprint of a spiral stair can be as small as 22 square feet (2 m²) without exceeding the maximum riser criteria and while meeting the minimum tread depth requirement of the applicable code. (See also Figure 2-28.)

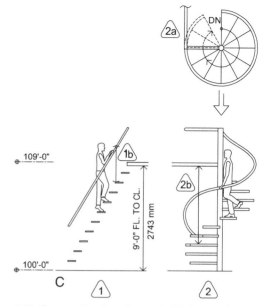

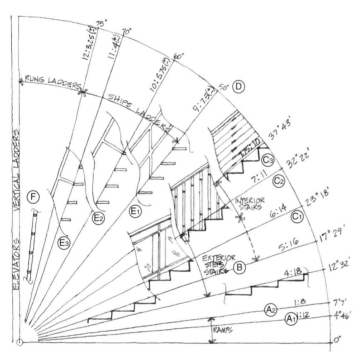

Figure 2-12 The range of configurations required for functions that involve vertical and/or horizontal movement and the generally accepted angle limits of each mode of vertical movement (e.g., answering the question, when is a stair a stair rather than a ladder?).

A. Ramps.
   A₁. 1:12 slope (1 unit of vertical rise/drop in 12 units of horizontal distance); legal maximum slope for unassisted wheelchair use per ADAAG; with appropriate width: 4 feet (1219 mm); landings (5 feet [1524 mm]) at 30 feet (9144 mm) maximum distance apart; and handrails on both sides.
   A₂. 1:8 slope; suitable for small vertical rises in residences; minimum ramp and landing width is 3 feet (914 mm), with handrails required on open sides and at least one side. For use by the ambulatory who have difficulty with steps and by wheelchair users, most of whom will need assistance at the 1:8 slope (see also the "Related Codes and Constraints" section of this chapter).
B. Exterior steps/stairs. Slope can vary a great deal; the limits of range of slope shown is not absolute but is a good rule-of-thumb range. For example:
   4-inch riser with an 18-inch tread
   (102 mm)   (457 mm)
   5-inch riser with a 16-inch tread
   (127 mm)   (407 mm)
   6-inch riser with a 14-inch tread
   (152 mm)   (356 mm)
   7-inch riser with an 11- to 12-inch tread
   (178 mm)   (279 to 305 mm)

The tread surface should slope slightly (1 to 2 percent) to shed water. The exact tread/riser ratio of the exterior steps is often influenced by the adjacent ground slope and how much horizontal space is available to accomplish the vertical transition.

C. Interior steps/stairs (with appropriate/required handrails). 23(+) to 37(+) degrees.
   C₁. 6:14 represents a reasonable, working minimum slope (there is no legal minimum); a lesser slope would require an inordinate amount of space (e.g., a 5-inch R/15-inch TR [127-mm R/381-mm TR] stair would take 33 feet [10,058 mm] of horizontal distance [with required top and bottom landings] to handle a modest 9-foot [2743-mm] floor-to-floor height [total vertical rise]).
   C₂. 7:11 represents the maximum slope for a stair in a public building (ADA and IBC requirements).
   C₃. 7¾:10 represents the maximum residential stair slope allowed by code (IRC), the exception being spiral stairs. Certain local codes may allow an 8-inch (203-mm) riser (maximum) and 9-inch (229-mm) tread (minimum)—for an 8:9 stair slope.
D. 50 degrees; generally considered to be the point at which even an able-bodied, well-coordinated adult can no longer go up or down the stair without assistance of handrails. However, all stairs/ship's ladders are required to have at least one handrail, so the point becomes moot.
E. Ship's ladders are allowed by some codes for access to open lofts of limited size or attics; the IRC does not allow ship's ladders unless the ladder serves a space where a legal means of egress is not required, or as an access in addition to a legal exit stair. Legal minimum width for ship's ladders is 20 inches (508 mm). Examples of ship's ladders (50 to 60 degrees) follow below:
   E₁. 9 inches R–7½ inches TR.
      (229 mm R–191 mm TR.)
   E₂. 10 inches R–5¾ inches TR.
      (254 mm R–146 mm TR.)
   Note: the IRC requires a tread depth of not less than 5 inches (127 mm) and a rise height of not more than 9½ inches (241 mm).
F. Vertical, or near vertical, rung ladders have rungs 12 to 18 inches (305 to 457 mm) O.C.; minimum width of ladder: 18 inches (457 mm)–24 inches (610 mm) if confined by walls.

while the *rise* is the sum of all risers. Figure 2-13 provides an illustration of stair elements, terms, and constructions.

A stair *landing* is, as the term implies, a place to "land" if you were to fall. The IRC calls for a landing every 12 feet (3658 mm) of vertical rise and a 36-inch (914-mm) landing at the top and bottom of every stair run. Obviously, the top landing is required because it is not a good idea to reach the top of a stair only to be knocked back down by running into a wall a few inches away. For more information on codes, refer to the "Related Codes and Constraints" section of this chapter.

It is worth noting that vertical movement on stairs can be hazardous; it would be an unusual person who has never had a fall of some sort on a stair. Thousands of people are hospitalized each year in the United States for accidents occurring on stairs; thousands more are injured and not hospitalized. Given such statistics, safety should be a significant consideration in stair design. One safety rule of thumb: The steeper the ascent and descent, the more risk is involved, making ladders more dangerous than stairs.

Most of us can think back to our own incidents with stairs and note that when accidents have occurred, they likely did so in the act of descending the stair rather than ascending. Older people often take to traversing stairs in their homes by descending the stairs backward (like younger people would come down a ladder). This is done because such an approach offsets many of the risks inherent in descending stairs. Refer to the "Ergonomics and Required Clearances" section for a more complete analysis of this phenomenon.

Interestingly, one- and two-step stairs can prove as hazardous as multiple steps; this is not because one falls as far as a full floor-to-floor stair, but because fewer steps are more difficult to see—and the most dangerous steps/stairs are the ones you don't see. This does not mean that such configurations should be avoided, but they require strong visual cues to the user. Such visual cues can be provided through a change of flooring materials, the sloping appearance of handrails, a change of color/texture/materials, and, of course, adequate lighting.

In terms of safety, it is important to see the stairs, but once movement within the stairs is in process, there should not be any surprises. In fact, one of the first rules of stair design is to create no surprises. An example of a hidden surprise, one that is not likely discernible from the initial assessment, is a difference in riser height or tread depth from step to step. Nothing will trip up the stair user faster than a shift in anticipated rhythm.

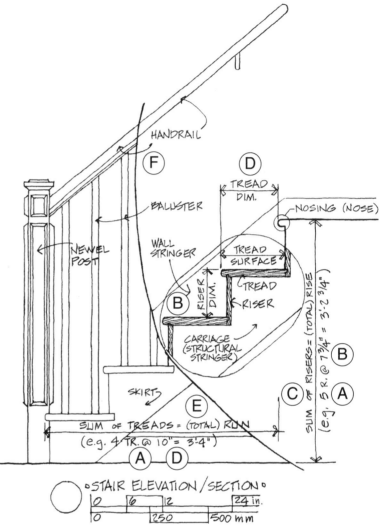

Figure 2-13 An illustration of stair elements, terms, and construction.

A. The term *step* (vis-à-vis the term *riser* or *tread*) can be somewhat ambiguous, since there is, in any given run of stairs (between floors/landings), always one less tread than the number of risers. As a general rule, refer to the number of risers when describing rudimentary information about any stair.

B. The riser dimension is from tread surface to tread surface, and it should always be constant in any given run of stairs.

C. The sum of all the risers is the rise of the stair, which will be the floor-level-to-floor-level (or landing-to-landing) dimension. In this case, 5R at 7¾ inches (196 mm) = 3 feet, 2¾ inches (984 mm), per IRC, Section R311.7.5.1.

D. The tread dimension is the horizontal measurement from nose to nose, rendering the "tread surface" almost always larger. (See also "Ergonomics and Required Clearances" section of this chapter.)

E. The sum of all tread dimensions equals the "run" of the stair. In this case, 4TR at 10 inches (254 mm) = 3 feet, 4 inches (1016 mm).

F. The odds of a safe trip up (or especially down) the stair are enhanced by the ability to steady oneself with a hand on a suitable handrail during those times during each step that support is only on one foot. The handrail needs to be stable (sturdy) and either/or:

F. Wall mounted (on a wall or half wall)

F. On open balusters

ACCESSIBILITY NOTE

Designing accessible spaces requires that adequate circulation be seriously considered and provided. Indeed, allowing universal entrance into a home is a key element of visitable design, as is allowing accessible circulation to a ground-floor bathroom. These are generally accomplished by providing 32 inches (813 mm) of clear space (clear of the door stop, jamb, and the door thickness) at doorways and 36 inches (914 mm) of clear space at hallways. Throughout the ground floor, providing adequate clear space for wheelchair movement is required, as is allowing for adequate turning space or space that allows for changing direction of the wheelchair.

In designing accessible vertical circulation, ramps or elevators must be provided, as stairs are problematic for wheelchair users and those with mobility limitations and significant difficulty with balance. It is also worth noting that many people benefit from the use of well-designed handrails as a component of vertical circulation. Handrails provide stability for a range of users throughout their life span. They should therefore be incorporated into the design of stairs and ramps. In addition, most codes require them. There is more detailed information about handrails in the "Related Codes and Constraints" section of this chapter.

Circulation Accessibility Checklist

☐ 32 inches (813 mm) clear space at doors. For swinging doors, doors with a minimum width of 36 inches (914 mm) are used because 34-inch (864-mm) doors are not a standard size.

☐ Hallways and/or paths of travel must be a minimum of 36 inches (914 mm) wide (see also Figure 2-6).

☐ For wheelchair users, provide clear turning space (5 feet [1524 mm] minimum diameter) or room for T-shaped turn (as shown in Figure 2-14b).

☐ Stairs are problematic for wheelchair users and others with mobility limitations, requiring that ramps or elevators be provided in place of stairs.

☐ Well-designed handrails are required in areas of vertical circulation (stairs and ramps).

For detailed information about required clearances, spatial requirements, and dimensional information for accessible circulation, refer to the "Ergonomics and Required Clearances" and "Related Codes and Constraints" sections of this chapter.

While spiral and curved (also known as winding) stairs do not have treads that are uniform in depth (across the width of the stair), users tend to compensate for that phenomenon by perhaps being more careful and counting on the fact that treads are all the same shape (or consistency). The principal safety issue with spiral stairs is the difficulty of meeting another user coming in the opposite direction, forcing one of the users toward the inside where the treads are at their narrowest. This potential hazard is often avoided by one user waiting for the other to complete the trip.

Specific information about required clearances and dimensions for vertical and horizontal circulation can be found in the "Ergonomics and Required Clearances" section of this chapter, whereas information about traffic flow and organization can be found in the "Organizational Flow" section. For the most part, this chapter covers circulation related to moving from one room or space to the next, rather than circulation within rooms. Information about circulation within rooms and spaces can be found in the individual chapters; for example, bedroom circulation is covered in Chapter 5.

ERGONOMICS AND REQUIRED CLEARANCES

Hallways and stairs are designed for the average adult. In motion, the average adult will have a 24- to 26-inch (610- to 660-mm) pace and require a clear space a minimum of 22 inches (559 mm) wide. That rule of thumb may be in a state of flux because the average adult size keeps growing—in both directions. Figure 2-14a illustrates the space required for human movement.

The current code minimum in a residential setting is 36 inches (914 mm) wide for a hallway or stair. However, this is not optimal, as persons meeting in such a space will have to pause, slow down, and possibly turn sideways. In the case of stairs, one of the persons may need to wait at the head or foot for the other person to complete the trip. It is a relatively minor inconvenience that many occupants/owners are willing to put up with in a residential setting. In contrast, this minimal dimension is too intimate as well as time consuming for circulation within a public building, where the minimum widths of stair and corridor passages are 44 to 48 inches (1118 to 1219 mm), depending on the specific code jurisdiction.

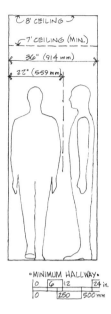

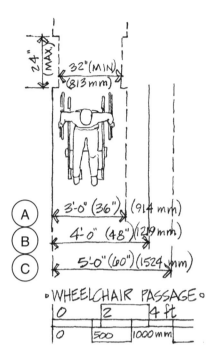

Figure 2-14a Hallway/horizontal circulation clearances required for ambulatory human movement.

The average adult requires a clear space 22 inches (559 mm) wide minimum for movement.

The hallway width code requirement is 36 inches (914 mm) for a hallway or stair. As indicated in the illustration, at 36 inches (914 mm) the hallway does not grant passage to two adults moving forward; typically one will have to move sideways.

Figure 2-14b Hallway/horizontal circulation clearances required for wheelchair use.

A. Clear width of a wheelchair-accessible route: 36 inches (914 mm).
B. Required space for one wheelchair and one ambulatory person: 48 inches (1219 mm); this is a minimum and not ideal.
C. Minimum required space for two wheelchairs: 60 inches (1524 mm).

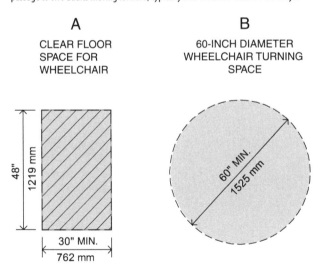

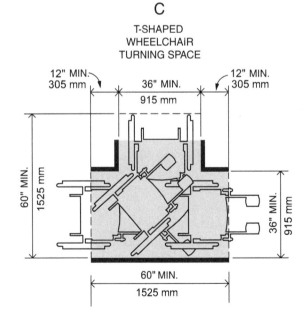

Figure 2-14c Additional circulation clearances for wheelchair users.

A. A minimum of 30 by 48 inches (762 by 1219 mm) of clear floor space should be provided at areas intended for use by wheelchair users. Note that this is not a minimum hallway space; it is the space taken up by the wheelchair and the user and can be considered a landing space for the chair and user.
B. Turning space must be provided in the form of a 60-inch (1525-mm) diameter circle or a T-shaped turning area as shown in C.
C. T-shaped turning space may be provided as an alternative to the circular space shown in B.

ACCESSIBILITY NOTE

There are additional passage requirements for wheelchair users, as shown in Figure 2-14b. In addition to planning for required passage space for wheelchairs, turning space and general clearance must be provided. As shown in Figure 2-14c, wheelchairs require a turning area at least 60 inches (1524 mm) in diameter or a T-shaped turning area. Clear space for the wheelchair must be provided in areas where the user must access items such as closets, plumbing fixtures, and other items for daily use; this clear space should be a minimum of 30 by 48 inches (762 by 1219 mm).

If stairs are designed for the pace and ambulatory capabilities of an average adult, then it can also be said that they are not designed for small children, who may have to struggle a bit to handle adult stairs. Nor are stairs designed for the tall and/or athletic adult, who will often compensate by taking two steps at a time on the ascent. Also, stairs are not designed for the elderly, arthritic, or inflexible, even though stair riser maximums have been, over time, reduced. That is the paradox: People, and consequently average strides, are getting bigger, but the population is also getting older. What used to be the maximum riser in a nursing home stair (7 inches [177 mm]) is now the maximum for all public stairs (IBC and ADAAG), and residential stair riser dimensions have dropped ¼ to ½ inch; for example, the IRC now requires 7¾ inches (197 mm) maximum.

The typical stair user can, generally speaking, handle a larger riser as he or she ascends the stair; a smaller riser would be desirable on the descent. It can be argued that the ideal, but of course impractical, stair system would have larger risers for the ascent, smaller for the descent, thereby requiring two sets of steps. Anecdotal evidence is provided by the fact that people can be frequently seen climbing a stair two steps (risers) at a time and often without railing support, but rarely do you see anyone descend a stair two steps at a time and even more rarely without the aid of a handrail.

Therefore, a compromise is struck in favor of the descent. The descent is inherently the more hazardous. The feet are in much more stable positions on the ascent and if a fall occurs, the person falls into the plane of the stair—a relatively short trip. As stated previously, those with mobility limitations and/or difficulty with balance often feel safer descending a stair backward, just as people typically descend a ladder.

A person can move up or down a hallway or ramp at any step increment (pace). This is very different from stairs, which must be traversed at the pace determined by the designer; a person can take two steps at a time, but one cannot take a ½ step or a 1¼ step, for example. So, it is important that the pace be comfortable for the average user, and, in most cases, such a pace is more likely to be safe. It is also important that every stair, although certainly not identical, be designed within reasonable pace parameters. The average indoor stride translates into a commonly used formula for proportioning riser/tread ratios (in the equation, R stands for riser, T for tread):

$2R + T = 25$ inches (24 inches min. to 26 inches max.)
(610 mm min. to 660 mm max.)

Examples using the given formula:

7-inch risers / 11-inch treads: 2 x 7 inches + 11 inches = 25 inches

7½-inch risers / 10-inch treads: 2 x 7½ inches + 10 inches = 25 inches

Maximum (IRC)/Minimum (IRC)

7¾-inch risers / 10-inch treads: 2 x 7¾ inches + 10 inches = 25½ inches

Note:

- 7 inches = 177.8 mm
- 7 ½ inches = 190.5 mm
- 7 ¾ inches = 196.9 mm
- 10 inches = 254 mm
- 11 inches = 279.4 mm

In ascending a stair, it is not necessary to place one's entire heel on the tread surface. However, in a descent mode, there must be room on the tread surface for the heel to rest (lightly or heavily). This means that the tread size must not be too small and the stair nose must be limited in size and/or designed in a manner that will not easily catch a stair user's heel in the descent mode (see Figure 2-15).

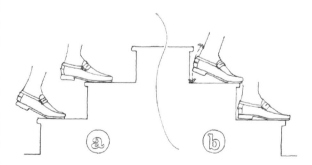

Figure 2-15 Ascending and descending stairs. In ascending a stair, heels are not necessarily placed on the entire tread surface. However, descending requires room on the tread surface for the heel to rest fully, requiring that the tread size not be too small and that the stair nose be limited in size and be detailed in a manner that will not easily catch a stair user's heel; too small a tread will put the toe too far out beyond the nosing and compromise the footing.

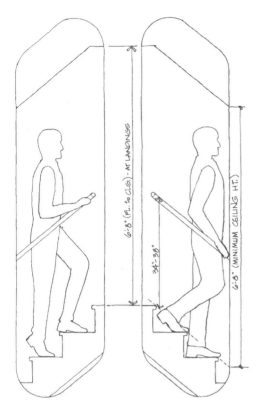

Figure 2-16 Headroom clearances at stairs and landings, and handrail heights at stairs. The code minimum for clear headroom heights is 6 feet, 8 inches (2032 mm); handrails are called for at 34 to 38 inches (864 to 965 mm).

Furthermore, too small a tread will put the toe too far out beyond the nosing and compromise the footing. Even an

adequate (legal) tread may prove to be difficult for people with very large feet, as they may be forced to set the foot askew on the tread to get full support. Consideration of headroom at stair locations is required for safety and comfort and by most codes. Headroom is defined as the clear vertical space from a stair tread (at the nosing) to any overhead obstruction, as shown in Figure 2-16.

Another safety consideration relates to materials used for the tread surface and especially the nosing. These must not be slippery or become slippery with wear. Slippery surfaces are likewise to be avoided on ramps; the steeper the ramp and the more exposed to the elements (rain/ice/snow), the more care that is required of the designer regarding suitable material selection.

A stable and easily graspable handrail is the final component in the design of a safe and comfortable stair/ramp to ascend and descend. A well-placed handrail will ensure that the user will always have the possibility of at least two points of body support (a hand and a foot) at any point in time. The designer should ascertain the best railing height in any given setting, within the parameters set by the code: generally 34 to 38 inches (864 to 965 mm) vertically above the nose. (See Figure 2-16.) As stated previously, the code minimum for clear headroom heights is 6 feet, 8 inches (2032 mm). While there are distinct code requirements for handrails, balusters, and railings, a variety of design and material options can meet requirements. Some are shown in Figure 2-17. For additional information, see the "Related Codes and Constraints" section of this chapter.

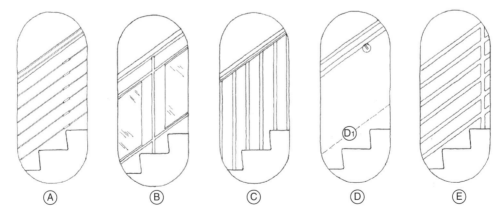

Figure 2-17 A range of handrail/railing design options that meet code requirements. As required, these do not allow passage of a sphere 4 inches (102 mm) or more in diameter of clear/open railing space (as described in the "Related Codes and Constraints" section of this chapter), and handrails are at 34 to 38 inches (864 to 965 mm).

A. Cable and turnbuckle with wood or metal handrail.
B. Glass and steel with wood or steel handrail.
C. Wood balusters and handrail.
D. Wood or metal handrail mounted on a half wall with metal rail brackets. D₁ shows a base or "skirt" at half wall.
E. Pipe railing; handrail: 1¼ to 2 inches (38 to 51 mm) in diameter.

ORGANIZATIONAL FLOW

Space that is devoted exclusively to circulation is often regarded as nonproductive and is to be minimized where possible. Exceptions would be found in those residences where the design statement is principally about circulation—the drama of movement, where the pleasure of the use of the residence is found in moving around in it.

Single-loaded circulation, as shown in Figure 2-18, item A, is twice as long and takes twice the time to negotiate as double-loaded circulation, shown in Figure 2-18, item B. This is true whether the circulation delivers access to rooms or simply to items such as equipment or furniture. Thoughtful design of the circulation space itself may involve the shape of the space and features along the way such as a view to the outside, an elevated view of other rooms, a gallery of artwork, the play of artificial or natural light, and so on. In creating views, in turn, circulation becomes more than a long, deadly corridor, as shown in Figure 2-18, item C.

The drama of movement, especially vertical movement, is a powerful tool in a designer's arsenal. The level of drama in vertical movement, for the observer as well as the mover, can be related to the relative speed of ascent or descent. For instance, stairs are generally more dramatic than ramps, a firehouse pole more dramatic than a stair (but, unfortunately, it works in one direction only). Vertical movement is also more hazardous than horizontal movement, an important issue for the designer. See the "Related Codes and Constraints" section of this chapter for a more complete discussion of safety issues.

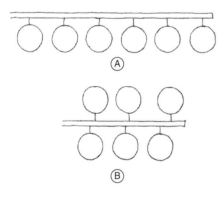

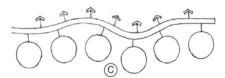

Figure 2-18 Simple diagrams illustrating a range of approaches to flow of circulation.

A. Diagram depicting single-loaded circulation flow, where rooms or areas flow in a single direction.

B. Diagram depicting double-loaded circulation flow and the efficiency thereof. Here rooms or areas flow in more than one direction using the same circulation space to access far more square footage.

C. Diagram depicting single-loaded circulation flow that is enhanced visually through the creation of views or emphasis, illustrating that in some cases the experience of space is improved by less efficient approach to circulation.

Stair design, in any given circumstance, is driven (at a minimum) by the following factors:

Flow within the residence

Floor (level) to floor (level) vertical distance

Minimum requirements of the applicable code(s)

Within the given parameters, the stair can be a design statement in and of itself—a piece of "sculpture" or fine woodwork/metalwork that becomes a dominant and memorable element in the residence.

Hallways (corridors) move the occupants horizontally from one part of the residence to another and, in the process, control the direction of flow. Ramps will do much the same thing, albeit with modest vertical gains or losses. Movement between floors (a full story) is seldom done with ramps because of the inordinate amount of space they take. For example, to move 9 feet (2743 mm) floor to floor would take a 1:12 ramp (required to move unassisted in a wheelchair), 125-plus lineal feet (38,100 mm) including landings every 30 feet (9144 mm), and approximately 400 total square feet (37 m²).

Well before that point (25 square feet [2.3 m²], plus or minus), it becomes less expensive to build a shaft and install a small residential elevator. Compared to most stairs that involve some horizontal movement (to the other side of the house in the case of a straight-run stair), one can enter and exit an elevator in the same relative horizontal position; in other words, you can enter and exit through the same wall of the shaft and find yourself directly above (or below) where the trip was started. It is also possible to enter through any given shaft wall and exit through the opposite or adjacent shaft wall (thereby necessitating a 90-degree turn). It has become increasingly common in recent years for clients to request framing a rough opening for future installation of an elevator. Often the future shaft is used as a closet or pantry on the floors where the elevator will have stops in the future. This type of planning is often done in cases where clients wish to "age in place."

A spiral stair comes close to an elevator in terms of requiring virtually no horizontal movement for the floor-to-floor traveler as well as a minimal footprint, just 20 square feet (1.86 m²) for a minimal spiral stair, which, for all practical purposes, is 5 feet (1524 mm) in diameter. Unlike an elevator, however, a spiral staircase is obviously not suitable for wheelchair use. That, coupled with the problem of moving large objects, such as furniture, up and down, relegate its use to secondary stairs or where there is access to open balconies (lofts, etc.) that provide an alternative route (albeit difficult) for moving furniture. The "Related Codes and Constraints" section of this chapter contains spiral stair examples.

Some projects call for monumental curved stairs; in such cases, creating the curve requires that each tread must vary (identically to all other treads) from one end to the other, but the tread/riser ratio should ideally be reasonable at both ends of each tread. This likely will result in a large radius to the curve of the stair: for example, 24 feet (73,151 mm). This, in turn, leads to a modest (less than 90 degrees) change in direction from the top to the bottom (see Figure 2-19, item D). A larger range of change

Figure 2-19 Stairs used to control direction of flow in the residence.

A. Straight-run stair; no change in direction.
B. An L stair; 90-degree change in direction.
C. Single U stair; 180-degree change in direction.
D. A curved (monumental) stair will commonly yield a 15- to 90-degree change in direction, but can be manipulated to be 1 to 180 degrees.
 D_1. Minimum tread depth should be 10 inches (254 mm) at the walkline
E. 1- to 90-degree change in direction.
F. 91- to 180-degree change in direction.

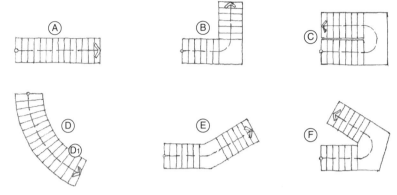

in direction (0 to 180 degrees) of a stair can be achieved with the use of landings, as shown in Figure 2-19. As already stated, curved stairs may result in very narrow treads at the inner radius; a *walkline* is an imaginary line a distance from the inner edge where people are meant to walk. Building codes specify a minimum depth at the walkline (see Figure 2-19, item D_1).

Figure 2-20 highlights some common errors and bad practices in stair design and delineation. In this example, the stairs occupy prime real estate within the home and are poorly planned and/or delineated for the reasons outlined in the caption.

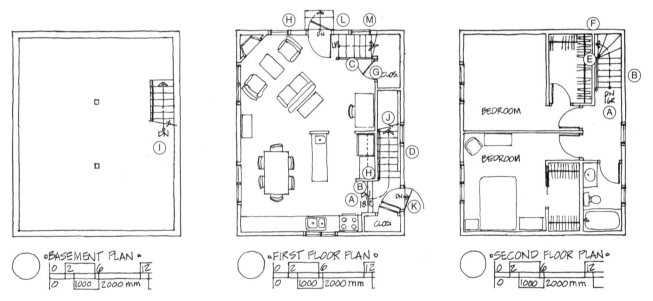

Figure 2-20 Negative (bad practice) examples meant to serve as illustrations of some common errors and/or bad practices in stair design and delineation. The stairs shown occupy prime real estate within the home, including exterior walls that might be better used for some exterior exposure/windows for light and air for the interior of the house. A central location for the stairs is often but certainly not always preferable from the standpoint of ease and efficiency of circulation. Stairs that do not stack *directly,* one over the other, result in greater horizontal travel distance; for example, the travel distance from basement to second floor involves an extra-long transfer distance (through two rooms) on the first floor.

A. The likelihood of there being more steps to the basement (18R) (first floor to basement) than to the second floor (16R) is minimal; 16R indicates that the first-floor ceiling is likely 9 feet (2743 mm), plus or minus. Though possible, 18R (10 feet [3048 mm], plus or minus), floor to floor, is not common for a basement.
B. Tread depth is insufficient; 10 inches (254 mm) is the required minimum.
C. Treads need to be a uniform depth in any given run of stair, not changed partway into the run.
D. The basement walls will likely be 2 to 6 inches (51 to 152 mm) thicker than the first-floor exterior walls; a basement stair that starts out at (a legal minimum) 3 feet (914 mm) wide on the first-floor plan becomes too narrow as the stair descends.
E. "Winder stairs" need a prescribed minimum tread depth at the narrow end; stair at corner is not legal as shown.
F. Insufficient head clearance (6 feet, 8 inches [2032 mm] required); the floor will have 12 inches (305 mm), plus or minus, of thickness and the head must clear the bottom-most portion of the floor structure.
G. Doors under stairs; check height available. In this case, the door would have to be shorter than a standard 6-foot, 8-inch (2032-mm) door.
H. Handrail not required by some codes (when less than four risers), but it would be considered good practice to install a handrail in this situation. See L below.
I. Directional arrows (and notation "UP"/"DN") should point from the floor level that is being shown; in this case, an "up" arrow should be shown starting at the bottom of the stair.
J. No break line should be shown on the "down" run of a stair; all the risers will be shown, or they will disappear under a floor/wall or the "up" run of another stair.
K. If there are steps at the "front door," it's almost a certainty, in the example shown, that exterior steps will be necessary at the "back door" in addition to those on the interior, Additionally, the maximum step from a secondary door to the ground is 7¾ inches (196.8 mm). See the "Related Codes and Constraints" section of this chapter.
L. Exterior steps. 3 by 3 feet (914 by 914 mm) minimum landing required; 3-foot-wide (914-mm) steps minimum (or as wide as the door); handrails required.
M. Windowsill may not be able to be as low as the symmetrical window on the other side of the "front door"; stair may partially block it.

Figures 2-21 to 2-23 provide examples of houses with different floor-to-floor heights, and each illustrates a different type of stair. As shown, common ceiling heights of 8 feet (2438 mm), 9 feet (2743 mm), and 10 feet (3048 mm) are going to result in floor-to-floor heights of 9 feet (2.74 m), plus or minus; 10 feet (3048 mm), plus or minus; and 11 feet (3353 mm), plus or minus, respectively. The floor thickness will vary, but a 12-inch (305-mm) thickness is a good preliminary assumption, and all of the examples use that assumption. In most projects, the floor thickness is frequently but not always in the 11- to 14-inch (279- to 356-mm) range.

Most stairs involve horizontal movement as well as the sought-after vertical movement. As shown in Figure 2-21, a straight-run stair involves the most horizontal movement. Information about L-shaped stairs can be found in Figure 2-22. U-shaped stairs, also known as scissor stairs and detailed in Figure 2-23, take a 180-degree turn over roughly half a floor.

U-shaped stairs, also known as scissor stairs and shown in Figure 2-23, take a 180-degree turn over roughly half a floor.

Any residential stair is often the dominant factor in the flow throughout the entire residence; it is imperative that the designer consider the stair not as an afterthought but as a critical element that can be as important as any other space in the residence. Bad decisions regarding a stair can ruin an otherwise fine design.

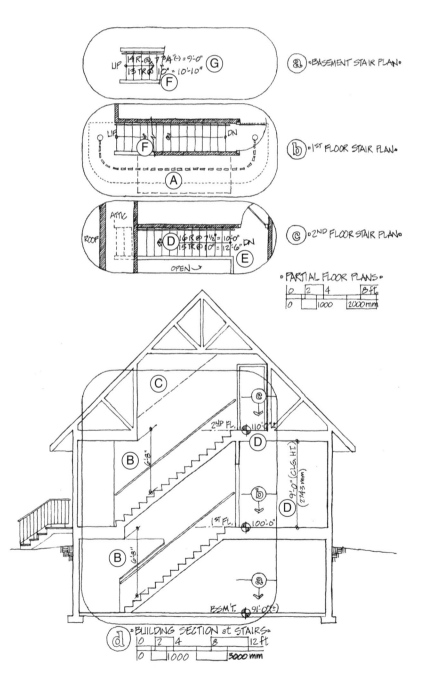

Figure 2-21 Straight-run stairs. Most stairs involve horizontal movement as well as vertical movement; a straight-run stair requires the most horizontal movement. In a modest-sized house, the stair will carry the user to the other side of the house, and then, continuing to another level, involves doubling back to the head or foot of the next stair, thereby requiring dedicated circulation space on the middle (transfer) level(s).

A. Movement from the second floor to basement (or vice versa) will require circulation space at the middle level (first floor in this case) to be able to get to the head or foot of the next stair; at a minimum, the total footprint (stair and first-floor circulation and landings at the top and bottom of each stair) can easily amount to more than 100 square feet (115 square feet [10.68 m²] in this example).
B. Required head clearance. Commonly 6 feet, 8 inches (2032 mm) in most codes.
C. Alternate ceiling, to reduce stair volume and consequent maintenance.
D. First floor to second floor stair total rise (with 9-foot [2743-mm] ceilings) is 10 feet (120 inches [3048 mm]) floor to floor.
   Design Calculation Options
   120 inches (3048 mm) divided by 15 risers = 8 inches (203.2 mm) each riser (may still be legal in some codes, but not the IRC).
   120 inches (3048 mm) divided by 16 risers = 7½ inches (190.5 mm) each riser (a suitable choice).
   120 inches (3048 mm) divided by 17 risers = 7.06 inches (179.3 mm) each riser (an easier stair to climb but will add 26 inches [660 mm] of length to the total run).
E. First floor to second floor stair, given the selection of 7½-inch risers above, total run:
   (2R + T = 25)
   2 x 7½ + T = 25
   T = 25 − (2 x 7½)
   T = 10 inches each tread (254 mm)
   Total run: 15 treads @ 10 inches (254 mm) = 150 inches, or 12 feet, 6 inches (3810 mm).
F. Break line—shown in all "up" runs.
G. Basement stair:
   14R at 7¾ inches (197 mm) = 9 feet (2743 mm)
   13TR at 10 inches (254 mm) = 10 feet, 10 inches (3302 mm)

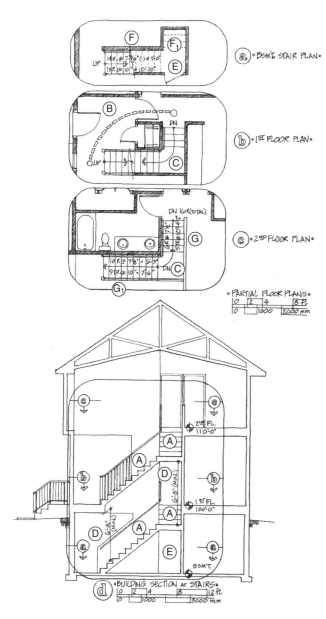

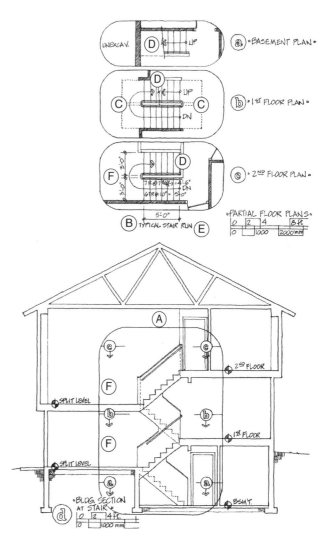

Figure 2-22 The L-shaped stair. This type of stair creates a 90-degree change in direction, which can be used to the designer's advantage to improve the circulation throughout the residence in certain situations. Less space is required to move from one stair to the other, on the first floor, than in the straight-run stair.

A. The two runs forming the L need not be identical in length.
B. Circulation route required at the first-floor level to be able to move easily to all three levels.
C. Minimum landing: 36 by 36 inches (914 by 914 mm); minimum stair width: 36 inches (914 mm).
D. Minimum head clearance at stair and landings: 6 feet, 8 inches (2032 mm) in most codes.
E. Door(s) located under stairs; check door height (in this case, the maximum door height would be about 5 feet, 8 inches [1727 mm]).
F. Break line on the "up" runs; steps above the break line can be shown with dashed line, if doing so helps with the drawing's clarity (F₁).
G. 6R at 7½ inches (190.5 mm) = 3 feet, 9 inches (1143 mm)
 5TR at 10 inches (254 mm) = 4 feet, 2 inches (1270 mm)
 G1. 10R at 7½ inches (190.5 mm) = 6 feet, 3 inches (1905 mm)
 9TR at 10 inches (254 mm) = 7 feet, 6 inches (2286 mm)

Figure 2-23 U stairs. This type of stair, also known as scissor stairs, takes a 180-degree turn every half (plus or minus) floor; therefore, the stair user winds up directly above or below where he or she started (every full story traveled). The resultant stair shape is quite square, as compared to the straight-run or L stair. The midlevel landings can be as small as 3 by 6 feet (914 by 1829 mm) plus or minus; conversely, landings can be as large as needed to accommodate the total design of the residence (e.g., to become part of a room that is at the landing level). The example shows equal runs: seven risers/seven risers on the top two stair runs; this is not required, as the 14 risers (floor to floor) could be divided: eight risers/six risers (as shown on the bottom two runs), nine risers/five risers, and so on.

A. Circulation path between all levels is the shortest of any of this set of examples shown in this and Figures 2-21 and 2-22.
B. Minimum footprint of (all) steps: 6 by 5 feet (30-plus-or-minus square feet [2.79 m²] is comparable to a 6-foot-diameter spiral stair with a 3-foot [914-mm] tread width: 28 square feet [2.6 m²]).
C. Landings: 36 by 36 inches (914 by 914 mm) required minimum landing at the top and bottom of each run. The stair minimum footprint, including landings, is 67 square feet (6.2 m²).
D. Break line shown on all "up" runs; "down" runs are shown in their entirety—until they disappear under the floor or the stair above.
E. Typical stair run:
 7R at 7¾ inches (197 mm) = 4 feet, 6 inches (1372 mm)
 6TR at 10 inches (254 mm) = 5 feet (1524 mm)
F. Landing or room.

RELATED CODES AND CONSTRAINTS

Interior stairs, hallways, exterior doors, and, less commonly, ramps may, at some point in the life of the structure, need to be used as a means of emergency egress from the residence. That egress needs to be safe and must therefore comply with applicable portions of the code. Stairs are also an inherently hazardous element in the residence during normal daily use as well as when used for emergency egress. For these reasons, building codes are quite specific and rigorous in their delineation of minimum requirements for those elements (doors, hallways, stairs, and ramps) that facilitate or impede movement.

Section R311 of the IRC requires that dwellings have a means of egress that provides a continuous and unobstructed path (vertical and horizontal) from all areas of the dwelling to the exterior, without going through a garage.

In addition, Section R311.2 states that not less than one egress door must be provided for each unit. The door must be side-hinged and provide a minimum clear width of 32 inches (813 mm) and a clear minimum height of not less than 78 inches (1981 mm); for practical purposes, this requires a standard door size of 3 feet by 6 feet, 8 inches (914 by 2032 mm) or larger. The egress door must be openable from the inside without a special key or specialized knowledge. The IRC does not require that other doors comply with these minimum dimensions. Some codes may require a secondary door as well as bedroom egress windows (see Chapter 5). These stated requirements for an egress door also create a door that is wheelchair accessible if coupled with a compliant threshold.

The code (Section R311.3) also requires that there be a floor or landing on each side of every exterior door and that the landing have a minimum dimension of 36 inches (914 mm) running in the direction of the path of travel with a width not less than the door. There are exceptions for other exterior doors such as patio doors that are less restrictive; these can be found in Sections R311.3.2 and R311.3.3. For example storm doors are allowed to swing out over exterior steps and/or landings.

Another important egress and circulation issue covered by the IRC is hallway width. Section R311.6 requires a minimum hallway width of "not less than three feet (914 mm)." This is also the appropriate minimum for wheelchair-accessible hallways and paths of travel.

The following is a list of code-related requirements as well as health/life safety con-

siderations and suggestions related to the design of stairs and stairways. Figures 2-24 to 2-28 illustrate the items.

Checklist of Code-Related Requirements and Health/Life Safety Considerations for Stairs and Stairways (see also Figures 2-24 to 2-28).

☐ As stated previously in this chapter, avoid designing stairs that are too steep. Some codes may allow a riser to be as much as 8 inches (203 mm). The IRC maximum is 7¾ inches (197 mm). The corollary tread is 9 inches (229 mm) minimum in some codes; 10 inches (254 mm) minimum in the IRC. See Figure 2-26.

☐ Avoid slippery tread surfaces; the stair nose is a particularly critical surface.

☐ Provide adequate width, enough that it is possible for two average adults to meet and pass on the stairs and not necessitate contortions, on the part of one or both, sufficient to force them off balance.

☐ Provide adequate headroom. A residence is required to have 6 feet, 8 inches (2032 mm) of head clearance at

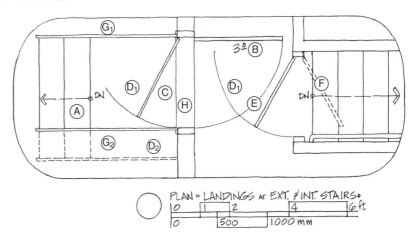

Figure 2-24 An illustration of various code regulations for entry steps and doors, as well as landings and doors at stairs.

A. The number of steps will vary to accommodate the site and the type of house construction (such as basement/no basement); in many geographic areas where basements are not common, no exterior steps will be necessary.

B. Required 3-foot (providing 32 inches [813 mm] minimum clearance) residential entrance/exit door.

C. Screen/storm door is a climatic requirement only.

D₁. Landing or floor on each side of each exterior door. 3 by 3 feet (914 by 914 mm) minimum (Section R311.3).

D₂. Extra width (beyond minimum) is desirable; it serves as a place for the user to stand while opening an out-swinging door.

E. A floor or landing is at the top and bottom of each stairway, and the landing must have a minimum dimension of 36 inches (914 mm) running in the direction of the path of travel with a required width not less than the stairway served by the landing (Section R311.7.6). A door may be at the landing with limitations; see F below.

F. Do not swing a door *into* a stair at the top of a flight of stairs.

G₁. The IRC requires that porches, balconies, or raised floor surfaces located more than 30 inches (762 mm) above the floor or grade below must have guards that are not less than 36 inches (914 mm) in height. In addition, open sides of stairs with a total rise of more than 30 inches (762 mm) are required to have guards not less than 34 inches (864 mm) in height (Section R312).

G₂. Railing not required in this case (stoop is approximately 24 inches [610 mm] above grade), but good practice would call for installation of a railing—especially in this case where the stoop is code minimum width.

H. Door threshold.

doors/doorways. That should be matched or exceeded on a stair. The possibility of the user bumping his or her head while traversing a stair is, obviously, to be avoided. The IRC allows for a minimum of 6 feet, 8 inches (2032 mm), but this is not ideal. Avoid built-in tripping hazards. The nosing detail is critical in minimizing this hazard. See Figure 2-25.

☐ Provide lateral support for the upper body. Support, in the form of a handrail, is mandatory. The rail needs to be easily graspable, sturdy, and at an optimal height. See Figures 2-25 and 2-26.

☐ In order to eliminate falls off the side of a stair, railing assemblies need to be solid or the components need to be spaced close enough together to disallow the passage of a small child's or baby's head. The actual dimensions for this vary by code, but they are consistent in concept and are often roughly described as not allowing the passage of a sphere 4 inches (102 mm) or more in diameter through the clear/open railing space; 6 inches (152 mm) may be allowed at the juncture of a tread and the adjoining riser. See Figure 2-26.

☐ Limit the potential falling distance. Provide landings at no more than every 12 feet, 3 inches (3734 mm) of vertical distance; provide a substantial landing (3 feet [914 mm] minimum by the width of the stair) in the path of travel (Section R311.7.3). See Figure 2-25.

☐ Provide good illumination for the stair. The IRC minimum is 1 foot-candle at the center of every tread and landing (and should be seen as a minimum).

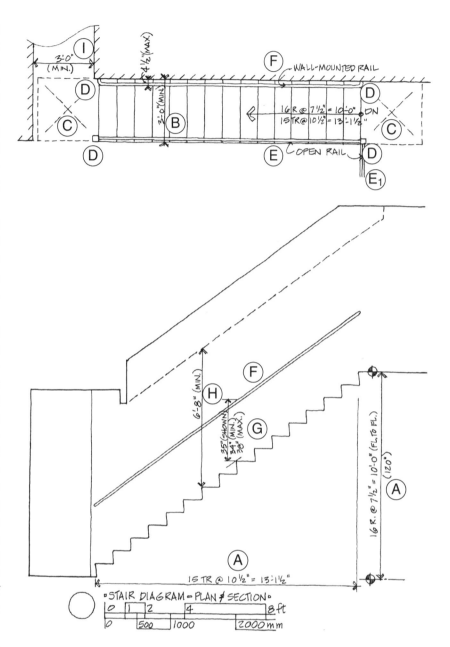

Figure 2-25 An illustration of various code requirements for interior stair design.

A. See Figure 2-21, items D and E, for detailed information on stair design/calculation.
B. Stair width: 36 inches (91 mm) minimum (Section R311.7.1).
C. 36-inch (914-mm) landing (in this case stair width and the code minimum) required at top and bottom (Section R311.7.6), or match the stair width if wider than 36 inches (914 mm).
D. Terminate handrail at newel post or return to wall at a point directly above lowest and highest riser (Section R311.7.8.2).
E. One handrail (minimum) is required in any stair with four or more risers (Section R311.7.8). In addition, a railing (guard) is required on open side of stairs measuring more than 30 inches (762 mm) from the floor below.
E₁. The IRC requires that railings at balconies and open landings be 36 inches (914 mm) high (Section R312.1.2).
F. Railing at wall. Optional in this case (given the railing on the other side); cannot project more than 4½ inches (114 mm) into the required minimum width of stair (3 feet [914 mm]) and must clear the wall by 1½ inches (38 mm) (Section R311.7.8.2).
G. Handrail height. Minimum 34 inches (864 mm), maximum 38 inches (965 mm); measured vertically from a typical nose (Section R311.7.8.1).
H. Stair headroom. 6 feet, 8 inches (2032 mm) minimum; measured vertically from the plane of the nosings or any landing (Section R311.7.2).
I. Hallways. 36 inches (914 mm) wide minimum (Section R311.6).

Figure 2-26 An illustration of code regulations related to riser, tread, nosing handrail, and guard rail requirements.

A. Riser height. "The maximum riser height shall be 7¾ inches (196 mm)" (IRC 311.7.5.1). There is no absolute minimum, but a good rule-of-thumb working minimum is 7 inches (178 mm), plus or minus.

B. Tread depth should be a minimum of 10 inches (254 mm) (IRC 311.7.5.2). The depth of the tread should increase as the riser decreases. (Refer to the "Ergonomics and Required Clearances" section of this chapter.)

C. Nosing. The IRC requires that the "radius of curvature at the leading edge of the tread shall be no greater than 9/16 inch (14.3 mm)" and requires a nosing of not less than ¾ inch (19 mm), not more than 1¼ inches (32 mm) on stairways with solid risers (IRC 311.7.5). Where the tread depth is a minimum of 11 inches (279 mm), nosing is not required.

D. The IRC permits open risers as long as the opening between treads does not permit the passage of a sphere 4 inches (102 mm) in diameter (IRC 311.7.5.1).

E. The IRC requires a handrail height of 34 inches (864 mm) minimum, 38 inches (965 mm) maximum (IRC 311.7.8). In addition, handrails for stairways should be continuous for the full length of the flight. Code also requires that handrail ends return or terminate in newel posts or safety terminals. Handrails can be interrupted by a newel post at the turn and a "volute, turnout, starting easing or starting newel shall be allowed over the lowest tread" (IRC311.7.8.2). See E₁.

F. Code requires guards (railings) on open sides of "stairways, raised floor areas, balconies, and porches" with intermediate rails or ornamental closures that do not allow passage of a "sphere 4 inches (102 mm) or more in diameter" (see F₁); while there are exceptions (see

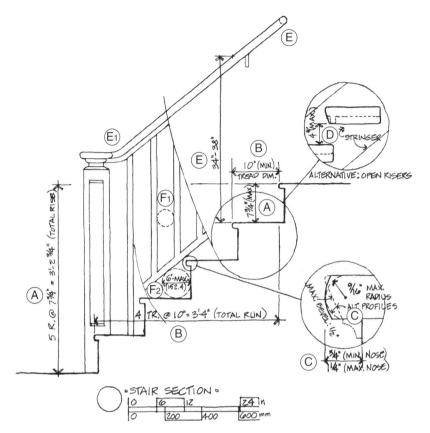

F₂), this is a good rule of thumb for guardrail design (IRC312). The railing requirement is applicable to all stairs, landings, porches, and balconies that are 30 inches (762 mm) or more above adjacent floor or grade. Local codes may be more restrictive; for example, railings may be required at 18 inches (457 mm) above floor or grade.

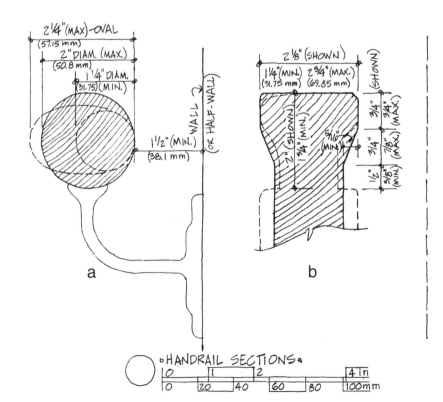

Figure 2-27 Illustrations of the requirements for "graspability."

Type **a** handrail requirements are relatively straightforward: minimum perimeter is 4 inches (102 mm), maximum is 6¼ inches (153 mm).

Type **b** has much more varied possible profiles; two of many possible profiles are shown with dashed lines. This figure delineates only a very limited interpretation of the code requirements described in the IRC.

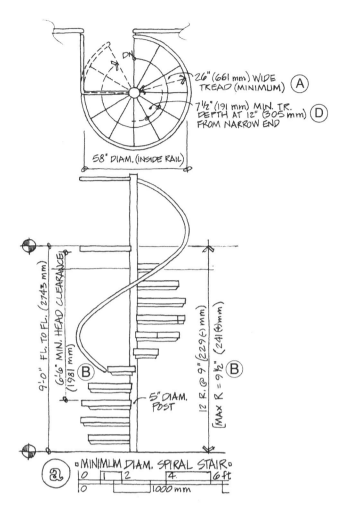

Figure 2-28 An illustration of spiral stairs that meet the minimum requirements of the IRC. The example shown is for a 9-foot (2743-mm) floor-to-floor height. Floor-to-floor height varies with the specific residence design.

A. Stair **a** (shown) illustrates the code minimum tread width spiral stair; all tread widths must be identical.
B. All risers are identical and must be no more than 9½ inches (241 mm). The IRC requires a tread depth of not less than 6¾ inches (171 mm) at the walkline of travel. Minimum headroom of 6 feet, 6 inches (1982 mm) is required for this type of stair (Section R311.7.10.1).
Note that for clarity and ease of drawing, balusters are not shown, but are required similar to straight-run stair requirements.

The design of ramps is similar to the design of stairs in terms of the need and standards for handrails and for landings at the top, bottom, and where ramps change direction (minimum landing is 3 by 3 feet [914 by 914 mm]; see Section R311.8). There is a significant difference between what is allowed for ramps in public accommodations versus private residences in terms of slope, width, length, and landing size. In residential use, ramps serving a required egress door must meet the 1:12 slope requirement. The amount of space consumed by a ramp (the footprint) should not be underestimated. It will be significant, and the designer should take that reality into account in the initial stages of the design process.

ELECTRICAL AND MECHANICAL

Much like other areas of the home, circulation areas require general electrical outlets at minimum for cleaning and maintenance. Following general rules of thumb for outlet spacing and placement will suffice in most instances; these can be found in Chapter 1. Keep in mind, however, that specialized situations may require additional outlets or unusual placement or mounting heights.

LIGHTING

Lighting for circulation spaces varies greatly based on the type of space involved. For example, decorative lighting for an elegant open stair located in or near an entry foyer may be supplied by a chandelier and layered with additional ambient

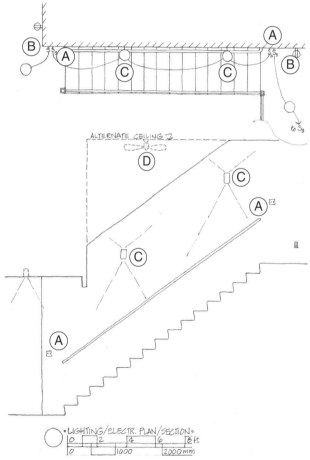

Figure 2-29 Lighting/electrical plan and section at a stairwell.

A. Stair lighting requires a switch (S3, a three-way switch) at both the head and the foot of every stair.
B. Hallway lighting should also be switched at each end of any hall.
C. Light distribution is important. Wall sconces are shown providing up- and down-light (in this case, mounted at 6 feet, 8 inches (2032 mm) above the finished floor).
D. If the HVAC system requires a ceiling fan, a high ceiling in a stairwell can be an unobtrusive location.

light provided by wall sconces or adjustable downlights. On the other hand, lighting in more utilitarian circulation spaces may be provided without decorative fixtures and supplied instead by recessed downlights, surface- or ceiling-mounted luminaires, or cove- or soffit-mounted fluorescent fixtures.

Given the range of types of circulation spaces within most houses, careful consideration of any desired aesthetic effects as well as the use and requirements of each space must occur. Great drama may be provided in some foyer/entry areas and hallways through the use of chandeliers, pendant fixtures, and wall sconces, and, in fact, many such spaces with higher-than-standard ceilings call for this kind of decorative lighting. In some homes, long hallways serve as gallery spaces, and these are well served by accent lighting in addition to general/ambient lighting. In other cases, hallways and other circulation spaces may benefit from a simple approach to lighting that provides adequate light levels for safe passage in a way that makes a minimal visual impact.

The previous two paragraphs point to the need to establish specific lighting design criteria for circulation spaces. This requires noting any specific visual or aesthetic requirements for each space as well as the basic functional requirements of adequate lighting for safe passage, in addition to the architectural parameters, and making design decisions accordingly.

Because circulation spaces are designed to facilitate movement, the location of switches and controls provided in such spaces must work to support that movement. This often requires providing switching at both ends of any particular circulation space, for example, at the top and bottom of a run of stairs and at each end of a hallway, as shown in Figure 2-29. It is not uncommon for central controls or home security system controls to be placed within a circulation space, although this varies based on layout and design.

REFERENCES

Contains both works cited and recommended reading.

Abercrombie, Stanley. 1991. *A Philosophy of Interior Design*. New York: HarperCollins.

Alexander, Christopher, et al. 1977. *A Pattern Language*. New York: Oxford University Press. A seminal work worth owning.

International Code Council. 2015. "2015 International Residential Code for One- and Two-Family Dwellings." Country Club Hills, IL: International Code Council.

Rumberger, Janet, ed. 2003. *Architectural Graphic Standards for Residential Construction*. Hoboken, NJ: John Wiley & Sons.

Whitehead, Randall. 2004. *Residential Lighting: A Practical Guide*. Hoboken, NJ: John Wiley & Sons.

CHAPTER 3
Social and Leisure Spaces

INTRODUCTION

Living room, gathering room, great room, family room—all of these terms describe a space where people gather to interact and take part in various forms of entertainment, from reading to playing video games to watching movies. For many current homeowners, a formal living room—"where no one ever goes"—is no longer desired. Instead, a great room or gathering room where all family members can come together and take part in a range of activities is preferable. However, some homeowners desire a room for more formal events, and there may be a desire for a room used by the adults in the family, with younger family members using a separate room, often called a family room or den. Similarly, formal dining rooms are not favored by some current homeowners, who prefer a more casual eating area that is open or partially open to the kitchen, forming a cooking, eating, and entertainment area.

Formal living rooms and parlors, casual youth-oriented entertainment rooms, informal and/or formal dining areas, and media rooms (including home theaters) are all places where people gather for interaction and entertainment. Careful client interviews and programming are required in order to design spaces that reflect family interests and support interaction. In planning such spaces, the first steps involve a thorough review of the owner's spatial requirements, day-to-day activities, and interests. Armed with a clear understanding of a homeowner's actual needs and activities, the designer can undertake the design of such places.

Although the various leisure spaces differ in terms of formality, size, and, to some degree, activities undertaken, they all share the primary need for furniture groupings that support interaction (such as conversation). Interestingly, while dining areas can be seen as supporting very different functions than, say, formal parlors, they share the similarity of seated activities being the focus of the experience conducted in the room. Therefore, we can see all of these rooms as being based, to some degree, on the organization of seating and related furnishings.

Media rooms (including home theaters) and home gyms are increasingly favored by homeowners, particularly those with large residences and/or those involved in large-scale renova-tion and building additions. The design of home theaters and specialized media rooms requires an understanding of equipment and acoustics that goes beyond the scope of this book. Refer to the references at the end of this chapter for information on publications that cover home theater design. The design of home theaters and media rooms has become a design specialty, with a number of firms and studios available for design or design/build services. Home gym design and layout vary, depending on room size, equipment used, and manufacturers' suggested clearances. See Chapter 7 for more information on home gyms and home office design.

Spaces that are specifically meant to support conversation require seating and/or furniture that can accommodate a certain number of people, arranged at appropriate distances for speaking and discussion. In addition, such spaces, as well as all others used for leisure activities, require adequate circulation. Additional information about furniture layout and clearances is provided later in this chapter.

In addition to furniture placement supportive of interaction and appropriate circulation, many leisure spaces are designed in relation to some focal point. A fireplace or wood stove, window(s), views, or a television or screen may become focal points and therefore major influencing factors on the design of the space and the layout of furnishings. Artwork may be displayed in leisure spaces and can also influence or be influenced by furnishings.

The discussion of room design in this chapter is less technical and in some ways more general than discussions of most other rooms covered in this book. This was done in order to adapt to the many types of rooms, situations, and architectural parameters that may present themselves in the design of leisure spaces. In this chapter, we approach leisure spaces broadly, in order to aid in the design of a wide range of spaces and a wide range of room types and combinations that may present themselves in current design practice. Therefore, readers will find fewer illustrations of specific room designs and prototypes than in previous chapters and a more general discussion of the design of leisure spaces.

Regardless of the relative size of the room or its specialized nature, there are some general rules that can be of help in planning leisure spaces. Areas that are meant to support inter-action are best planned for a minimum of six seated individuals. This is not true for dining spaces but generally holds true for other rooms where other forms of interaction take place. When there is not room for six actual seats—such as in the case of small rooms or rooms used for a range of purposes—it is helpful to find an area for standing interaction for six. This could be done by providing four seats plus room for two people to stand. Another option is to allow space for pulling up a small chair or chairs.

The authors have found that it is best to cluster seating arrangements in seating groups of six people, when possible; therefore, we can consider seating areas for six both a minimum and a maximum—or an ideal. We have found that groups larger than six tend to splinter into smaller conversations, dividing the larger group into *conversation clusters,* or create a situation where individuals are "left out" of conversations. We have also found that dividing larger leisure spaces into a series of areas for smaller-group interaction (groups of six and smaller) also provides for better acoustics, because groups are clustered away from one another.

Because of the limits of human hearing and issues related to social interaction, furniture within the cluster should be spaced from approximately 4 to 10 feet (1200 to 3048 mm) apart. Depending on furniture size and room configuration, the actual area of a conversation cluster should be approximately 12 to 13 feet (3658 to 3962 mm) in diameter to best support interaction. Figure 3-1 illustrates conversation clusters with a range of seating options.

Conversation clusters may be created within larger spaces by simply arranging furniture into separate groupings. When possible, architectural elements such as alcoves can serve as the setting for conversation clusters. Alcoves also work well to articulate areas in which different activities take place—for example, a home office or computer space works well set into an alcove within a larger room. In addition to architectural features that reinforce clusters of seating, rooms may be divided into clusters based on focal points, such as windows, fireplaces, or televisions, or on other uses, such as a game table area. Figure 3-2 illustrates a room with two seating clusters with different functions and/or focal points.

As with all spaces described in this book, the overall square footage, general layout, and activities engaged in will greatly alter the furnishings within the space. The most basic seating cluster will consist of varied forms of seating, such as a sofa and two chairs or two sofas and a chair, plus some type of table upon which to place items such as drinks, reading material, and remote controls. Specialized areas such as game areas, very small rooms, and media rooms may require furnishings other than those mentioned.

Actual furniture sizes and ergonomics must be considered as arrangements are designed. Furniture sizes have kept up with the ever-increasing size of American houses, with larger and oversized leisure space furnishings becoming increasingly popular. One issue with larger furnishings is that deep seats can be less comfortable for shorter people who may not be able to place their feet comfortably on the floor while seated. Figure 3-3 depicts a range of sizes for various types of seating for non-dining areas. Figure 3-4 depicts sizes of some tables and storage units for leisure rooms. Figure 3-5 depicts sizes of some dining furnishings. For additional information on furniture arrangement and layout of specific types of spaces, refer to the "Ergonomics and Required Clearances" and "Organizational Flow" sections of this chapter. Note that metric furniture dimensions are listed in centimeters, following most manufacturers' standards.

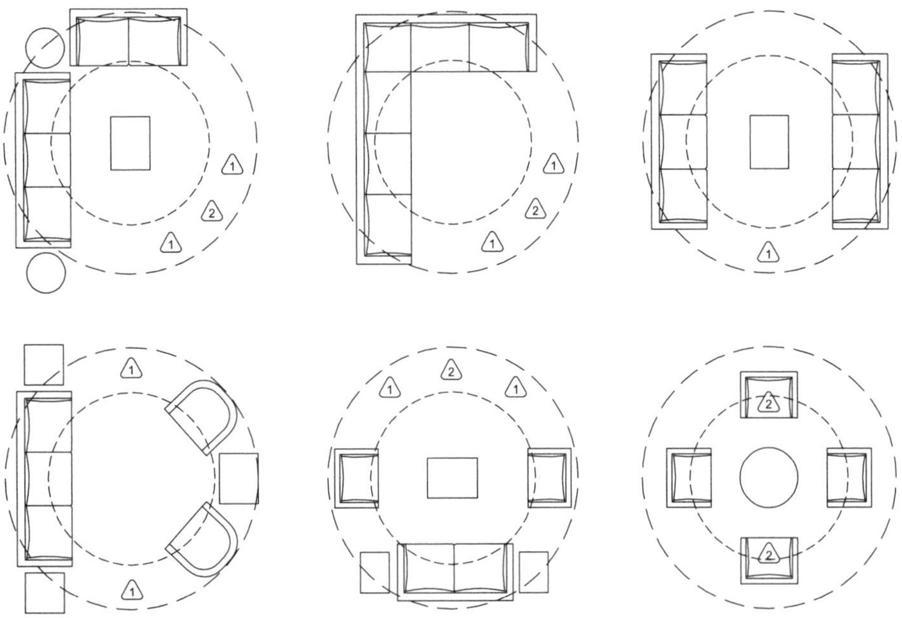

Figure 3-1 Large groups tend to break into smaller groups of four to six people, creating conversation clusters. Conversation clusters support interaction. The outer dashed circle on each illustration depicts the outer limits of furniture arrangement that will support successful interaction, roughly 12 to 13 feet (3658 to 3962 mm) in diameter; limits for face-to-face interaction are indicated by the inner dashed circle, roughly 6 to 10 feet (1200 to 3048 mm).

1. Room for standing interaction or for seating to be pulled up on occasion.
2. Could be a seating location or a focal point.
   For dimensions of furniture, see Figures 3-3, 3-4, and 3-5.

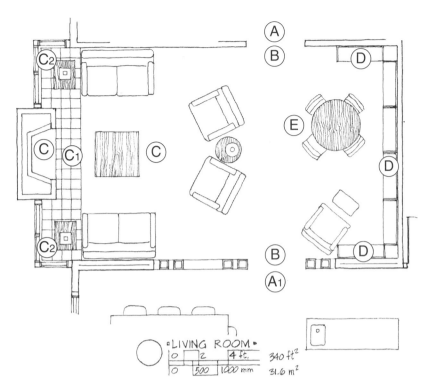

Figure 3-2 Furniture can be arranged into separate groups or clusters within the larger space. This room contains two seating clusters with differing functions and different focal points.

A. Access to bedroom(s).
   A_1. Access to dining/kitchen/utility spaces beyond.
B. Through traffic is straightforward and does not go through any of the activity/furniture clusters.
C. Focus of the seating cluster is a fireplace and/or television (the location of the television above the fireplace is too high for some clients). Also, the furniture placement shown is not ideal for television viewing by larger groups.
   C_1. Keep a fireplace low (hearth at floor level) if there is a television in addition to the fireplace; a wood-burning fireplace requires a noncombustible hearth 16 to 20 inches (406 to 508 mm) from the fire area opening; check local codes.
   C_2. Hearth shown extends to the side walls; this is not a code requirement.
D. Bookshelves.
E. Game table or library/study/homework table.

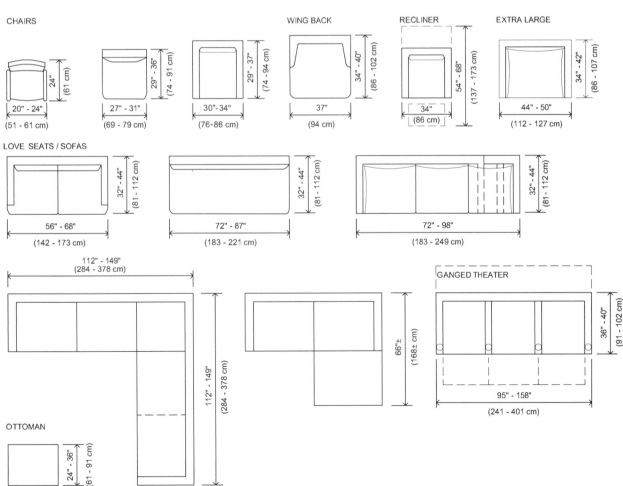

Figure 3-3 Sofa, love seat, and chair sizes. These are for preliminary planning purposes; consult manufacturers for actual product dimensions. Sectionals often consist of armless/single-armed models; consult manufacturers for dimensions/details.

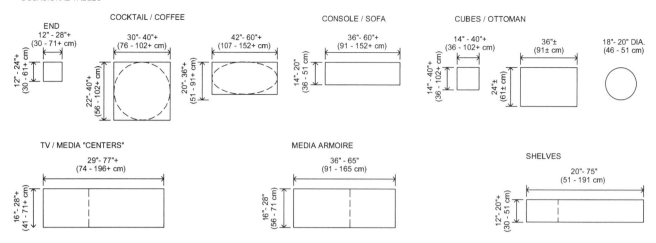

OCCASIONAL TABLES

Figure 3-4 Occasional, coffee, and media-center table sizes. These are for preliminary planning purposes; consult manufacturers for actual product dimensions; cabinets meant to sit below flat-screen televisions may be 16 inches (46 cm) deep.

In many ways, dining areas offer fewer options for laying out spaces than do other leisure spaces because they are typically focused on a single table with appropriate seating. Generally, the only options dining rooms present are the size and shape of the table and, in some cases, table location. Room size, shape, and the level of formality required will influence table shape and other furnishing selections. Views and window locations and the existence of some other focal point—such as a fireplace—will also influence table shape and location. Also, as noted in the "Lighting" section later in this chapter, the table shape and location can influence—or be influenced by—decorative lighting location(s).

Round tables can nurture conversation within smaller groups of four to six people and work well in small alcoves such as breakfast nooks and are useful as game tables. Placement of additional furnishings such as buffets and china hutches generally involves consideration of circulation space and location of walls or corners (for use of corner hutches).

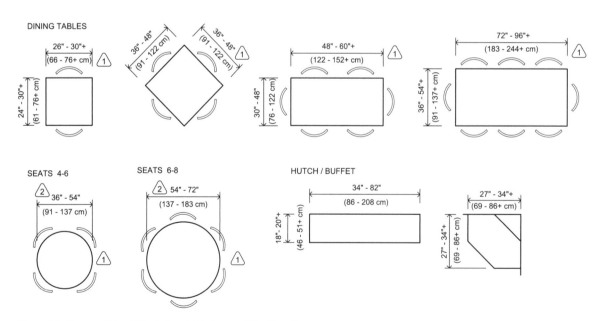

Figure 3-5 Common dining table, chair, and dish storage unit furniture sizes.

1. Tables shown have the potential for extensions and leaves, which will add to the overall dimensions (or, in some cases, reduce the table size). Extensions and leaves vary in size, often adding 10 to 18 inches (254 to 457 mm) for each extension. These are for preliminary planning purposes; consult manufacturers for actual product dimensions.
2. The smaller dimension indicated seats the smaller number of people indicated.

These issues are discussed further in the "Ergonomics and Required Clearances" and "Organizational Flow" sections later in the chapter.

ACCESSIBILITY NOTE

In contrast to chapters on other spaces covered in this book, there is little technical information provided regarding accessibility of leisure spaces. Compared to kitchens and baths, leisure spaces tend to have fewer built-in cabinets and other elements that can create barriers to those using wheelchairs or walkers or those with mobility limitations. However, access to and enjoyment of leisure spaces by all requires careful planning of circulation routes, locations of switches and controls, and arrangement of furnishings. These issues are addressed in this chapter in the appropriate sections.

Making sure that access to the leisure space requires no steps is a major factor in making the space wheelchair accessible as well as visitable. It is also worth noting that selection of furnishings must be made with special attention to the ease of sitting on and getting out of chairs and sofas, which can be an issue for a range of individuals of various heights and those with mobility problems. Huge, overstuffed chairs with low or unsupportive seats can be very difficult to get out of for individuals with mobility

limitations. With an aging population, this will be an increasing problem. Also, very deep seats may not allow shorter people to place their feet comfortably on the floor while seated.

ERGONOMICS AND REQUIRED CLEARANCES

Planning leisure spaces requires consideration of providing adequate space for each individual to sit and conduct the desired activity (e.g., television viewing or conversing while playing games) as well as adequate circulation. Figure 3-6 illustrates the room required for comfortable adult seating.

Screen Size and Viewing Distance

When planning seating in relationship to screen viewing the below rules of thumb can be helpful.

Screen Size, inches (mm)	Distance from Sofa/Seat to Screen, feet (mm)
40 (1016)	5–8 (1524–2438)
46 (1168)	6–10 (1829–3048)
52 (1016)	7–11 (2134–3353)

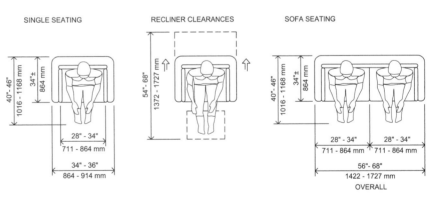

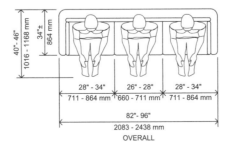

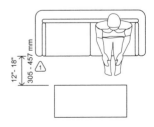

Figure 3-6 Space required for adult seating (sizes shown are for upholstered pieces). The space requirements shown are based on male and female adult averages. The 12-inch (305-mm) dimension shown (1) is a minimum and only possible in cases where the table length is also minimal; longer tables, such as that shown, require greater access space for comfortable movement.

Dining tables require adequate space for each seated individual as well as for serving pieces, dishes, and table decorations. The areas allotted for serving pieces, dishes, and decorations are considered shared access zones. More formal dining areas generally require more space in the access zone in order to accommodate more formal dining as well as room for more formal place settings. Peninsulas and dining bars generally have minimal shared access zones because of the casual nature of the dining experience. These are covered in detail in Chapter 4. Figure 3-7 shows required spaces for place settings and shared access zones for various table shapes. Figures 3-8a and 3-8b illustrate clearances for dining areas, including necessary space for circulation to and within the area.

Generally speaking, outdoor dining spaces have the same spatial requirements as those given in Figures 3-7, 3-8a, and 3-8b.

ORGANIZATIONAL FLOW

Circulation and flow through leisure spaces is dependent on the relationship of doors and the related circulation patterns that flow from doors and doorways to adjacent rooms, spaces, and furnishings. Put simply, the locations of doors and passageways influence the flow through a leisure space and the related arrangement of furnishings. Numerous doorways and passageways into leisure spaces can negatively impact furniture arrangement, as can the location of poorly placed doors, as shown in Figures 3-9a to 3-9c. Additional influencing factors in organizing leisure spaces include the relationship of furnishing groupings to windows, additional architectural elements and focal points, and a consideration of conversation clusters, as previously discussed.

Doors and passageways can also have a negative impact upon dining room furniture arrangement because doors and doorways dictate the circulation through the room and because the dining table often occupies a central location within the room, as shown in Figures 3-10a to 3-10c. In temperate climates and/or on certain building sites, a door leading to the exterior from leisure and dining spaces can be desirable (see Figures 3-11a and 3-11b). The location of such doors requires consideration of circulation patterns and furniture arrangements. See Figures 3-9a, 3-9b, and 3-9c.

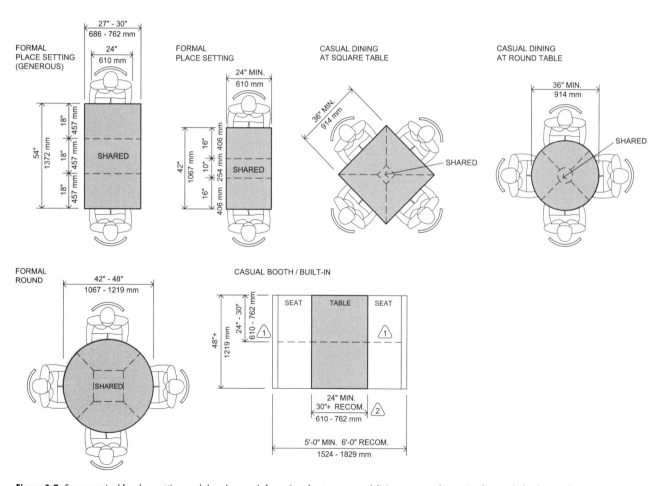

Figure 3-7 Space required for place settings and shared access. Information about more casual dining spaces such as eating bars and islands, as well as chair heights, can be found in Chapter 4.

1. Area required for a single seat.
2. Minimum table dimension shown is very tight for dining; 36 inches (914 mm) is ideal for full-meal dining.

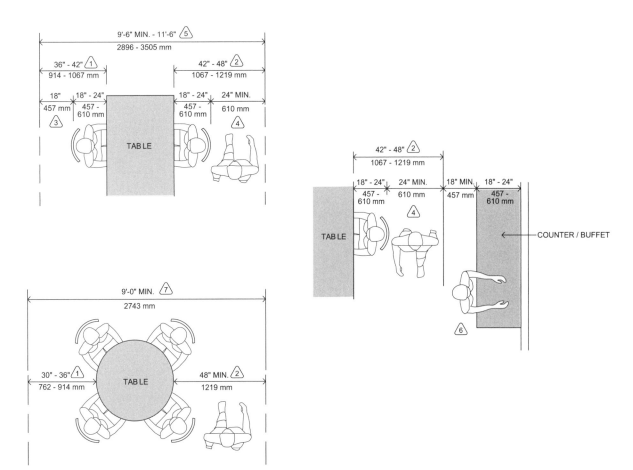

Figure 3-8a Required clearances at and for circulation to and around dining areas.

1. Required clearance from table edge to wall or obstacle to allow access to chair and clearance for chair movement; total dimension is dependent on chair size. The use of round tables can allow for a minimum of 30 inches (762 mm), as shown in the lower left illustration, but this varies depending on chair size and room form.
2. Required clearance for through circulation and seating.
3. This shows the minimum required for seating space (18 inches [457 mm]) and the minimum required for chair movement and body placement (18 inches [457 mm]), which allows for seated individuals to pull away from the table to relax or stand at their chair; total dimension is dependent on chair size. Note: Using the minimum spacing does not allow for through traffic in the area behind seated user. See item 4.
4. 24 inches (610 mm) is required for forward movement/through traffic circulation in addition to the minimum clearance required for seating (18 inches [457 mm] minimum).
5. Minimum room width for activities shown.
6. Minimum clearance for standing activity, such as a buffet line.
7. Minimum casual or breakfast room dimensions—round table.

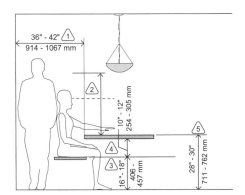

Figure 3-8b Sectional view of required seated dimensions and clearances in dining areas.

1. This shows the minimum required for seating space and the minimum required for chair movement and body placement (36 inches [914 mm]), which allows for seated individuals to pull away from the table to relax or stand at their chair; total dimension is dependent on chair size. Note: Using the minimum spacing does not allow for through traffic in the area behind seated user. Providing room for through traffic requires a minimum of 18 inches (914 mm) for the chair and 24 inches (1067 mm) for circulation, with more than the minimum space required for ease of movement.
2. Eye level varies greatly; 27 inches (686 mm) is at the low range and 34 inches (864 mm) is at the high range; hanging luminaires should be placed above this height or be adjustable (30 inches above table height is a good average standard).
3. Seat height varies: height of seat back also varies.
4. A minimum space of 7½ inches (190 mm) must be provided between seat top and table bottom; 10 to 12 inches (254 to 305 mm) is a more comfortable range for most seated users.
5. Standard table height varies from 28 to 30 inches (711 to 762 mm).
   Note: See Appendix C for dimensions related to seated wheelchair use.

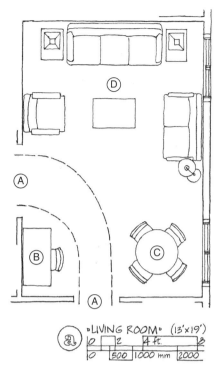

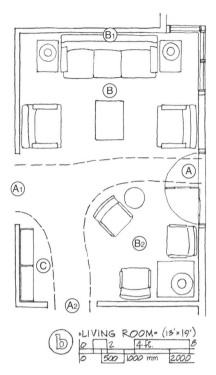

Figure 3-9a Door and passageway placement has an impact upon furniture arrangements and conversation clusters.

A. Through traffic originating from two adjacent walls allows for a range of options in seating arrangements.
B. A desk for working on a computer/writing/reading in a corner that is not suited for much more.
C. A game table corner for study/games/projects.
D. Seating cluster for six; as shown, there is no focal point; to allow for a focal point, seating could be rearranged.

Figure 3-9b Door and passageway placement has an impact upon furniture arrangements and conversation clusters.

A. Although traffic to French or sliding doors leading to a patio or deck may be sporadic, it is necessary to locate furniture in a manner that will leave an access route open.
A₁. Access to house entry, dining/kitchen, and, secondarily, utility spaces.
A₂. Access to bedrooms.
B. The larger of the two seating clusters could be turned 180 degrees and allow for a focal point (B₁); cluster B₂ is quite tight and limited in terms of arrangement possibilities.
C. Shelves.

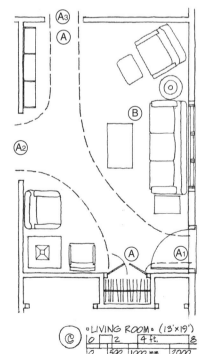

Figure 3-9c Door and passageway placement has an impact upon furniture arrangements and conversation clusters.

A. Traffic moving from end to end in a rectangular space is most disruptive and leads to a very constrained situation in terms of options for arranging furniture.
   A₁. House entrance; very minimal in terms of space provided for the transition from outside and for receiving guests.
   A₂. Access to dining/kitchen and, secondarily, to bedrooms.
   A₃. Access to owner's suite (also referred to as master bedroom).
B. While this room shape is similar to that shown in Figures 3-9a and 3-9b, the door locations significantly limit options for furniture arrangement, and, as arranged, the room is not particularly comfortable or functional.

As mentioned, homes increasingly contain "great rooms" or "gathering rooms" that include dining, entertainment, and kitchen areas all within a single open space. As with other types of spaces mentioned, the location of doors in these large open areas requires careful consideration. While often fewer doors are required than for individual rooms, the placement of openings and doors in such rooms has a significant impact upon the use of the room and the placement of furnishings, as shown in Figures 3-11a to 3-11e.

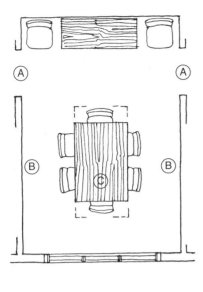

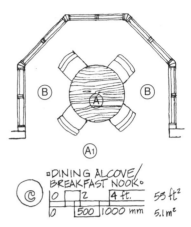

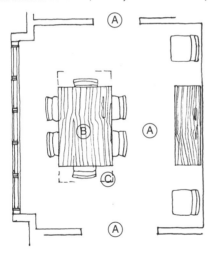

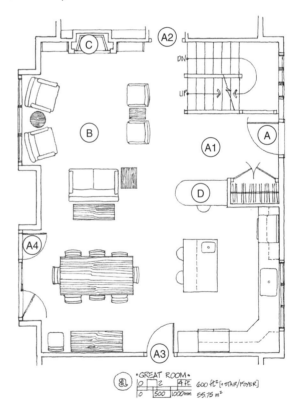

Figure 3-10a Door and passageway placement has an impact upon furniture locations in dining areas.

A. Any required through circulation is straight across the short dimension of the room.
B. At 10 feet, 6 inches (3200 mm) wide, there is insufficient room for auxiliary furniture on either side of the table.
C. Table shown is 5 feet (1524 mm) long by 3 feet, 6 inches (1067 mm) wide but could be longer (6 to 7 feet [1829 to 2134 mm]). A pendant fixture centered in the ceiling could work well in this room, as the layout dictates a centrally placed table.

Figure 3-10b Door and passageway placement has an impact upon furniture locations in dining areas.

A. Door openings that are located centered in the walls create a more meandering path of travel through the room than that shown in Figure 3-10a.
B. A light fixture placed in the center of this room will not fall in the center of the table. In situations such as this, it is important that the designer convey the desired location of the pendant luminaire or chandelier so the luminaire does not end up (by default) poorly located.
C. Table shown is 5 feet (1524 mm) long by 3 feet, 6 inches (1067 mm) wide but could be longer (6 to 7 feet [1829 to 2134 mm]).

Figure 3-10c Door and passageway placement has an impact upon furniture locations in dining areas.

A. The table shown is 42 inches (1067 mm) in diameter; this comfortably accommodates four adults and would be a tight fit for five. Increasing the table size may be possible but would require that the table extend outside of the alcove into A_1, where the appropriate amount of space would be required.
B. Chair locations work best at the angles shown for ease of movement and comfort of those already seated.

Figure 3-11a Door and passageway placement has an impact upon room use and furniture locations in large, open great rooms.

A. Primary entrance to house.
 A_1. Generous entry corridor with convenient coat storage and view of adjoining areas/exterior views.
 A_2. Access to owner's suite.
 A_3. Access to utility spaces/mudroom/garage.
 A_4. French door access to patio/deck.
B. Seating cluster for six.
C. Gas fireplace (focal point).
D. Work area for computer/mail center/desk, small hobby area, or charging station.

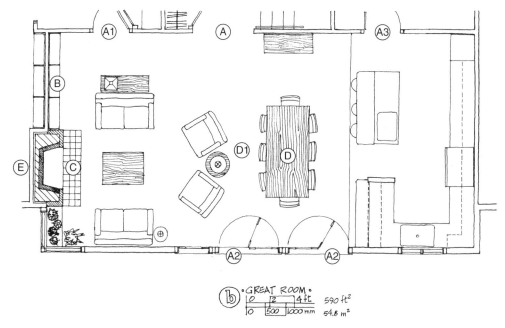

$\textcircled{b}$ •GREAT ROOM•
590 ft²
54.8 m²

Figure 3-11b Door and passageway placement has an impact upon room use and furniture locations in large, open great rooms (see also Figure 3-12).

A. Access to foyer/stairs.
  A_1. Access to owner's bedroom suite.
  A_2. French door access to patio/deck.
  A_3. Access to utility spaces.
B. Shelves.
C. Wood-burning fireplace with floor hearth. Television above mantel.
D. Dining table seats 8 with space to expand to 10.
  D_1. Potentially tight with chairs in use.
E. Frame walls surrounding masonry fireplace must be noncombustible and nonstructural or provide clear space (gap), as shown.

Figure 3-11c A T-shaped great room; this is the smallest in this sequence of examples shown, at 465 net square feet (43 m²).

A. Entrance foyer with stair to second floor; stair is open to great room (A_1).
B. Seating cluster consisting of six seats with room for two additional chairs pulled in as needed.
C. Gas fireplace set at floor level with a television above (C_1).
D. Dining alcove, which can seat up to 10 (10 square feet [0.93 m²] per person). The alcove is glazed on three sides, providing abundant daylight, but no dish storage.
E. A two-cook kitchen (see Chapter 4) with informal eating at a counter that is 42 inches (1067 mm) high with 30-inch (762-mm) stools.
F. Utility/mudroom with pantry cabinets suitable for food/utensil storage or general utility storage.

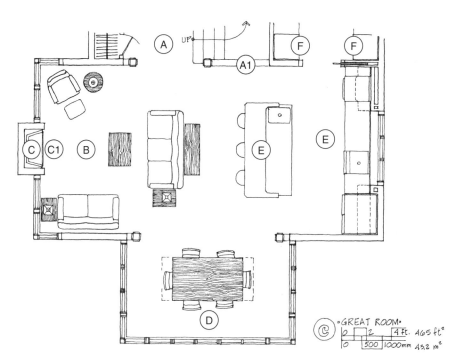

$\textcircled{c}$ •GREAT ROOM•
465 ft²
43.2 m²

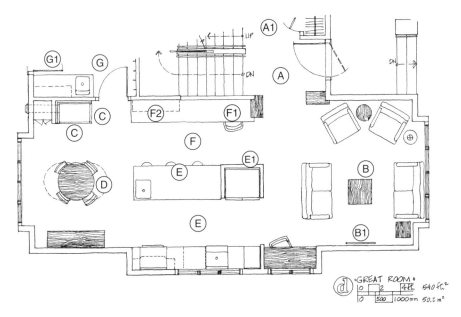

Figure 3-11d This long, narrow great room is 540 net square feet (50 m²), with a central kitchen.

A. Entrance foyer with a guest closet and stair access to the upper level and basement and access to the remainder of the first floor (A₁).
B. Seating cluster accommodates six seats and allows for television viewing (B₁).
C. Two-sided gas fireplace at 48 inches (1219 mm) above floor level, which is also visible from the kitchen and is located to create a focal point for dining.
D. The small dining area can accommodate seven comfortably (with table extensions) with 11.7 square feet (1.08 m²) per person.
E. A small two-cook kitchen (see Chapter 4) with informal eating at a counter that is 36 inches (914 mm) high with 24-inch (610-mm) stools. The walled refrigerator (E₁) screens most of the kitchen from the entrance area.
F. Primary circulation with desk/charging/mail counter (F₁) at 30 inches (762 mm) high. This area also contains dish storage (F₂) near the dining area and serves a secondary function as a buffet line for entertaining at 36 inches (914 mm) A.F.F.
G. Utility/mudroom with auxiliary entrance (rear of house G₁).

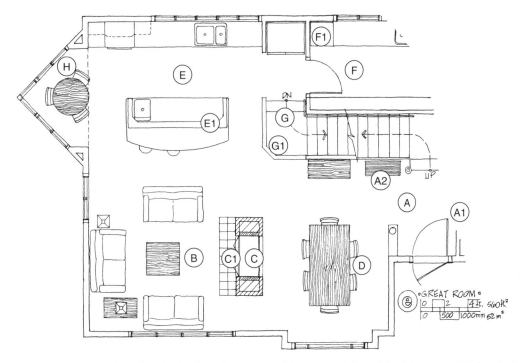

Figure 3-11e An L-shaped great room with an informal eating alcove. Access to most of the great room is through the dining area—with adequate circulation space, this type of traffic flow can work well. Some visitors to this home may never move beyond the dining area, while others may enter these more casual spaces. This example is 560 net square feet (52 m²).

A. Entrance area with stair access to the upper level and owner's suite, guest closet (A₁), and bench (A₂). Dining table is distant from kitchen.
B. Seating cluster accommodates six seats with room for three more with pulled-into-place seats.
C. Two-sided masonry fireplace with floor hearth. A television could be placed above fireplace (C₁).
D. Dining for six (up to eight with table extensions).
E. A two-cook kitchen (see Chapter 4) with a screening element at a height of 48 inches (1219 mm) (E₁) and informal eating at a counter that is 42 inches (1067) high with 30-inch (762-mm) stools. This counter could seat up to four.
F. Utility/mudroom with pantry for food and portable kitchen equipment storage (F₁).
G. Stairs down to lower level with a half wall (G₁) at a height of 48 inches (1220 mm).
H. Breakfast nook.

The examples shown in Figures 3-11a to 3-11e range in size from 465 square feet (43 m²) to 600 square feet (56 m²), with an average of roughly 500 square feet (46 m²); the areas given are for great room spaces only and do not include stairs, foyers, or closets. The examples shown are not oversized great rooms with massive furniture but are relatively modest in size and show furniture that is not overly large.

Well-designed residences often provide a *hierarchy of experience,* with the great room, gathering room, or living room (and less often the dining room) providing a culminating experience that can be seen as the height of experience within the building. This is often done through the use of a focal point, such as a view or fireplace; through enhanced spatial definition, such as raised or specialized ceilings or floors; or through the special use of materials and finishes. Thought should be given to the hierarchy of experience within the structure and the role of the leisure space in this hierarchy.

Often an important leisure space that serves as the culmination of the building hierarchy has an adjacent or significant relationship to the building entry or foyer and related hallways and circulation spaces to the rest of the building. There is often a strong relationship among the building entry, the "most important" room or rooms (in terms of hierarchy), and the major circulation corridors.

It is also worth noting that there should be some balance between room size and the number of rooms. For example, a home with several large leisure spaces is best balanced with an appropriate number of bedrooms, bathrooms, general storage, and kitchen facilities to make use of the entertainment potential provided by the generous leisure spaces. This is not only an issue of supporting leisure spaces with appropriate kitchen, storage, and toilet facilities, but it can be an issue for the resale value of the property as well. For publications that provide information about design related to the hierarchy of space and plan balance, see the references at the end of this chapter.

RELATED CODES AND CONSTRAINTS

Many of the constraints related to the design of leisure spaces are considered in subsequent chapters covering habitable spaces. The International Residential Code (IRC) includes living rooms as habitable spaces. Section R303.1 of the IRC states that habitable rooms should be provided with "aggregate glazing area of not less than 8 percent of the floor area." The code also states that natural ventilation should be "through windows, doors, louvers, or other approved openings to the outdoor air." The minimum openable area to the outdoors must be "4 percent of the floor area being ventilated."

The exception to these requirements allows for rooms to be provided with acceptable mechanical ventilation systems (more common in bathrooms). In addition, there may be exceptions or broader requirements in some state and local codes.

Regardless of possible exceptions, it is a good general rule to meet or exceed the ventilation and daylight requirements. The

positive effects of exposure to daylight for both health and energy efficiency, as well as solar gain potential, are well documented. Therefore, designing daylight into interior spaces is generally seen as a worthy goal, as is effective use of natural ventilation.

Section R304 of the IRC covers minimum room areas and requires that in any dwelling unit all habitable rooms are "not less than 70 square feet (6.5 m²) of gross floor area." In addition, "habitable rooms shall not be less than 7 feet (2143 mm) in any horizontal dimension." This is a very minimal code requirement and is easy to meet or exceed in most rooms used for leisure spaces.

Section R305 of the IRC covers ceiling height and requires that habitable rooms have ceilings not lower than 7 feet (2134 mm), measured from the finished floor to the lowest projection in the ceiling; this includes the habitable areas of basements. Therefore, according to the IRC, leisure spaces—even those found in basements—must have ceilings that are 7 feet (2134 mm) or higher, with the exception of beams, which can be no lower than 6 feet, 4 inches (1930 mm). An illustration of code-related ceiling height limitations for sloped habitable spaces can be found in Chapter 1 (Figure 1-5).

Some additional issues related to leisure spaces located in basements are covered in the IRC under "Emergency Escape and Rescue Openings" in Section R310. Detailed descriptions of code requirements for basements with habitable spaces are covered in Chapter 5 and detailed in Figure 5-23. The code issues mentioned to this point relate to single-family homes only, which are governed by the IRC. State or local codes may be more stringent.

ELECTRICAL AND MECHANICAL

Unlike some other rooms in a home, most leisure spaces are not influenced to any large degree by plumbing or unusual electrical requirements. Mechanical provisions for such spaces are rather straightforward. Because Section R303.9 of the IRC calls for heating to a minimum of 68°F (20°C) when the winter temperature is below 60°F (15.5°C), most leisure spaces in the United States are required to have some source of heat (portable heaters do not suffice). The location of the heat source or its registers or diffusers, as well as those used by any air-cooling source, must be considered by the interior designer as lighting, furnishings, and window and door locations are planned. The actual engineering of the heating and cooling system is, of course, done by professionals other than the interior designer. However, it is worth noting that in colder northern climates, heat is often delivered low on or near exterior walls (radiant floor heat is also an option). In warmer climates, cool air can be delivered at higher locations, at interior walls, or by ceiling diffusers near the center of the room.

There are some general rules for locating electrical switches and convenience outlets, and these are discussed and illustrated in Chapter 1. Figure 3-12 shows outlets and switching locations for a larger leisure space.

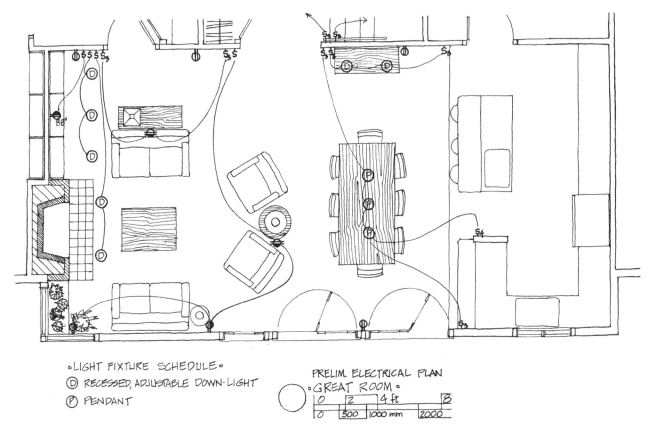

Figure 3-12 Outlet and switching location for the space illustrated in Figure 3-11b; switching/lighting for the kitchen area is not shown (see Chapter 4 for a kitchen outlet and switching example). In this room, switching is included at the multiple room entry points for convenience and safety. See Figure 1-14b for more information about electrical and lighting graphic symbols.

LIGHTING

One key to planning lighting for leisure spaces is to properly identify the activities the space is meant to support and to provide some level of flexibility for special occasions. For example, a space meant primarily for conversational interaction and occasional reading will require ambient lighting to support conversation and task lighting for reading. Flexibility in such a space could be provided through the use of dimmers, and additional focal lighting could be provided by wall washers (for lighting artwork or special room locations). Other options for flexibility are to place adjustable recessed luminaires that adjust to accommodate changes in both furniture and artwork.

Layering lighting within living rooms, gathering rooms, dens, and family rooms so that ambient lighting, task lighting, and focal lighting are all provided is a goal worth trying to achieve. Simply placing fixed downlights above seating areas in leisure spaces is not a good choice because it can create harsh shadows and make people look quite unattractive. Given the fact that leisure activities are often conducted from a seated position, bringing lighting "down" near seated eye level is worthwhile. This can be done with portable fixtures such as table and floor lamps.

Ceiling height is a major factor in making luminaire selection and placement choices. Standard 8-foot (2438-mm) ceilings are rather low for pendant fixture placement because of clearance limitations and the actual limitations of the fixture height. In rooms with lower ceilings, wall sconces can provide attractive ambient lighting. Freestanding torchères are another option in such areas, although the lighting they provide tends to be less balanced than that provided by two well-placed sconces. Both sconces and torchères work best in pairs to create even ambient lighting. Uplights provide the most illumination when directed up at light- or white-colored ceilings.

Rooms with higher ceilings allow for more options in luminaire selection and placement; ceilings that are 9 feet (2743 mm) or higher allow for pendant placement, as well as cove lighting or perimeter lighting, which can create attractive ambient lighting. Sloped and beamed ceilings offer the opportunity to place lighting on top of beams and on tall walls (often using sconces or concealed fixtures). Figure 3-13 illustrates lighting for leisure spaces in rooms with varied ceiling heights.

Task lighting is most often supplied through the use of portable table and floor luminaires, as these bring the light down to the appropriate height. For reading, luminaires with shades that direct light down onto the reading surface are generally

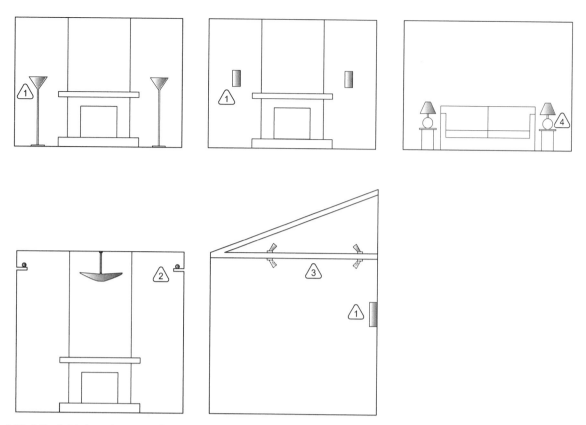

Figure 3-13 Ceiling height has an impact upon luminaire selection for ambient light in leisure spaces.

1. Sconces and torchieres can provide comfortable ambient light in rooms with 8-foot (2438-mm) ceilings (as well as those slightly higher).
2. Cove lighting can work well in rooms with ceilings over 9 feet (2743 mm) high, as can multiple pendant luminaires.
3. Structural beams can serve as mounting surfaces for luminaires (on top or bottom surface of beam); sconces can be used to light higher portions of wall. Pendants can also be hung from ceiling surface (not shown).
4. Portable luminaires work well to bring lighting down to seated eye level.

Regardless of room height, adjustable recessed downlights and wall washers can provide accent lighting, as can track lighting (in situations where using other fixtures is not possible).

best; these often offer some degree of adjustability so that the height can be varied to accommodate various users. Standard table and floor models also provide light at a lower height for reading but may not direct light to the reading surface and may provide overwhelming bright spots of light at various locations throughout the room. In cases where reading lamps and other portable luminaires are used in the middle of a room, installing floor outlets solves the problem of stepping over cords. Locating such floor outlets requires that a variety of furniture arrangements be considered so that the use of the room is not limited for future furniture arrangements—or to only one furniture arrangement.

As in many rooms, accent lighting may be provided with wall washers, recessed downlights, adjustable recessed downlights, and track lighting. Many lighting designers currently employ adjustable recessed downlights because they provide a level of flexibility that is very helpful in leisure spaces. Track lighting is not the first choice of many lighting designers, although it is used where constraints prevent adjustable recessed down-

lights and wall washers. Using track lights around the perimeter of the room much like one would lay out wall washers can work in situations where using downlights or wall washers is not possible. Track lights allow flexibility, but the tracks can become a highly visible design element.

Lighting design in dining rooms is very much like that described for other leisure spaces in that it requires layering of ambient and accent lighting (some types of accent lighting may also serve as task lighting in buffets and cocktail bar areas). The one element that makes dining areas different is the largest piece of furniture in most dining rooms: the table.

Traditionally, a decorative luminaire such as a chandelier is hung in a prominent central position above the dining table. This continues to be the preferred choice for many homeowners, while others prefer a more flexible approach that allows them to move the table around a bit. Locating a decorative luminaire a bit higher than a standard chandelier, or installing it in a raised portion of the ceiling, makes it a less conspicuous design element and can allow some flexibility with table placement.

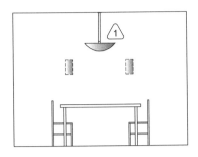 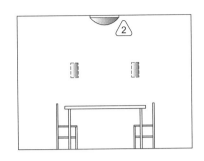 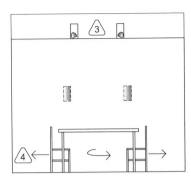

Figure 3-14 Selected dining area lighting options.

1. Central chandelier and/or pendant placement can limit table placement options; as such, placement creates a "visual expectation" that the table be placed directly under the luminaire. In addition, luminaire height must be carefully considered so that it does not obscure the vision of diners or create a physical barrier to movement. Wall sconces add pleasant fill light.
2. A luminaire mounted tightly to the ceiling surface in a central dining room location allows for greater flexibility with table placement; this location doesn't create the same "visual expectation" and allows for a variety of table locations. Wall sconces can be added to this arrangement.
3. Adjustable recessed luminaires can provide cross-illumination, making people and food appear attractive, with fewer hard shadows than those created with fixed downlights. Wall sconces can be added to this arrangement.
4. The lack of a fixed highly visible luminaire (such as a chandelier or pendant) allows for flexible table placement. In this illustration, the arrows indicate that the table can be moved elsewhere.

Placing a chandelier requires consideration of the proportions of the room as well as possible future locations for the dining table. Central placement can create such a strong visual presence in the room that it creates a "visual expectation" that the table be centered directly under it. If the table appears in another location, the chandelier can seem awkward and out of place.

Chandelier or pendant placement height above the table requires consideration of the eye levels of those seated at the table (see Figure 3-8b).

Use of a centrally placed, decorative luminaire does not eliminate the need for additional ambient light sources. Currently, many lighting designers are employing adjustable recessed downlights in dining areas both as sources of fill light, used with a decorative luminaire, and as the primary source of ambient light in the room. When used as the primary source, the lights should not be pointed directly down, as this creates harsh shadows. Instead, the light should be directed to cross-illuminate various areas within the room. Sconces also work particularly well to supplement the light provided with a centrally placed decorative luminaire. See Figure 3-14 for illustrations of some dining area lighting design options.

REFERENCES

Contains both works cited and recommended reading, with occasional annotation.

Alexander, Christopher, et al. 1977. *A Pattern Language*. New York: Oxford University Press.

Briere, Danny, and Pat Hurley. 2003. *Home Theater for Dummies*. Hoboken, NJ: John Wiley & Sons. A general guide.

Castle, Steve, and Phillip Ennis. 2003. *Great Escapes: New Designs for Home Theaters by Theo Kalomirakis*. New York: Abrams. A lavish coffee-table book covering the work of Theo Kalomirakis; not a planning guide but instead a review of home theaters for the very wealthy.

Ching, Francis. 1983. *Home Renovation*. New York: Van Nostrand Reinhold.

Driver, Nicole. 2015. "64 Important Numbers Every Homeowner Should Know." *This Old House Magazine*. http://www.thisoldhouse.com/toh/photos/0,,20797929,00.html. This is the source for dimensional information about screen viewing and a good general reference for residential dimensional information.

Jacobson, Max, Murray Silverstein, and Barbara Winslow. 1990. *The Good House: Contrast as a Design Tool*. Newtown, CT: Taunton Press. This publication contains wonderful sketches and drawings and follows up on some issues raised in *A Pattern Language*. What the authors refer to as "studies of contrast" provide some guidance to hierarchy of experience and plan balance.

Karlen, Mark, and James Benya. 2004. *Lighting Design Basics*. Hoboken, NJ: John Wiley & Sons.

Leslie, Russell, and Kathryn Conway. 1993. *The Lighting Pattern Book for Homes*. Troy, NY: Rensselaer Polytechnic Institute.

Panero, Julius, and Martin Zelnik. 1979. *Human Dimension and Interior Space*. New York: Whitney.

Susanka, Sarah. 1998. *The Not So Big House: A Blueprint for the Way We Really Live*. Newtown, CT: Taunton Press.

Whitehead, Randall. 2004. *Residential Lighting: A Practical Guide*. Hoboken, NJ: John Wiley & Sons.

CHAPTER 4
Kitchens

While the house as a whole is among the more traditional and conservative elements of society, the kitchen is quickest within the house to reflect new concepts of comfort and convenience. It is here one finds technology changing fastest. Yet the kitchen's traditional role as the hub of family life remains.

Merritt Ierley, *The Comforts of Home*

INTRODUCTION

Residential kitchens have a rich history related to sociological, cultural, technological, and economic factors. With an open hearth, early colonial kitchens formed the heart of the house. Later, kitchens were located in the basement, at the rear of the house, or outside—depending on geography, climate, and economics. Evolving further, the kitchen later became a private, enclosed room often adjacent to a formal dining room or pantry.

Various societal influences have brought about the American kitchen's common present incarnation, often open to adjacent dining and entertainment areas, allowing family and guests to join in food preparation. As Ellen M. Plante, author of *The American Kitchen,* writes, "the kitchen as hearth has come full circle," indicating that kitchens are once again the social center of the home.

Current trends include the kitchen performing as a multifunctional space with casual seating areas and an office and/or hobby zone (which may include various personal electronic devices and charging stations). Additional trends include a continued interest in islands, kitchens open to other social spaces, large expanses of windows often combined with limited wall cabinets, and an interest in second sinks or appliances, as well as designs that include functional spaces for a second cook. Outdoor kitchens continue to be popular, and secondary kitchens (or outpost kitchens) are a growing trend. See Figures 4-1 to 4-4b for images of kitchens of the past and present.

Kitchens that meet the lifestyles, culinary interests, and aesthetic preferences of owners are important components

Figure 4-1 A colonial kitchen hearth served as the heart of the home. Parry Mansion Museum, New Hope, Pennsylvania.

Photograph courtesy of the New Hope Historical Society.

of custom home design, new home construction, and home remodeling projects.

In his book *Bobos in Paradise,* political commentator David Brooks discusses high-end kitchen remodeling projects as status symbols:

> When you walk into a newly renovated upscale home . . . you will likely find a kitchen so large it puts you in mind of an aircraft hangar with plumbing. The perimeter walls of the old kitchen will have been obliterated, and the new kitchen will have swallowed up several adjacent rooms.

Figure 4-2 Two women standing in a kitchen of the late 1800s. The stove, sink, and cupboards are located very close to one another, and the room is enclosed and separated from the rest of the house, which is typical of the era.

Photograph courtesy of the Minnesota Historical Society.

This contrasts with what the designer Bill Stumpf has discussed in relation to his research of Julia Child's kitchen:

> Julia was more than a cook; she had these ideas about where to be in a space while doing other things. She had a view of cooking that was essentially social. . . . She was very philosophical about its central location,

about the importance of sitting around the kitchen table and talking.

The information contained in this chapter supports the creation of kitchens that provide the active, social space sought by Julia Child rather than Brooks's description of a kitchen as an "airplane hangar with plumbing." The focus here is on function, ease of use, and economy of space. For information about outdoor kitchens and outpost kitchens, refer to Appendix E. For specific information about remodeling kitchens, refer to Chapter 10.

Getting Started

A thorough review of a client's requirements, lifestyle, and budget, as well as the project's architectural parameters and related building codes, is required in order to provide a new kitchen or major kitchen remodeling design that meets the client's aesthetic and functional needs. Part of understanding a client's functional needs can be accomplished with a review of his or her lifestyle as it relates to his or her cooking and dining requirements.

A review of the following "Kitchen Programming Questionnaire" can provide a guide to understanding those needs and requirements and aid in the design of a functional, comfortable kitchen, and should be considered part of the programming phase of the kitchen design. Included within the questionnaire are references pointing to pertinent sections of this chapter.

Figure 4-3 A more open kitchen with a peninsula, on the journey to the open kitchen popular today.

Photograph dated 1952 by Norton & Peel, courtesy of the Minnesota Historical Society.

Figure 4-4a A newer kitchen complete with a hearth-like cooking area, bringing the kitchen full circle.

Photograph courtesy of KraftMaid Cabinetry.

Figure 4-4b A newer kitchen that incorporates an office area, electronic charging station and varying counter heights and is open to adjacent rooms.

Photograph courtesy of KraftMaid Cabinetry.

Kitchen Programming Questionnaire

Number of Cooks

One?

Two people working together?

One primary cook with helper(s)?

Multiple cooks?

Will the kitchen be used by caterers or a professional chef?

Is there often an additional helper for cleanup?

Review the "Organizational Flow" section for guidance related to these items.

Meals Prepared

Frequency of Meals Prepared:

Which meals are prepared at home: breakfast, lunch, dinner, other?

Meals Served in the Kitchen/Number of Diners:

- Which meals are served in the kitchen?
- How many people should the in-kitchen seating serve?

Types of Meals Prepared:

Does the family eat a limited or wide variety of food types (this is similar to identifying the menu in commercial kitchens)?

Are there any special meal requirements, such as kosher?

Do members of the family have food preferences that require specialized equipment such as woks or grills, or large quantities of fresh foods?

What small appliances are used most frequently (those used daily and weekly)?

Are any specific appliances or fixtures desired or heavily used by homeowners?

Do the clients require specialized work areas within the kitchen, such as baking centers?

Review the "Fixtures and Appliances," "Ergonomics and Required Clearances," and "Kitchen Storage and Cabinetry" sections for guidance related to these items.

Entertaining

Do homeowners entertain frequently, and what is the typical number of guests?

In entertaining, do the homeowners prefer to have guests join them in the kitchen?

When homeowners are entertaining, what is the style of dining (e.g., buffet or more formal seated dining)?

Are some events catered, or is cooking for all events done by the homeowners?

Review the "Fixtures and Appliances" and the "Ergonomics and Required Clearances" sections for guidance related to the above items. Note that in cases where guests will be invited to join in on kitchen work, additional space should be provided for circulation and required clearances (these must exceed recommended dimensions shown).

Additional Functional Areas Required

Do the clients require additional work areas located within the kitchen, such as sewing centers, charging stations, or homework or office areas?

Review Chapter 7, "Utility and Work Spaces," if such spaces are desired within the kitchen.

Storage

Is a walk-in pantry or butler's pantry desired?

Is tall storage, undercounter storage, or wall storage desired?

It is helpful to do an inventory of the kitchen-related items to determine storage needs. The inventory should include small appliances, dry good and perishable food storage, as well as dish, pan, and silverware storage.

Are there any special desires in terms of cabinetry?

Review the "Kitchen Storage and Cabinetry" section for guidance related to these items.

Visual and Spatial Characteristics

Is there a desire for the kitchen to be open to other areas/rooms? If so, which rooms?

What are the desired visual qualities of the space?

Are there any particular finishes or materials that are desired or that should be avoided?

There are not specific areas in this chapter that relate to these items; rather, these responses will be used to develop a visual direction for the design.

Special Needs and Circumstances

Do any members of the family have specialized needs relative to counter heights and heights of storage elements?

Is there a desire for specific switch or outlet placement?

Is there a current range of ages in the family or future plans for a range of ages of users?

Is childproofing an issue?

Does any member of the family use a wheelchair or walker? If so, is he or she a cook or a helper?

Do the homeowners have an interest in designing the kitchen for aging in place?

Review each Accessibility Note in this chapter for guidance related to these items.

Budget

Develop an understanding of the homeowners' budget for the project. This may require clarifying with them the reality of both new and remodeling costs.

Architectural Parameters, Existing Conditions, and Code

Develop an understanding of the architectural parameters and constraints of the project. Typically this involves measuring the existing conditions and gaining an understanding of structural issues.

Develop an inventory of existing appliances, fixtures, and equipment for remodeling situations, or a wish list of these items for new construction.

Conduct code and zoning research.

Review the "Related Codes and Constraints" and "Electrical and Mechanical" sections of this chapter as well as Chapters 8 and 9 for guidance related to these items.

ORGANIZATIONAL FLOW

The highly functional nature of the kitchen makes its layout paramount to making it efficient. Because of the importance of kitchen layout, this chapter has a different structure than others, with organizational flow covered first. This chapter is structured to provide an understanding of the functional, organizational requirements of the kitchen as a foundation. Details about appliances, storage, ergonomics, and code requirements are provided later.

For many years, conventional wisdom held that there were three kitchen *work centers*, and most writing on kitchen design adhered to this thinking. The following list describes these work areas:

Conventional Kitchen Work Areas

1. *Primary sink center.* For food preparation (such as washing) and cleanup. This could be considered the most heavily used area of the kitchen, and its location therefore provides an important base or anchor for the other work centers.

2. *Primary refrigerator center.* For storage of perishable foods. Food is received into this area and then removed for preparation and cooking; therefore, reasonable access to

entry/exit areas should be considered, as should the relationship to the sink center. The conventional approach identified this area as part of a preparation and mixing center and therefore indicated that mixing utensils should be stored in this location. The authors of this book argue that preparation is often done in other locations, and that therefore the preparation area is sufficiently important to be considered a separate center.

3. *Cooktop/range center.* For cooking and serving food (in terms of placing it in serving platters, bowls, etc.).

These three major work centers make up a conventional *"work triangle,"* which is an imaginary triangle linking each of the work centers in a three-point arrangement and constrained by certain dimensions described in the following list.

Conventional Work Triangle Dimensional Information

- Each leg of the triangle should be more than 4 feet (1219 mm).
- Each leg of the triangle should be less than 9 feet (2743 mm).
- The measurement of the three legs combined should total at least 12 feet (3658 mm).
- The measurement of the three legs combined should not total more than 26 feet (7925 mm).
- According to the National Kitchen and Bath Association, "A work triangle leg should not intersect an island or peninsula by more than 12 inches (305 mm)."
- Measurements for the dimensions above should be made from the center of each appliance/fixture in each work center.
- The cumulative total (recommended maximum) has grown from 22 (6706 mm) to 26 feet (7925 mm) over the years. Such minimum and maximum footage recommendations are guidelines meant to aid in creating a kitchen that is neither cramped nor so spacious as to require excess movement to complete basic tasks.

Additional Conventional Work Triangle Information

- The sink center should be in between the refrigerator center and cooking center.
- Through room traffic should avoid the center of the triangle; this area should not be seen as a through circulation area.
- Ideally, taller obstacles such as tall cabinet units and wall ovens should be placed outside the work triangle. In cases where this cannot be achieved, use of cabinets and storage elements that preserve as much counter space as possible should be used.
- Built-in wall ovens and microwave ovens are not considered part of the work triangle, as they are not part of any of the three work centers; however, placement of these should be

well considered in terms of work flow and room organization.

■ At each of the work centers storage should be provided to adequately support the work being performed. Items used most frequently should be readily available, whereas items not frequently used may be placed in more remote locations. For example, everyday dishes and glassware should be conveniently located near the sink area/dishwasher and the areas where items are served; serving pieces used rarely may be placed in more remote locations.

Based on the notion of the work triangle, the following basic kitchen configurations have been identified: single wall (which contains a flattened triangle), corridor (also known as parallel, Pullman, or galley), L-shaped, U-shaped, and G-shaped, most of which are illustrated in Figure 4-5.

The notion of the kitchen triangle was developed over 50 years ago based on research carried out at the University of Illinois (the Small Homes Council) and Cornell University, and a great number of changes have occurred in appliances, technology, and lifestyle in the ensuing years. The addition of a second cook, a second sink, and frequent use of microwave ovens, just to name a few changes, have greatly impacted the way kitchen work is done and the overall organization of the kitchen.

Introducing the "Major Preparation Work Area"

The authors believe that the idea of the kitchen triangle is useful in providing rule-of-thumb guidelines for distances between each of three work centers. In addition, the notion of each center linked and considered part of a system is a good one. As part of this system, each work center should be seen as containing the appliance/fixture (for example, the sink) as well as a clear "landing" area on the adjacent counter for dishes, pans, and elbow room. (For a detailed discussion of these clear counter spaces or landing areas, please see the "Fixtures and Appliances" section of this chapter.)

Although the notion of the conventional work triangle is helpful, we find that the conventional triangle is improved through inclusion of another area: the *major preparation/work area* for standard single-cook kitchens. Providing a major preparation/work area in a single contiguous counter space of 36 inches (914 mm) minimum, rather than several chopped-up counter locations, can aid in creating a functional kitchen. See Figure 4-6.

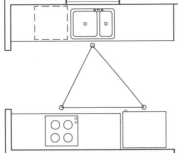

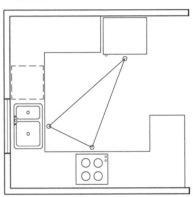
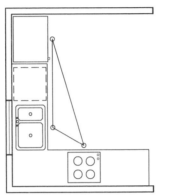

CORRIDOR/GALLEY   U-SHAPED

L-SHAPED   G-SHAPED

Figure 4-5 The conventional wisdom describes a single work triangle linking the sink center, refrigerator center, and cooking center, resulting in the following shapes: corridor or galley, L-shaped, U-shaped, and G-shaped.

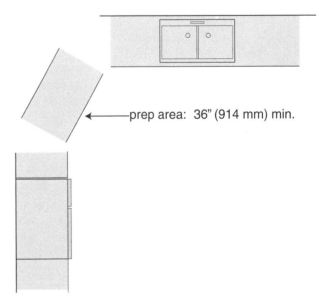

prep area: 36" (914 mm) min.

Figure 4-6 Adding a major preparation work area can create a more functional kitchen.

The preparation/work area should be provided in a single contiguous counter space of 36 inches (914 mm) minimum, ideally between the sink and refrigerator. Shown here at an angle only for illustration purposes, the preparation area may be part of a counter adjacent to either the refrigerator or sink and need not be angled.

This major preparation/work area can be seen as anchoring a secondary triangle linking the refrigerator and sink. This secondary preparation/work triangle aligns with one leg of the standard work triangle; the authors refer to this configuration as the *double work triangle*. See Figure 4-7a, where a secondary triangle is anchored by the major prep area.

Increasingly, more than one cook is at work in the kitchen. When accommodating a second cook is desired, it is worth considering including a second work triangle. In order to provide a true *secondary work triangle,* a secondary sink is generally necessary. In addition, the work triangle provided for the second cook should not cross the primary work triangle but may align with one leg of it (that containing the refrigerator and range). Taking the idea of the double work triangle mentioned in the previous paragraph and adding these triangles to the two primary work triangles can form *doubled-double work triangles,* shown in Figure 4-7b.

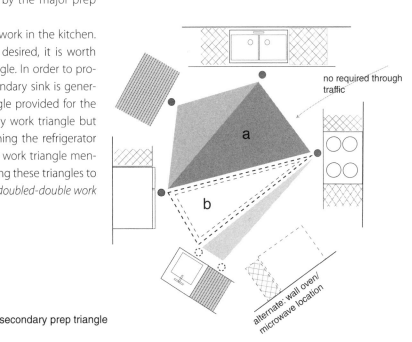

Figure 4-7b The two-cook kitchen can be designed based on doubled-double work triangles. It consists of two triangles (a and b) connecting the major centers (using two sinks) and two secondary triangles connecting preparation/work areas with the sink and refrigerator (the primary prep area should be 36 inches [914 mm] wide).

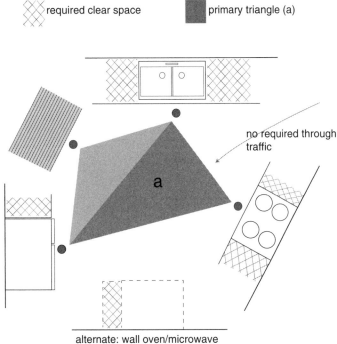

Figure 4-7a The one-cook kitchen can be improved by designing double work triangles, which include a *primary triangle* (a) connecting the major centers and a *secondary triangle* anchored by the *preparation/work* area, 36 inches (914 mm) wide minimum, connecting the sink and refrigerator.

The notion of these double work triangles is a new way of considering the organizational flow of the kitchen and of planning for how many homeowners cook today, in that it provides a major preparation space and/or a second complete work triangle for a secondary cook. We find this notion very useful and worth considering.

It is also worth noting that the L-shaped, corridor, and U-shaped kitchens shown in many publications do not reflect the variations and options available in the design of work islands and peninsulas, which are extremely popular in new construction and home remodeling. In order to accommodate kitchen islands and peninsulas as well as secondary work triangles and two-cook kitchens, the authors have identified 13 kitchen configurations or prototypes, shown in Figure 4-8 and detailed in figures in the "Prototype Kitchen Illustrations" section of this chapter.

Figure 4-8 Prototype kitchen diagrams.

The authors have identified this range of kitchen layout prototypes in a review of recent buildings and publications; these go above and beyond traditional notions of L-shaped, corridor, and U-shaped layouts. Additional detailed prototypes can be found in the "Prototype Kitchen Illustrations" section of this chapter.

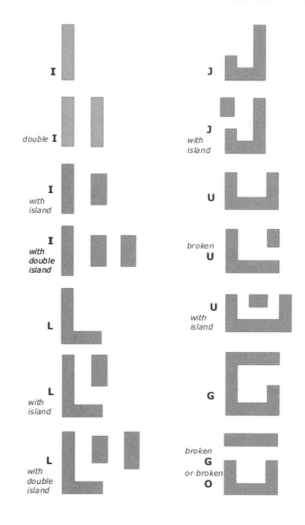

ACCESSIBILITY NOTE

According to the Paralyzed Veterans of America's *Kitchen Design for the Wheelchair User* by Kim A. Beasley and Thomas D. Davies Jr.:

> For most wheelchair users, none of the functional spaces in a home is a more complex design problem than the kitchen. The process of food preparation—as well as the cleanup afterwards—involves a series of interrelated tasks requiring an array of different appliances, plumbing fixtures, storage components, food items, and utensils.

Designing a space that accommodates these interrelated tasks requires careful consideration of the user's specific needs. While the American National Standards Institute (ANSI) and Uniform Federal Accessibility Standards (UFAS) provide standards for creating residential kitchens that are wheelchair accessible, these do not necessarily best suit the specific needs of individual users or family groups. In most cases, such standards can be modified to suit specific needs. In cases where a wheelchair user resides alone, the kitchen is best designed with counters and clear spaces that suit that individual alone. In contrast, for situations where a kitchen is shared by wheelchair users and others, a range of counter heights and accommodations is necessary. In addition, if resale and/or resale value is a concern, the kitchen design should suit a range of users. This can be accomplished with adjustable kitchen components, and wheelchair clearance spaces can be provided, as discussed later in this chapter.

Given that kitchens present significant challenges to individuals with special needs as well as to those who fall outside the range of adult averages in terms of stature, this chapter provides information about accessibility, adaptability, and universal design as they relate to appliances, fixtures, clearances, and workflow. Specific information about appliances and design for accessibility is set off in this chapter for easy reference. Information on standards and guidelines that apply to certain multiple-family housing units (ANSI/UFA and FHAA) can be found in the "Related Codes and Constraints" section of this chapter, as well as in Chapter 1 and Appendix B.

FIXTURES AND APPLIANCES

This section covers appliances and fixtures found in kitchens. An overview of appliances is presented, as well as a brief overview of considerations related to accessibility. For additional information regarding placement, mounting heights, and wheelchair clearances, see the "Ergonomics and Required Clearances" section of this chapter.

Given that kitchen design is based on the functional relationship of design elements and appliances, it is difficult to discuss those fixtures and appliances without first noting the interrelationship between the placement of primary fixtures and appliances. In-depth discussion of the relationship of work areas is found in the previous "Organizational Flow" section. As indicated, it is useful to begin the discussion of appliances with an understanding of the fact that the *placement* of the primary sink, refrigerator, and cooktop/range is key to successful kitchen design.

Another key factor in designing highly functional kitchens is the concept of providing clear areas adjacent to fixtures and appliances. For example, clear counter space adjacent to each side of the primary sink must be provided to serve as a "landing space" for dirty dishes, vegetables ready to be washed, and items that have been washed. This type of clear or landing space must be provided adjacent to the cooking area and the refrigerator.

In addition to providing these clear spaces, providing adequate preparation/work space and circulation space is fundamental to creating a functional kitchen design. Detailed information about these required spaces is in the "Ergonomics and Required Clearances" section of this chapter. While the information about appliances is covered separately here, it important to consider the sections on ergonomics and organizational flow in tandem with the following information on appliances and fixtures as one begins to tackle kitchen design.

Sinks

The sink area can be seen as the primary work area in the kitchen, as it forms the base of the primary cleanup center, which often includes a dishwasher, garbage disposal, and garbage (and perhaps recycling) bins. Increasingly, kitchens are used by more than one cook at a time, a situation that can be improved with adding a secondary sink. A second sink can be part of a secondary preparation and cleanup area (for use by a second cook) or as part of an entertainment/bar area. Some cooks prefer a sink adjacent to the cooktop as well as one adjacent to the dishwasher. Others require only a faucet (without a sink) near the cooktop for filling large pots (although this has fallen out of favor in recent years).

Some homeowners prefer a single-bowl (or -basin) sink and rely primarily on the dishwasher for dish and pan cleanup, whereas other homeowners prefer a double- or even a triple-bowl sink because they wash a lot of dishes by hand or prepare a great deal of food. For years, the double-bowl sink was the most popular type, yet single-basin sinks have been gaining in popularity. In addition, deep sinks are very popular, as they allow for washing large items. In tight spaces, single-bowl sinks may perform best because they have the larger single basin rather than two small basins; small basins can prohibit the washing of large items such as pots and pans. The following list contains additional key kitchen sink information.

Key Kitchen Sink Information

- According to the National Kitchen and Bath Association's *Kitchen Basics,* in the United States standard double sinks are 33 inches (838 mm) wide and standard single-bowl models are 24 inches (610 mm) wide. In addition to these standard sizes, a range of sizes, shapes, and configurations is available, as shown in Figure 4-9.

- One-, two-, and three-bowl sink configurations are readily available.

- One popular option is a two-bowl configuration with one larger, deeper sink for washing and a smaller, shallower sink with a garbage disposal for cleaning and prep. Three-bowl varieties often include two larger deep sinks and one smaller shallow sink for disposal and prep.

- Sinks with integral accessories are a current trend. With these sinks, items such as cutting boards, drain grids, rails for holding bins and bowls, and lock-in colanders can be combined to create a sink station.

- Some one-, two-, and three-basin sinks have a drainboard integrated into the unit (often made of the same material as the sink).

- In planning sink location and configuration it is important to take into account the location of the dishwasher; considering the user holding a dish and rinsing it, then easily placing it immediately into the dishwasher. Having the garbage disposer on the same side as the dishwasher is ideal; for double sinks. For sinks with both a small shallow bowl and a large bowl, ideally the disposer should be placed in the small shallow bowl, adjacent to the dishwasher.

- Secondary sinks for a second cook/helper or for entertaining are often smaller than standard sinks and can be found in various shapes, including square, round, somewhat freeform, and an elongated rectangular form known as a trough sink. Figure 4-9 shows some options for secondary sinks.

- Sinks are available in several depths, ranging from roughly 6 to 9 inches (152 to 229 mm) for standard sinks and 10 to 12 inches (254 to 305 mm) for especially deep models. Deeper sinks tend to splash less than shallow sinks and obviously allow for handling larger items. Selection of the proper sink depth requires careful consideration of counter heights relative to the heights of users and to needs for accessibility. For example, taller users may find deep sinks require bending and stooping; shallow sinks allow greater knee space for wheelchair users.

- Additional issues to consider in sink selection relate to the overall size and design of the kitchen. For example, in areas where counter space is limited, a sink with a cutting board that fits over the basin can be used to gain usable work space. The overall size of the kitchen, its layout, the lifestyle of the homeowner, and the project budget greatly influence sink selection.

- When selecting a sink, consider the size of the sink relative to the cabinet base size, as the interior width of the sink base cabinet is a key constraint for sink size. A standard kitchen sink base cabinet is 36 inches (914 mm) by 24 inches (610 mm) and will accept a standard 33-inch (838-mm) sink. Most manufacturers provide information about the recommended base cabinet size for a given sink; this should be reviewed carefully.
- Faucet selection is best done in tandem with sink selection, as the sink type and mounting methods influence faucet placement (see the faucet section of this chapter).

Common materials for sink construction include stainless steel, vitreous china, fireclay, enameled cast iron, solid-surface material, composite materials, stone, and decorative metals. Stainless steel continues to be the most popular material for kitchen sinks.

For sinks, stainless steel is available in a range of gauges and finishes. It does not chip or rust but can scratch, which can be more evident with certain finishes. Copper sinks are also available. Vitreous china is a ceramic product, usually with a durable glazed finish. Fireclay is also a ceramic product, fired at very high temperatures and available in high-gloss finishes. Artisan versions of ceramic and metal sinks are available in a range of designs. Enameled cast iron is available in a wide range of colors, shapes, and configurations. Unlike stainless steel, chipping can be a problem with ceramic and enameled cast iron sinks. Some people prefer ceramic sinks because they can be less noisy than stainless steel and enameled cast iron sinks, although this varies based on gauge and design. In addition, some sinks have noise-attenuating design features.

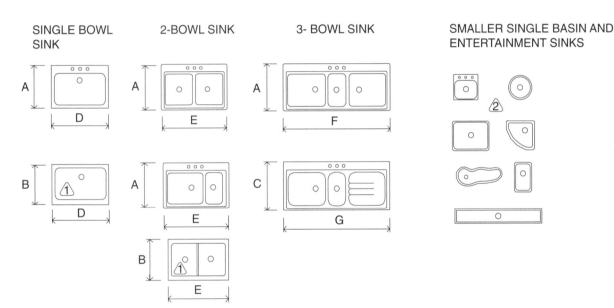

Figure 4-9 Sink sizes and configurations.

In United States, the standard double sink is 33 inches (838 mm) wide and the standard single-bowl model is 24 inches (610 mm) wide. While these are considered standard, a range of sizes, shapes, and configurations is available as noted in the dimensions and notes below. In selecting the configuration of double- and triple-bowl sinks, the location of the garbage disposer and dishwasher must be considered (see notes on sink configurations above) in addition to sink base cabinet size.

1. Apron-front sinks tend to be shorter in length and are placed forward on the counter, with faucets placed on counter rather than within sink.
2. The sinks shown range in size from 12 by 12 inches (305 by 305 mm) to 8 by 60 inches (203 by 1524 mm) for the trough sink and can be used singly or combined to serve as two- or three-bowl configurations.

Options such as integrated cutting boards and drain grids are available for most of the sinks shown (with the exception of smaller single sinks).

Dimensions:
    The interior width of the sink base cabinet is a key constraint for sink size; a 36-inch (914-mm) kitchen sink base cabinet will accept a standard 33-inch (838-mm) sink.

Legend:
    A. 22 inches +/- (559 mm); undermount sinks tend to be shorter in this dimension; some models are dual mounts.
    B. 18 to 22 inches +/- (457 to 559 mm).
    C. 22 to 25 inches (559 to 635 mm); some larger multiple-bowl sink assemblies consist of integrated drainboards on one or both sides and may be so large as to replace a countertop at sink location (these are typically 24 to 25 inches [610 to 635 mm]).
    D. 24 to 36 inches (610 to 914 mm).
    E. 31 to 48 inches (787 to 1219 mm); standard double-bowl sinks are roughly 33 inches (838 mm); however, some units are as large as 48 inches (1219 mm).
    F. 43 to 48 inches (1092 to 1219 mm); at the larger end of this spectrum are sinks with large bowls and/or integrated drainboards.
    G. 60 inches (1524 mm); this is an unusually large sink assembly with an integrated drainboard and counter option; it does not require additional counter surface material in the sink location.

Solid-surface sinks are created from the same type of surfacing material used to make solid-surface countertops. Some of the sinks are available as integral to the counter surface, while others are made separately and mounted in countertops of similar or varying materials (most often mounted under the counter). These sinks tend to be quiet and offer the durability of solid-surface material. Composite sinks are a combination of stone and acrylic polymers; this material generally resists cuts, scratching, stains, and fading. These sinks are available in a range of mounting options. Figures 4-10a to 4-10d, 4-11a, and 4-11b depict various sink types and styles.

Sinks are also available in materials such as stone and marble as well as terrazzo. These are used less frequently than those made of the materials discussed previously. Special artisan-created sinks in various stones and metals such as copper are

Figure 4-10c A trough-shaped stainless steel entertainment or secondary sink (an undercounter installation in this example).

Photograph courtesy of Kohler Co.

Figure 4-10a A double-basin cast iron sink (self-rimming in this example).

Photograph courtesy of Kohler Co.

Figure 4-10d A single-basin vitreous china entertainment or secondary sink (an undercounter/undermount installation in this example).

Photograph courtesy of Kohler Co.

Figure 4-10b Two single-basin cast iron sinks used in combination (an undercounter installation in this example).

Photograph courtesy of Kohler Co.

also available. Often these sinks are very expensive; however, they can serve as focal points of a particular room or as secondary sinks to be enjoyed for their beauty.

A range of mounting styles and options are available for kitchen sinks, including self-rimming, metal frame or rimless, undermount, apron front, and wall mounted. See Figures 4-11a and 4-11b. As in bathrooms, the choice of countertop material and overall design determines the mounting style used.

Self-rimming sinks have a rim or lip that fits over the top surface of the counter. This type of sink is readily available in

Figure 4-11a Cast iron metal frame sink.

Photograph courtesy of Kohler Co.

Figure 4-11b A fireclay tile-in apron-front sink.

Photograph courtesy of Kohler Co.

various styles, colors, and materials. One drawback with self-rimming sinks is that the rim prevents water from being drawn back into the sink bowl, which can cause water and soil to collect where the rim meets the countertop, making it difficult to clean.

Metal frame or rimless sinks use a metal mounting rim and clips attached below the countertop, which hold the sink in place, as shown in Figure 4-11a. Undermount sinks attach to the bottom surface of the countertop, as shown in Figures 4-10b, 4-10c, and 4-10d.

Tile-in sinks allow tiles to be taken flush to the edge of the sink, as shown in Figure 4-11b. Apron-front sinks, or farm sinks, have an exposed panel in the front that is often the same material and depth as the sink bowl; this is also shown in Figure 4-11b. Wall-mounted, or wall-hung, sinks feature a basin that is hung from the wall at a desired height.

ACCESSIBILITY NOTE

Wheelchair-accessible sinks require open space under the sink, as well as some form of protection from hot pipes, usually in the form of an angled protective panel or insulation-wrapped pipes. In addition, accessible sinks are mounted lower than the standard countertop height. Some users prefer shallow sinks for better access.

Additional options for accessibility include sinks in adjustable countertops, as well as adaptable base cabinets with removable fronts or with fold-back or bifold doors (shown in Figures 4-19a through 4-19c). It is worth noting that some garbage disposals can interfere with open knee space required under sinks and may not fit within protective panels. Detailed information about mounting heights and clearances

for wheelchair-accessible sinks can be found in this chapter under "Ergonomics and Required Clearances." Dimensions for seated wheelchair use can be found in Appendix C.

Faucets

Faucet selection is best done in tandem with sink selection because the various types of sinks and mounting methods require differing faucet placement. Faucets come in a vast range of styles, from high gooseneck styles that make filling pots easy to low-slung models that tend to splash less and make less of a visual impact upon the room. Faucets are available with separate hot and cold controls (called control valves) as shown in Figure 4-12a, or with single controls as shown in Figure 4-12b.

Figure 4-12a A gooseneck faucet with separate controls.

Photograph courtesy of American Standard.

Figure 4-12b A single-control low-slung faucet with a double control.

Photograph courtesy of American Standard.

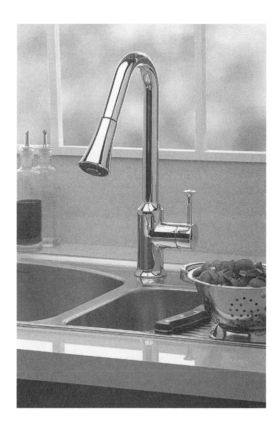

Faucets with two separate controls may be constructed with the spout and valves grouped over a single hole or with three to five separate holes. There is also a type of single control with a joystick-like handle. Faucets may be mounted on the deck of the sink or on the counter behind the sink; wall mounting is also an option. In planning for deck mounting, the number of holes in the sink deck must be considered. As already stated, sink decks may have one or more holes located behind the bowl(s); these exist for accessories such as soap dispensers, spray hoses, and hot and/or filtered water. In cases where there are more holes than required, plates (called base or deck plates) can be used to cover the unused holes.

Self-rimming sinks generally have holes predrilled for faucets, whereas undermount sinks often have faucet holes drilled in the countertop. Apron-front sinks vary; some have predrilled holes within the body of the sink and some have the holes drilled into the counter. In other types of apron sinks, the faucets are wall mounted. Many wall-mounted sinks are predrilled for faucets.

Pullout or pull-down faucets are equipped with a spray device that pulls out of the spout of the faucet to allow for use of the spray mechanism, as shown in Figures 4-12c and 4-12d. This allows a single faucet to deliver a standard stream or a spray and creates a cleaner, more minimal appearance with fewer visible controls.

Many cooks prefer single-control faucets with easy-to-use levers, because when they are preparing foods it is easy to reach and touch a lever with a clean hand in order to wash the other dirty hand. In addition, single-lever controls are recommended for universal accessibility in kitchens because they can be used more easily by a wide range of individuals. Single-lever sinks require at minimum a single hole but may require additional holes for accessories such as handheld sprays or dispensers.

Figure 4-12c and 4-12d A single-control gooseneck faucet with pull-down spout.

Photographs courtesy of American Standard.

"Hands-free" or touchless faucets use motion and/or light sensors. These faucets can cut down on germs spread from raw meats and other foods. In some cases hands-free faucets are installed next to standard faucets.

There are also faucet-mounted water filtration systems. Options include aftermarket units that are designed to be added to a standard spout (these do not work with most pullout types) and built-in filters located in the base or spout area.

Other options include undercounter/undersink units; these are available with a separate dispenser or with a dedicated waterway connected to an undercounter filter (referred to as dual delivery because the faucet provides dual delivery).

Additional sink and faucet options include instant hot water dispensers, which offer instant delivery through a sink-top spout. Speed and efficiency are the primary advantages with this item; it delivers very hot water far faster than a teakettle or microwave oven can and delivers only the amount of water needed, with little waste. These units heat water to 190°F (87.7°C), which can cause severe burns in a matter of seconds. Another option is a pot-filler faucet located at or next to the cooktop/range. These are often wall mounted.

ACCESSIBILITY NOTE

Faucet options available for universal accessibility include faucets with single-control levers, crosses, or loops (in place of other handle styles); faucets with nonslip textures; faucets with easy-to-control flow rate and/or temperature, pedal-operated options; hands-free faucets; and side-mounted options.

Garbage Disposers

Garbage disposers, also referred to as garbage disposals (or food waste grinders in many codes and standards), grind food scraps in a chamber with blades and use water to wash the churned-up bits down the drain.

Disposers are available in ⅓-, ½-, ¾-, and 1-horsepower models, with some models available with an auto-reverse mode for clearing jams. There are two basic feed types: continuous feed, which works as the name implies, and batch feed, which requires loading and putting a stopper in place in order to activate the blades. Batch feed types can be more costly and time-consuming but are considered safer because they keep hands out of the chamber.

Sustainability Note

Many homeowners appreciate the convenience of being able to remove dish scraps into the sink and then directly down the drain using a garbage disposer. There is some debate, however, about the ecological implications of garbage disposers. Because the disposers shift food scraps away from landfills and into wastewater treatment systems, some cities require disposers in new homes.

However, food waste can increase the burden on sewers. In addition, food waste can generate added nitrogen and perhaps wastewater in septic systems, prompting some municipalities to ban disposers in residences. In some areas with specialized systems, on the other hand, food waste from disposers can be beneficial. Therefore, it is advisable to check local codes prior to installing disposers.

According to the Consumer Reports website Greener Choices, it takes roughly "2 gallons [8 L] of water per minute for most sinks, or about 700 gallons [2650 L] per year to flush food waste through a disposer. Besides potentially increasing your water bill, a disposer's added demand can be a concern in drought areas." Composting food scraps is an alternative to use of a disposer (for plant-based items), and the resulting compost can provide fertilizer for gardens.

Dishwashers

Dishwashers are considered part of the primary sink area because of the work required at the sink to prepare items for the dishwasher and because of the need for drainage of the dishwasher. Standard built-in dishwashers are roughly 24 inches wide (610 mm) and fit into a space under a kitchen countertop and are attached to a hot water pipe, a drain, and an electrical line.

Ideally the dishwasher should be placed immediately adjacent to the sink and no further than 36 inches (914 mm) from the primary sink. For further information, refer to the "Ergonomics and Clearances" section of this chapter.

In addition to the standard built-in type dishwashers, other sizes and styles are available. Compact, typically 18 inches (457 mm) wide, as well as larger models, 30 inches (762 mm) wide, are also available. In addition, some manufacturers are producing double or single pullout-drawer-style dishwashers. Portable dishwashers are available in full-sized models as well as compact countertop models. Additionally, some manufacturers produce double sinks with a small dishwasher located within one of the sink basins. Figure 4-13 depicts dishwasher sizes.

Options for dishwashers include super-quiet operation, dirt-detecting sensors (these can aid in energy efficiency), special cycles, "turbo boosting" (for added speed or greater cleaning power, depending on the manufacturer), loading flexibility, the option of a third rack, greater rack adjustability, energy and water efficiency, hidden controls, and various finish options, including fittings for custom panels.

Sustainability Note

The U.S. federal government sets minimum standards for dishwashers in addition to the Energy Star and EnergyGuide ratings. Some states ban the sale of detergents with more than 0.5 percent phosphorus, while others are banning detergents with phosphates. Some utilities and governmental agencies offer tax incentives and rebates for replacing old dishwasher units with new, more efficient models.

Figure 4-13 Dishwasher sizes.

1. Standard dishwashers fit under the counter, are roughly 24 inches (610 mm) wide, and have front controls. Compact versions, 18 inches (457 mm) wide, and large versions, 30 inches (762 mm) wide, are available.
2. Dishwashers are available with hidden controls; the controls are not visible when the door is shut.
3. Select models can be fitted with panels to match cabinetry.
4. Drawer-style models are available as single-drawer or double-drawer models (lower drawer front can overlap toe kick in some models/installations).

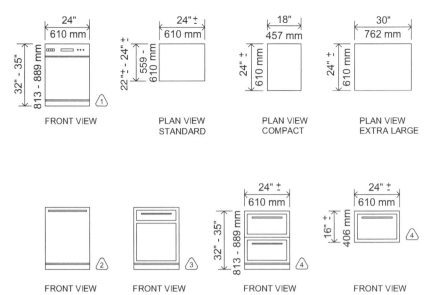

ACCESSIBILITY NOTE

Standard dishwashers require bending for loading and unloading. A higher-than-standard mounting location is required for wheelchair use or for individuals with mobility limitations (see Figure 4-21 b). In some instances, using a compact dishwasher in a wheelchair-accessible kitchen allows for more open knee space for access to work counters, and this option is worth considering if space is at a premium. In addition, drawer-style dishwashers can be useful for some individuals with limited mobility. Additional issues to consider in terms of universal design include location of the detergent containers and simplicity and ease of reading/using controls.

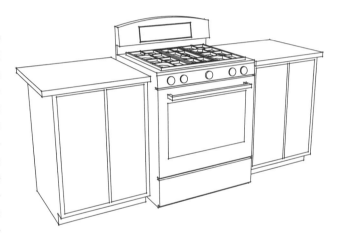

Figure 4-14a A freestanding range sits independently and is finished on both sides.

Ranges

The term *range* is used to describe an appliance that combines surface cooking elements and oven functions in one unit. *Free-standing* ranges are those that are completely independent of cabinet and counter surfaces; these are generally finished on the sides. *Slip-in* ranges rest on the floor but have a cooktop that protrudes slightly, allowing it to sit above the countertop on each side yet fit in between cabinets. This type requires that cabinets be placed on each side, as the range is unfinished on the sides. *Drop-in* ranges rest on a drawer or cabinet frame; these are generally unfinished on the sides. See Figures 4-14a to 4-14c for illustrations of range types. Ranges with more than one oven are available; in some cases, a microwave or second oven is placed above the cooktop.

Common materials for range exteriors include porcelain enamel or stainless steel. Glass and ceramic cooking surfaces are also an option. Energy sources for ranges include electric or

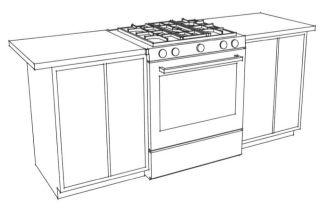

Figure 4-14b A slip-in range rests on the floor and is unfinished on both sides; it typically has no dash.

Figure 4-14c A drop-in range rests on a cabinet, base, or drawer; it typically has no dash.

gas. Some homeowners prefer the more precise heat control of gas burners, while others prefer electric coil or smooth-top (heated by covered radiant elements) models.

Ratings for gas ranges (and cooktops) are measured with the British thermal unit (Btu). Standard ranges generate from 8000 to 15,000 Btu per burner. Many current models offer one high-heat element of at least 15,000 Btu, as well as a simmer burner (often in the range of 5000 to 6000 Btu). Professional-style ranges, similar to those used in restaurant kitchens, generate 15,000 Btu or more on each burner. Such a high Btu allows food to heat more quickly and allows for specialized cooking techniques such as stir-frying. More information on professional-style ranges can be found later in this chapter.

Electrical cooking elements include electric coils as well as radiant elements covered by a glass and/or ceramic surface. There are also induction units that employ a magnetic field under a smooth top, which heats the pan, rather than the surface, when the cooktop surface comes in contact with an iron or steel pan; copper-bottomed and aluminum pans do not heat on these units. Another, less common heat source employs halogen-filled glass tubes under a smooth-top surface.

In terms of cooking surfaces, some homeowners prefer the smooth-top surface, which are easy to clean. Others prefer gas burners, as they heat more quickly and generally allow for more precise heat control. Options with gas burners include sealed burners, which can be easier to clean than standard burners. Other options include heavy-duty cast iron grates, as well as a single continuous grate over the entire top, allowing pots to be placed in various locations. Smooth-top models often come with indicator lights to let the users know that the burner is hot.

Like gas versions, electric models may contain a high-heat element (of at least 2500 watts) as well as elements that provide a simmer function. Smooth-top electric models may have heating elements that allow for switching between a large,

high-powered element and a smaller, lower-powered element contained within the larger one. Additional information on cooking surfaces may be found in the cooktop section that follows.

Standard electric and gas ranges, with four burners, are commonly 24 inches deep by 30 inches wide (610 by 762 mm). Smaller-size ranges—from 20 to 24 inches (508 to 610 mm) wide—are available as well. Many 30-inch (762-mm) models offer five burners. See Figure 4-15 for standard and larger range sizes.

Some manufacturers offer ranges with gas burners and electric ovens (known as dual-fuel ranges), because some homeowners prefer the even heating of electric ovens, with the control and Btu of a gas range. New types of ranges include units that combine an induction cooktop and electric oven, and a built-in microwave oven drawer in combination with a convection oven and electric cooktop.

The energy source used and the number of Btu generated are important considerations in range and cooktop selection and relate directly to the price of the unit, as well as to the need for ventilation. Ranges most commonly used in residences may be broadly divided into standard and professional-style ranges. Professional-style ranges offer the higher Btu of commercial ranges but generally have added insulation, which is not present in many true commercial fixtures. True commercial ranges (often with no insulation) must generally be installed as completely freestanding units a certain distance from cabinetry and other flammable elements for purposes of fire safety.

Professional-style ranges and cooktops *look* similar to true commercial models and allow very high Btu but can be placed within or close to cabinetry. They also require very good ventilation. Although sizes are not completely standardized among manufacturers, professional-style ranges are generally available in 24- and 30-inch (610- and 762-mm) deep models, in widths of 30, 36, 48, and 60 inches (762, 914, 1219, and 1727 mm), with some specialized manufacturers making larger units up to 72 inches (1829 mm). The widest units accommodate as many as six or eight burners, with accessories such as griddles, grills, and large double ovens (see Figure 4-15).

Another type of range, the best-known of which is made by Aga and called a *cooker,* employs radiant heat in multiple ovens at constant preset levels, with top cooking surfaces that are preset at consistent levels. This type of range is consistently warm at a range of settings. The temperature is controlled by selecting the oven or cooking surface location that meets the level of heat required. These are available in sizes roughly 24, 39, and 59 inches (610, 991, and 1499 mm) wide and roughly 27 inches (686 mm) deep.

The designer must keep in mind that ranges require adequate ventilation. This is covered later in this chapter in the "Electrical and Mechanical" section.

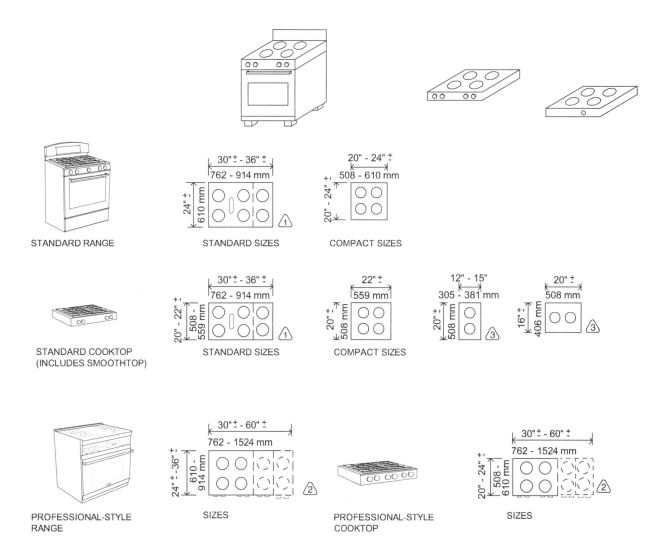

Figure 4-15 Range and cooktop sizes.

1. Standard versions can include five or more burners, as well as grills, steamers, and other options.
2. Larger versions can include six to eight burners, and/or grills, steamers, and other options; 60-inch (1524-mm) versions often have two ovens.
3. Smaller compact cooktops come in two-burner and modular configurations.

ACCESSIBILITY NOTE

Ranges are not considered ideal for use by individuals in wheelchairs because the cooking surface is too high for many seated users and because ranges require a parallel approach rather than allowing open knee space below the cooking surface; open space below the cooking surface is a far superior cooking position to a parallel approach. While ranges are permitted under ANSI 4.32.5.6 and UFAS 4.34.6, in order to meet these standards, controls must be mounted along the front or side of the range so that the user is not required to reach across a hot burner to adjust the controls. In most cases, a cooktop with a separate built-in oven (installed at a reasonable seated reach height) is considered best for wheelchair users. See the "Ergonomics and Clearances" section for more information about wheelchair-accessible cooking units.

Cooktops

Cooktops are cooking surfaces that don't include an oven. These can be built into islands and countertops. Cooktops are available in a standard width of 30 inches (762 mm); wider versions are also available, as are compact two-burner versions. Materials of construction include glass, porcelain enamel, and stainless steel. Professional-style cooktops are available, and these offer the same advantages and disadvantages as professional-style ranges. See Figure 4-15 for cooktop sizes. The information on burners and cooking surfaces found in the previous section holds true for cooktops as well. As with ranges, cooktops require adequate ventilation. This is covered in this chapter in the "Electrical and Mechanical" section.

ACCESSIBILITY NOTE

Cooktops can be placed in countertops with open space underneath for seated wheelchair use. Such an installation also allows for the countertop to be mounted at various heights or, in some cases, to be adjustable. The bottom of the cooktop unit must be insulated and covered in order to prevent users from being burned. Smooth-top cooktops are recommended for wheelchair users because pans can be easily moved on the smooth surface, although care must be taken to ensure that users can easily read temperature indicators in order to prevent burns, since smoothtops do not have flames or the bright red coils of standard burners to denote heat.

Cooktop controls must be placed at the front or side of the unit for wheelchair use so that users are not forced to reach over hot surfaces to use controls. In selecting a cooktop, the designer should give special attention to the ease of reading and using controls for users with limited eyesight or difficulty gripping. In addition, cooktops with

a staggered burner arrangement or cooking elements aligned on the front of the cooktop are ideal for wheelchair users, as these minimize reaching over hot surfaces. Including an angled mirror above the cooktop surface is helpful for wheelchair users as well. See the "Ergonomics and Clearances" section for more information about wheelchair-accessible cooking units.

Wall Ovens

Wall ovens are separate units that are not contained within a range and are placed within wall cabinets. Several factors come into play in the decision to use wall ovens. Wall ovens allow for a separate oven area, add storage under the cooktop (as there is no oven there), and allow for double ovens. Also, a separate cooktop (open underneath) and wall oven(s) are preferable for wheelchair users. Additional information about wall ovens and wheelchair users can be found in the following discussion and in the "Ergonomics and Clearances" section of this chapter.

Wall ovens are available in several types and sizes with gas or electric heat sources. However, the most product choices, technological advancements, and new options are available in electric models. Figure 4-16 illustrates wall oven sizes.

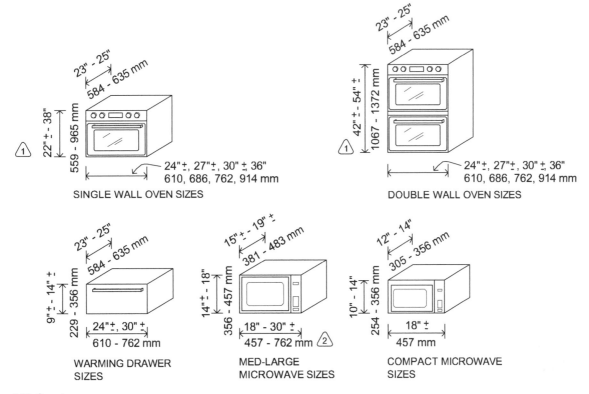

Figure 4-16 Oven sizes.

1. Gas and electric ovens vary greatly in height; consult manufacturer's specifications.
2. Medium to large microwave ovens include range-top and countertop models. Vented range-top models tend to be 16-plus inches (406 mm) in height and roughly 30 inches (762 mm) wide.

Conventional ovens (also called thermal or radiant ovens) cook using a combination of radiant energy from a heat source and the convection that occurs naturally from the heated air inside the oven. Such ovens can be fired by gas or electricity. Convection ovens employ an electric heating element in tandem with a fan that circulates the hot air within the oven cavity.

Some convection models have shorter interior depth because of the location of the fan, while in other models very thin, highly insulated oven walls allow for a deeper cavity. Combination ovens are also readily available; these combine conventional elements with the addition of a fan to circulate air. Combination convection/microwave ovens are also available. Wall ovens with both a conventional oven and a warming oven are also available.

Space and price are factors to consider in deciding to include a wall oven (or ovens) within a kitchen. Wall ovens offer a much more convenient working height, but this comes at the cost of counter space that is typically given up to accommodate the wall oven and cabinet. Similarly, including multiple wall ovens can remove storage or counter space but has the payoff of allowing for cooking multiple items at varying temperatures, which some cooks find very useful. Costs for separate cooktop and oven units are typically higher than for a single range unit (for equal-quality products).

The height of the actual wall oven unit varies based on whether it is a single or double unit, as well as by manufacturer. Typical wall oven widths are roughly 24, 27, 30, and 36 inches (610, 686, 762, and 914 mm). Installed height and placement of wall ovens varies greatly and is dependent on the cabinet that the oven is placed within (more information about wall oven cabinets may be found in the "Kitchen Storage and Cabinetry" section).

Warming drawers are used to keep food warm, have various temperature settings, and can also be used to warm plates. Warming drawers are available in sizes to match ovens so that they can be installed below ovens; they are also available in 24- and 36-inch (610- and 914-mm) sizes so that they fit in standard cabinet boxes for installation. In addition to being available in wall units, warming drawers are available in some ranges. Figure 4-16 illustrates warming-drawer sizes.

ACCESSIBILITY NOTE

Oven height and placement for use by people using wheelchairs requires careful thought. Optimum wall-mounted oven height for universal use allows for ease of use by those in wheelchairs, as well as use by standing individuals without the need to bend to retrieve heavy objects. Drop-front (standard), side-hinged, and double swinging door styles offer various advantages. Side-hinged and double swinging oven doors can be helpful for seated users; these require a pullout shelf underneath the oven for placement of hot

objects (and to protect from hot spills) or a permanent ledge (such as one at the front edge of the base cabinet).

Non-self-cleaning ovens require an open knee space adjacent to the oven for cleaning access. In side-hinged models, this must be on the latch side. When possible, an open knee space adjacent to the oven (often a roll-under counter space) located adjacent to the oven is helpful. The controls must be on the front or side panel of the oven. Specific information about shelf/counter placement and open knee spaces and mounting heights can be found in the "Ergonomics and Required Clearances" section of this chapter.

Microwave Ovens

Microwave ovens use radio waves, or microwaves, to heat and cook food. These ovens come in a range of sizes from compact to large; compact versions are often 600 to 800 watts, whereas larger versions offer 850 to 1600 watts. Oven capacity is a factor to consider when selecting a microwave. Larger-capacity ovens hold more food or larger items, but they can eat up substantial counter or storage space in smaller kitchens.

Microwave ovens can be placed in various locations, such as on the countertop, over the range (often integrated with a hood), over the counter (attached under wall cabinets), or as a component of a double wall oven.

Increasingly, homeowners are installing microwaves directly underneath countertops, especially in islands and peninsulas as part of a snack-making area (this can require bending for access and can allow small children to see and reach controls, which is usually not a good thing). Placing a built-in microwave at countertop height but incorporated into a cabinet that sits directly on the counter is currently a popular placement as well. Microwaves are typically hinged on the left side. Counter space is needed to the right side or on top of the oven, as described in the "Ergonomics and Required Clearances" section of this chapter.

Microwave sizes vary based on the location selected for the oven as well as the oven capacity and special features. Compact models as well as larger countertop and above-range models are shown in Figure 4-16.

ACCESSIBILITY NOTE

According to the Center for Inclusive Design and Environmental Access (IDEA Center), microwaves placed on a counter location are "usable for the broadest population," and an adjoining counter space facilitates transfer of hot items. Simplified programming and controls as well as backlit controls make standard built-in ovens as well as microwaves most useful for a wide range of individuals.

Refrigerators

Like many of the appliances discussed in this chapter, refrigerators are available in a variety of styles and arrangements and offer a wide array of options. Freestanding models are deeper than counter/cabinet depths. Built-in models are intended to fit flush or nearly flush with cabinets and counters. Some of these can be fitted with custom panels (sometimes called overlay models). Counter-depth models are freestanding refrigerators that are just slightly deeper than counters and cabinets and offer the look of built-in models. Built-in and built-in-style refrigerators offer a sleeker look but may provide less overall space than deeper models. Figure 4-17a illustrates refrigerator model types. Separate built-in refrigerator and freezer units may be used for maximum cold and frozen storage. In rare cases, commercial walk-in refrigerators may be used in residential settings.

Freestanding models can be surrounded with cabinetry to make them appear like the more expensive built-in models (this is sometimes referred to as "framed"). Care must be taken to ensure that there is adequate clearance for doors to open fully and for ease of moving (in remodeling situations, one must make sure there is adequate clearance to move the refrigerator into position). In some cases, a wall can be recessed directly behind the refrigerator location, allowing the refrigerator to fit into the pocket created by the recess. This allows the refrigerator to align with the countertop depths.

Top-freezer, side-by-side, and bottom-freezer styles are the most widely used refrigerator types currently available in the United States. Figure 4-17b provides illustrations of these configurations and sizes.

According to *Consumer Reports* magazine, top-freezer models tend to be less expensive to purchase and more space efficient than side-by-side models. Top-freezer models have become available with through-the-door water dispensers as well as internal water dispensers. Side-by-side models offer narrow doors (with correspondingly narrow swings) that can be handy in tight or awkward spaces and offer through-the-door ice and water dispensers. Proportionally more of the total capacity space goes to freezer space in side-by-side models as compared to top- and bottom-freezer models.

Bottom-freezer models provide easy reach and eye-level storage for frequently used items in the refrigerator section, but they require bending or squatting to retrieve frozen items (rather than doing so to retrieve refrigerated items in other models) and generally have less area for frozen items than side-by-side models. Increasingly popular are French door models, with side-by-side access to the refrigerator area above a freezer unit. Top-freezer and bottom-freezer models are commonly available with reversible handle locations, allowing the flexibility to change from left-hinged doors to right-hinged doors. This is not true of all models, so the issue should be researched prior to purchase.

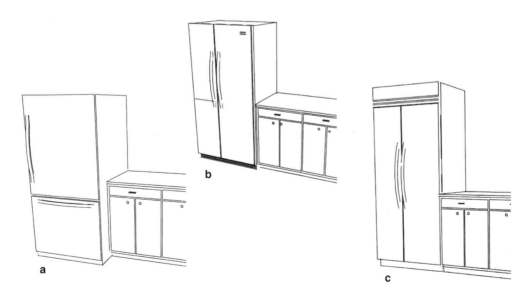

Figure 4-17a Built-in and freestanding refrigerators.

a. Freestanding. Deeper than cabinets.
b. Counter-depth. Almost flush with counter.
c. Built-in. Flush or nearly flush with counter.

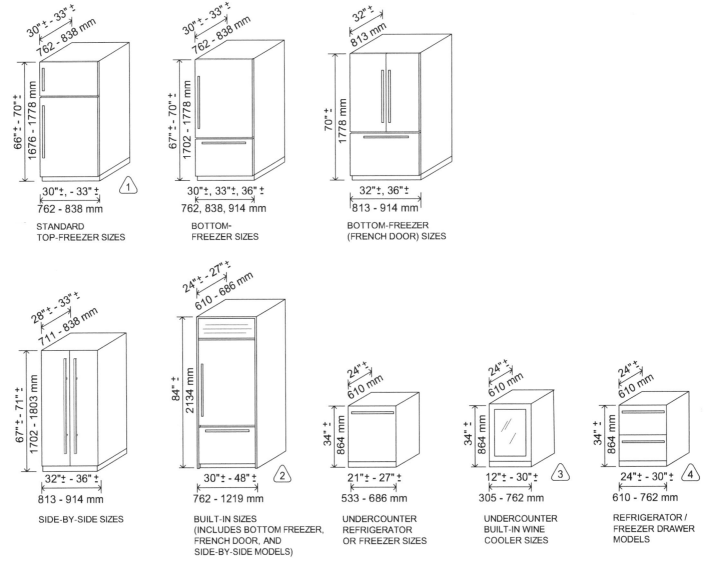

Figure 4-17b Refrigerator configurations and sizes.

1. Compact versions (not undercounter) are available from 46 inches (1068 mm) high by 22 inches (559 mm) wide by 24 inches (610 mm) deep.
2. Other sizes and configurations are available.
3. Full-height wine chillers are available up to 84 inches (2134 mm) high.
4. Drawer-style models are available with trim/panels that can conceal toe kicks as shown.

Note: Not shown are large single refrigerator and single freezer models; these are most often built-in models and vary in size similar to combination units.

Undercounter models are less common than full-sized models in the United States but are used widely elsewhere as the primary cold storage space and are increasingly being used in the United States for entertainment and bar areas. Combination refrigerator/freezers as well as separate refrigerator and freezer-only undercounter models are available. Wine chillers, also known as wine coolers, are available in undercounter models as well as taller models, most often 24 inches (610 mm) deep, as shown in Figure 4-17b.

Several companies currently produce refrigerator and freezer drawer units. These can be used alone much like undercounter models or in conjunction with refrigerator and freezer units with doors. A combination of drawer and door units can create a range of customized cold storage areas throughout the kitchen. Single refrigerator and single freezer models are also available. Often these are built-in models, and they vary in size similar to the combination units shown in Figure 4-17b.

ACCESSIBILITY NOTE

Side-by-side refrigerator models are often recommended for wheelchair accessibility because of narrow door swings and relatively easy access to large portions of the refrigerator and freezer units. In-door storage gives some side-by-side units exceedingly heavy doors, making them difficult for some individuals to open. Slimmer built-in and built-in-style units can open up floor space in front of the refrigerator for wheelchair users. Easy-to-read, simple controls as well as lighted in-door water and ice delivery can help make side-by-side refrigerators more universally accessible. As an alternative to side-by-side models, undercounter refrigerators can be mounted in an accessible location for wheelchair users (this would place them on a toe kick a minimum of 8 inches (203 mm) above the floor and create a higher-than-standard countertop).

Sustainability Note

Those refrigerators manufactured after April 2008 are required to be 5 percent more efficient than previous models to achieve Energy Star qualification. While there have been advances, refrigerators use significant electricity. It is worth noting that in 2010 tests, *Consumer Reports* found that several refrigerators used far "more energy than their EnergyGuide labels indicated."

Trash Compactors

Trash compactors compress glass, cartons, paper, plastics, and dry food waste to less than half their original volume. However, with the current mandatory and voluntary recycling programs in most areas, trash compactors are less common in new home construction and kitchen remodeling. For homeowners that prefer to include compactors within the home, there are under-counter and freestanding models available in widths ranging from 12 to 15 inches (305 to 381 mm), with 15 inches (381 mm), plus or minus, the most common size. A key-activated on/off switch is a safety feature that prevents children from operating the compactor.

ERGONOMICS AND REQUIRED CLEARANCES

The specialized nature of kitchens requires that designers consider ergonomics and required fixture clearances in order to design useful, comfortable kitchens. Because a good percentage of the work of daily living is performed in the kitchen, ergonomics, workflow, and clearance requirements must be considered in the design of a successful kitchen.

Work Counters and Cabinets

Stock cabinetry comes in standard counter heights that can work for adults of average size; however, in seeking universal design of kitchen elements or tailoring a kitchen to a particular user, careful consideration of reaching heights, comfortable standing, and seating work heights is required.

Standard dimensions are a compromise meant to meet the needs of "average" adults. Therefore, veering greatly from standards can affect resale value, which is a reason to explore adaptable design features such as adjustable counters and/or varying counter heights. Figure 4-18a illustrates standard reach and work counter height information. Figure 4-18b illustrates clearances at cabinets and counters. Figure 4-18d shows dimensional information for dining surfaces. Appendix C gives dimensional information for wheelchairs, including seated height information.

Detailed information about cabinetry, including construction, standards, and additional design considerations, can be found in the "Kitchen Storage and Cabinetry" section of this chapter.

ACCESSIBILITY NOTE

Creating accessible cabinets and work counters requires careful consideration of seated reach range and wheelchair (and arm rest) height. In addition, accessible work counters are best planned with a front approach and clear knee space access as shown in Figure 4-18c.

Designing Dining Spaces For Interaction

When planning dining surfaces such as eating islands, bars, and peninsulas, the designer should not only follow dimensional requirements but also provide spaces that foster conversation and interaction. This means that meeting minimum dimensional requirements is important, but considering how those eating will interact with one another is also important. It is essential to go beyond simply creating a row of diners and instead consider how they will interact. Curving the dining surface and providing two-sided dining are both ways to foster interaction.

STANDARD REACH AND WORK DIMENSIONS

TYPICAL <u>STOCK</u> CABINET DIMENSIONS

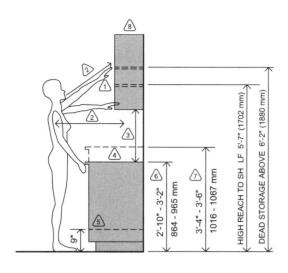

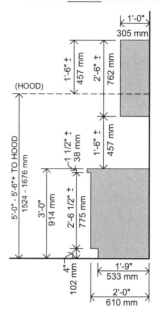

Figure 4-18a Standard reach and work counter information and stock cabinet dimensions.

1. High shelf. Adult reach: back 4 feet, 11 inches (1499 mm) plus; this dimension refers to the need to reach the back portion of a shelf.
2. Adult reach radius. 1 foot, 11 inches to 2 feet, 3 inches (584 to 686 mm) plus.
3. Work counter clearance. 1 foot, 3 inches to 1 foot, 8 inches (381 to 408 mm); 1 foot, 6 inches (457 mm) recommended minimum.
4. Depth of work counters. 1 foot, 9 inches to 2 feet (457 to 610 mm); 2 feet (610 mm) is standard.
5. Low comfortable reach. 9 inches (229 mm); it is best to store frequently used items above this height.
6. Work counter height. 3 feet (914 mm) is standard.
7. High counter.
8. Standard depth of wall cabinets is 1 foot (305 mm) to allow for access to counter surface.

CLEARANCES AT COUNTERS

CLEARANCES AT COUNTERS

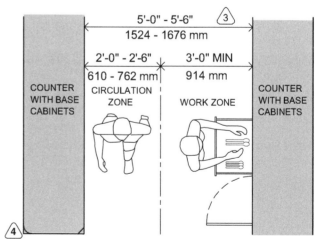

Figure 4-18b Clearances at cabinets and counters.

1. Work zone minimum between cabinets with no additional through-traffic circulation.
2. This clearance is also useful between counter/cabinet and nearest physical obstruction. In cases where there is only a wall (no cabinets or appliances) and no through circulation, 4 feet (1219 mm) is required for a two-cook kitchen and 3 feet, 6 inches (1067 mm) is required for a single-cook kitchen.
3. Total clearance of 5 feet (1524 mm) minimum is required between cabinets when the work zone is combined with (required) through circulation.
4. When possible, "clip" or round corners of countertops for safety, especially in high contact and/or island areas. Human contact with a clipped or rounded corner is less painful than contact with a sharp corner.

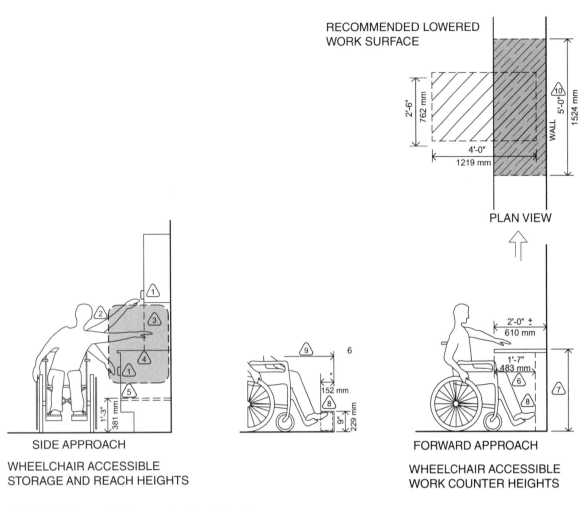

Figure 4-18c Wheelchair-accessible storage, reach, and work dimensions.

1. Accessible handles/pulls should be at top edge of base cabinets and lower edge of wall cabinets.

2. Obstructed side reach is 10 inches to 2 feet (254 to 610 mm) maximum from side of wheelchair (the obstruction in this case is the cabinet itself; seated side wheelchair reach is 2 feet [610 mm] maximum over an obstruction that is 34 inches [864 mm] maximum in height).

3. Because shaded area indicates ideal storage locations, standard wall cabinet installation heights do not provide much accessible storage. Storage at these locations can be provided with wall cabinets placed low (at countertop level), tilt-out drawers, stacked drawers, plate racks, and/or other accessories.

4. As much storage as possible should be located between 2 and 4 feet (610 and 1219 mm) above the floor (shaded dashed area). Items outside of this range are not accessible to wheelchair users; provide a device for grasping items out of this range.

5. Low reach from wheelchair is 1 foot, 3 inches (381 mm) above the floor.

6. Provide minimum clear space 1 foot, 7 inches (483 mm) deep by 2 feet, 6 inches (762 mm) wide for knee space.

7. Counter height for seated (including wheelchair) users varies from 2 feet, 4 inches to 2 feet, 10 inches (711 to 864 mm) and in rare cases is as high as 3 feet (914 mm); this range allows for variations in user/armrest height and for a 1½-inch counter thickness. (The ADAAG calls for kitchen counters at 2 feet, 4 inches [865 mm] except in cases where the counter is adjustable.)

8. For front approach, provide toe clearance 9 inches (229 mm) high by 6 inches (152 mm) deep (maximum).

9. Clear knee space at this location may be used as part of maneuvering clearance/turning space.

10. Lowering a continuous counter area with an open clear space underneath (see shaded, angle dashed area) for a forward approach creates a work and prep area. Lowered counters like this must be balanced with higher counter areas to accommodate dishwashers and other kitchen elements. The 5-foot (1524-mm) open area shown is helpful, but, at minimum, the open area should accommodate the wheelchair forward approach zone as indicated.

Note: Appendix C gives dimensional information for wheelchairs, including seated height information.

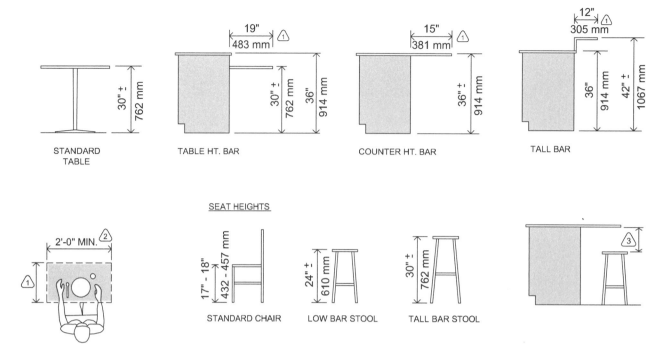

Figure 4-18d Dimensional information for dining/eating. Additional dining-related information can be found in Chapter 3. Appendix C gives dimensional information for wheelchairs, including seated height information.

1. Depth for eating area varies based on the nature of the meal being consumed; the narrow dimension shown is for snacking, while the deeper dimensions may be appropriate for dining with plate/placemats. All depth dimensions shown can vary as needed (from 12 to 19 inches (305 to 483 mm) for the range of bar heights shown).
2. Width per person should be a minimum of 2 feet (610 mm); 2 feet, 2 inches (660 mm) is recommended.
3. 10 to 12 inches (254 to 305 mm) distance between stool and countertop is the comfortable range for most seated users.

ACCESSIBILITY NOTE

As stated, in some cases adjustable countertops are a good idea. Multiple users of varying abilities, including wheelchair users, benefit from adjustable work surfaces, sinks, and cooktops. There are several methods for creating this type of adaptable countertop, as shown in Figures 4-19a to 4-19c.

Creating pullout cutting boards or work boards at an appropriate height is another way to provide additional work areas for seated users. These are a very cost-effective way of creating universal design in the kitchen. Another accessible/adaptable kitchen feature is a pull-down shelf, shown in Figure 4-19d.

Other considerations for creating counters for universal use include using contrasting values or colors at countertop edges to aid in visual location. In addition, using contrasting colors in floor areas to aid in visual location of elevation changes or to highlight certain portions of work areas can be helpful. Nonslip flooring is another option that should be considered in the design of kitchens for universal use.

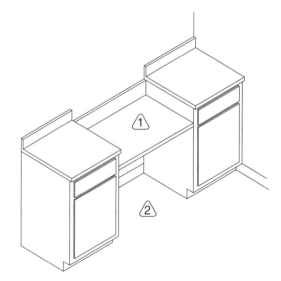

Figure 4-19a Adjustable counter.

1. An adjustable counter can be attached by means of wood support strips or an apron, supported by heavy-duty shelf brackets or supported by tracks mounted to walls.
2. Floor and wall finishes continued under counter.

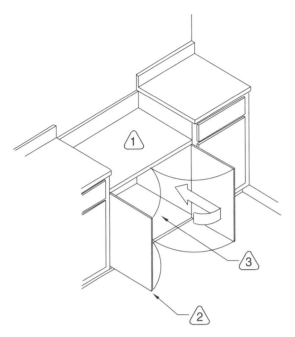

Figure 4-19b Adjustable/adaptable counter and cabinet.

1. An adjustable counter, as shown in Figure 4-19a.
2. Swinging or retractable doors allow for wheelchair access.
3. Optional hinged/fold-up cabinet bottom allows for wheelchair access.

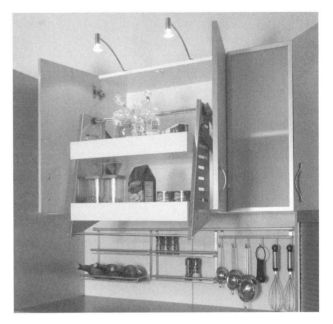

Figure 4-19d The EZ Shelf, distributed by Häfele, allows for the shelf to be pulled down by wheelchair users and some individuals with mobility limitations.

Photograph courtesy of Häfele America.

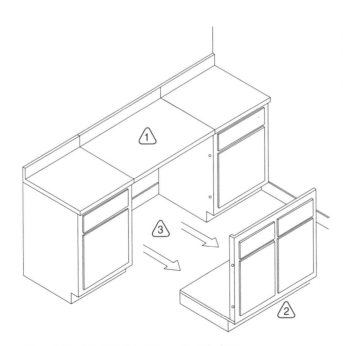

Figure 4-19c Adjustable/adaptable counter and cabinet

1. An adjustable counter, as shown in Figure 4-19a.
2. Special removable base cabinet.
3. Floor and wall finishes continued under cabinet.

Shallow shelves (10 to 12 inches [254 to 305mm]) in closet-style pantries allow users to see all contents with one quick look. When placed very close to or within the kitchen, such pantries afford a convenient storage solution. This type of pantry can also be placed farther from the kitchen. In such instances, the items stored tend to be those used less frequently in day-to-day cooking. See the "Kitchen Storage and Cabinetry" section of this chapter, Figures 4-30a and 4-30b, for pantry options.

Walk-in pantries have the advantage of containing the most actual storage space, allowing for an array of storage options such as shelves, cabinets, work areas, and storage bins. Like the closet-style versions, walk-in pantries containing infrequently used items can be located well outside of the kitchen, whereas those containing frequently used food preparation items are best located immediately adjacent to the kitchen.

In addition to considering dimensions of work and storage or reach areas, the designer must consider adjacent counter space for each appliance for preparation, cooking, and cleanup. Clear floor space for access as well as clear areas to allow for operation of appliances—such as opening and shutting doors—is required. The following are descriptions of required clearances and required counter space at major appliances.

Sinks

When planning primary sink areas, the designer must consider the space required to approach and use the sink. Sinks also require clear counter space adjacent to the sink for use in food preparation and for washing/drying. A portion of the counter should be the same height as the sink, as shown in Figure 4-20a.

Secondary sinks (those used by a second cook or for entertainment/snack areas) also require clearance space the same height as shown in Figure 4-20a.

ACCESSIBILITY NOTE

Sinks intended for use by those in wheelchairs require specific clearances in approach; optimum wheelchair access to the sink is provided with a front approach and clear knee space, as shown in Figure 4-20b.

REQUIRED CLEAR SPACES
AT PRIMARY SINK

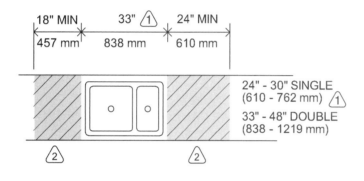

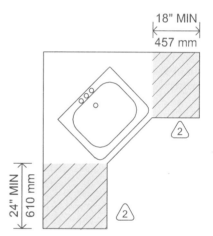

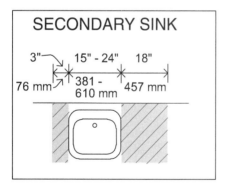

Figure 4-20a   Standard sink clearances and clear counter spaces (landing spaces).

1. Sink sizes vary; see sink sizes in Figure 4-9 .
2. Clear areas to each side of sink are required; a clear area of 24 inches (610-mm) to one side and 18 inches (457 mm) to the other. Clear areas should be the same height as sink. Areas adjacent to sink and below clear counter space can accommodate dishwasher/trash/recycling. The 24-inch (610-mm) clear area is a logical location for a dishwasher (at standard height).

WHEELCHAIR ACCESS TO SINK

FORWARD APPROACH WITH KNEE SPACE:
RECOMMENDED

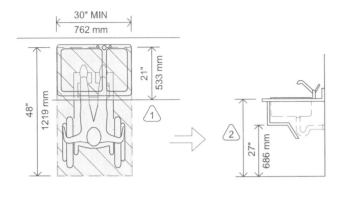

SIDE APPROACH:
NOT IDEAL

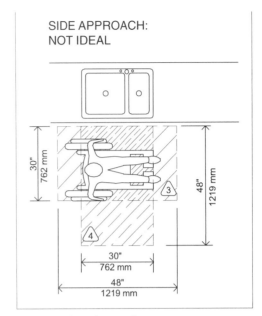

Figure 4-20b Sink clearances for wheelchair users. Forward approach with knee space is recommended, though not shown in all images.

1. Additional clear space to the side of the sink is helpful (see Figure 4-20c).
2. Counter height for seated users varies (see Figure 4-18c, item 7). While ANSI/ADA call for 27-inch (686-mm) clear height for knee spaces, individual residential preferences may differ. Sink bowl depth varies (while the ADA calls for a maximum depth of 6½ inches (165 mm), individual preferences vary). As stated previously, single-family residences need not meet ADA/ANSI. These requirements are given for reference only.
3. Parallel/side approach is not ideal, as it does not allow access to controls or for user to roll under the sink.
4. Front approach with no knee space provided does not allow wheelchair user to work comfortably at sink.

ACCESSIBLE SINK
WITH CLEAR SPACES

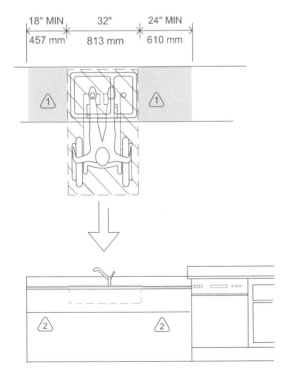

Figure 4-20c Clear counter spaces at sink for wheelchair users and accessible sink with garbage disposer.

1. Clear counter spaces at sink should be provided for wheelchair users, when possible (see Figure 4-20a). Clear counter spaces should be the same height as sink and be adjacent to sink.
2. While clear spaces are shown here with open space for knee access, this is not always possible. Typically the dishwasher is raised (see Figure 4-21b) and the counter above the dishwasher is not considered part of the clear counter space.
3. A garbage disposer can be included by using a two-bowl sink with knee space under one bowl and disposer located under the second bowl behind a cabinet. In cases where there is no disposer, the entire area under the sink should be left open; some homeowners opt for saloon-type swinging doors under sinks, which allow access but retain a "traditional" look.

ACCESSIBLE SINK
WITH GARBAGE DISPOSER

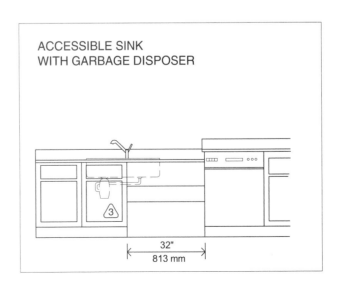

Dishwashers

Dishwashers must be considered in relationship to an adjacent sink and be convenient to storage for frequently used utensils and dishes. For standard use, a minimum of 21 inches (533 mm) of clear floor space should be allowed for using the dishwasher; wheelchair users would require more space. In larger kitchens, placing the dishwasher so that more than one person may use it at a time is useful. See Figure 4-21a for illustrations of dishwasher clearance and counter space requirements.

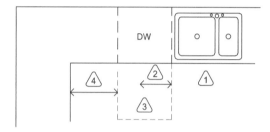

Figure 4-21a Standard dishwasher clearances.

1. Allow clear space for access to dishwasher; this space is often directly in front of sink.
2. Placement of dishwasher immediately adjacent to sink is helpful. This keeps drips within a close range of sink and dishwasher and allows one to rinse dishes and place them immediately into dishwasher. The absolute maximum distance from dishwasher to edge of sink is 36 inches (914 mm) but closer, as shown, is better.
3. Plan for open floor space at door location. Location of door should not conflict with doors of opposite appliance (when open).
4. Clear floor space of 21 inches (533 mm) is helpful between the edge of the dishwasher and a corner (this allows another person access to the corner).

ACCESSIBILITY NOTE

As stated previously, a higher-than-standard mounting location is required for wheelchair users or for individuals with mobility limitations. See Figure 4-21b. Standard undercounter dishwashers are made to fit under a standard counter (36 inches [914 mm] high), but this is not a useful arrangement for wheelchair users. Placing the dishwasher higher than standard, often on a raised toe kick (a minimum 8 inches [203 mm] above the floor—the actual ideal height varies), can make all interior racks accessible for various users and require less bending and stooping for standing users. Obviously, such a placement raises the countertop above a workable height for those using wheelchairs or standing; therefore, this is generally done in larger kitchens or those with adequate counter space in other areas. Dishwashers require clear space for the user to access controls, as well as a clear parallel approach for the user to unload dishes, as shown in Figure 4-21b.

Ranges and Cooktops

Providing adequate counter areas adjacent to each side of the cooktop or range allows for ease of use and allows the cook to slide a heavy pot directly from the burner to the counter area without lifting in case of emergency. With this in mind, such adjacent countertops must be the same height as the cooktop and should be fabricated of heat-resistant materials. Figure 4-22a illustrates standard cooktop/range clearances and clear counter spaces required.

Figure 4-21b Dishwasher clearances for wheelchair users.

1. Knee space (shaded) under counter can also serve as clear floor space. Additional clear floor space locations (shown) can be included in cases where room allows; this provides space for two individuals to use dishwasher/sink.
2. Open dishwasher door should not obstruct clear floor space for nearby appliances.
3. The dishwasher should be raised for wheelchair access; standard dishwasher installation height is not ideal for seated users. The *minimum* mounting height is 8 inches (203 mm) above floor (higher for some users); the maximum mounting height is 18 inches (457 mm) above floor (shaded area denotes mounting location for dishwasher). Raising the dishwasher as required requires raising the countertop (at dishwasher) well above a workable height for those using wheelchairs or standing.
4. The area immediately above dishwasher is ideal for dish storage.

PARALLEL CLEAR SPACE REQUIRED AT DISHWASHER

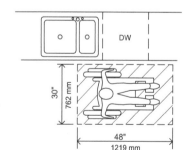

DISHWASHER MOUNTING HEIGHT

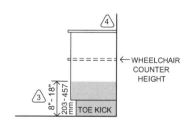

FORWARD-APPROACH CLEAR SPACE REQUIRED TO LOAD/UNLOAD DISHWASHER

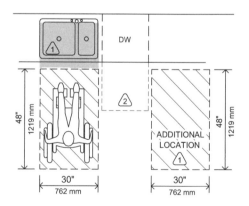

ENCLOSED (BY WALL)

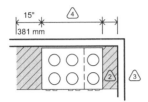

3" MIN. (76 mm)
9" RECOM. MIN (229 mm)
12"+ IDEAL (305 mm)

OPEN-ENDED LOCATION

3" MIN. (76 mm)
9" RECOM. MIN (229 mm)
12"+ IDEAL (305 mm)

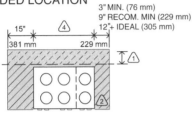

Figure 4-22a Standard range/cooktop clearances and clear counter spaces (landing spaces).

1. Island/peninsula locations require 9 inches (229 mm) minimum behind the cooktop if the counter height is the same as the cooktop.
2. Ideally, clear counter spaces (landing spaces) should be provided to each side of range/cooktop; one 15 inches (381 mm) and another 12 inches (305 mm). In smaller kitchens or tight areas, the clear space may be reduced as noted. Required clear spaces provided should be the same height as cooktop/range to form one continuous plane.
3. Minimum 3-inch (76-mm) clearance required at end wall with flame-retardant surface.
4. Sizes vary; see Figure 4-15 .

ACCESSIBILITY NOTE

Optimum wheelchair access for cooktops is provided with a front approach and clear knee space, as shown in Figure 4-22b. Ranges are not recommended for wheelchair users as they require a parallel approach. Information about clearances required for a parallel approach is provided, but it is not a recommended solution for accessible cooking.

Ventilation

Proper location of a ventilation system requires adequate clearance between the cooking surface and the hood. In cases where there is no hood or flame-resistant surface above, more clearance is often required, as shown in Figure 4-23. Cooking surfaces should not be placed below an operable window unless there is proper clearance and a protected wall surface behind and above the cooking surface, also shown in Figure 4-23.

Ovens and Microwaves

Wall ovens should be placed so that open oven doors do not dangerously protrude into high-traffic areas and so that hot items may be easily transferred to a resting space on the adjacent counter surface or another nearby counter surface that is removed from major traffic areas, as shown in Figure 4-24a.

RECOMMENDED
FORWARD APPROACH
KNEE SPACE AT COOKTOP

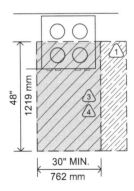

PARALLEL APPROACH: CLEAR SPACE
AT RANGE (NOT IDEAL)

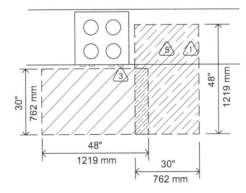

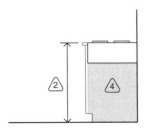

Figure 4-22b Range/cooktop clearances for wheelchair users.

1. Additional space at side(s) preferred.
2. Height for seated users varies from 2 feet, 4 inches to 2 feet, 8 inches (711 to 813 mm) and, in some cases, 3 feet (914 mm), to allow for variation in armrest height and countertop thickness.
3. Access to controls must not require reaching over burners.
4. Knee space (shaded) allows ideal access; the knee space must be insulated to protect from burns, abrasions, and electrical shocks.
5. If possible, provide knee space under counter adjacent to range in cases where open space under a cooktop is not possible.

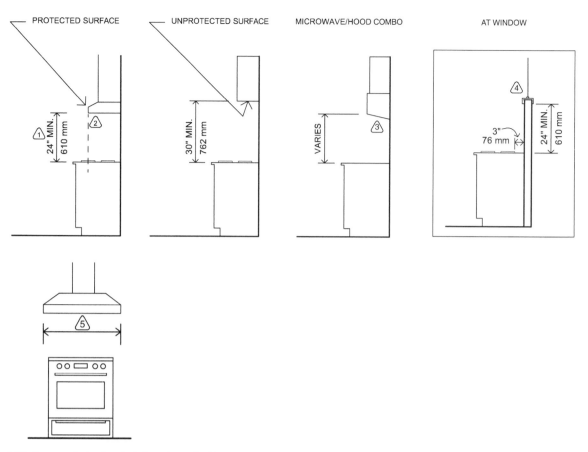

Figure 4-23 Clearances for hoods and windows at range/cooktop.

1. Hood distance above range/cooktop: 24 inches (610 mm) minimum to 36 inches (914 mm) in most cases. Increasing the height within this range is helpful for capturing steam/odors. Verify height requirements with manufacturer's guidelines.
2. Hood should extend at least as far as the middle of the first burner (dashed line), often 17 to 21 inches (431 to 533 mm).
3. Manufacturer-suggested clearances for protected surfaces such as microwave/hood combinations may be less than 24 inches (610 mm), as shown in the first drawing; access to oven/rear burners must be considered.
4. Cooking surfaces should not be located below an operable window unless these minimum dimensions are met.
5. Hood should be 3 to 6 inches (76 to 152 mm) wider than cooktop.

Ideally, ovens are not located directly next to refrigerators. In cases where this occurs, counter space should be provided next to the refrigerator and next to/across from the oven. Oven heights vary depending on whether single, double, or combination ovens are used.

ACCESSIBILITY NOTE

As discussed previously, wall ovens are well suited for wheelchair users; see Figure 4-24b. Side-hinged and swinging doors require a pullout shelf, which pulls out a minimum of 10 inches (254 mm), underneath the oven or a permanent shelf (such as one at the front edge of the counter). In cases where the oven is not self-cleaning, an adjacent counter with open knee space is required on the latch side. Non-self-cleaning ovens with drop-front doors also require an adjacent counter with open knee space below, as shown in Figure 4-24b. In self-cleaning models, adjacent clear knee space is recommended where possible. For many seated users, ovens installed with the cavity between 30 and 40 inches (762 and 1016 mm) above the floor work well, but this varies based on the individual.

Generally, microwave ovens are comfortably located with the oven bottom between 24 and 48 inches (610 and 1219 mm) above the floor, although those set at counter height—36 inches (762 mm) or slightly lower—are considered best for many wheelchair users. Microwave units that are part of built-in ovens or over cooktops are sometimes higher than 48 inches (1219 mm). Microwaves require open adjacent counter space or open space below or above the oven. See Figures 4-24a and 4-24b.

WALL OVEN/MICROWAVE CLEARANCES

WALL OVEN MOUNTING HEIGHTS

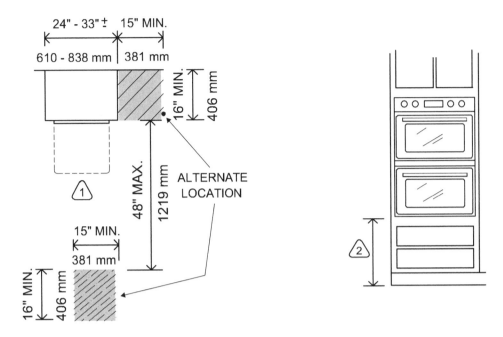

MICROWAVE MOUNTING HEIGHTS

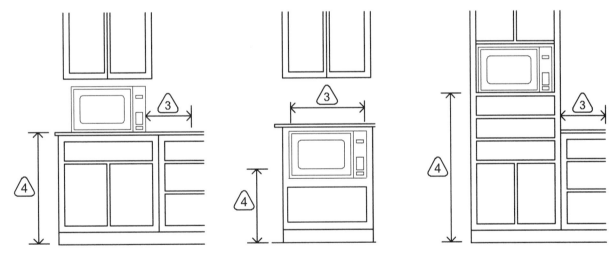

Figure 4-24a Standard wall oven/microwave clear counter spaces and heights.

1. Door should not open into major traffic aisle.
2. Wall oven height relates to the cabinet the oven(s) are placed within. Single ovens are convenient at heights from 30 to 36 inches (762 to 914 mm) above the floor. The placement of double ovens varies. In larger kitchens ovens are placed side by side rather than one on top of another. Ovens are usually placed within tall cabinets; typically, single ovens are placed in *universal oven cabinets* and double ovens are place in *double oven cabinets* where height is based on oven location within the cabinet; see Figure 4-27a.
3. Clear space of 15 inches (381 mm) is required above, below, or adjacent to a microwave oven.
4. Bottom of microwave oven should be 24 to 48 inches (610 to 1219 mm) above floor; heights vary based on location/user.

Figure 4-24b Wall oven/microwave clearances and clear counter space for wheelchair users.

1. Non-self-cleaning ovens require an adjacent 30-inch (762-mm) open knee space (on latch side of side-hinged doors); this clear space is helpful for self-cleaning models as well.
2. Side-opening doors require a shelf that pulls out a minimum of 10 inches (610 mm).
3. Counter location is best for microwaves for a range of users; however, this placement eliminates counter space.
4. Clear counter space required adjacent to microwave and oven.

ACCESSIBLE OVENS/MICROWAVES

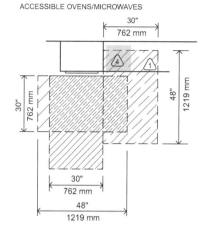

FOLD-DOWN OVEN DOOR

SIDE-HINGED OVEN DOOR

Refrigerators

Refrigerator placement requires thought about the swing of the door(s) and the need for clear counter space nearby. Single-door units require clear counter space next to the refrigerator or across from the refrigerator. In two-door models, where open space is not available on both sides of the refrigerator, it is important to have the available open counter space accessible to the fresh food (refrigerator) section, as this is used more often. The refrigerator door side should be hinged so that the flow of food to counters and work centers takes precedence over the freezer section. As stated previously, side-by-side models offer the best access for wheelchair users; one rule of thumb calls for 50 percent of freezer space below 54 inches (1372 mm) for universal access. Figure 4-25 illustrates standard accessible refrigerator clearances as well as wheelchair-accessible refrigerator floor clearances.

ACCESSIBILITY NOTE

Information about required clearances for wheelchair-accessible refrigerators can be found in Figure 4-25. A side-by side refrigerator is the best choice for users of wheelchairs as these allow access to both frozen and refrigerated items.

KITCHEN STORAGE AND CABINETRY

The location and quality of storage is paramount to the overall usefulness of the kitchen. Food, cooking gear, small appliances, dishware, flatware, and cleaning supplies as well as trash/recycling can be found in kitchens and must be stored in a manner that makes these items reasonably easy to locate, retrieve, and put away. The location and use of these items—particularly those used frequently—must be considered as kitchen work areas are designed. (Information about work areas can be found in the "Organizational Flow" section of this chapter.)

The layout of cabinetry and storage areas requires knowledge of cabinet design and an understanding of the placement of storage. These go beyond issues of style and fashion and relate far more to the day-to-day function of the kitchen. For example, ideally there should be ample dish storage near the sink and dishwasher. This may seem obvious, but some beautiful kitchens lack decent dish and utensil storage near where those items are used or washed, making the kitchen less than functional.

The design of storage spaces can be seen as adding to the previous discussion of kitchen work areas and organization, as one must consider what dishes, utensils, and small appliances

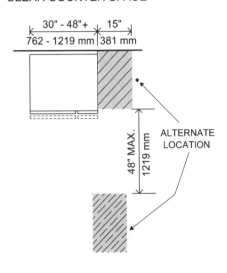

STANDARD REFRIGERATOR
CLEAR COUNTER SPACE

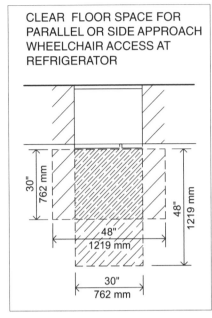

CLEAR FLOOR SPACE FOR
PARALLEL OR SIDE APPROACH
WHEELCHAIR ACCESS AT
REFRIGERATOR

Figure 4-25 Standard refrigerator clear spaces (landing spaces) and wheelchair-accessible clearances. A minimum of 15 inches (381 mm) of clear counter space should be provided on the latch side of single-door refrigerators or at an alternate location that is not more than 48 inches (1219 mm) from the refrigerator. Side-by-side models require this clear counter space to be convenient to the fresh food section or in an alternate location as shown. Wheelchair-accessible refrigerator clearances are shown at right. Side-by-side models are recommended for wheelchair users.

are used in each area and to provide handy storage for those items. In addition, storage for consumables and cleaning items must be provided.

According to literature produced by Blum, a manufacturer of cabinet and furniture fittings, "Every kitchen can be divided into five kitchen zones regardless of size or shape." This zone approach is based on the notion that items used together should be stored together in the following zones:

Five "Kitchen Zones" Identified by Blum:

- **Consumables Zone**: Food items should be stored together; this includes refrigerated as well as nonperishable items. One approach to this is placing tall cabinet or pantry units adjacent to the refrigerator area.

- **Non-Consumables Zone**: Dishes, cutlery, glasses, and storage containers should be stored together, and ideally the dishwasher is close by.

- **Cleaning Zone**: The sink and dishwasher are the foundation of this zone, and cleaning utensils and supplies should be stored here. This is a key area for storage of items as they come out of the dishwasher. Some studies indicate that this is the most heavily used area in the kitchen. (See additional information in the following "Concepts to Consider" list.)

- **Preparation Zone**: Items needed for food preparation are kept here. This zone has overlap with the nonconsumable zone in that some items are required for dining and for preparation. Kitchen knives would be kept here, as would cutting boards and gadgets used in food preparation. (This is the 36-inch (914-mm) area described in the "Organizational Flow" section of this chapter.)

- **Cooking:** Pots, pans, lids, and cooking utensils should be kept here. Again there may be some overlap with preparation in that some utensils are used for both preparation and cooking.

Some additional concepts to consider related to kitchen storage are included in the following list:

Additional Kitchen Storage Concepts to Consider:

- The sink center (or cleaning zone) requires a significant amount of storage. The National Kitchen and Bath Association's Kitchen Planning Guidelines recommends specific quantities of storage near the sink:

    Small Kitchen (less than 150 square feet [14 m²]):

    400 inches (10,160 mm) of shelf/drawer frontage

    within 72 inches (1829 mm) of the center of sink

    Medium Kitchen (between 150 and 350 square feet [1395 to 32.52 m²]):

    480 inches (12,192 mm) of shelf/drawer frontage

    within 72 inches (1829 mm) of the center of sink

    Large Kitchen (greater than 350 square feet [3252 m²]):

    560 inches (14,224 mm) of shelf/drawer frontage

    within 72 inches (1829 mm) of the center of sink

- Another consideration for the sink area is the relationship of items such as flatware, glassware, and dishes, which are often stored by the sink/dishwasher so that they are convenient to put away; these items should also be convenient during cooking and preparation. Another approach to dealing with this is to store items where they are first or last used; for example, coffee mugs could be stored near the coffee brewing area or the dishwasher.

- Corner cabinets present some interesting challenges. When two built-in cabinets are perpendicular to one another, the space created at the corner is not easily usable. A blind corner cabinet can allow storage but is typically not easy to access; various lazy Susan and specialized pull-out drawers and unusual door and hardware configurations can add greatly to the usability of corner cabinets. (See Figure 4-26a and 4-26b for examples of specialized corner drawers.)

- Drawers are increasingly replacing doors in lower base cabinets in many kitchens. This is because drawers work well to contain a range of utensils, tools, and cookware and also work effectively behind doors as rollouts for pans, canned goods, and other items. (See Figure 4-26c.) Drawers installed at appropriate heights and locations can also work well for wheelchair users.

- Manufacturers are creating a range of innovative products to allow for greater ease of accessing storage; see Figures 4-26a through 4-26d for examples of innovative approaches to storage.

- When possible, cluster tall elements such as refrigerators, wall ovens, and tall cabinets. This will create more uninterrupted counter space and better visual cohesion. Clearly there is some complexity to this, in that it is not ideal to have wall ovens immediately adjacent to refrigerators. However, tall pantry units next to wall ovens or refrigerators can work well.

- In kitchens with limited counter space and limited storage, wall cabinets that are placed at counter height can be a good option; this provides a good deal of storage space yet offers a bit of counter surface at these areas.

Figure 4-26a and 4-26b The SPACE CORNER cabinet, by Blum Inc., is an innovative approach to corner cabinet storage. Options include metal or wood drawers as shown and a range of drawer storage systems.

Photographs courtesy of Blum Inc.

Figure 4-26c Drawers are increasingly replacing doors because they offer greater ease of access. Full extension hardware allows the drawer to open fully so that all items are within view.

Photograph courtesy of Blum Inc.

Figure 4-26d Blum's AVENTOS HF bifold lift system allows doors to be lifted up and out of the way with minimum effort and allows full access to the interior of cabinet.

Photograph courtesy of Blum Inc.

More on Cabinets and Built-In Storage

Cabinets and shelving provide much of the storage in most kitchens, so an understanding of the basic construction, production types, styles, arrangements, and available options is therefore required. When specifying cabinets, the designer should keep in mind that there are three production method options: *stock*, *semicustom*, and *custom*.

Stock cabinets are mass-produced and warehoused, awaiting quick shipment (in most cases); they come in standard sizes and finishes. Stock cabinets are generally the least expensive type, the most popular in terms of sales, and available in a variety of sizes, shapes, styles, and wood species. But they are limited in terms of options and may not fit the desired space exactly, in which case filler strips are used to close gaps.

Stock cabinets are available in standard widths starting at 9 inches, in 3-inch increments up to 24 inches, and in 6-inch increments from 24 to 48 inches. Standard depths are 12 inches for wall cabinets and 24 inches for base, oven, and utility cabinets. Figures 4-27a to 4-27c depict common stock cabinetry units. Note that dimensions for stock cabinets have not been converted into millimeters because stock cabinets are sold based on inch dimensions, as noted.

Stock-Cabinet Terminolgoy

Kitchen cabinet manufacturers employ a basic code for referencing stock cabinets in which the type of cabinet (such as base) is listed by the first initial, followed by the cabinet width. Therefore, a 36-inch-wide base cabinet is referred to as a B36, whereas a 36-inch-wide sink base could be referred to as an SB36. W3030 describes a wall cabinet that is 30 inches wide and 30 inches high.

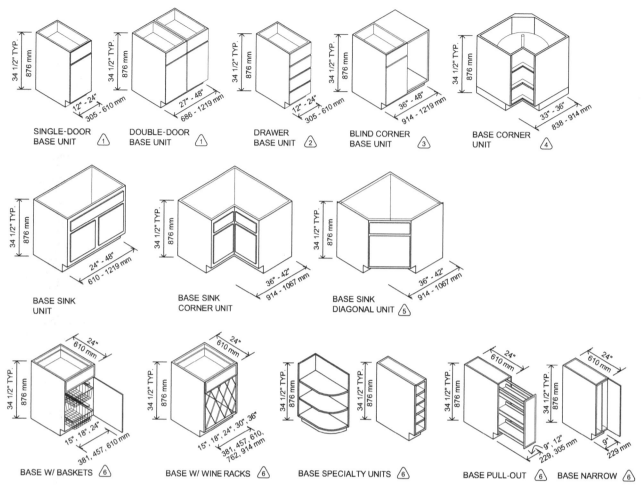

Figure 4-27a Base cabinet configurations and sizes for stock cabinets.

1. Single- and double-door units are available with open shelves and many options such as rollout shelves. Double-door units may have single top drawers or double top drawers.
2. A wider/deeper version is available as a cooktop base (without top drawer).
3. These have very small doors unless unit is more than 39 inches wide.
4. Not all corner units contain a lazy Susan; they are a useful option (see also Figures 4-26a and 4-26b).
5. Given the depth of this unit, it is very difficult to reach from front to back.
6. There are many interior options available, such as pullout trays, wastebaskets, and shelf-tray combinations. These options are available in both single- and double-door units.

It is worth noting that European modular cabinets are built to different stock dimensions. Additional information about European stock cabinets can be found in Appendix F. Information about standard reach and work counter height can be found in Figure 4-18a.

Semicustom cabinets are also preassembled but are typically constructed when the order is finalized so that custom modifications can be made, which increases delivery time. Semicustom cabinets are the second most popular type in terms of sales and can allow greater flexibility than stock cabinets in terms of cabinet size, construction materials, color, and other options. Widths start at 9 inches (229 mm), with 3-inch (76-mm) incremental increases up to 48 inches (1219 mm). Depths can

be reduced and increased from standards as required, within manufacturers' guidelines. Semicustom cabinets are more costly than stock and are generally not accepted for return if they do not fit.

Custom cabinets are built to completely custom specifications—either by a craftsperson or manufactured on a made-to-order basis. There are few limitations in terms of size, design, arrangement, construction materials, color, wood species, and options. Custom cabinets can be quite expensive depending on materials and construction techniques used, and they have long lead/delivery times. However, custom cabinetry remains an option for certain clients and can offer excellent results. See Table 4-1 for an overview of cabinet production information.

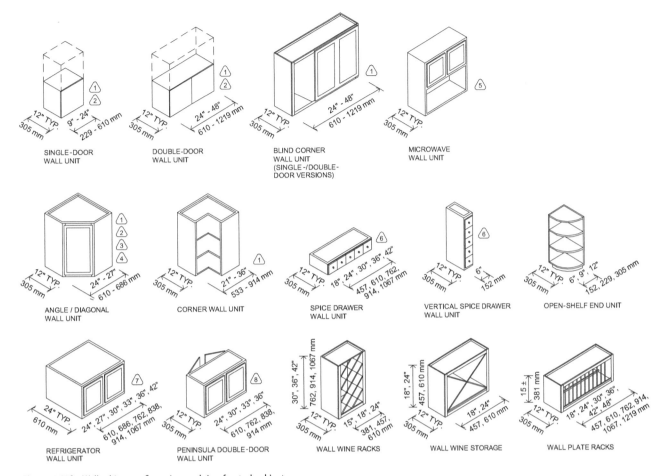

Figure 4-27b Wall cabinet configurations and sizes for stock cabinets.

1. Heights vary: 12, 15, 18, 21, 24, 27, 30, 36, 39, 42, and 48 inches.
2. Available with lower tambour door cabinet (in tall versions).
3. Available with rotating shelves/lazy Susan or specialized drawers.
4. Special units accommodate curved doors.
5. Height varies: 36, 45, and 48 inches, depending on whether they are compact or full-sized ovens. There are also other options used for microwaves.
6. Many options are available; this is only a small sampling. Wall end units with doors are also available.
7. Heights vary: 12, 15, and 18 inches.
8. Heights vary: 12 to 42 inches in 3-inch increments.

Table 4-1 Cabinet Production Types

Type	Production Information	Comments
Stock	Mass produced. Standardized sizes, although there are many options in terms of size, color, and materials used.	Most common. Least expensive (although costs vary widely). Limited options due to standardization.
Semicustom	Typically produced when ordered to allow for customization. More options in terms of cabinet dimensions and customization. Cabinet widths begin at roughly 9 inches and run to 48 inches; depths can be modified.	Generally more expensive than stock types, with no return option after delivery.
Custom	Built to precise custom specifications for the individual project.	Can be quite expensive, with long lead times.

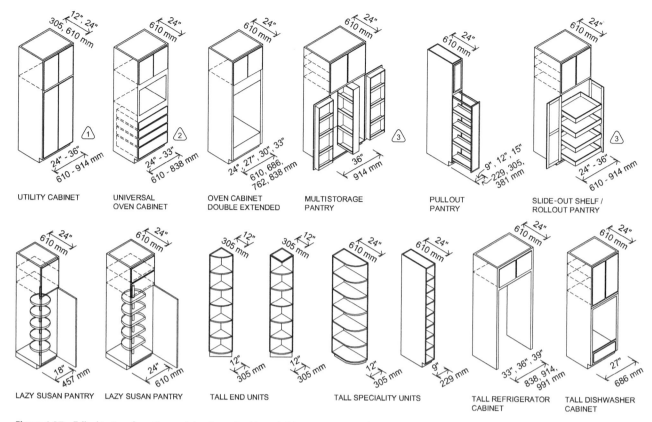

Figure 4-27c Tall cabinet configurations and sizes for stock cabinets; heights vary: 84, 90, and 96 inches.

1. Heights vary: 84, 90, and 96 inches; depths vary: 12 and 24 inches. Available in single-door units: 9, 12, 15, 18, and 24 inches wide.
2. Universal unit accommodates single or double oven by eliminating drawers; microwave versions available. Some single-oven units are as wide as 39 inches. Microwave cabinets are also available.
3. Single-door versions available (12, 18, and 24 inches wide).

Stock, semicustom, and custom cabinets are production techniques and do not refer directly to cabinet quality; overall quality is determined by the construction of the cabinet box. The quality and thickness of the material chosen for construction as well as the joinery and bracing all contribute to the overall quality of the cabinet box.

Two additional terms related to cabinet construction describe general cabinet structure or assembly: framed (or face-framed) and frameless. *Framed* cabinets are common in North America and consist of a frame (referred to as a face frame) that is attached to the front of the cabinet box with doors attached to the frame. This frame is composed of horizontal members

Table 4-2 Door and Drawer Types

Type	Comments	Used with Cabinet Types
Inset	Door/drawers are inset within the face frame and sit flush with the edges of the frame.	Framed only
Traditional overlay	Door/drawers rest against the frame, overlaying it and exposing at least a portion of the frame.	Framed only
Lipped	Door/drawers have grooves cut around the door on the back edge, allowing the cut portion to sit back inside the frame and giving the appearance of an overlay door.	Framed only
Full overlay	Door/drawers completely cover the face frame with less than 1/8 inch between the door/drawer and frame and have concealed hinges.	Both framed and frameless

(known as rails) and vertical members (known as stiles). Typically, double cabinets wider than 24 inches (610 mm) have a center stile, although these may also be found on smaller cabinets. Figure 4-28a illustrates framed and frameless cabinets.

Frameless cabinets have no face frame on the front of the cabinet box, as shown in Figure 4-28a. Without the frame and the center stile (on two-door cabinets), frameless cabinets provide more open access to interior contents. Hinges are concealed on frameless cabinets and doors cover the entire opening—these are known as full-overlay doors/drawers.

Frameless cabinets were invented in Germany and are also known as European or Euro-style. In most cases, frameless cabinets have two parallel, vertical rows of predrilled holes (known as system or hardware holes) that are spaced 32 millimeters (1.26 in.) apart and are 5 millimeters (0.197 in.) in diameter. Given the 32-millimeter hole spacing, cabinet elements such as hinges, slides, and drawer and door faces are also spaced in 32-millimeter increments. Refer to

Figure 4-28a for illustrations of frameless cabinets and Figure 4-28b for door styles.

When first introduced into the United States in the 1980s, frameless cabinetry was considered new and innovative, but it has now become common with many American manufacturers using this system. While the 32-millimeter (1.26-in.) spacing and frameless cabinets have become commonplace in the United States, overall cabinet dimensioning and sizing are not based on metric measurements in the United States as they are in other parts of the world. An example of European cabinet configurations and sizes can be found in Appendix F.

Various door and drawer styles can be used on framed cabinets, whereas frameless types only have one option: a full overlay door. Table 4-2 contains some door/drawer options and information.

Another type of door, known as a tambour, works similarly to the rolling portion of a rolltop desk. It uses separated pieces or strips attached to a backing sheet and set in a track, allowing

Figure 4-28a Framed and frameless cabinets. Framed cabinet is shown with face frame portion shaded; frameless cabinets do not have a face frame.

1. Framed cabinets can accommodate door and drawer fronts that are inset within frame or overlay type (overlay shown).
2. Frameless cabinet accommodates overlay type door and drawers only.
3. Framed cabinet hinges attach to frame.
4. Frameless cabinet hinges attach inside box.
5. Predrilled holes for shelf supports.
6. Frameless cabinets are available with adjustable legs as shown or can have a standard toe kick or base.

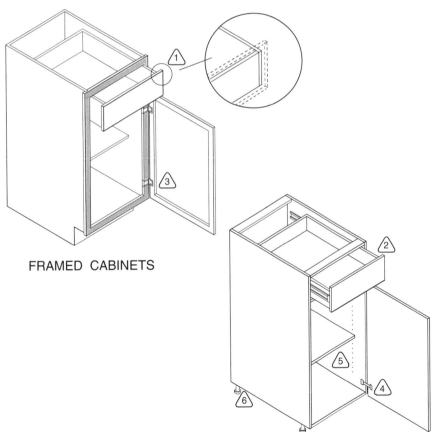

FRAMED CABINETS

FRAMELESS CABINETS

DOOR/DRAWER TYPES

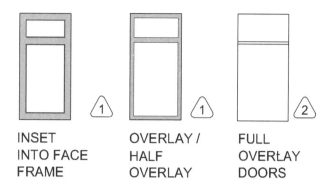

INSET
INTO FACE
FRAME

OVERLAY /
HALF
OVERLAY

FULL
OVERLAY
DOORS

DOOR/DRAWER STYLES

SPECIALTY DOORS

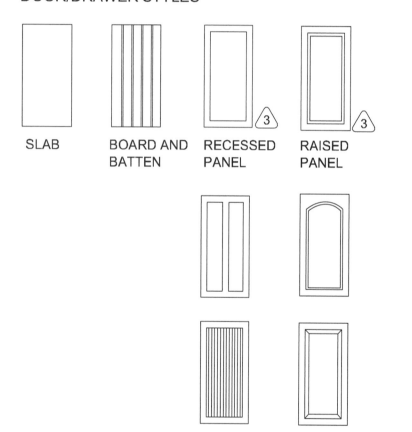

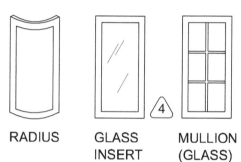

SLAB

BOARD AND
BATTEN

RECESSED
PANEL

RAISED
PANEL

RADIUS

GLASS
INSERT

MULLION
(GLASS)

Figure 4-28b Cabinet door and drawer styles.

1. Shaded portion depicts visible face frame on framed cabinets; inset and half overlay used only on framed cabinets.
2. Full overlay is the only door/drawer option for frameless cabinets and can be used on framed cabinets as well.
3. Recessed panel and raised panel styles are available in a variety of style options.
4. Glass insert types consist of single glass planes inserted into the center panel area within a door; a range of types of glass may be used. Mullion styles consist of multiple smaller glass panels placed within mullions.

    Note: Door styles listed include matching panels for hoods and refrigerator and dishwasher doors.

it to roll up. This type of door is helpful in areas where a door should remain open without getting in the way, such as for an appliance garage.

Both framed and frameless cabinets can be found in stock, semicustom, and custom production. Cabinet doors are also available in a range of specialty options, including curved doors (generally called radius doors). Doors without center panels can be inset with glass or with mullions (thin strips of wood) and glass. See Figure 4-28b for specialty door styles.

Cabinet hardware includes hinges, latches, pulls, and knobs. Hinge choices can be limited depending on manufacturer's standards (this is not usually an issue in custom installations), whereas pulls (also called handles) and knobs are available in a vast array of designs, materials, and finishes. The selection of pulls and knobs can greatly impact the visual quality of cabinetry and therefore requires consideration of size, shape, and finish as part of the total composition of the design. In addition, functional issues such as the relative size and position of these will impact day-to-day use of the cabinet. In terms of universal design, larger U-shaped pulls are considered most useful for a wide range of individuals.

A variety of interior accessories and fittings are available for use in stock cabinetry. In semicustom and custom cabinetry, the options are endless. The "Ergonomics and Required Clearances" section of this chapter describes some additional accessories and adaptable/adjustable cabinets for wheelchair users.

The discussion of kitchen cabinetry to this point has been about built-in cabinetry rather than "unfitted" storage elements. Unfitted storage is typically freestanding, often furniture-like, movable, and not restricted by the size and construction limits discussed in this section.

Accessibility Note

Stock base cabinets come in a standard height of 34½ inches (876.3 mm) with toe kicks 4 inches (101.6 mm) high. Generally, these heights work for a range of able-bodied adults of average stature; however, for smaller/taller individuals or those with mobility limitations, standard counter heights are problematic. Several cabinet manufacturers offer stock cabinets in what is sometimes referred to as universal access or universal design cabinetry, which include stock base cabinets that are 32½ inches (825.5 mm) high (without countertop) and with toe kicks that are 9 inches (228.6 mm) high and 6 inches (152.4 mm) deep for wheelchair accessibility, as shown in Figures 4-29a to 4-29c. For additional information on counter heights, see the "Ergonomics and Required Clearances" section of this chapter.

Figure 4-29a The Passport Series from KraftMaid Cabinetry is an example of universal access stock cabinetry that allows wheelchair access.

1. A raised dishwasher base cabinet with adjacent plate rack and lowered wall cabinets creates convenient storage near dishwasher/sink.
2. Sink, open underneath for forward approach.
3. Lowered countertop heights.
4. Open area under cooktop allows for forward approach. A tambour door is shown in the base cabinet next to the cooktop.
5. Oven cabinet puts oven within convenient seated reach range.
6. High, deep toe kicks.

Courtesy of KraftMaid® Cabinetry

Figure 4-29b This pullout table provides a work surface for seated use.

Courtesy of KraftMaid® Cabinetry.

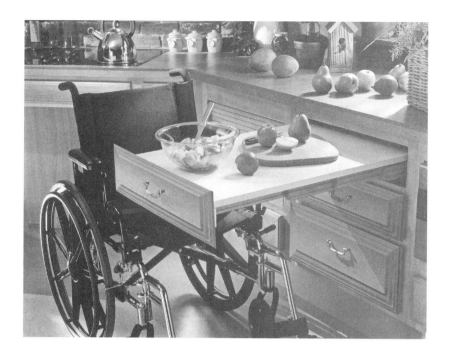

Figure 4-29c Pullout shelves can provide universal access to stored items.

Courtesy of KraftMaid® Cabinetry.

THE PANTRY

While pantries have drifted in and out of favor over the years, many homeowners currently desire them. The term *pantry* can refer to a wide assortment of storage units: tall (deep or shallow) cabinets within the kitchen, small closets lined with shelves, or separate walk-in rooms with cabinets, shelves, and bins. Each type of pantry brings with it advantages and disadvantages.

Pantries in kitchen cabinets are available in stock or custom cabinetry. Stock cabinets that serve as pantries are available

with a range of options and fittings, as described and illustrated in the previous section (Figure 4-27c). In some cases, multiple tall cabinet units can be used to provide extensive storage. This type of pantry located within the kitchen provides handy access to items for cooking and cleaning.

Closet-style pantries can be equipped with shelves alone, as well as with shelves, cabinets, and bins for such things as garbage and recycling. Shelf depths of 10 or 12 inches (254 or 305 mm) work well to contain various sizes of food packaging (from cereal boxes to canned goods); some designers find that deeper shelves simply obscure stored items, making items difficult to see and retrieve. Dinnerware, serving items, glassware, and appliances often require deeper shelving, and shelving depths may therefore vary accordingly.

Some walk-in pantries are outfitted with exquisite cabinetry to display beautiful dishware and/or collections, while others are more utilitarian in terms of materials/finishes and are meant primarily as functional storage areas. A recent trend involves creating pantry rooms that can be used as future elevator shafts in multistory homes so that owners may age in place (see Figure 4-30a, item A_1).

A butler's pantry is a pantry-like space, traditionally housed between the kitchen and the dining room, meant to store glassware, silver, and additional dining-related items. Currently, butler's pantries may be used to house wine and wine accessories or to display dishes and glassware. They may also serve as a bar, or, in some cases, as a secondary service area to set out appetizers or food. They may include refrigerators or sinks, as shown in Figure 4-30b. When designing a butler's pantry that is meant to function as a bar or secondary serving area, one should follow the information in the following section in order to incorporate the necessary elements. For example, when a sink is included, one must follow the required clearances for a sink and provide adequate circulation space.

Figure 4-30a Pantry plans and configurations. A₁ and A₂ are walk-in pantries with adequate storage and access space; these require a minimum of 2 feet (610 mm) of circulation/aisle space. B₁ and B₂ are reach-in pantries. C₁ shows built-in, reach-in pantry cabinets. C₂ is a reach-in pantry housed in tall cabinetry (see Figure 4-27 c for more information about tall pantry units).

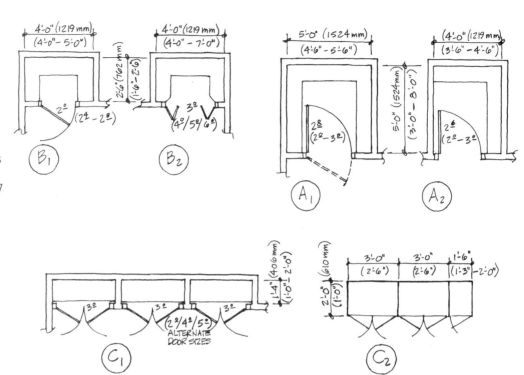

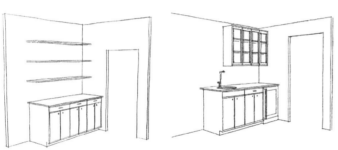

Figure 4-30b A butler's pantry may simply supply storage for dishware and glasses or may serve more as a bar or buffet counter. In cases where sinks, dishwashers, and other appliances are included, information from the "Organizational Flow" section should be followed to ensure that the space functions well.

Secondary Kitchens

Outdoor kitchens are desired by some homeowners. In addition, in some larger homes an extra, secondary kitchen is desired. Also known as outpost kitchens, they are often on a different level than the primary kitchen, adjacent to a social/leisure space. For information on the design of outdoor kitchens and outpost kitchens, see Appendix E.

RELATED CODES AND CONSTRAINTS

Many of the constraints related to kitchen design have been covered in previous discussions of recommended appliance and fixture clearances. As stated in previous chapters, all code information provided here is presented for general informa-

tion based on the International Residential Code (IRC). The designer should always consult local codes, as they may vary.

The IRC considers kitchens "habitable space," and Section R303.1 requires that all habitable rooms "be provided with aggregate glazing area of not less than 8 percent of the floor area." It also calls for natural ventilation through "windows, doors, louvers or other approved openings" and for the minimum openable area to the exterior to be 4 percent of the floor area being ventilated. There are exceptions to this rule allowing for adequate mechanical ventilation, and artificial light may serve as a substitution for natural ventilation in certain rooms (such as kitchens) that do not require an escape opening. Additionally, in cases where kitchens are open to adjoining rooms, they may share approved natural ventilation with some contingencies.

The required ventilation discussed covers room ventilation, not the ventilation of the range or cooktop. A detailed discussion of ventilation of cooking surfaces can be found in the next section, including further IRC requirements related to cooking ventilation.

The following list covers some additional IRC kitchen-related code requirements and their related sections.

Selected IRC Kitchen-Related Code Items

- Section R304 allows kitchens to be the exception to the requirement that all habitable rooms have a floor area of not less than 70 square feet (6.5 m²) (Section R304.2). Kitchens are also an exception to the requirement that a room not be less than 7 feet (2134 mm) in any horizontal dimension (Section R304.3).

- Section R305 of the IRC covers ceiling height in detail and requires that habitable rooms have ceiling heights of "not less than 7 feet (2134 mm)," with no portion of the required space to have a ceiling height lower than 5 feet (1524 mm). An illustration of this height requirement is shown in Chapter 1. This section contains several exceptions related to beams, soffits, and sloped ceilings, as discussed in Chapter 5.

- Section R306 requires that dwelling units be provided with a kitchen area with a sink. Section R306.4 requires that all plumbing fixtures be "connected to an approved water supply" and that kitchens be "provided with hot and cold water." Section P2706.3 prohibits plumbing fixtures from receiving the discharge of an indirect waste, although "a kitchen sink trap is acceptable for use as a receptor for a dishwasher."

- Section M1503 covers range hoods and indicates that they must "discharge to the outdoors through a single-wall duct"—with exceptions based on natural and mechanical ventilation provided through other sources. An exception is granted to "approved" ductless range hoods.

- Section M1507 (table 1507.4) shows minimum requirements for ventilation in kitchens to be 100 cfm (cubic feet per minute) for intermittent ventilation or 25 cfm for continuous ventilation. Additional information on range and cooktop ventilation can be found in the next section of this chapter.

- Section E3901 covers electrical outlet placement in kitchens. See the "Electrical and Mechanical" section for information on outlet placement and the related code.

As stated previously, federally financed multiple-family dwellings must meet accessibility guidelines required by the Fair Housing Amendments Act (FHAA), which requires "usable kitchens . . . such that an individual in a wheelchair can maneuver about the space." This generally requires wheelchair turning clearance in U-shaped kitchens and 36-inch (914-mm) clearance at all passageways and circulation areas, but the guidelines do not address counter heights.

UFAS requires a 40-inch (1016-mm) clearance between kitchen cabinets (providing knee space) and opposing walls, appliances, and cabinets. It also requires specific parallel or front clearance at appliances and adjustable counters or counters that are 34 inches (864 mm) high. See Appendix B for comparative information about ANSI and UFAS related to kitchen design.

ELECTRICAL AND MECHANICAL

The work done in a kitchen brings in smoke, odors, grease, and toxic fumes (in gas ranges and cooktops). With newer homes increasingly airtight due to improvements in construction and insulation, proper ventilation of cooking equipment is a necessity.

Four cooking area ventilation choices are available: a ventilating hood over the cooktop vented to the outside, a ductless hood with a recirculation fan, a downdraft range/cooktop that draws contaminants into connected ductwork downward and then outside, and a wall fan that exhausts to the outside. According to the NKBA's Kitchen Basics, the ductless hood and wall fan are the least effective, with the vented hood the best option. The limitations of the downdraft system can involve tall pots and pans limiting ventilation and dependence on the proximity to the substances being vented. Both the vented hood and the downdraft systems work to filter out grease, odors, and smoke, whereas the other options primarily move the air only.

Downdraft systems may vent directly outside or use ducting running beneath the floor between joists. Ventilated hoods may exhaust outside: vertically through the roof, directly through an exterior wall, or horizontally through a soffit or through exposed ductwork. Sizing the ventilation hood and fan requires careful thought. According to the NKBA, hoods should be roughly 3 inches (76 mm) wider on each side than the cooking surface, although in the authors' experience, this is seldom seen in standard residential construction.

According to the NKBA, ventilation of 150 cfm is recommended for surface cooking appliances. This recommendation exceeds that required by the code and may vary from that called for by manufacturers; therefore, familiarity with manufacturers' guidelines is imperative. The length of ductwork, how many bends are required, and its location all affect the sizing of the ventilation fan. If ductwork is located in uninsulated attics in some colder climates, it may need to be wrapped with insulation.

Because the IRC (Section R303.9) calls for heating to a minimum of 68°F (20°C) when the winter design temperature is below 60°F (15.5°C), most kitchens in the United States (with the possible exception of portions of Hawaii and Florida) are required to have some source of heat.

The location of the heat source or its registers or diffusers, as well as those used by any air-cooling source, must be considered in relationship to the location of appliances and counters. The actual engineering of the heating and cooling system is, of course, done by professionals other than the interior designer. However, it's worth noting that in colder northern climates, heat is often delivered low—for example, at toe spaces—and on outside walls. Conversely, in warmer climates, cool air can be delivered at higher locations on interior walls.

The National Electrical Code calls for ground fault interrupters (GFIs) to be used for electrical outlets in kitchens and other wet locations. These are designed to protect from electrical shock by detecting currents as minor as a few milliamperes and tripping a breaker at the receptacle or at the breaker panel to remove the shock hazard.

Most electrical guidelines call for two 20A/120V circuits for kitchens; these are for small-appliance use. In addition, special single-outlet circuits are required for larger appliances such as ranges/cooktops and ovens. In some cases, these are directly wired to a junction box. In other cases, a heavy-duty receptacle (and plug for the appliance) is used. Further information about the electrical system can be found in Chapter 1.

Kitchen outlet (duplex receptacle) placement is based on the organization of the room and the location of countertops and appliances. Generally, outlets are located above counter-top height, where they are needed for appliances, and at wall locations for general use.

One rule of thumb requires duplex receptacles every 4 feet (1219 mm) along counters at roughly 6 to 8 inches (152 to 203 mm) above counter height (depending on backsplash height) to a maximum height of 48 inches (1219 mm) above the floor. This rule provides a helpful guideline; however, specific conditions vary widely and may require different outlet placement. It is also generally useful to place outlets to one side of the sink and cooktop. Where counters are lower than the standard 36 inches (914 mm), especially at accessible counters, outlets should be a maximum of 3 feet, 6 inches (1067 mm) from the floor—and often lower. Figure 4-31 illustrates outlet/receptacle placement.

The rule of thumb given in the previous paragraph should be considered in relation to code requirements, which state the following:

A receptacle outlet shall be installed at each wall countertop space 12 inches (305 mm) or wider. Receptacle outlets shall be installed so that no point along the wall line is more than 24 inches (610 mm), measured horizontally from a receptacle outlet in that space.

According to the IRC, the exception to this requirement occurs on the wall behind the range, cooking unit or sink, which is where the rule of thumb mentioned comes into play. Portions of a counter may have receptacles placed 24 inches (305 mm) apart except at the sink, range, or other cooking units where receptacles may be placed to the side of these appliances and roughly 4 feet (1219 mm) apart.

Sections E3901.4.2 and E3901.4.3 require that each island or peninsular countertop have at least one receptacle installed. This is required of island and peninsular countertops larger than 12 inches (305 mm) by 24 inches (610 mm).

The on/off switches for general lights are best located close to the room entry door on the latch side of the doorway when possible. In addition to lighting and power outlets, some clients request various communication lines for telephone, cable, and stereo/audio for use in kitchen areas.

LIGHTING

Kitchens can be places of work, entertainment, and relaxation. Lighting a space where such varied activities take place requires providing a range of light sources at various heights and locations.

Providing task lighting for areas where work is done as well as general or ambient lighting for the room makes the kitchen attractive and functional. Creating soft ambient light will make people and food appear more attractive; doing this generally requires more than a single centrally located downlight. Also, a person working at a counter can block the light coming from a single centrally located downlight, causing a darkened work area—the opposite of helpful task light. Some lighting designers find that using only a series of recessed downlights can create rather harsh shadows, which is less than ideal in lighting a kitchen. Figure 4-32 illustrates some kitchen lighting concepts.

Adding undercabinet lighting helps create ambient light and can serve as task lighting at countertop areas. Such lighting does not put those working at the counters in a position to cast shadows. Undercabinet lighting can be provided by linear fluorescent or incandescent luminaires and/or spot luminaires (called puck lights because of their shape), which are available in incandescent (including halogen and xenon). In some cases, incandescent luminaires produce enough heat to affect food inside of cabinets. Location of food and luminaires should be planned accordingly.

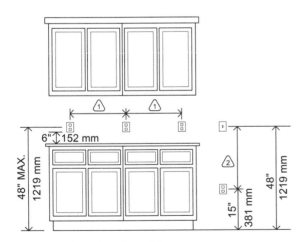

Figure 4-31 Kitchen outlet and control placement.

1. The IRC requires that at kitchen counters: "no point along the wall line is more than 24 inches (610 mm), measured horizontally from a receptacle outlet." The areas behind the range and sink are the exception to that rule; for those areas, placing outlets to the side of the appliance and roughly 48 inches (1219 mm) apart is a good rule of thumb. Local codes may vary.
2. The best height for wheelchair users (or those with limited mobility) is 24 to 48 inches (610 to 1219 mm) above the floor. However, counters may obstruct the reach of wheelchair users.

Note: Wall-mounted outlets and switches should be 15 to 48 inches (381 to 1219 mm) above the floor (to the center of the actual controls, not the bottom of the plates).

Undercabinet luminaires should be mounted so that they are not visible from seated locations, which can happen when they are placed at the rear of the cabinet (without some type of concealing trim) or when they are not recessed into the bottom of the cabinetry. See Figure 4-32. Undercabinet fixtures can be a problem in cases where countertop materials are highly reflective, as this can create significant glare. In such instances, a different type of luminaire may be a better choice.

Linear luminaires may be placed above cabinets to create indirect overhead lighting. This is often done with fluorescent fixtures. Some cabinets with deep top framing or molding allow for the installation of luminaires that are not seen from a standing position, while others require the addition of trim pieces in order to cover existing soffits above cabinets. These can be fitted with crown molding to accommodate linear luminaires and strip luminaires. See Figure 4-33 .

While undercabinet luminaires can provide excellent task lighting, certain locations, particularly the sink area and areas such as islands and peninsulas, may require a different approach. Many clients prefer downlights at the primary sink area; depending on the size and design, one or two incandescent downlights in the sink area may work well. Islands and peninsulas that serve as dining or conversation areas are often lit with downlights, with pendant fixtures, or with a combination of the two.

Pendants in such areas are currently popular, and a variety of fixtures are available that can enhance the dining experience and provide an interesting aesthetic component. Height, location, and design of pendant fixtures must be well considered in order to avoid creating glare at seated eye level, as well as uneven lighting. Care must also be taken so that the fixtures do not block vision or cause people to bump into them.

Some kitchens require accent lighting in order to display art and collections or to show off appliances. Adjustable downlights, track or canopy fixtures, and wall washers can provide accent lighting. Enhancing certain areas to the desired effect requires careful consideration of fixture placement, and beam spread of these fixtures requires careful study of product information. Figure 4-34 shows an electrical/lighting plan illustrating some of the lighting choices discussed.

In cases where fluorescent fixtures are used, color rendition is important in making food look appetizing. Lamps at 3000K

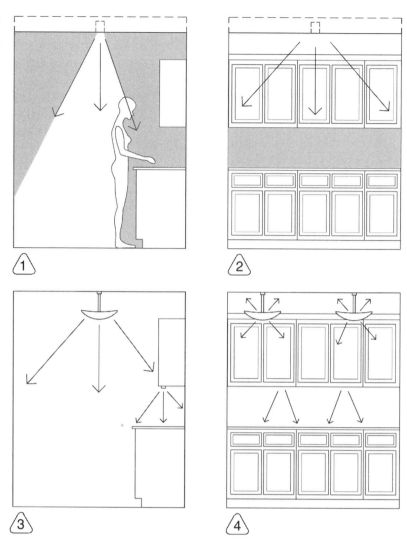

Figure 4-32 Kitchen lighting concepts.

1. A person working at a counter can block light cast by a single/centrally located downlight.
2. Downlights can create dark areas under cabinets.
3. Undercabinet lighting washes the counter and backsplash with light.
4. Multiple pendants combined with undercabinet lights provide ambient lighting and some task lighting at counters.

and with a CRI of 80 or higher will render food and beverage colors more pleasing than will those used in areas where color rendition is less important. However, local codes may restrict lamp choices. Additional lighting information can be found in Chapter 1.

The discussion of lighting to this point has included using a variety of luminaires set at a range of mounting heights, which can create attractive ambient light, task light, and visual interest. However, some clients are focused on energy efficiency, and some states and municipalities have codes that regulate energy use; these may limit the type and number of fixtures used.

Figure 4-33 Undercabinet and above-cabinet lighting.

1. Small surface-mounted spot or puck (or puc) lights, as well as linear fluorescent or incandescent luminaires, may be used under cabinets.
2. Linear undercounter fixtures may require concealing trim (as will deeper puck lights).
3. Luminaires may be placed above cabinets to supply indirect uplighting; trim may be required.
4. Luminaires may be placed at soffits to supply indirect uplighting; trim may be required. Sconces may also be used at these locations, if the vertical dimension of the soffit is adequate.
5. Recessed luminaires or other downlights may be helpful at soffit/ceiling locations above sink.

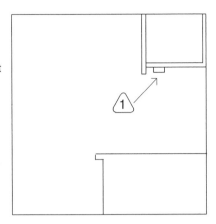

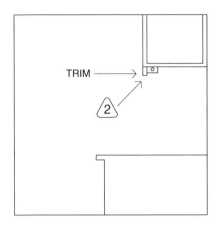

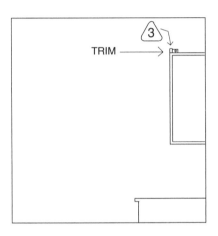

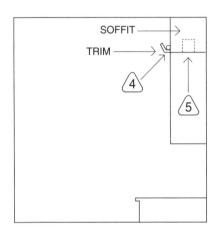

CALIFORNIA TITLE 24

California's Energy Commission issued updates to the Title 24 Energy Code in 2013.

Title 24 requires that *more* than 50 percent of installed lighting wattage in kitchens meet standards for high efficacy. The remaining wattage may be exempt from the high-efficacy requirement only when specific conditions have been met, as indicated in Table 4-3.

While Title 24 regulates only those residences in California, it mandates an energy-efficient way of lighting kitchens that could prove useful in other locales. While somewhat limiting, California's Title 24 requirements do allow for light layering with the use of uplights, undercabinet lights, and other fixtures that are switched separately and on dimmers, as indicated in Table 4-3.

Table 4-3 California Title 24 Kitchen Lighting Standards*

California Title 24	2013
Definition of a kitchen	Kitchen in a residential dwelling unit is a room or area used for cooking, food storage and preparation, and washing dishes, including associated countertops and cabinets, refrigerator, stove, oven, and floor areas.
Required kitchen lighting wattage	At least 50 percent of installed wattage of luminaires must be high efficacy (this does not necessarily include lighting inside cabinets).
Adjacent areas	Adjacent areas are considered part of kitchen lighting when "they are not separately switched from kitchen."**
Undercabinet lighting (or lighting that projects light outside cabinetry)	Is considered permanently installed lighting and counts toward the 50 percent efficacy requirement.
Lighting for the interior of cabinets (that does not project into room)	Can use up to 20W of lighting per linear foot of cabinet.

California Title 24	2013
Switching	All high-efficacy luminaires must be controlled (switched) separately from all low-efficacy luminaires. Controls must be installed according to manufacturers' instructions. Exhaust fans must be switched separately from low-efficacy luminaires. Switches must be readily accessible and permit manual on/off switching.
Earning more low-efficacy lighting	If all lighting (both low- and high-efficacy) in kitchen is controlled by vacancy sensor, dimmer, EMCS, or multi-scene programmable control, the standards allow low-efficacy lighting beyond the maximum up to: 50 watts per dwelling units ≤ 2500 square feet (232 m²); 100 watts per dwelling units > 2500 square feet (232 m²)

* Additional recommendations that are not currently requirements: 1) switch nooks, dining areas, and other adjacent spaces with controls separate from those used for kitchen; 2) install task lighting over sink; 3) use light-colored, low-glare countertops to increase light reflectance while minimizing glare; 4) consider LED luminaires for recessed and undercabinet lighting.

** When switched separately, lighting for these areas is not included in the 50 percent high-efficacy calculation.

Sources: California Energy Commission, "Residential Compliance Manual for California's 2013 Energy Efficiency Standards," 2014; California Lighting Technology Center, "2013 Title 24 Part 6: Residential Lighting, a Guide to Meeting or Exceeding California's 2-13 Building Energy Efficiency Standards," 2014.

Figure 4-34 Sample kitchen electrical and lighting plan.

A. The IRC (Section E3901.4.1) requires a receptacle outlet at each counter wall space 12 inches (305 cm) or wider and that no point along the wall line be more than 24 inches (610 mm) measured horizontally from a receptacle outlet.

B. The IRC (Section E3902.6) states, "All 125-volt, single-phase, 15- and 20-ampere receptacles that serve countertop surfaces shall have ground fault interrupter protection."

C. Switched outlet for garbage disposal inside base cabinet in this example; not required if disposal is wired directly.

D. Separate 15-amp circuit for refrigerator/freezer is a good practice (not required by IRC or many other codes).

E. Downdraft exhaust fan with switch.

F. Duplex convenience outlet set horizontally to fit in between the two counter heights. The IRC (Section E3901.4.2) requires a minimum of one receptacle outlet at each island counter "with a long dimension of 24 inches (610 mm) and a short dimension of 12 inches (305 mm) or greater." The code also requires a duplex receptacle at peninsula counters.

G. Referred to by some as puck lights.

H. Dishwasher, fan, and oven are wired directly.

I. A switched, split-wired duplex outlet placed on wall above cabinets for a variety of possible uses (such as lighting or decorative elements).

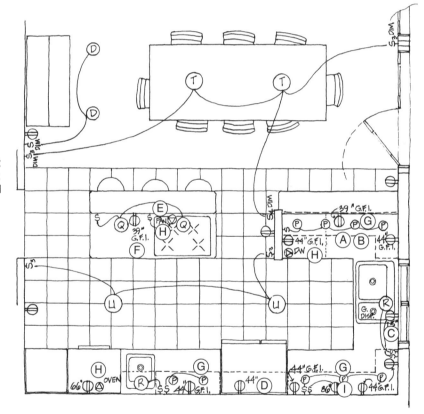

℗ UNDER CAB. LOW VOLT. QUARTZ HALOGEN

Ⓠ INCAND. PENDANT FIXT.

Ⓡ RECESSED INCAND. SOFFIT FIXT.

Ⓓ RECESSED ADJUSTABLE DOWNLITE

Ⓣ INCAND. PENDANT FIXT.

Ⓤ FLUOR. CEILING FIXT.

PROTOTYPE KITCHEN ILLUSTRATIONS

The following is a range of prototypes that have been developed to illustrate the workflow, work triangles, and basic clearances discussed in this chapter and to introduce readers to various advantages and disadvantages of certain design choices and layout options. These provide detailed illustrations of the concepts covered in Figures 4-6 through 4-8, and support the author's interest in inclusion of a dedicated preparation area included within the work triangle; some examples also support a second cook.

Each of the following kitchen prototypes is detailed in an illustration showing the following:

- Location of appliances and fixtures in a range of sizes, all with the goal of meeting the clearance standards mentioned previously.
- Dimensions of various appliances and fixtures.
- The primary work triangle and either a second major preparation area triangle forming double triangles or a double-double set of triangles with adjacent preparation triangles.

- A 1-square-foot floor grid to give a sense of scale to each kitchen.
- Primary sinks in the prototypes are generally shown in window locations, but this is not required by code and is not always feasible, especially in multifamily housing or remodeling situations.
- Additional notes include a general caution about avoiding inside corners for primary sink areas—when possible—as one cook in the corner location blocks access to substantial cabinetry.
- Islands and peninsulas used as seating/eating bars are shown in many prototypes, with a focus on grouping people in a way that fosters interaction and discussion rather than in a line, where interaction can be difficult.
- Figures 4-35 to 4-38 are variations on the single-wall or **I**-shaped kitchen. The **L**-shaped prototypes are shown in Figures 4-39 to 4-41. **J**-shaped kitchens are shown in Figures 4-42 and 4-43. **U**-shaped prototypes are illustrated in Figures 4-44 to 4-46. Figures 4-47 and 4-48 illustrate **G**-shaped plans.

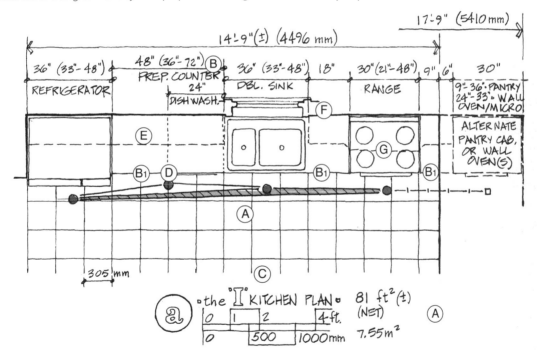

Figure 4-35 The "I" kitchen.

A. This is a one-cook kitchen that involves a lot of steps for the cook. The work triangle becomes a virtual straight line that can easily exceed recommended maximum travel distance, as noted in B below. This is not an ideal design but can work when space is limited.

B. Increasing the prep area to the full 72 inches (1829 mm) will cause the work triangle to exceed the recommended 26-foot (7925-mm) maximum.

B₁. When expanded, the total counter space still falls short of what is recommended.

C. If the kitchen is open to adjacent spaces, it forces the cook to stand facing away from family/guests. Where a wall exists at C, the room becomes long and tunnel-like.

D. Primary preparation center is 8 feet (2438 mm) from the range, and clear counter space at the range is very limited.

E. Location for dish storage in wall cabinet is convenient to cleanup area.

F. Shown as an exterior wall with a window, but this would not be required when the kitchen is open to an adjoining room with an operable window (natural ventilation and daylight are provided) or when mechanical ventilation and artificial illumination are provided.

G. Range hood with microwave.

Shaded triangle indicates primary work triangle. The secondary adjoining triangle anchors the major prep area. Dimensions given in parentheses indicate a range of possible dimensions.

Figure 4-36 The "double I" kitchen (also known as a corridor, galley, or Pullman kitchen).

A. This can work as a two-cook kitchen, providing reasonable counter and cabinet storage; it packs a lot of kitchen into a relatively small area with generally efficient double triangles.

B. Work triangle: (a) 14 feet, 6 inches (4420 mm), (b) 15 feet, 6 inches (4724 mm), lineal dimensions.

C. Window/bar as shown can be an informal dining bar, a pass-through, a window on an exterior wall, or a wall with wall cabinets.

D. An interior or exterior wall (with a window possible at sink).

E. Preparation center also serves as part of cleanup center; microwave is built into cabinet at E₁.

F. Cleanup center has convenient wall cabinets for dish storage (F₁).

G. Width of work corridor is 4 feet (1219 mm) as shown; 3 feet, 6 inches (1067 mm) is the absolute minimum; 5 feet (1525 mm) is a good rule-of-thumb maximum. Excessive width only leads to more steps between major work/appliance stations.

H. Mandatory through traffic is to be avoided; this type of kitchen works best with major circulation routes located outside of the kitchen.

I. Recess in wall to accommodate depth of refrigerator and mitigate projection into galley. Recess not easy to accomplish on an exterior wall.

Shaded triangle indicates primary work triangle (a) with a secondary adjoining triangle for the major prep area. Second cook's triangle (b) also has an adjoining prep area. Dimensions given in parentheses indicate a range of possible dimensions.

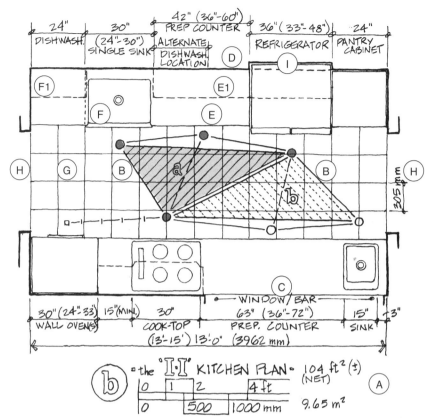

Figure 4-37 The "I with island" kitchen.

A. This works as a two-cook kitchen, providing room for others to gather and contribute to meal preparation. The double triangles in this layout are not as efficient as those in previous layouts (see Figure 4-29 b), but are reasonably efficient.

B. Work triangle: (a) 19 lineal feet (5791 mm), (b) 18 lineal feet (5486 mm).

C. Kitchen is very open to adjacent spaces, allowing interaction with family and guests.

D. Standard location for a window (and preferred by many clients) but not required or necessary at exact location shown.

   D1. French doors shown; or substitute window.

E. Prep center also serves as part of cleanup center.

   E₁. Cleanup center has convenient wall cabinets for dish storage, with additional dish storage in island (drawers).

F. Island contains a 36-inch (914-mm) range with downdraft vent, a small secondary sink, a work/preparation center (36 inches above floor), and a curved shelf 42 inches (1067 mm) above floor (F₁). There is also room—30 inches (762 mm) or 36 inches (914 mm) above finished floor—for an informal eating area that allows for conversation (F₂).

G. Open-island-based kitchens often provide limited storage due to limited wall cabinets. Pantry cabinets and/or dish storage drawers can compensate for this. Shaded triangle indicates primary work triangle (a) with a secondary adjoining triangle for the major prep area. Second cook's triangle (b) also has an adjoining prep area. Dimensions given in parentheses indicate a range of possible dimensions.

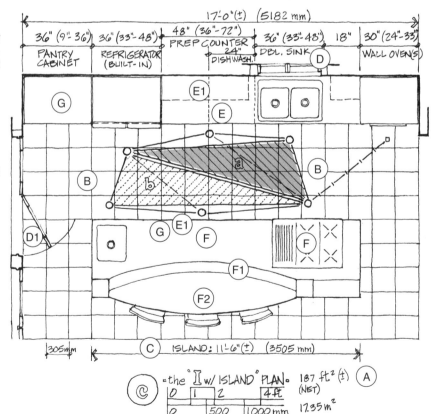

Figure 4-38 The "I with double island" kitchen.

A. This works as a two-cook kitchen, with the second island serving as a snack/preparation area for a third cook. It is a very large kitchen, two or three times the size of more efficient layouts.

B. Work triangle: (a) 18 lineal feet (5486 mm), (b) 15 lineal feet (4572 mm). The triangle B₁ (secondary triangle) is not composed of straight lines and requires moving around the corner of the island to fully access the prep area from the side.

C. Islands and exterior windows provide a very spacious feeling but result in very few wall cabinets; this must be offset with a pantry and dish storage drawers.

    C₁. Some of the windows could be replaced with wall cabinets.

D. Traffic through the primary work triangles can be avoided by taking alternate routes.

E. A snack/sandwich preparation area with sink, under-counter refrigerator, and undercounter microwave oven is readily available.

    E₁. A counter, 42 inches (1067 mm) above finished floor, with refrigerator and microwave raised (6 inches [152 mm]) to a more accessible/visible height.

F. A second cleanup area with dishwasher or dishwasher drawers and adjacent dish storage drawers.

G. Informal dining at 29 inches (737 mm), 36 inches (914 mm), or 42 inches (1067 mm) above finished floor, with dish cleanup and storage close at hand (see F above).

H. Suitable for open shelves under the counter for cookbooks, decorative accessories, collectibles, and so on.

I. Primary cleanup area, especially for pots, utensils, and large items.

J. Preparation counter with small sink (and garbage disposal); convenient for filling pots with water.

K. Pantry suitable for any/all of the following:

    K₁. Pantry cabinets.

    K₂. Base cabinets.

    K₃. Small upright freezer.

Shaded triangle indicates primary work triangle (a) with a secondary adjoining triangle for the major prep area. Second cook's triangle (b) also has an adjoining prep area. Dimensions given in parentheses indicate a range of possible dimensions.

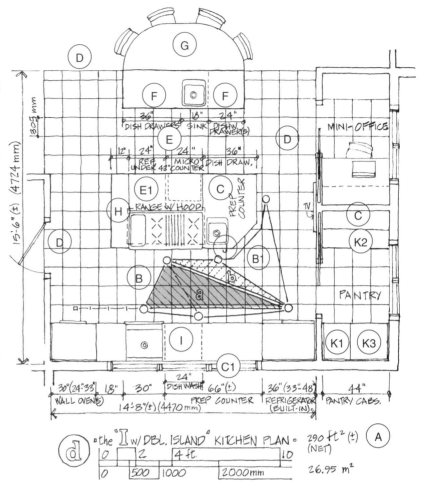

Figure 4-39 The "L" kitchen.

A. The kitchen is, as shown, a one-cook kitchen with a relatively large work triangle.

B. Work triangle: 20 lineal feet (6096 mm).

C. This prototype yields a natural spot for in-kitchen informal dining. As shown, the kitchen is open to other spaces but the cook would have his or her back to others. Often L-shaped kitchens are enclosed by a wall or walls to create a less open space than that shown.

D. Corner windows provide plentiful daylight for a secondary work/preparation area; however, wall cabinet storage is lost in the use of many windows—the use of a pantry or additional storage can offset the loss (D₁).

E. This preparation/work center can serve as part of the cleanup center; convenient dish storage is provided near sink and dishwasher.

F. Range with microwave above.

Shaded triangle indicates primary work triangle. The secondary adjoining triangle anchors the major prep area. Dimensions given in parentheses indicate a range of possible dimensions.

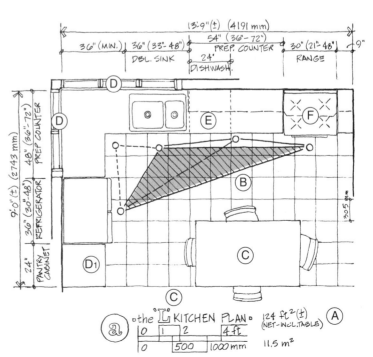

Figure 4-40 The "L with island" kitchen.

A. This kitchen, at 154 square feet (14.3 m²), is roughly average in size for an American home and accommodates two cooks with two nearly equal efficient triangles.

B. Work triangle: (a) 16 feet, 6 inches (5029 mm), (b) 16 feet, 6 inches (5029 mm), lineal dimensions.

C. As shown, the kitchen is open to two adjoining spaces, and combined with the open island and windows, wall cabinet storage is lost and dish storage would have to be provided by pantry and/or island drawer storage.

D. This prototype accommodates a very generous work/eating island 36 inches (914 mm) above finished floor; a sink installed at this location allows for a second work triangle/cook.

E. Dish storage would be required in base drawer cabinets because of the small quantity of wall cabinets.

F. The open nature of this design combined with easy access to the second sink and the refrigerator results in minimal traffic intrusion into the work triangles.

G. A third alternative workstation, conveniently located to range and oven(s), is available.

H. Corner sink location creates a space here that is useful for some clients and annoying for others.

Shaded triangle indicates primary work triangle (a) with a secondary adjoining triangle for the major prep area. Second cook's triangle (b) also has an adjoining prep area. Dimensions given in parentheses indicate a range of possible dimensions.

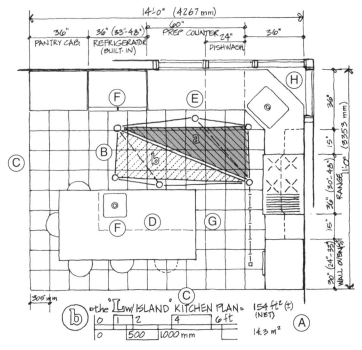

Figure 4-41 The "L with double island" kitchen.

A. This kitchen allows for two cooks and multiple helpers; it can be a social center with guests/family eating, drinking, and helping.

B. Work triangle: (a) 14 feet (4267 mm), (b) 12 feet, 6 inches (3810 mm), lineal dimensions.

C. As shown, the kitchen is set into a large alcove, open to adjoining spaces yet set apart. Traffic through work triangles can be avoided by creating alternate routes to adjoining areas/exits.

D. A prep/work center with abundant daylight results in a significant loss of wall cabinets.

E. A secondary prep/cleanup center at 36 inches (914 mm) above finished floor.

F. Two dishwasher locations are shown: F_1 primarily for dishes (with dish storage nearby) and F_2 for cooking utensils, pans, and bowls as needed.

G. A 36-inch (914-mm) range with hood, with limited adjacent clear counter space.

H. Counter at 48 inches (1219 mm) above finished floor, with microwave under counter (at a convenient height) and room for dish storage drawers; counter at this height has limited use but allows for standing, eating, and drinking.

I. Counter shown at 29 inches (737 mm) above finished floor, with seating at chairs; alternatively, the counter could be 36 or 42 inches (914 or 1067 mm) high with 24- or 30-inch (610- or 762-mm) stools.

Shaded triangle indicates primary work triangle (a) with a secondary adjoining triangle for the major prep area. Second cook's triangle (b) also has an adjoining prep area. Dimensions given in parentheses indicate a range of possible dimensions.

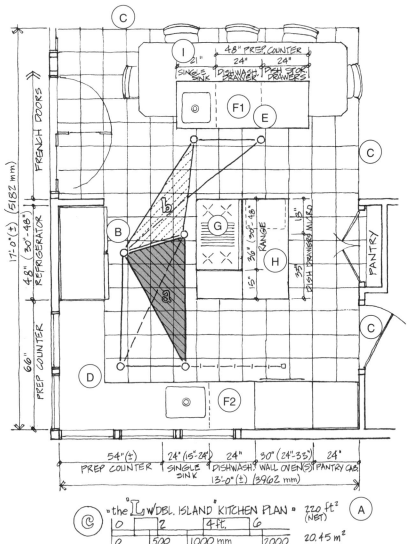

Figure 4-42 The "J" kitchen.

A. This "J" kitchen is a modestly sized, one-cook kitchen that includes an eat-in kitchen table.

B. Work triangle: 16 lineal feet (4879 mm).

C. The degree of openness to adjoining spaces varies in relation to the wall here; for example, only base cabinets with no full wall or a partial wall to 42 inches above the floor, or a full wall with wall cabinets (dashed).

D. Placing windows only at the sink, as shown, maximizes space for wall cabinets. However, this window placement minimizes daylight at the other end of the room (table).

E. There are two prep/work centers (one small and one large) but only one primary work triangle, making this less than ideal for two cooks. The distance between work center counters is 5 feet, 3 inches (1600 mm), plus or minus, to accommodate the space required for the sink and dishwasher.

F. The cleanup center and convenient dish storage (in wall cabinets) can be screened by C from adjoining rooms for clients who desire this visual separation.

G. Through circulation/traffic does not require penetration of the work areas.

Shaded triangle indicates primary work triangle. The secondary adjoining triangle anchors the major prep area. Dimensions given in parentheses indicate a range of possible dimensions.

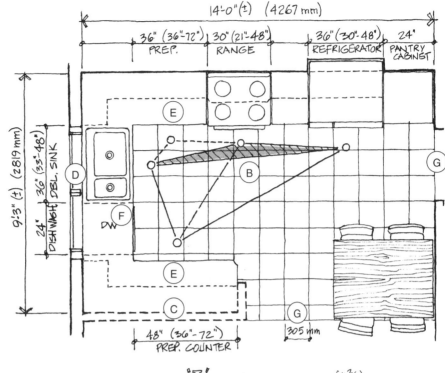

Figure 4-43 The "J with island" kitchen.

A. This is a larger-than-average two-cook kitchen that is 170 square feet (15.8 m²); the length required for the kitchen relates directly to the size of the island, which incorporates a cooktop to better serve two cooks.

B. Work triangle: (a) 15 feet, 6 inches (4724 mm), (b) 12 feet, 3 inches (3734 mm), lineal dimensions.

C. The room is open to adjoining spaces with limited screening provided by a shelf/bar 42 inches (1067 mm) high.

  C₁. Dish storage in suspended wall cabinets with doors on both sides (C₂).

D. As shown, there is available daylight only from the window at the sink; this maximizes space for wall cabinets but minimizes daylight.

E. Space must be provided for loading the dishwasher (dashed); while the minimum space is provided, this location could be awkward (see Figure 4-31 a for an alternative sink/dishwasher configuration).

F. In addition to two primary preparation/work counters (F₁), there are two other smaller work centers (F₂).

G. A counter 42 inches (1067 mm) high with three 30-inch (762-mm) barstools.

H. Cooktop with downdraft vent instead of hood to maintain visual connection to adjoining areas.

I. Single sink with high wall cabinets (mounted at 60 inches [1524 mm] above the floor).

J. Centrally located refrigerator is convenient but can create a circulation problem, especially with dishwasher door open.

K. A second microwave is located in a wall cabinet here.

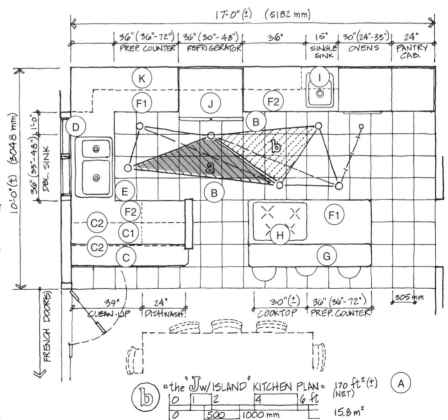

Shaded triangle indicates primary work triangle (a) with a secondary adjoining triangle for the major prep area. Second cook's triangle (b) also has an adjoining prep area. Dimensions given in parentheses indicate a range of possible dimensions.

Figure 4-44 The "U" kitchen.

A. This is a small and efficient for one cook; it provides plentiful wall and base cabinet storage and counter frontage in relatively small square footage (105 square feet [9.75 m²]); there is no through traffic/circulation.

B. Work triangle: 16 feet, 6 inches (5029 mm), lineal dimensions.

C. The room is open on one side only, separating the cook from adjoining spaces (some clients prefer this, while others find it isolating). Depending on the design of adjoining rooms, walls could be partially opened at C_1 and C_2 (with the range adjusted); in both cases, this would drastically reduce the quantity of wall cabinets.

D. There are two inside corners, and while these aid in efficiency for a single cook, a second person in the room at these locations blocks access to a disproportionate amount of storage and counter space.

E. Counter space is divided into unequal segments in order to create a major prep/work center.

F. A lazy Susan at these locations is useful. Additionally, countertop appliances, television, and so on can be located in these relatively inaccessible (to reach) corners. A microwave is placed in wall cabinet adjacent to range (F_1).

G. Sinks are shown in the traditional location under windows; windows are not required by code at this location.

H. Optional adjoining dining area (formal or informal).

I. Standard 30-inch (762-mm) range with vent/hood mounted under raised wall cabinet.

Shaded triangle indicates primary work triangle. The secondary adjoining triangle anchors the major prep area. Dimensions given in parentheses indicate a range of possible dimensions.

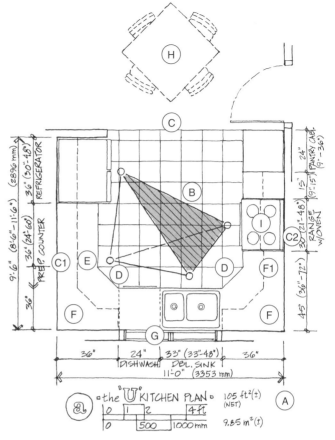

Figure 4-45 The "broken U" kitchen.

A. This is a small, efficient layout, and with the addition of a secondary sink (A_1), it can function as a two-cook kitchen. It provides plentiful wall and base cabinet storage and counter frontage in a relatively small footprint (117 square feet [10.86 m²]).

B. Work triangle: (a) 13 feet, 6 inches (4115 mm), (b) 14 feet, 6 inches (4420 mm), lineal dimensions.

C. Shown with two doorway openings; an alternate route should be provided for circulation/traffic outside of kitchen.

D. This inside corner has disadvantages/issues discussed in Figure 4-44 , items D and F.

E. Dish storage is close to but not immediately above dishwasher.

F. Two prep centers are provided; the larger also serves as part of the cleanup center (F_1).

G. Width of work corridor is at recommended maximum of 5 feet (1524 mm).

H. Windows at sink may create a pleasing vantage point but introduce daylight only to the far end of the room.

I. Range placement does not provide recommended clear counter space to the left of the cook; however, this placement allows a larger, more useful preparation counter/work center (F_2).

J. Range hood with microwave.

Shaded triangle indicates primary work triangle (a) with a secondary adjoining triangle for the major prep area. Second cook's triangle (b) also has an adjoining prep area. Dimensions given in parentheses indicate a range of possible dimensions.

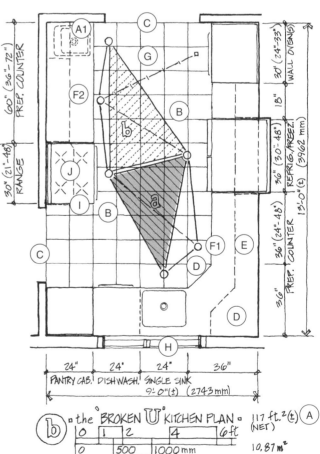

Figure 4-46 The "U with island" kitchen.

A. This 160-square-foot (14.86-m²) kitchen accommodates two cooks with an imbalance in the work triangles (one large, one small); it provides plentiful wall/base cabinet storage, and counter frontage is provided in part by the island.

B. Work triangle: (a) 21 feet (6401 mm), (b) 12 feet (3658 mm), lineal dimensions.

C. This plan demonstrates the dilemma of creating an island within a U-shaped plan; as the size of the island increases, the size of the room necessarily increases; it can quickly reach the point where the work triangle(s) become too big. As shown, the room is open to adjoining spaces on one side only and a modest amount of windows provide adequate daylight.

D. Work/prep centers are modest in size; an additional work center (D₁) is the largest when the counter with the cleanup center is included. A microwave could be placed under the counter in this area.

E. Cleanup center has convenient base and wall cabinets for dish storage.

F. A 36-inch (914-mm) vent/hood mounted under a raised cabinet.

　F₁. Secondary sink is well placed for filling pots and drawing water at range, but it eliminates recommended counter space at one side of the range.

G. Inside corners have disadvantages/issues discussed in Figure 4-44 , items D and F.

H. Work/eating island is 36 inches (914 mm) high and is not large enough to include a range or sink and still provide, as shown, adequate counter space to the kitchen at large.

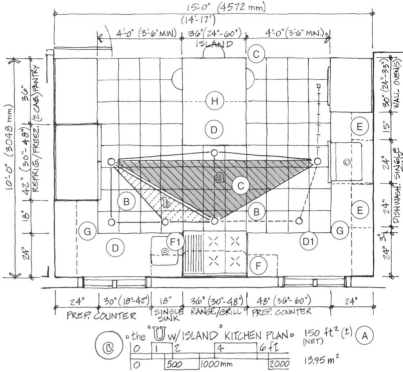

Shaded triangle indicates primary work triangle (a) with a secondary adjoining triangle for the major prep area. Second cook's triangle (b) also has an adjoining prep area. Dimensions given in parentheses indicate a range of possible dimensions.

Figure 4-47 The "G" kitchen.

A. This is a medium-sized kitchen (144 square feet [13.38 m²]) that accommodates two cooks; it provides plentiful wall and base cabinet storage and counter frontage.

B. Work triangle: (a) 16 feet (4877 mm), (b) 16 feet, 6 inches (5029 mm), lineal dimensions.

C. As shown, windows at cleanup center also provide daylight/view for the counter/bar seating.

D. Room is open to adjoining spaces on one side only; however, the enclosing walls provide abundant location(s) for appliances and storage.

E. Work/prep center (E₁) receives direct daylight, while E₂ allows for interaction (and exposure) to diners; both locations contain inside corners and related disadvantages/issues discussed in Figure 4-44 , items D and F.

F. Dish storage cabinets are convenient to dishwasher but remote from the dining counter (C₁).

G. A single opening to kitchen can become a bottleneck with heavy traffic; the only route to triangle a is through triangle b.

H. Potential microwave locations at H₁ and near range.

Shaded triangle indicates primary work triangle (a) with a secondary adjoining triangle for the major prep area. Second cook's triangle (b) also has an adjoining prep area. Dimensions given in parentheses indicate a range of possible dimensions.

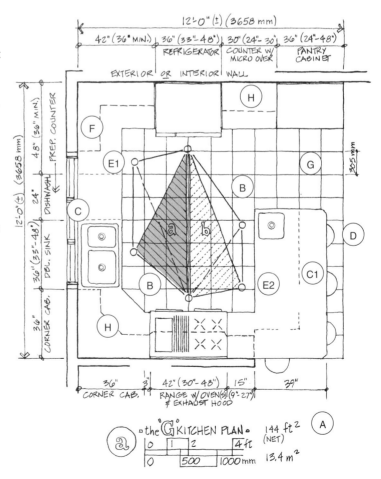

Figure 4-48 The "broken G" kitchen.

A. This is a medium-sized kitchen, accommodates two cooks, and has adequate base and wall cabinet storage and counter frontage. However, one of the work triangles can be interrupted by through traffic, making it less useful than other plans for some clients.

B. Work triangle: (a) 13 feet, 9 inches (4191 mm), (b) 16 feet, 3 inches (4953 mm), lineal dimensions.

C. As shown, the room is open on one side to adjacent rooms.

D. D_1 and D_2. Work centers; part of D_1 also serves as cleanup center.

E. Cleanup center has convenient dish storage in wall cabinets, with adjacent open pass-through to eating area(s).

F. Limited window area could be expanded at the expense of convenient wall cabinet storage.

G. A 30-inch (787-mm) cooktop with downdraft/exhaust.

H. Wall is recessed to accommodate a deep refrigerator and allow refrigerator doors to be flush with front of cabinets.

I. Sink location (close to corner) can block access (by others) to adjacent cabinets when sink is in use.

J. Casual eating bar 42 inches (1067 mm) high with three 30-inch (787-mm) stools at 27 inches (686 mm) on center; minimum knee space of 15 inches (381 mm) is required.

K. A wall oven and microwave; K_1 is a second microwave.

Shaded triangle indicates primary work triangle (a) with a secondary adjoining triangle for the major prep area. Second cook's triangle (b) also has an adjoining prep area. Dimensions given in parentheses indicate a range of possible dimensions.

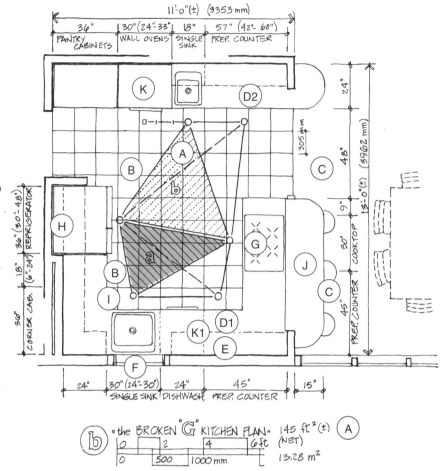

Not shown in the prototypes are specialized items and work centers requested by some homeowners, such as baking centers, which generally have a relationship to the mixing center or oven, and work well located between the refrigerator and oven. Another specialized residential kitchen is the kosher kitchen, which requires the separation of items used in the preparation and serving of dairy and meat items. Depending on the level of observance, kosher kitchens may require two separate sinks, two disposals, two ovens, or the separation of storage and prep areas, with the sink and cooktop centered between the two. Clearly, designing these highly specialized kitchens requires specialized expertise not detailed in this chapter.

Also not shown in detail are offices or desk areas and craft/hobby areas that could be included but should be located outside of work triangles.

Nor do the prototypes include indoor wood-fired ovens. These often form a strong focal point, but they also have spe-

cific spatial and ventilation requirements and may need to be located outside of the primary work triangle.

ACCESSIBILITY NOTE

Prototypes of wheelchair-accessible kitchens are shown in Figures 4-49, 4-50, and 4-51. These have been provided by the Ability Center of Greater Toledo, Ohio.

Figures 4-51 to 4-53 illustrate negative examples of kitchen design in which there are significant problems with planning, organization, and/or flow. In these examples, much like many kitchens that are not well designed, work triangles do not meet the standards discussed here, and appliance placement does not allow clear adjacent spaces. In addition, there is insufficient prep space and the circulation is problematic. Improvements to these examples could be made by following the appliance clearances provided and rethinking the flow of work triangles.

Figure 4-49 A prototype of a minimum-sized ANSI/UFAS-compliant kitchen; this is not ideal, merely compliant. While this kitchen is wheelchair accessible, it may be inadequate for many disabled or nondisabled people because of its small size. This kitchen would be suited for small efficiency apartments only.

1. Adjustable-height sink; a sink with open area underneath for forward approach would be ideal. Both sink and range lack ideal clear "landing spaces."
2. Range with front controls (only allows a parallel approach); accessible but not ideal.
3. Adjustable-height work counter.
4. ANSI/UFAS-compliant refrigerator with 50 percent of storage within reach range.
5. Recommended position for single-handled door; position refrigerator so door can swing back 180 degrees; a side-by-side refrigerator is recommended but not possible in such a small space.

Design courtesy of the Ability Center of Greater Toledo, Ohio.

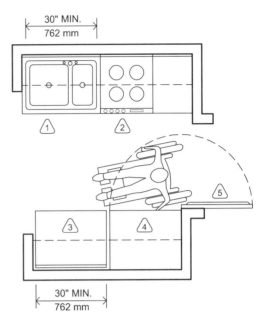

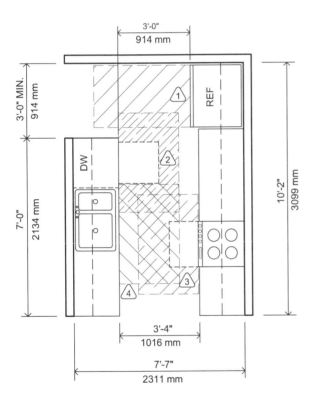

Figure 4-50 A wheelchair-accessible, small-corridor kitchen prototype; this is not an ideal plan, as it allows only a parallel approach to sink and cooktop. Providing knee space at cooktop, sink, and work counter would make the kitchen more useful and would require more space (a wall oven would replace the range).

1. Because there is no opposing counter/cabinet, the refrigerator may encroach on the 3 feet, 6 inches (1016 mm) required by ANSI/UFAS. When space allows, a side-by-side model is recommended.
2. This space provides a parallel approach to the dishwasher/counter surface.
3. Space for a parallel approach to range; a cooktop with open area underneath for forward approach would be ideal.
4. Parallel approach at sink permits a forward approach to dishwasher baskets when pulled out of dishwasher; a sink with open area underneath for forward approach would be ideal.

Design courtesy of the Ability Center of Greater Toledo, Ohio.

Figure 4-51 Negative example. Problematic kitchen plan.

A. Primary work triangle totals less than 9 feet (2743 mm), which is too small.
B. Counter is inaccessible; work space is behind refrigerator and over a range.
C. Inaccessible base cabinet storage.
D. Difficult to access wall cabinet over the range.
E. Counter space area totals 24 square feet (2.23 m²), but much of it is fragmented and difficult to access.
F. Dishwasher and oven doors will conflict.
G. Refrigerator and oven doors will conflict.
H. Main aisle width is minimal and reduced even further by refrigerator.

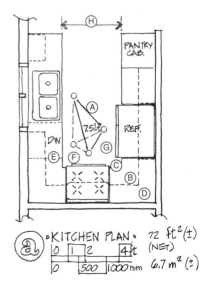

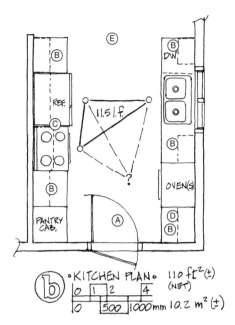

Figure 4-52 Negative example. Problematic kitchen plan.

A. Mandatory through traffic should be avoided; here it is required (through to door).
B. Counter space is fragmented into equal small pieces and there is no major preparation/work counter.
C. Refrigerator and range should not be immediately adjacent (conflicting heat/cold appliances). Also inadequate clear "landing space" for appliances.
D. Not a useful counter space—a dead corner; would be better located elsewhere.
E. A width of 5 feet, 6 inches (1676 mm) is wider than necessary but gains little, other than adding more steps and partially accommodating through traffic.

REFERENCES

Contains both works cited and recommended reading, with occasional annotation.

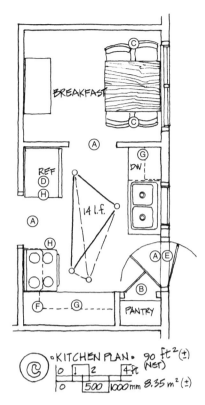

Figure 4-53 Negative example. Problematic kitchen plan.

A. This is a small kitchen that is made less effective because multiple doorways chop up the room/work areas and create mandatory through traffic, which interrupts the primary work triangle.
B. Door swings conflict; pantry door left ajar may prevent exterior door from opening.
C. Tight for two people.
D. Refrigerator is too large for available wall space and isolated with no clear counter to serve as "landing space" for items.
E. Direct, abrupt entrance from exterior; especially problematic in cold climates.
F. Relatively inaccessible—requires reaching over a hot range.
G. Inadequate counter frontage, base, and wall cabinet space.
H. No adjacent clear counter "landing space."

Ability Center of Greater Toledo. "Usable Kitchens." www .abilitycenter.org.

Beasley, Kim A., and Thomas D. Davies. 1999. *Kitchen Design for the Wheelchair User.* Washington, DC: Paralyzed Veterans of America.

Blum. 2015. "Put Your Kitchen to Work for You: Workflow— Everything Where You Need It." http://www.blum.com/us/ en/03/10/10.

Bouknight, Joanne Kellar. 2001. *The Kitchen Idea Book.* Newtown, CT: Taunton Press. Contains beautiful examples and many helpful ideas.

———. 2003. *The Storage Idea Book.* Newtown, CT: Taunton Press. Contains helpful examples and innovative ideas.

Brooks, David. 2000. *Bobos in Paradise.* New York: Simon and Schuster.

California Energy Commission. 2014. "Residential Compliance Manual for California's 2013 Energy Efficiency Standards." http:// www.energy.ca.gov/title24/2013standards/residential_ manual.html.

California Lighting Technology Center. 2014. "2013 Title 24 Part 6: Building Energy Efficiency Standards." http://cltc.ucdavis. edu/title24.

Ching, Francis, and Cassandra Adams. 2001. *Building Construction Illustrated.* 3rd ed. Hoboken, NJ: John Wiley & Sons.

Ching, Francis, and Dale E. Miller. 1983. *Home Renovation.* New York: Van Nostrand Reinhold. A great reference for renovation and residential construction.

Consumer Reports Online. 2010. "Has 'Live-in Value' Replaced ROI When It Comes to Kitchen Remodeling?" http://blogs. consumerreports.org/home/2010/04/kitchen-remodeling- return-on-investment-builder-magazine-cost-vs-value- report-kitchen-planning-guide.html.

———. 2010. "Refrigerators: Form Meets Function at an Affordable Price." http://www.consumerreports.org/cro/ magazine-archive/2010/august/appliances/top-rated- refrigerators/overview/index.htm.

Consumer Reports Greener Choices. "*Products for a Better Planet: Garbage Disposers.*" http://www.greenerchoices.org/ products.cfm?product5garbagedisposer&pcat5appliances.

———. "*Products for a Better Planet. Refrigerators*, What Government and Industry Are Doing." http://www.greenerchoices.org/products.cfm?product5fridge&page5GovtIndustry.

Galvin, Patrick K., and Ellen Cheever. 1998. *Kitchen Basics: A Training Primer for Kitchen Specialists*. East Windsor, NJ: Galvin Publications. A kitchen guide sponsored by the National Kitchen and Bath Association that covers principles and standards for kitchen design.

International Code Council. 2015. "2015 International Residential Code for One- and Two-Family Dwellings." Country Club Hills, IL: International Code Council.

Ierley, Merritt. 1999. *The Comforts of Home: The American Modern House and the Evolution of Modern Convenience*. New York: Three Rivers Press.

Karlen, Mark, and James Benya. 2003. *Lighting Design Basics*. Hoboken, NJ: John Wiley & Sons.

Kitchen and Bath Business Online. July 2005. www.kitchen-bath.com/kbb.

McGowan Maryrose, and Kelsey Kruse. 2003. *Interior Graphic Standards*. Hoboken, NJ: John Wiley & Sons.

"The Metropolis Observed: Kitchen Confidential." *Metropolis Magazine* 24 (3), November 2004. An interview with designer Bill Stumpf.

National Association of Home Builders. 2004. *"Housing Facts, Figures, and Trends 2004: What 21st Century Home Buyers Want."* Washington, DC: NAHB Advocacy/Public Affairs and the NAHB Economics Group.

National Kitchen and Bath Association. 2013. *Kitchen Planning, Guidelines, Codes, Standards*. 2nd ed. Hoboken, NJ: John Wiley & Sons.

Newmark, Norma, and Patricia Thompson. 1977. *Self, Space, and Shelter: An Introduction to Housing*. New York: Harper and Row. This is an excellent survey of environmental psychology and social history related to the residential environment. Out of print, but worth seeking out.

Pile, John F. 1995. *Interior Design*. 2nd ed. Englewood Cliffs, NJ: Prentice Hall.

Plante, Ellen M. 1995. *The American Kitchen: 1700 to the Present: From Hearth to Highrise*. New York: Facts on File.

"Plumbing Trends: Kitchen Sinks." *Plumbing and Mechanical Magazine*. 2007. http://www.pmmag.com/articles/89523-plumbing-trends-kitchen-sinks?v=preview

Rumberger, Janet, ed. 2003. *Architectural Graphic Standards for Residential Construction*. Hoboken, NJ: John Wiley & Sons.

Smith, Steve. 2004. "Special PM Survey: Kitchen Plumbing." http://www.pmmag.com/articles/86057-special-i-pm-i-survey-kitchen-plumbing?v=preview

State University of New York at Buffalo. 1996. "Technical Report: Accessible Appliances Universal Design."

Susanka, Sarah. 1998. *The Not So Big House: A Blueprint for the Way We Really Live*. Newtown, CT: Taunton Press.

Whitaker, Ellen, Colleen Mahoney, and Wendy Jordan. 2001. *Great Kitchens: At Home with America's Top Chefs*. Newtown, CT: Taunton Press.

Whitehead, Randall. 2002. *Residential Lighting: A Practical Guide*. Hoboken, NJ: John Wiley & Sons.

CHAPTER 5
Bedrooms

INTRODUCTION

It has been said that roughly one-third of our lives is spent sleeping, an activity that often takes place in the bedroom. In addition to being a room for sleep, the bedroom also serves as a private sanctuary or retreat, a place to take refuge from the world outside.

As stated in Chapter 1, various zones of privacy can be identified in homes. The bedroom is unique in that it serves a variety of purposes far more private than any other in the home, with the possible exception of the bathroom. Because of this need for privacy, a bedroom's placement within the residence must be well considered as it relates to family circulation patterns and outside noise.

If we break the bedroom down into its most essential functions, it is used for sleeping, dressing, sexual intimacy, and as a place of recovery from illness. In terms of space, at the most minimal extreme, a bedroom consists of a place to lie down, store clothing, and get dressed. Figure 5-1 illustrates the absolute minimum space required by most codes for a single bedroom. While this minimal approach may meet certain building standards, it is certainly less than ideal in terms of the access space required to make the bed, dress comfortably, and navigate within the room.

In simple terms, bedrooms are ruled by bed size and location. Beds are quite large and therefore tend to dominate the

use of the room in terms of both circulation and the related placement of additional furnishings. Most bedrooms include a bed, some furnishings for various types of storage, and some sort of closet.

Many bedrooms go well beyond the minimal to include various ancillary functions such as entertainment, study, and reading and therefore can include an array of furnishings, such as dressers, chests, shelves, night tables, and clothing or media armoires. Seats or chairs, lamps, and mirrors are often included, as are desks. It is especially common to include desks in rooms meant for children or students, as the bedroom commonly serves as a study area.

The overall square footage and general layout will dictate the amenities that can be found in a given bedroom. A king-size bed, two night tables, two or more dressers, a small office nook, a sitting area, a fireplace, an entertainment console or armoire, and two walk-in closets, or some combination of these items, can be found in some of the larger custom homes popular today. Figure 5-2 shows a very large, fully furnished bedroom, which serves as an extreme contrast to the minimal bedroom shown in Figure 5-1.

It is often the smaller dwelling, found in dense settings and/or in less costly housing, that necessitates that the bedroom serve multiple functions such as sleeping, entertainment, and office/study area. This means that a smaller room is fulfilling multiple functional requirements, a situation that requires careful planning and design. In larger houses, on the other hand, specialized rooms are used for home offices and study areas, allowing the bedroom to serve fewer functional requirements.

A thorough review of the project, including careful client interviews, enables the designer to uncover the functional requirements as well as the reality of the budget and square footage limitations, thus leading to the design of the best bedroom for a given situation. With that said, it is worth noting that most design solutions should not only meet short-term requirements but should, in addition, be able to withstand changes in the needs of the client or resale of the home.

This chapter provides detailed information about furnishings, closets, organizational flow, required clearances, and ergonomics, and is meant as a general aid in the planning of bedrooms for a range of clients with varying needs. Figures 5-3a through 5-6 illustrate the sizes of furnishings commonly found in bedrooms. Note that metric furniture dimensions are listed in centimeters, following most manufacturers' standards.

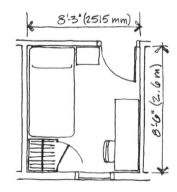

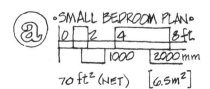

Figure 5-1 This floor plan represents a minimum of space and includes minimal functional elements required for a bedroom. At 70 square feet (6.5 m²), it meets the absolute minimum code requirements of square footage for habitable rooms.

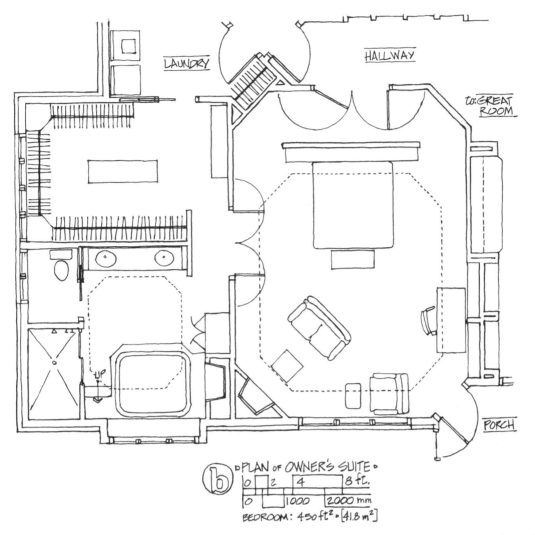

Figure 5-2 Although there is no upper limit on the size of a bedroom, this floor plan represents what could be called the maximal bedroom. It includes substantial room around a king-size bed, a study/library area, a sitting area with fireplace, and a large bathroom with a full range of plumbing fixtures and an additional fireplace, as well as a large closet with an island adjacent to a laundry.

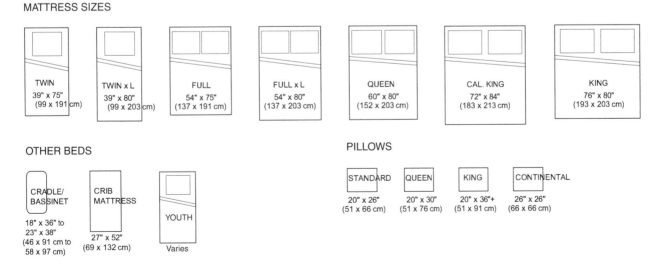

Figure 5-3a Bed/mattress sizes—plan views.

SOFA BEDS

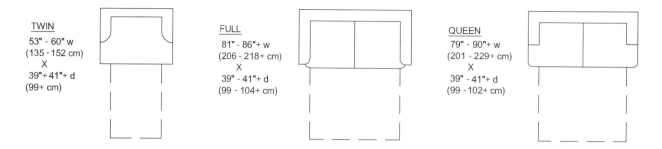

TWIN
53" - 60" w
(135 - 152 cm)
X
39"+ 41"+ d
(99+ cm)

FULL
81" - 86"+ w
(206 - 218+ cm)
X
39" - 41"+ d
(99 - 104+ cm)

QUEEN
79" - 90"+ w
(201 - 229+ cm)
X
39" - 41"+ d
(99 - 102+ cm)

FOLDING BEDS ①

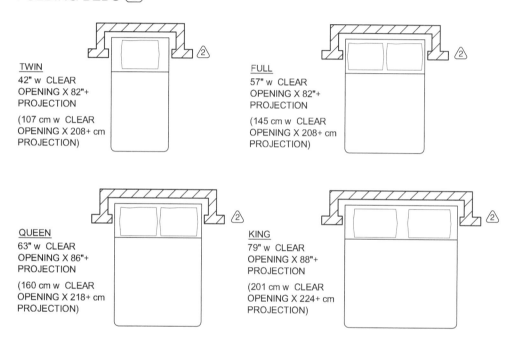

TWIN
42" w CLEAR
OPENING X 82"+
PROJECTION

(107 cm w CLEAR
OPENING X 208+ cm
PROJECTION)

FULL
57" w CLEAR
OPENING X 82"+
PROJECTION

(145 cm w CLEAR
OPENING X 208+ cm
PROJECTION)

QUEEN
63" w CLEAR
OPENING X 86"+
PROJECTION

(160 cm w CLEAR
OPENING X 218+ cm
PROJECTION)

KING
79" w CLEAR
OPENING X 88"+
PROJECTION

(201 cm w CLEAR
OPENING X 224+ cm
PROJECTION)

Figure 5-3b Sofa beds and folding bed sizes—plan views.

1. Also known as wall beds or murphy beds.
2. Verify requirements for walls and ceilings (construction and dimensions) with manufacturer. With the bed in the upright position, the floor area of the room opens up dramatically.

The closet, much like other parts of homes, has become larger to accommodate an increase in the quantity of clothing, personal belongings, and leisure activities of current homeowners.

Anyone having lived in an American home built before 1945 can attest to the minimal closet space in individual bedrooms in older homes. As closet space has grown in terms of quantity, the arrangement and organization of closets has evolved to the point that closet design and fabrication is now a billion-dollar industry. Various storage systems and organizational elements are employed to create closets that allow appropriate, accessible storage for all of one's personal items.

Some firms specialize in designing and building closets outfitted with fine hardware, stone countertops, specialized lighting, and beautiful custom cabinetry. Such luxurious elements do not necessarily improve the functional qualities of the closet. They do, however, appeal to some homeowners. Closets need not be outfitted with such luxurious elements to serve the homeowner well; a suitable and useful closet is a matter of design and careful planning, which is covered in detail in the "Ergonomics and Required Clearances" section.

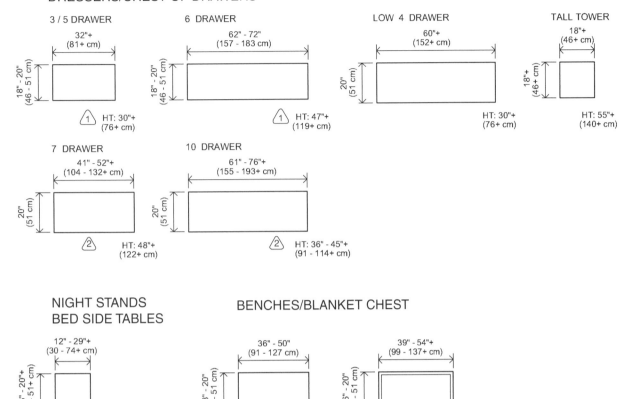

Figure 5-4 Dresser storage—plan views.

1. Taller, six-drawer versions are 36 inches (91 cm) wide by 20 inches (51 cm) deep by 50 inches (127 cm) high.
2. Taller versions are available.

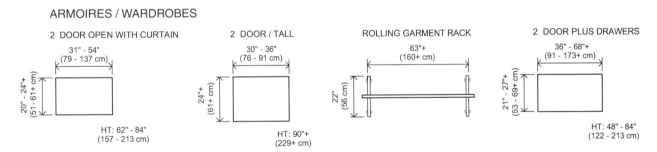

Figure 5-5 Armoire/wardrobe storage sizes—plan views.

ERGONOMICS AND REQUIRED CLEARANCES

The specialized nature of bedrooms requires that designers consider several ergonomic factors in order to design useful, successful rooms for sleep. Figures 5-7 and 5-8 depict bedroom circulation area requirements. The work of making and cleaning around the bed requires a minimum of 18 inches (457 mm) but is most comfortably designed at 24 (610 mm) inches.

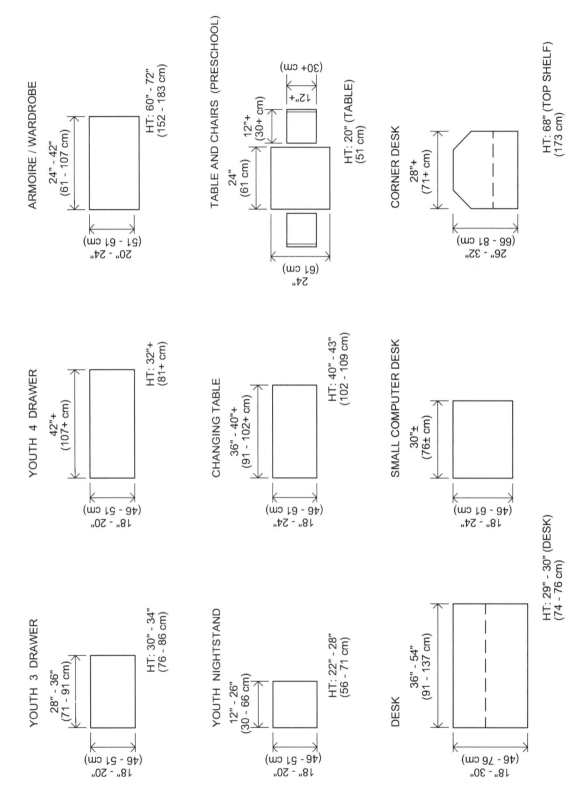

ARMOIRE / WARDROBE

24" – 42"
(61 – 107 cm)

HT: 60" – 72"
(152 – 183 cm)

20" – 24"
(51 – 61 cm)

YOUTH 4 DRAWER

42"+
(107+ cm)

HT: 32"+
(81+ cm)

18" – 20"
(46 – 51 cm)

YOUTH 3 DRAWER

28" – 36"
(71 – 91 cm)

HT: 30" – 34"
(76 – 86 cm)

18" – 20"
(46 – 51 cm)

TABLE AND CHAIRS (PRESCHOOL)

12"+
(30+ cm)

12"+
(30+ cm)

24"
(61 cm)

HT: 20" (TABLE)
(51 cm)

24"
(61 cm)

CHANGING TABLE

36" – 40"+
(91 – 102+ cm)

HT: 40" – 43"
(102 – 109 cm)

18" – 24"
(46 – 61 cm)

YOUTH NIGHTSTAND

12" – 26"
(30 – 66 cm)

HT: 22" – 28"
(56 – 71 cm)

18" – 20"
(46 – 51 cm)

CORNER DESK

28"+
(71+ cm)

HT: 68" (TOP SHELF)
(173 cm)

26" – 32"
(66 – 81 cm)

SMALL COMPUTER DESK

30"±
(76± cm)

18" – 24"
(46 – 61 cm)

DESK

36" – 54"
(91 – 137 cm)

HT: 29" – 30" (DESK)
(74 – 76 cm)

18" – 30"
(46 – 76 cm)

Figure 5-6 Youth bedroom furniture sizes—plan views. Items labeled "youth" can range from ages 3 to 12 and can be up to 5 feet (152 cm) in height, depending on the manufacturer. Items may be categorized into school age, preschool, etc.

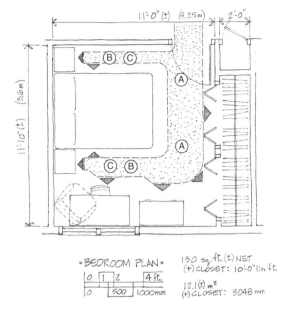

Figure 5-7 Standard circulation space and bed access.

A. Major circulation occurs at the entrance and most-traveled areas; major circulation areas require 36 to 48 inches (914 to 1219 mm) of clear floor space (minus door swings).
B. Minor circulation areas—those less traveled—are most comfortable designed at 24 inches (610 mm). However, they can function at 22 inches (559 mm) and can be tightly sized at 18 inches (457 mm); see B₁.
C. The area required to make the bed is a minimum of 18 inches (457 mm) and is more comfortably designed at 24 inches (610 mm).

ACCESSIBILITY NOTE

Accessible bedrooms require access to the room through a door with a minimum clear opening of 32 inches (813 mm), which requires—for all practical purposes—using a 36-inch (914-mm) door. In addition, accessible bedrooms require clear circulation space for a wheelchair (also 32 inches [813 mm] minimum) for access to the bed, closet, and additional clothing storage; see Figures 5-8 and 5-9. Providing clear turning space for the wheelchair within the room is also recommended (see Figure 2-14b). In addition to providing clear circulation space for movement of the wheelchair, space must also be provided for opening doors and drawers.

The following section of the chapter covers more specifics related to circulation and clear spaces required for wheelchair users.

The following guidelines checklist can be used in creating accessible bedrooms.

Bedroom Accessibility Guidelines Checklist

☐ **Provide a minimum clear space of 32 inches (813 mm) at doors—use 36-inch (914-mm) doors to accomplish this.**

☐ Provide a minimum clear circulation space of 32 inches (813 mm) for access to bed and closet/storage.

☐ Provide a clear turning space (5 feet [1524 mm] in diameter) or room for a T-shaped turn (see Figure 2-14b) conveniently located within the room.

☐ Provide clear space to access doors (clear area on latch side of door).

☐ Provide clear space to access drawers and other storage areas.

☐ Adjust mounting heights of clothing rods and shelves (see Figure 5-10b).

Many of the checklist items are illustrated in Figure 5-8.

Consideration of mounting heights for clothing rods, shelves, and additional storage elements is important in order to provide useful storage space for wheelchair users and those individuals with limited mobility. This information is also provided in the following section of the chapter.

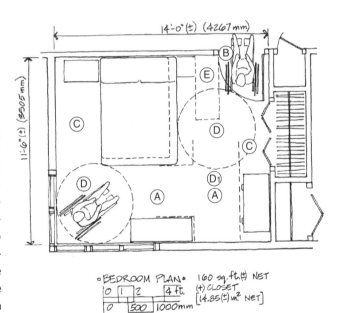

Figure 5-8 Circulation space and bed access for wheelchairs. The solid lines at the bed area indicate a queen-size bed; dashed lines indicate a full-size bed.

A. Major circulation areas require 36 inches (914 mm) minimum for wheelchairs.
B. For wheelchair users, all circulation space is best kept at 36 inches (914 mm) or more, with 32 inches (813 mm) clear the minimum required for wheelchairs.
C. A clearance of 36 inches (914 mm) around beds is required for wheelchairs, with a clear space 48 by 36 inches (1219 by 914 mm) next to the closet (not drawn).
D. The minimum turning radius for wheelchairs is 60 inches (1524 mm). T-shaped turns may be used in place of the 60-inch (1524-mm) turning radius in cases where there is not adequate room to provide the full radius (D₁).
E. Clear space is required on the latch side of doors opening inward for wheelchair access to the door when opening and closing the door (minimum of 18 by 48 inches [457 by 1219 mm], as shown with dashed lines at E).

Storage furnishings such as dressers, dressing tables, shelves, and nightstands often require the user to bend down rather low to use the furniture and require clearance for drawers to pull out. For access to storage items from a wheelchair, a clear space (30 by 48 inches [762 by 1219 mm]) adjacent to storage furnishings with doors and drawers is necessary. Figure 5-9 illustrates requirements for using bedroom storage furnishings.

As stated previously, closets present specific dimensional requirements related to reaching and retrieving items, which are influenced by the sizes of garments and accessories. Figures 5-10a and 5-10b illustrate reaching heights and storage information.

Because closets are generally enclosed by some sort of door or visual screen, the type of door selected requires serious consideration. Doors and their frames can strongly influence the ease with which the closet is accessed, as illustrated in Figure 5-11.

ACCESSIBILITY NOTE

As noted in the previous "Bedroom Accessibility Guidelines" checklist, wheelchair users require clearance for access at closets as well as consideration of rod/shelf height and seated reach heights, as illustrated in Figure 5-10b.

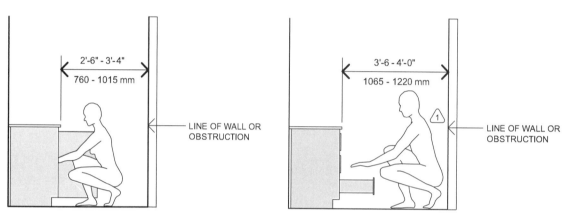

Figure 5-9 Required clearances for bedroom storage; note that storage with drawers requires greater clearance space.

1. In some cases, a bed can be located closer than indicated here; this requires that users use the drawers while sitting on the bed, which is not ideal.

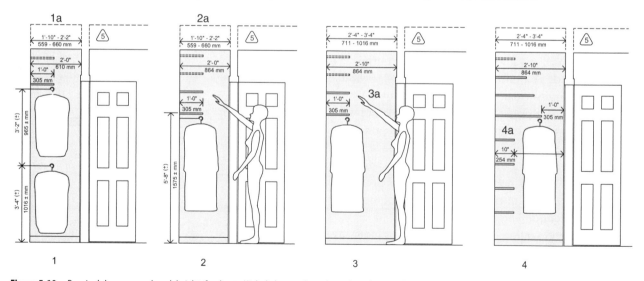

Figure 5-10a Required clearances and reach heights for closets. High shelves, as shown in reach-in closets with 9-foot (2743-mm) ceilings, can be difficult to access and are best for items that are not used frequently. *Note:* Shaded areas convey depth and offer a comparison of usable space; 1 and 2 offer more useful/efficient for storage than 3 and 4.

1. Two-row (-rod) hanging clothing storage. Depths shown (1a) offer the greatest efficiency of storage for area used.
2. Single rod for long coats, dresses, and pants. Depths shown (2a) offer the greatest efficiency of storage for area used.
3. Closets deeper than 24 inches (610 mm) offer limited benefits as shown. Note that the extra space shown (3a) does not provide useful storage space.
4. Very deep closets may offer additional shelving storage behind hanging clothes; this can be awkward to access (4a) and useful only for storage of items that are seldom accessed.
5. 9-foot (2743-mm) ceiling height (dashed line).
6. 8-foot (2438-mm) ceiling height (solid line).

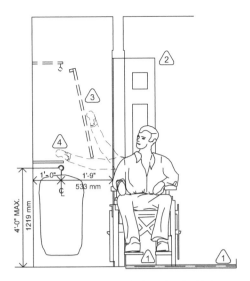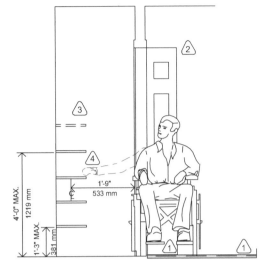

Figure 5-10b Required clearances and reach heights for closets for wheelchair users.

1. Provide a clear space 30 by 48 inches (762 by 1219 mm) adjacent to closet for parallel access.
2. Bifold doors can allow for greater clear space at closet.
3. Pull-down rods are accessible through the use of a wand; pull-down shelves are also available.
4. Average wheelchair reach dimension is 1 foot, 10 inches (559 mm), therefore placing rod no more than 1 foot, 9 inches (533 mm) from chair location is useful.
    Note: the height reach range for children using a wheelchair is 36 to 44 inches (914 to 1118 mm).

While many homeowners prefer the idea of a walk-in closet, such closets do not always provide the most effective clothing storage. This has to do with the fact that clothing rods generally run in a line and require access space for clothing retrieval. Reach-in closets use space efficiently because they share circulation space with the bedroom. In some cases, walk-in closets can limit actual clothing rod space because they require that access to the rod be contained within the closet area, while in other instances, walk-in closets may be preferable in that they can provide more wall space for placement of furniture and artwork in the bedroom because they require a narrower door opening. Therefore, it is important to discuss storage requirements and spatial constraints in detail with the individual client and to adjust closet location and type to the specific project plan. Figure 5-12 illustrates the use of floor space requirements relative to clothing storage in a range of closets.

As with all types of home storage, it is important to inventory items that will be stored in individual closets. Those items used least frequently can be placed in less-accessible areas (typically on a top shelf or an area that requires a bit of reaching). The most accessible portions of the closet (this varies based on door type) should contain the most commonly used items. Rods placed at varying heights allow for the appropriate amount and type of hanging space and free up space for racks and shelves.

Specialized closet storage systems are available. These run the gamut from simple shelves and rods to custom cabinetry. Within quite a range of options and costs, there are some common elements shared by many closet storage systems. Rods arranged at various heights, including areas of double rods, are part of most well-designed closets. Shelves, baskets, and drawers are used to store folded clothing and other accessories. These are often open but can be concealed behind doors as desired. Most shelves are adjustable, and some can pull out to the full dimension of the shelf. Shoes are commonly stored on shelves, angled racks, hanging racks, or in "shoe cubes." Other closet accessories include forward telescoping rods, tie racks, belt racks, and bottom-hinged doors with hamper inserts. Figure 5-13 provides information about elements used with various closet-organizing systems.

Larger, more elaborate closets may include an island with a finished top placed in a central location and used for folding and arranging clothes. Such islands are often roughly 36 inches (914 mm) high and require significant circulation space so that one may access both the island and the adjacent clothing storage areas. Closets may include specialized lighting, windows, or mechanical ventilation systems (useful where hampers are located), dressing tables, and vanities. These items can all be combined to create an entire dressing enclave that often includes or is adjacent to the bathroom area (see Figure 5-2).

ORGANIZATIONAL FLOW

The bed and its placement tend to dominate the layout of the room. Therefore, as a bedroom is designed, the location of the bed is best considered first. As stated previously, circulation space in a bedroom directly relates to the bed and to those spaces considered ancillary, such as the closet, additional stor-

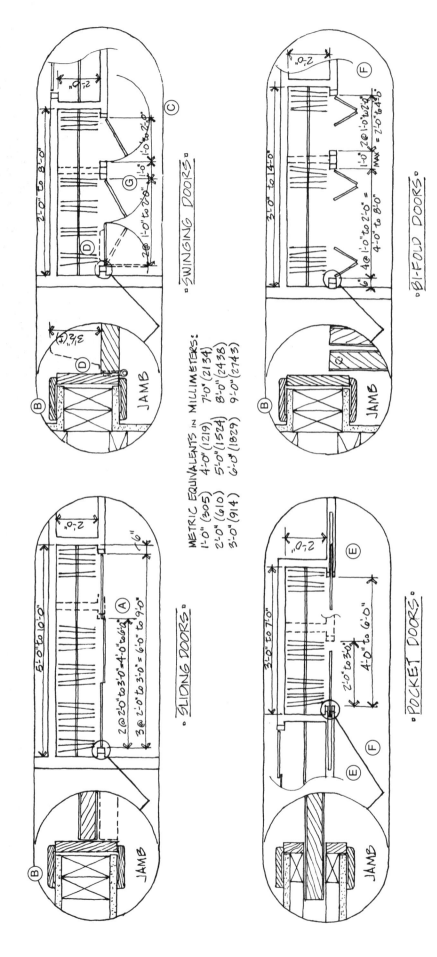

Figure 5-11 Closet doors and jamb details. These are intended to illustrate door and jamb details at closets and other interior door locations.

A. Three-door example shown. Additional doors can be added. The standard double track allows for only a 33 percent opening in this case. The addition of a third track allows for a 66 percent opening.

B. In all of the door examples shown, there must be an allowance for door trim, which commonly varies in width from 1½ to 5½ inches (38 to 157 mm), with 2¼ to 3½ inches (57 to 89 mm) the most common. Sliding and bifold doors can be installed without a doorframe and/or trim.

C. Unlike sliding doors, swinging doors require no track, creating fewer maintenance problems.

D. Swinging doors permit the back of the door (closet side) to be used for lightweight shallow storage, much like a refrigerator door.

E. There may not be wall space available for the location of a pocket on two sides. With adequate room in the adjacent walls for pockets, this type of door can allow up to a 95 percent opening.

F. Pocket and bifold doors can allow for a greater percentage of open area, with limited floor space taken up by door swings, making them helpful for some wheelchair users.

G. These doors (practical maximum of 2 feet [610 mm]) allow for a large opening (90+/- percent).

Figure 5-12 Closet type comparison. Generally, reach-in closets are more efficient because they share circulation space with the actual room rather than requiring internal space dedicated to circulation only. This is illustrated in the following drawings.

a. Closets a_1 and a_2 contain the same lineal footage of clothing rod space; however, because of the need for circulation space in closet a_2, far more square footage is required. a_2 does offer an area for shelving (dashed lines), but this may be a minimal advantage for some homeowners when weighed against the additional square footage required. a_1 will work using bifold, swinging, and sliding doors, while a_2 would generally use a swinging door and, less commonly, a pocket door.

b. Closets b_1 and b_2 contain the same lineal footage of clothing rod space; however, because of the need for circulation space in closet b_2, the square footage is tripled. b_1 will work using bifold or sliding doors, while, at this size, swinging doors (2 feet, 6 inches [762 mm] each) would project into the room excessively.

c. Closets c_1 and c_2 contain the same lineal footage of clothing rod space. Unlike the previous walk-in examples, c_2 offers the advantage of a "double-loaded" rod or storage areas sharing one circulation aisle, which offers a better economy of space than the single-loaded examples. This type of double-loaded walk-in closet can be extended quite a bit. As the closet depth increases, it is helpful to increase the closet width to 8 feet (2438 mm) or more to create a generous space, rather than

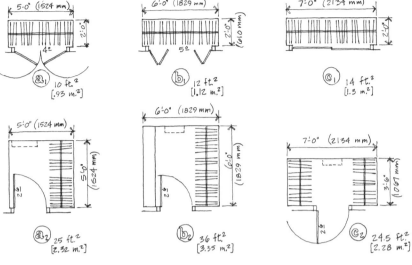

a tunnel-like space. As the width expands, accessing the closet through double swinging doors becomes possible, which appeals to some clients. c_1 will work using bifold or sliding doors, while, at this size (3 feet [914 mm]), swinging doors will project into the room excessively.

Note: This figure illustrates the comparative square footage in the various types of closets. In some instances, walk-in closets may be seen as preferable based on the overall room design. For example, walk-in closets may provide more wall space for locations of furnishings and artwork within the room or simply may be the preference of the homeowner/client.

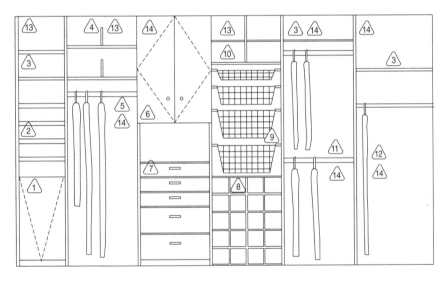

ELEVATION

PLAN

Figure 5-13 Closet storage elements and options.

1. Bottom-hinged door, useful as hamper. Coated wire inserts are also available.
2. Angled shoe shelves.
3. Open shelves, generally adjustable. Available in wood, laminate, glass, and coated wire.
4. Vertical acrylic/plastic shelf dividers.
5. Clothing rod for full-height clothes.
6. Doors available in a range of styles, including wood panel, laminate, wood with glass window, and clear acrylic panels.
7. Drawers available in a range of styles (similar to doors). Drawers range from 5 to 10 plus inches high (125 to 255 mm).
8. Shoe cubes.
9. Coated wire baskets available in a range of heights and lengths, with depths from roughly 10 to 13 plus inches (254 to 330 mm).
10. Shelves with dividers create cubbies.
11. Double clothing rod area (for shirts, blouses, jackets, some skirts, etc.).
12. Clothing rod for medium-length dresses and trousers hung by the cuffs.
13. Depth of some storage units ranges from 14 to 18 inches (356 to 457 mm); this is for items such as jewelry drawers, open shelving for folded clothing, and shoes.
14. Some storage units are deeper, running from 20 to 24 plus inches (508 to 610 mm); deeper units are for rod or drawer storage, most rod storage units are roughly 24 inches 610 mm) deep. There are also combined units that are deeper at the base and less deep above. Freestanding wardrobes and armoires can be as deep 27 plus inches (686 mm), to accommodate rod storage and door/drawer fronts.

age, other furnishings, and sometimes a bathroom, as well as access space to the main entry to the room.

When considering how elements in a room are used, the designer must also imagine the traffic flow. Circulation space is required as one approaches the bed, but traffic must also flow to the closet and additional clothing storage areas such as dressers when one requires a change of clothing. This means that, on some occasions, people enter the room with no intention of approaching the bed and instead are attempting to retrieve an item of clothing or to change clothes. With this in mind, it is generally most useful to place the closet close to the entry of the room instead of on the wall farthest from the room entrance. Figure 5-14 is a bubble diagram depicting the relationship between the room entry and closet area.

Because dressers and chests of drawers are used to store clothing and are often used at the same time as closets, it is helpful to place dressers relatively close to closets. This also helps with room layout relative to traffic flow. Those places used most often require more circulation space. As one moves from the dressing areas toward those areas less frequently accessed, less circulation space is required, as discussed previously.

Note that the location of the bedroom entrance relative to the location of exterior walls (and therefore windows) is a primary determinant of the form of the room. The authors have identified four basic bedroom form types based on relationships to exterior walls.

In one type, the exterior wall is opposite the entrance, as shown in Figure 5-15 (Room A). A similar situation occurs when there are two exterior walls in a room, with one of those walls opposite the entrance. This has the potential to create a "corner room," as shown in Figure 5-15 (Room B).

Another room form is created when one exterior wall is adjacent to the room entrance, as shown in Figure 5-15 (Room C). This room form is less common because it typically requires that a hallway terminate at the bedroom entrance, which can involve some wasted space in new construction. In other, also rare cases, a "bedroom wing" is created, with the entrance being flanked by three exterior walls, as shown in Figure 5-15 (Room D). This room form is often found in suites in custom homes and offers the possibility of taking great advantage of views, as it allows for daylight on three sides. The discussion of room form to this point relates to generic room types and is meant to be helpful as one plans the general disposition of rooms. In addition, this discussion of window location is based on windows placed at standard heights rather than above the height of furniture (for example, in a clerestory installation). Room size, furniture layout, closet design, window placement, and orientation are additional issues that must be considered as the room is developed further.

As the dimensions of the room are expanded, particularly in one direction, a more rectilinear room form is created. In this form, at roughly 150 square feet (14 m^2) or more, placement of storage furniture and bed(s) can occur on three walls—or more, depending on closet location. Furniture located in this manner requires space for major traffic flow to all three walls, which is easily accommodated in a room this size. This is shown in the "b" series of Figures 5-16 to 5-18. For a bedroom suite, the room sizes and configurations discussed to this point must be increased with considerable square footage to accommodate a walk-in closet and/or bathroom. Figure 5-19 shows a wheelchair-accessible owner's suite.

The overall size of the room will dictate where furniture may be placed and therefore where the circulation aisles and spaces are located, so that more than one major circulation space is created. A room that is roughly 130 to 140 square feet (12 to 13.5 m^2)—and relatively square in shape—allows for placement of major furniture (queen-size bed and dressers) on two walls, as shown in Figures 5-16 to 5-18. This two-wall placement creates a single major circulation aisle and one minor circulation space used for the secondary bed approach. Given this room size, it is not possible to load furnishings on additional walls, unless the bed size is reduced.

Figure 5-19a depicts the basic room size shown previously, with the areas for the larger closet and bathroom added to create an owner's suite. Figure 5-19b depicts a relatively small owner's suite in a configuration that is almost square in shape.

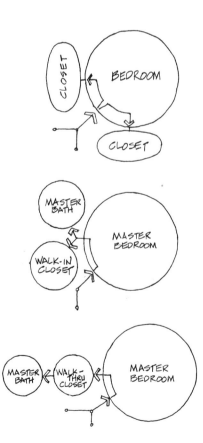

Figure 5-14 Bubble diagram depicting the entrance and its ideal relationship to closet space. Closets placed adjacent to the room entrance allow for easy retrieval of clothing and accessories, which may occur several times per day.

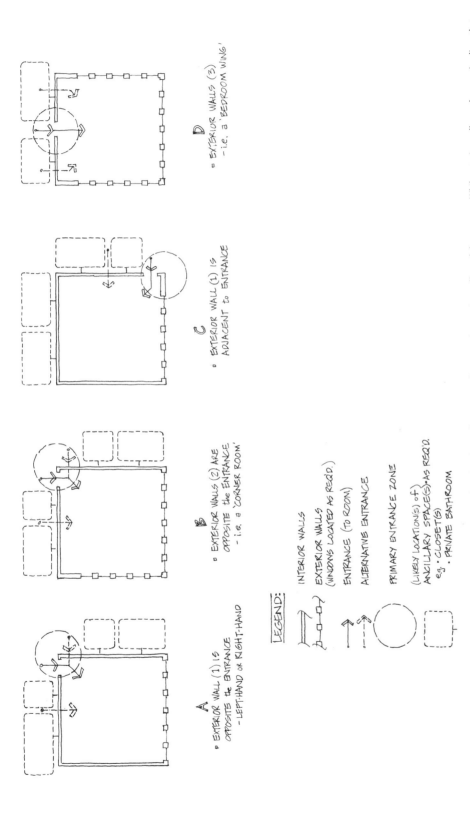

LEGEND:

‖ ‖ ‖ INTERIOR WALLS

◻—◻—◻—◻ EXTERIOR WALLS
(WINDOWS LOCATED AS REQ'D)

↑ ENTRANCE (TO ROOM)

↑ ↑ ALTERNATIVE ENTRANCE

◯ PRIMARY ENTRANCE ZONE

⬚ (LIKELY LOCATION(S) of
ANCILLARY SPACE(S) AS REQ'D.
e.g. • CLOSET(S)
• PRIVATE BATHROOM

A

▫ EXTERIOR WALL (1) IS
OPPOSITE the ENTRANCE
– LEFT-HAND or RIGHT-HAND

B

▫ EXTERIOR WALLS (2) ARE
OPPOSITE the ENTRANCE
– i.e. a 'CORNER ROOM'

C

▫ EXTERIOR WALL (1) IS
ADJACENT to ENTRANCE

D

▫ EXTERIOR WALLS (3)
– i.e. a 'BEDROOM WING'

Figure 5-15 Generic room forms. Drawings A, B, C, and D show generic bedroom plans based on the relationships among the room, the exterior walls, and the entrance. While exterior walls are shown using lines that represent windows, this is only an indication that windows may be placed at points along these walls. Actual window placement will vary based on a series of factors, including site orientation, aesthetics, climate, budget, and building context and style. If windows are located above furniture height, the notes below are less significant.

Room A. The exterior wall is opposite the entrance, offering one wall for window location and creating two possible locations for closet/bathroom placement and a range of possibilities for furniture placement. The door is best placed in an offset position, as centering it can cause traffic flow problems and limit furniture placement.

Room B. Two exterior walls are opposite the entrance, offering two walls for window location, allowing daylight from two sides (highly prized by some), and creating two possible locations for closet/bathroom placement and multiple possibilities for furniture placement. Window placement on each exterior wall must be well considered so that the most advantageous use of light and views takes place while at the same time not limiting furniture placement options. The door is best placed in an offset position, as centering it can cause traffic flow problems and limit furniture placement.

Room C. The exterior wall is adjacent to the entrance. This is rare, as it requires that a hallway terminate at an exterior wall (as shown). This type of room can be found in two-story houses, with a central stair creating a second-floor hallway with room entrances on opposite sides.

Room D. Three exterior walls are opposite the entrance, offering three walls for window location, allowing daylight from three sides (highly prized by some), and taking great advantage of available views. This room form is often found in suites in custom homes. It limits the placement of the closets, as there is only one location adjacent to the entry door. As with Room B, the placement of windows in such rooms requires careful thought in order to provide flexibility for furnishings. A bed with headboard would likely be required if the exterior walls were largely glass as shown.

Figure 5-16 Room size, circulation, and furniture layout.

A. This room size allows for furniture to be placed on only two walls with adequate major circulation space provided. See Figures 5-8a and 5-8b for information on spatial requirements. Major circulation space: A_1.

B. This larger room size allows for furniture to be placed on three walls with adequate major circulation space provided. See Figures 5-7 and 5-8 for information on spatial requirements. Major circulation space: B_1.

C. Minor circulation space to areas less traveled. See Figures 5-7 and 5-8 for information on spatial requirements.

D. It is often best to locate the bed off the exterior wall at the windows due to climate, the nature of furnishings (headboards), and, in the case of small children, safety.

E. Shown with a queen-size bed, currently the most popular bed size in the United States. Wheelchair access at the sides of the bed of 36 inches (914 mm) as well as a turning radius may require a reduction in bed size. Use of a king-size bed requires a larger room area or the elimination of some additional furnishings. Use of twin or full-size beds allows for a somewhat smaller room size or, in the case of a twin bed, the addition of furnishings.

F. Doors shown are 2 feet, 8 inches (813 mm); 3-foot (914-mm) doors are required for wheelchairs in order to provide 32 inches (813 mm) of clear passage space. Doors should be placed so that the arc of their swing works functionally and the door swings to an appropriate location and is kept out of the way.

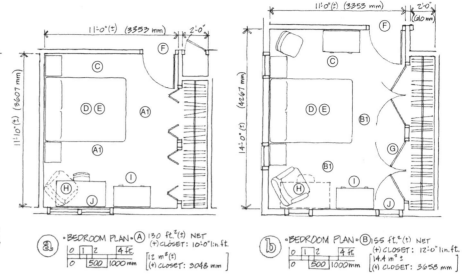

G. Swinging closet doors require adequate swinging space. For additional information on closet doors, see Figure 5-12.

H. Area shown for a variety of furnishings and uses.

I. Adequate area should be provided for opening doors and drawers. See Figure 5-9. In this case, access would be best accomplished by a user sitting on the bed.

J. At least one window must be of a size to meet code egress requirements (see Figure 5-23).

Figure 5-17 Room size, circulation, and furniture layout.

A. This room size allows for furniture to be placed on only two walls with adequate major circulation space provided. See Figures 5-7 and 5-8 for information on spatial requirements. Major circulation space: A_1.

B. This larger room size allows for furniture to be placed on three walls with adequate major circulation space provided. See Figures 5-7 and 5-8 for information on spatial requirements. Major circulation space: B_1.

C. Minor circulation space to areas less traveled. See Figures 5-7 and 5-8 for information on spatial requirements.

D. It is often best to locate the bed off the exterior wall at the windows due to climate, the nature of furnishings (headboards), and, in the case of small children, safety.

E. While this window is shown as centered, this is not necessarily the best placement relative to room layout, window style, and perhaps overall building design.

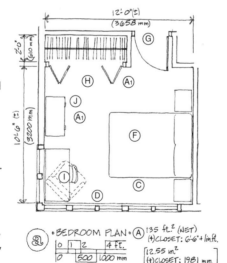

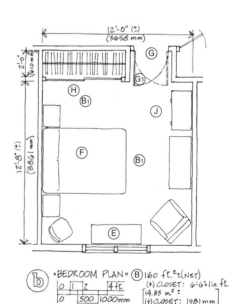

F. Shown with a queen-size bed, currently the most popular bed size in the United States. Wheelchair access at the sides of the bed of 36 inches (914 mm) as well as a turning radius may require a reduction in bed size. Use of a king-size bed requires a larger room area or the elimination of some additional furnishings. Use of twin or full-size beds allows for a smaller room size or the addition of furnishings.

G. Doors shown are 2 feet, 8 inches (813 mm). Doors should be placed so that the arc of their swing works functionally and the door swings to an appropriate

location and is kept out of the way. To make this room wheelchair accessible, 3-foot (914-mm) doors are required in order to provide 32 inches (813 mm) of clear space; the location of the door would need to be changed to allow 18 inches (457 mm) of clear space on the latch side of the door (G_1), or the closet could be shortened.

H. Swinging closet doors would require adequate swinging space. For additional information on closet doors, see Figure 5-11.

I. Area shown for a variety of furnishings and uses.

J. Adequate area should be provided for opening doors and drawers. See Figure 5-9.

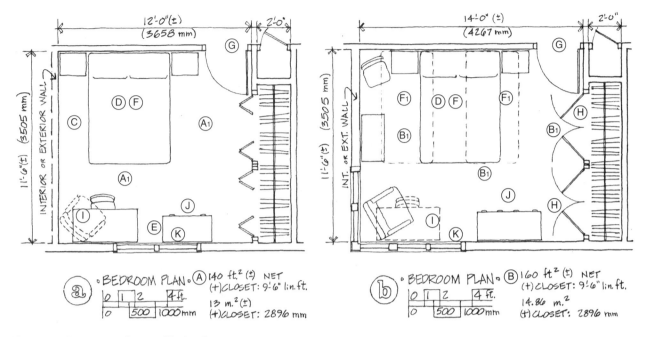

Figure 5-18 Room size, circulation, and furniture layout.

A. This room size allows for furniture to be placed on only two walls with adequate major circulation space provided (see D). See Figures 5-7 and 5-8 for information on spatial requirements. Major circulation space: A$_1$.

B. This larger room size allows for furniture to be placed on three walls with adequate major circulation space provided. See Figures 5-7 and 5-8 for information on spatial requirements. Major circulation space: B$_1$.

C. Minor circulation space to areas less traveled. See Figures 5-7 and 5-8 for information on spatial requirements.

D. It is often best to locate the bed off the exterior wall at the windows due to climate, the nature of furnishings, and, in the case of small children, safety.

E. While this window is shown as centered, this is not necessarily the best placement relative to room layout, window style, and overall building design; in this case, it may preclude locating the bed on that wall (see D above).

F. Shown with a queen-size bed, currently the most popular bed size in the United States. Wheelchair access at the sides of the bed of 36 inches (914 mm) as well as a turning radius may require a reduction in bed size. Use of a king-size bed requires a larger room area or the elimination of some additional furnishings. Use of twin or full-size beds allows for a smaller room size or the addition of furnishings. Two twin beds are shown with dashed lines (F$_1$). In spite of large room size, the window placement makes only one location work well for bed(s).

G. Doors shown are 2 feet, 8 inches (813 mm); 3-foot (914-mm) doors are required for wheelchairs in order to provide 32 inches (813 mm) of clear space. Doors should be placed so that the arc of their swing works functionally and the door swings to an appropriate location and is kept out of the way.

H. Swinging closet doors require adequate swinging space, 2-foot (610-mm) doors shown. For additional information on closet doors, see Figure 5-11.

I. Area shown for a variety of furnishings and uses.

J. Adequate area should be provided for opening doors and drawers. See Figure 5-9.

K. At least one window must be of a size to meet code egress requirements (see Figure 5-23).

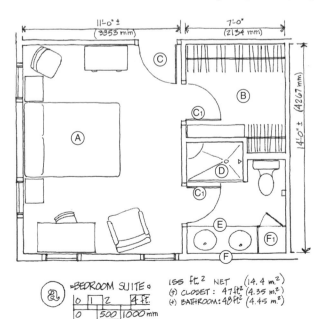

Figure 5-19a Bedroom suite. The addition of a walk-in closet and bathroom increases a room's square footage considerably. The room shown was covered in Figure 5-16 (plan b) and Figure 5-17 (plan b), and has been kept intact to demonstrate that, as suite size increases, basic room requirements can remain consistent. Bathrooms and large closets necessarily add to the room (suite) area and should not decrease the quality or function of the actual bedroom. When considering the options, the designer should keep in mind that all bedrooms require some form of closet and bathrooms can be seen as optional/located elsewhere.

A. A queen-size bed.

B. Walk-in closet with 9 feet, 8 inches (2946 mm) of clothing rod and/or closet system and 12-inch (305-mm) deep shelves behind the door.

C. A 2-foot, 8-inch (813-mm) door. A 2-foot, 6-inch (762-mm) door (C$_1$).

D. Shower module: 48 inches (1219 mm).

E. Vanity: 60 inches (1524 mm) long with two sinks.

F. No windows in the bathroom; the addition of a window would require the loss of one sink or linen cabinet (F$_1$).

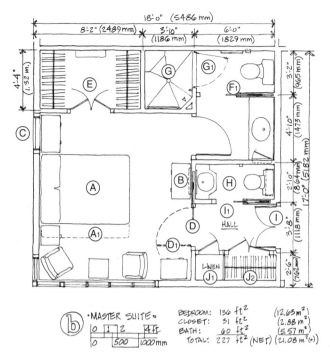

Figure 5-19b A small bedroom suite. The room shown is from the project featured in Chapter 8.

A. A queen-size bed is shown; a king-size bed would be possible if the chairs and table were eliminated.

B. A wall-mounted television.

C. Window sized to meet emergency egress requirements (see also Figure 5-23).

D. A 2-foot, 8-inch (813-mm) pocket door is used in part to eliminate dead space behind a swinging door (D_1).

E. A moderately sized walk-in closet with a pair of doors in a 3-foot (914-mm) opening.

F. A two-compartment master bath with no windows and no bathtub fixture, with a 2-foot, 8-inch (813-mm) pocket door (F_1).

G. A walk-in shower stall measuring 3 feet, 6 inches by 4 feet, 2 inches (1067 by 1270 mm), with a horizontal and vertical grab bar and a built-in seat with a 2-foot, 6-inch (762-mm) shower door (G_1). Options include a 2-foot, 8-inch (813 mm) opening with the door removed for access.

H. A minimal half bath with round bowl toilet (water closet) and a vanity sink. The small room size necessitates a 2-foot (610-mm) pocket door.

I. French doors (3-foot [914-mm] opening) allow the hall (I_1) and half bath (H) to become either part of the residence (a powder room) or to serve as a buffer and or a second toilet for the master suite.

J. A combination linen (J_1) and clothes closet (J_2), each with 1-foot, 6-inch (457-mm) doors. Given their location along the (semiprivate) hall, they can be used for master suite and/or household storage.

Figure 5-19c is a suite that includes laundry facilities. Figure 5-19d shows two bedrooms joined by a bathroom. Figure 5-19e is a wheelchair-accessible suite. Figures are meant to suggest some of the many possibilities of suite design; they do point to the need for the actual bedroom area to retain its relative size, which is augmented significantly with a large closet or closets and bathroom.

Poorly designed rooms that do not take into consideration the many issues covered thus far are illustrated in Figures 5-20

ACCESSIBILITY NOTE

Creating accessible bedrooms requires that all doors have clear openings of 32 inches (831 mm) minimum and allow for clear wheelchair access for the bed and clothing storage, as shown in Figure 5-8. Figure 5-19 illustrates a wheelchair-accessible suite, detailed information about accessible bathroom design is found in Chapter 6.

and 5-21. Figure 5-22 shows another negative example of a bedroom along with possible improvements to illustrate better design practice.

RELATED CODES AND CONSTRAINTS

Bedrooms meet the IRC's definition of habitable space in that they are intended for sleeping (and living), which means that bedrooms must follow the guidelines listed for habitable space, although there may be exceptions or broader requirements in some state and local codes. Regardless of possible exceptions, it is a good general rule to meet or exceed the ventilation and light requirements by providing the window area called for in bedrooms.

As stated in Chapter 1, the IRC calls for habitable rooms (including every sleeping room) to have a ceiling height of not less than 7 feet (2134 mm); this same height requirement is called for in basements and habitable attics. (See Figure 1-5 for an illustration of ceiling heights relative to room areas.)

Issues related to bedrooms are also covered in the IRC in the section on emergency escape and rescue openings (Section R310). This section describes regulations related to basements with habitable space as well as sleeping rooms and requires that they have at least one openable emergency escape and rescue opening.

The IRC also specifies that in cases where basements contain one or more sleeping rooms, emergency egress and rescue openings are required in each sleeping room. The codes set very clear requirements for the rescue openings, with specific requirements for sill heights, opening height and width, minimum openable area, and clear net openings; these are illustrated in Figure 5-23.

The IRC covers minimum room areas in Section R304 and requires that all habitable rooms not be less than 70 square feet (6.54 m²) of gross floor area and not be less than 7 feet (2143 mm) in any horizontal dimension. The previously discussed minimal bedroom (Figure 5-1) represents a room meeting these minimum standards. According to this section of the code, parts of any habitable room with sloped ceiling areas

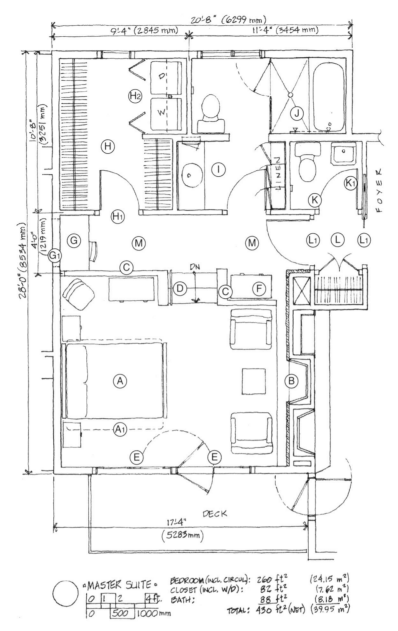

Figure 5-19c A fairly large bedroom suite with laundry facilities contained within a walk-in closet and full bathroom. There is deck access, which also serves as emergency egress. The suite is designed for future expansion into the attic area above the garage (G₁).

A. Queen-size bed; a king-size bed would also be an option (A₁).
B. Gas fireplace with raised hearth, within a stone veneer wall, housed in a fire-rated enclosure.
C. Half wall, 2 feet, 8 inches (813 mm) high, with a hardwood cap.
D. Three risers at 5⅜ inches (137 mm) with 12-inch (305-mm) treads.
E. Two pairs of 5-foot (1524-mm) French doors with transoms, which allow better view from raised circulation (M).
F. Small credenza serves in part as a charging station for electronic devices.
G. Temporary desk area, with a knock-out panel (G₁) to allow expansion for future studio in garage attic.
H. Walk-in closet with 14.75 lineal feet (4496 mm) of clothes hanging rod or closet system and a 2-foot, 8-inch (813-mm) door (H₁).
   H₂. Laundry closet with floor drain, overhead cabinets, and washer and dryer.
I. Vanity: 54 inches (1372 mm) in length.
J. A tub/walk-in shower room with glass enclosure that is 5 feet by 5 feet, 4 inches (1524 by 1626 mm).
K. A powder room that is 4 feet, 6 inches by 5 feet (1372 by 1524 mm); 2 feet, 8 inch door (813 mm) (K₁).
L. Hall linking (and buffering) master suite; both doors are 3 feet (914 mm) (L₁).
M. Circulation to suite entrance door and foyer beyond and to:
   -Sunken portion of bedroom.
   -Master bathroom.
   -Walk-in closet with washer and dryer.
   -Future studio.

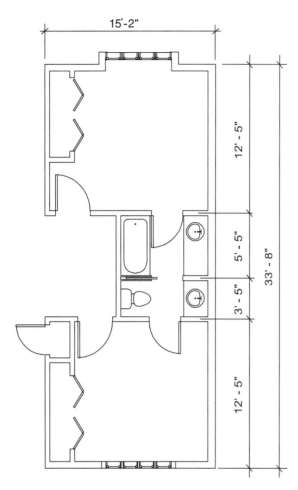

Figure 5-19d Two bedrooms joined by a shared bathroom. Some refer to this as "Jack and Jill" bedrooms/bathroom. In this example the shared bathroom has two sinks, in separate compartments, which allows for two to use the bathroom with privacy.

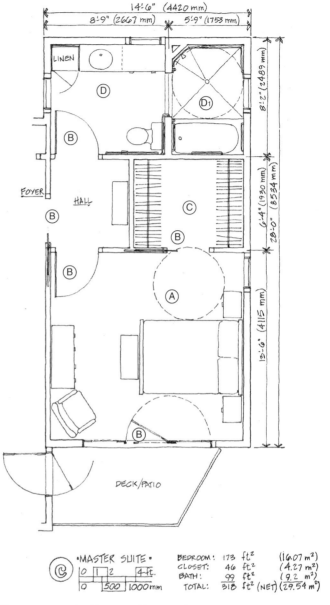

·MASTER SUITE·

BEDROOM:	173 ft²	(16.07 m²)
CLOSET:	46 ft²	(4.27 m²)
BATH:	99 ft²	(9.2 m²)
TOTAL:	318 ft² (NET)	(29.54 m²)

Figure 5-19e A wheelchair-accessible suite with a small hall, which enables double use of the bathroom: accessible for guests and allows the bath to become part of an accessible bedroom.

A. Wheelchair-accessible bedroom with queen-size bed with direct access to closet (C) and outdoor deck and patio.
B. Doors 3 feet (914 mm) throughout.
C. Walk-in closet.
D. Master bath with:
  -Knee space at sink.
  -Vanity height of 32 inches (813 mm).
  -Elongated toilet bowl (water closet); grab bars as shown.
  D₁. Bathtub and shower area:
  -Turning area 5 feet (1524 mm) in diameter.
  -Grab bars as shown (see also Figures 6-27b through 6-27d).

measuring less than 5 feet (1534 mm) or with a furred ceiling measuring less than 7 feet (2134 mm) above the finished floor do not count as contributing to the required minimum habitable area for any habitable room, including bedrooms (as shown in Figure 1-5).

Additional requirements found in the IRC relate to smoke alarms (Section R314) and carbon monoxide alarms (Section R315). Smoke alarm requirements are as follows: one in each sleeping room, and a second "outside each separate sleeping area in the vicinity of the bedrooms." Carbon monoxide alarms are required outside each separate sleeping area in the immediate vicinity of bedrooms (for new construction with fuel-fired appliances installed and in dwelling units with attached garages). See Figure 5-24 for an illustration of bedroom fire protection required by the IRC.

According to the IRC, effective 2011, automatic residential fire sprinkler systems are required (R313.2) for new one- and two-family dwellings. Over time, local codes may incorporate this requirement, often at first only with larger homes, so the designer should review the local codes.

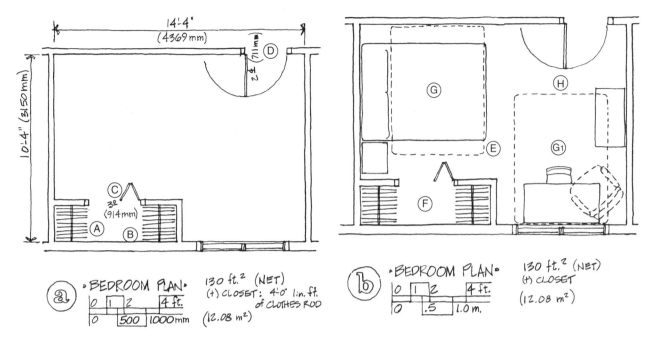

Figure 5-20 Negative examples.

Problematic bedroom plans. These illustrations depict a room of 130 square feet (12 m²) containing a poorly considered walk-in closet.

A. The closet location is very remote from the room entrance, requiring traveling the entire distance of the room to retrieve clothing. Additionally, the room is long and narrow, and the closet is located in a way that narrows the room further.
B. The closet occupies a prime room location on the exterior wall, eliminating possible window locations and limiting furniture placement options.
C. The bifold closet door is drawn too small (N.T.S.), thereby giving a false impression of how much space the door takes up.
D. The entry door at 2 feet, 4 inches (711 mm) is too small. The recommended code minimum is 2 feet, 6 inches (762 mm), and 2 feet, 8 inches (813 mm) is better. The door swing is awkward and would be better placed on the other side, where it would be out of the way when open.
E. The room contains adequate square footage, but the narrow design/closet location creates significant problems with circulation and furniture locations.
F. The closet contains only 4 lineal feet (1219 mm) of rod space; a similarly located reach-in closet with appropriate doors would allow 7 lineal feet (2134 mm) of rod space.
G. There is no good place for a queen-size bed and no room for adequate side clearances and circulation. Bed (dashed) at G_1 is against the only windows, with the related disadvantages.
H. This is wasted space, while other portions of the room are too tight to function well (for example, with the bed in G_1 location).

ELECTRICAL AND MECHANICAL

Unlike other rooms in the home, bedrooms are not typically influenced to any large degree by plumbing or significant (heavy) electrical requirements. Mechanical provisions for bedrooms are rather straightforward. Because the IRC (Section R303.9) calls for heating to a minimum of 68°F (20°C) when the winter temperature is below 60°F (15.5°C), most bedrooms in the United States are required to have some source of heat.

The location of the heat source or its registers or diffusers, as well as those used by any air-cooling source, must be considered by the interior designer as lighting, furnishings, window, and door locations are planned. The actual engineering of the heating and cooling system is, of course, done by professionals other than the interior designer. For additional information on heating, ventilation, and air conditioning, see the "Electrical and Mechanical" section of Chapter 1.

As with other general wall spaces, there are some general rules for locating electrical switches and convenience outlets in bedrooms:

Locating Switches and Convenience Outlets in Bedrooms

■ The on/off switches for overhead or general lights are best located close to the room entry door on the latch side of the doorway when possible. In larger suites with more than one entrance, a second on/off switch, known as a three-way switch, can be employed in another convenient location.

■ Where a number of light fixtures are used for ambient lighting, a single switch can be used to control a number of fixtures and outlets.

■ Vertical switch placement for bedrooms follows those described in Chapter 1 and illustrated in Figure 1-6.

Following general rules can be a good starting point; however, the placement of outlets must be considered in relation to the design and layout of the room. It is very important to consider the various possibilities for furniture placement in a bedroom so that the outlets can be designed in a way that is useful for a variety of scenarios. While a designer might have an initial plan for locating furnishings, years later the homeowner

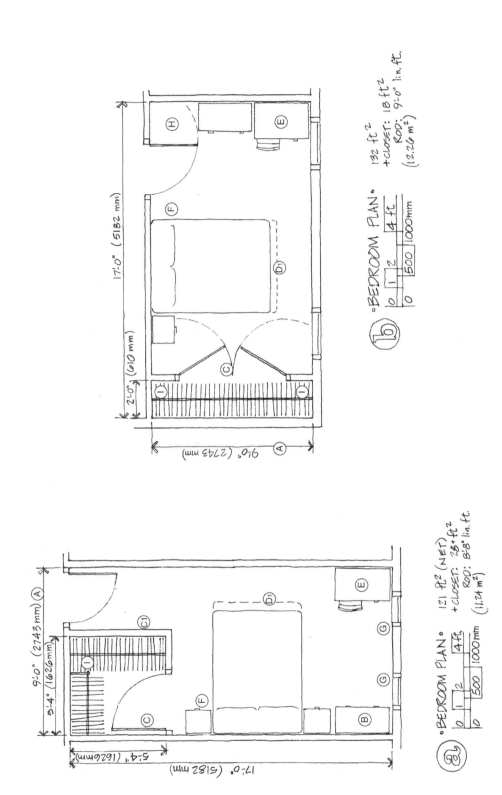

Figure 5-21 Negative examples. Problematic bedroom plans.

A. Identical shapes —9 by 17 (2743 by 5182 mm) —with different orientation to exterior wall feet (2743 by 5182 mm). Narrow width makes for circulation problems: square footage in a different shape (more square) would likely lead to better results.

B. Clothes storage (dresser) is distant from room entry, making it a long walk to retrieve an item.

C. 3-foot (914-mm) doors can be cumbersome to open and close often. In **plan b**, replacing the single pair of doors with two pairs of smaller doors would enhance this design. In **plan a:** moving the door around the corner (C1), together with reconfiguration of the closet, creates more efficient access.

D. Passage width is minimal and a bed frame (D_1) would make it too narrow, thereby limiting bed selection.

E. Area for a very small desk only.

F. Inadequate space for a nightstand at each side of bed.

G. Windows as shown are too small (narrow) to meet the escape/rescue route requirements found in the International Residential Code (IRC) (see Figure 5-23).

H. Dead corner is a waste of space and difficult to regain for useful purpose.

I. Inside corners in closets can be difficult to access.

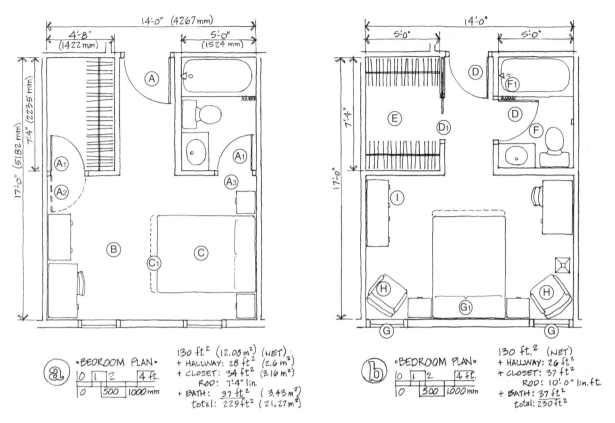

Figure 5-22 Negative example shown in **plan a,** with some improvements shown in **plan b.**

Problematic bedroom plans. **Plan a** has been improved upon in **plan b.** Both rooms are the same size: 14 by 17 feet (4267 by 5182 mm). Items A to C identify shortcomings in **plan a** that have been improved upon in **plan b.** The improvements include door location and size, window location, and furniture and fixture location as well as minor wall shifts. The revisions result in better circulation and space for more or larger furniture.

A. The 3-foot (914-mm) door does not provide many advantages beyond a good-size opening for moving furniture in and out of the room. It does not provide for accessibility unless doors to the bath and closet are also 3 feet (914 mm).

   A_1. These doors are remote in terms of circulation and ease of access.

   A_2. Shows alternate door swing, but this would accomplish little.

   A_3. Tight due to nightstand.

B. Space is overly generous in contrast to limited space provided in other areas.

C. Bed could be located against the opposite wall.

   C_1. Queen-size bed (mattress) shown; a bed with frame will be larger.

   Design improvements made in **plan b** are listed below.

D. All doors are 2 feet, 8 inches (813 mm).

   D_1. A pocket door allowing easy access to all hanging space; a swinging door would block some access to hanging clothes.

E. Double loading the closet creates more rod length (27 percent more rod space per square foot of closet area) than the version in **plan a.**

F. Relocation of door, toilet, and sink improves access to tub/shower controls.

G. Relocation of windows allows for a third location for the bed (G_1).

H. Added room for chairs, albeit with size limitations.

I. Added room for a larger dresser.

Figure 5-23 IRC emergency escape and rescue openings (egress windows). The code states that sleeping rooms and basements must have at least one openable emergency escape and rescue opening with specific requirements as follows:

- A sill height of not more than 44 inches (1118 mm) above the floor.
- A minimum net clear opening of 5.7 square feet (0.530 m²). There is an exception to this for grade-floor openings, which must have a minimum net clear opening of 5 square feet (0.465 m²).
- A minimum net clear opening height of 24 inches (610 mm) and a minimum net clear opening width of 20 inches (508 mm).
- The dimension shown in each window example is required to meet the 5.7-square-foot opening requirement when paired with the minimum horizontal or vertical dimensions shown.

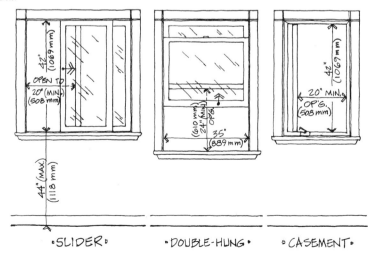

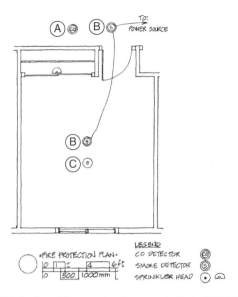

Figure 5-24 Smoke and fire protection plan as required by the IRC (R313, 314).

A. Carbon monoxide detector.
B. Smoke detector; the IRC calls for compliance with National Fire Alarm and Signaling Code (NFPA 72).
C. Sprinkler head (required effective January 1, 2011).

Note: Detectors can be combined per R314.7.5

may wish to move the furnishings around. With this in mind, the outlets should be designed to accommodate a range of furniture layouts, not simply the one planned for the short term.

See Figure 5-25 for drawings of outlet locations in a room with two different furniture layouts.

In addition to lighting and power outlets, bedrooms may require various communication lines. Owners may desire telephone, cable, and stereo/audio in bedrooms. As stated in Chapter 1, interior designers often designate the locations for lighting, outlets, switches, and various communication systems, while the actual engineering of the power, HVAC, and communication systems is done by professionals in those fields. Just as with electrical outlets, designers must consider a range of locations for cable and communication outlets so that various furniture layouts can be accommodated. With wireless communication more common, the location of communication outlets becomes less of a concern.

LIGHTING

Lighting for bedrooms has evolved and is now, in some cases, quite sophisticated. In years past, a single overhead ceiling-mounted light fixture, with its light pouring downward, was seen as a standard design feature in residential bedrooms. This is no longer considered standard, and in most cases, pleasant ambient lighting is supplied by sources other than a downlight. Pendant-mounted uplights bounce light off the ceiling and wall, creating ambient light that softens physical features—an excellent choice for the bedroom. In addition, cove and

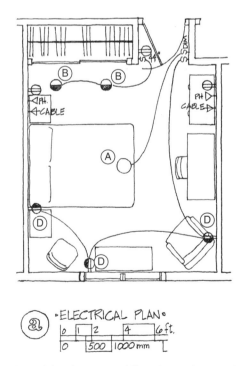

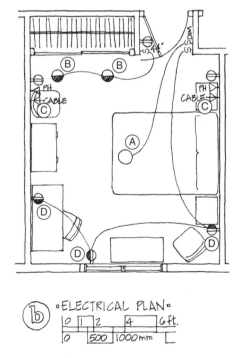

Figure 5-25 Electrical plans depicting two different furniture layouts, with identical light, convenience outlets, and switch locations for each room. The location of outlets and switches permits flexibility in furnishing the room. Note that the centered overhead fixture (A), wall washers (B), and wall outlets (D) are switched separately to provide general room light, allowing for flexibility. Also note that communication lines (phone and cable) (C) are provided to two locations to allow for flexibility with furniture placement. For additional information on electrical symbols and lighting, see Chapters 1 and 8.

cornice- and soffit-mounted luminaires can provide excellent, indirect ambient lighting.

Some rooms benefit from perimeter lighting as well as a ceiling-mounted fixture in the center for balance. Comfortable, adequate general lighting should be supplied in one manner or another, and the type of fixture used must be determined after careful discussions with the client so that the appropriate luminaires can be identified. Regardless of the type of fixture selected, the fixture or fixtures that supply general lighting should be switched at the wall adjacent to the room entry, as discussed previously.

In addition to adequate general lighting, the bedroom requires task lighting for reading, self-care, and, in some cases, work. Task lighting is often supplied by table, floor, or wall-mounted fixtures. Additionally, accent lighting can be used to create focal points, enhance artwork, and give focus to important objects or areas.

REFERENCES

Contains both works cited and recommended reading.

International Code Council. 2015. "*2015 International Residential Code for One- and Two-Family Dwellings*." Country Club Hills, IL: International Code Council.

Ramsey, Charles George, Harold Reeve Sleeper, and John Ray Hoke Jr. 2000. *Architectural Graphic Standards*. 10th ed. Hoboken, NJ: John Wiley & Sons.

Whitehead, Randall. 2004. *Residential Lighting: A Practical Guide*. Hoboken, NJ: John Wiley & Sons.

CHAPTER 6
Bathrooms

INTRODUCTION

A "typical" American bathroom, a room combining a toilet, bathtub and/or shower, and sink, is a relatively new development. It is only since the Victorian era that the functions of bodily washing and toileting have been brought together in one room inside the home. Until the advent of successful indoor plumbing, most bathing took place in a portable tub with water hauled, heated, and poured into the tub. The water closet, the ancestor to the modern toilet (still called a water closet by some), was invented in England in the mid-1800s and was refined with varying success into the early 1900s.

As indoor plumbing and water-heating devices evolved, the activities of washing and toileting came together in a single room in the American home, often called the bathroom. New grand houses of the late 1800s often boasted large, elaborate bathrooms with plumbing fixtures encased in decorative wood cabinets. In older homes of the day, bathrooms were often added through renovation of existing rooms such as smaller bedrooms and storage rooms. Figure 6-1 is a photograph of the interior of a plumbing fixtures shop taken in 1890.

In 1927, Kohler introduced bathroom sets—a bathtub, toilet, and lavatory—in matching colors. The matching set with various design options and available color choices was a step in the progression toward the myriad options available for the homeowner of today, such as that shown in Figure 6-2.

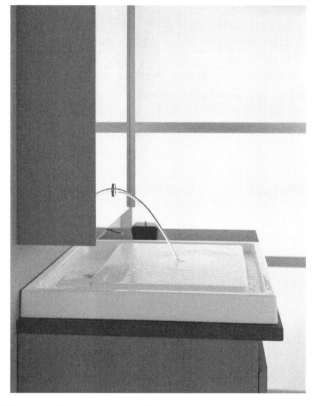

Figure 6-2 The Purist Lavatory by Kohler. Current manufacturers continue to develop inventive products such as this one to satisfy ongoing customer interest in new, innovative plumbing fixtures.

Photograph courtesy of Kohler Co.

Figure 6-1 Interior of a plumbing fixtures shop, 1890. This photograph shows some of the many plumbing fixtures available in the late 1800s and indicates consumer interest in the most up-to-date fixtures of the day.

Photograph courtesy of the Minnesota Historical Society.

According to the National Association of Home Builders (NAHB), 96 percent of American houses of the 1950s included one and a half bathrooms or fewer, whereas "the proportion of single-family homes with 1 or 1½ bathrooms has been below 10 percent for more than a decade."

The number of bathrooms has proliferated in quantity in our homes over time because many homeowners preferred a bathroom for each bedroom or, at the very least, an owner's suite with bathroom, a youngster's and/ or overnight guest's bathroom, and a partial bathroom (often called a powder room). With the economic downturn and increasing interest in sustainability, homeowners have begun to look for ways to create efficient and useful bathrooms—a search for quality over quantity.

This trend toward economy and quality of design was given voice by Sarah Susanka in her writing on residential design. In her book *The Not So Big House*, Susanka urges homeowners to reduce the number of bathrooms and to consider "which bathrooms can be shared." Susanka states that most master baths are "typically more an expression of fantasy than reality. With its whirlpool or soaking tub, the master bath implies a life of leisure and relaxation. Susanka continues by stating that for some families, a large shared bathroom makes sense, while for others, a private bathing sanctuary for adults is best.

Susanka's plea for well-thought-out bathrooms, those that fit with the reality of daily living, makes sense given the fact that building and outfitting bathrooms is expensive and can lead to a significant use of natural resources, not only in the fabrication of fixtures but also in the use of water, electricity, and natural gas. Issues of sustainability, cost, and use of space should be considered relative to the real needs of the family as bathrooms are designed.

A single well-designed bathroom can provide much of the privacy and comfort provided by two—or more—poorly considered bathrooms. Designing the bathroom to contain private chambers for differing activities, allowing more than one person to use the bathroom area at the same time, is a useful approach for lessening the overall number of bathrooms per home. For example, separating the sink area and/ or the bathing area from the toilet area allows one person to bathe or groom him- or herself while another person can use the toilet privately. Figure 6-3a illustrates a bathroom design that allows privacy for only one person. Figure 6-3b illustrates a bathroom design that provides private areas for more than one user.

Efficiency in terms of fixture location is another key bathroom planning consideration. The fixtures used most often are, in order: 1, sink; 2, toilet; and 3, bath/shower. Placing these fixtures so that the two most commonly used fixtures (sink and toilet) are most easily accessed upon entering the

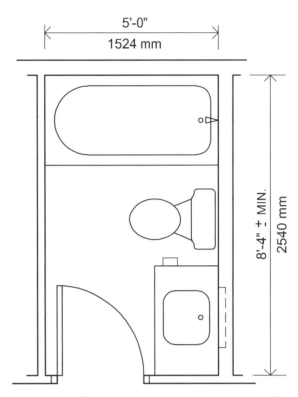

Figure 6-3a A plan of a commonly used single-wall bathroom design, which allows privacy for one user only.

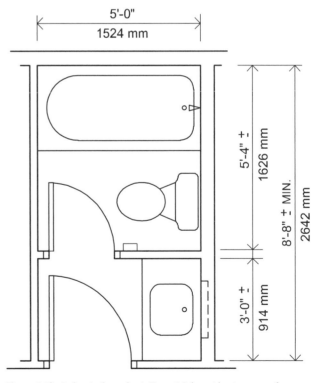

Figure 6-3b A plan similar to that in Figure 6-3, but with private areas for more than one user. This plan can be seen as providing almost the same level of privacy as two bathrooms in a far more economical manner.

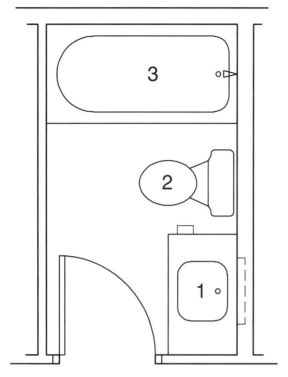

Figure 6-3c The fixtures used most often are, in order: 1, sink; 2, toilet; and 3, bath/shower. Placing these fixtures so that the most commonly used fixtures (sink and toilet) are most easily accessed upon entering the room is ideal; see the "Organizational Flow" section for additional information about fixture placement.

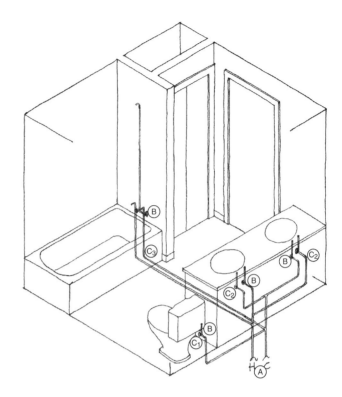

Figure 6-4 Bathroom supply pipes.

A. Water supply pipes can be fed from below or above and must be kept out of unheated spaces in areas subject to freezing.
B. Each fixture requires a shutoff valve for each line (hot and cold). This facilitates the repair or removal of the fixture or faucet.
C. Pipe sizes (branch lines to individual fixtures).
  C_1, Toilet (WC)—$\frac{3}{8}$ inch to $\frac{1}{2}$ inch (9.525 to 12.7 mm). See manufacturer's recommendations.
  C_2, Lavatories—$\frac{3}{8}$ inch (9.525 mm). See manufacturer's recommendations.
  C_3, Tub/shower—$\frac{1}{2}$ inch (12.7 mm).

Water supply pipes fabricated of copper will meet most codes. Certain plastics will also meet some codes. Check local codes for clarification.

room is worthwhile (see Figure 6-3c). While there is certainly room for variation in fixture location, ease of use and access should be considered in bathroom fixture layout and is covered in detail in the "Organizational Flow" section of this chapter.

In addition to considerations of privacy and efficiency of use, bathroom design is constrained by the basic nature of plumbing and the size and form of plumbing fixtures. All plumbing fixtures require water *supply lines*, or pipes, as well as drainpipes. The toilet requires a larger drainpipe known as a *soil pipe*. A network is formed as the independent branch drainpipes of other fixtures also lead to the soil pipe (also called a *soil stack*), and it is this larger pipe that leads sewage and wastewater out of the building.

The branch lines and soil pipes work using gravity and therefore require downward slopes (as called for in codes) for positive flow. In addition, the drainage system requires *venting*, which is generally supplied by an upward-rising vent line or pipe ultimately extending through the roof. Because the water supply system is under pressure, a continuous downward slope is not required by code. However, use of a continuous slope will facilitate the draining of the entire system, which is helpful in the prevention of frozen pipes in unoccupied

homes. Figure 6-4 illustrates the water supply pipes in a standard bathroom, and Figure 6-5 illustrates the drainage pipes in a standard bathroom.

Understanding the basics of bathroom plumbing is helpful as a means of understanding the interrelationships of fixtures and drains. Each wall that contains a plumbing fixture is considered a plumbing wall, and minimizing the number of these plumbed walls per bathroom can save money. However, the overall ease of use and creation of privacy zones must be considered as equally important—if not more important—than the simple economy of minimizing plumbing walls. Bathroom design requires a consideration of the best layout of space and fixtures for the given client and project, balanced with a careful look at the economy of plumbed walls.

Figure 6-5 Bathroom drainage pipes. Important rules of plumbing related to the waste system include the need to *trap all drains* and *vent all traps*. Wastewater must be trapped to prevent reentry of sewer gas, as methane can be lethal. There is no trap shown at the toilet because the fixture itself is shaped to form the trap. All traps must be vented in order to vent gas and to prevent siphoning action from pulling all of the wastewater out of the trap at times when a large quantity is released.

A. Vent stack—goes through roof. When possible, it is combined with plumbing vent pipes from other parts of the house to minimize the number of penetrations through the roof.

B. Soil stack—goes to house sewer line; 3 to 4 inches (76 to 102 mm) in size, depending on how many fixtures drain into it.

C. House sewer line with cleanout (known as C.O., shown in C_1). House sewer line runs to a municipal sanitary sewer main, most often in the street, or to an on-site private waste disposal system (septic tank and drain field).

D. All horizontal waste pipes slope 1 to 2 percent. Size (diameter of pipe) is dependent on length of run, number of fixtures serviced by the line, type, and distance from trap to vent. As shown:
D_1. Tub—2 inches (51 mm).
D_2. Lavatories—1½ inches (38 mm).
D_3. Toilet—3 inches (76 mm).

Waste pipes are most often polyvinyl chloride (PVC) plastic; however, some local codes may still require that certain pipes be cast iron, such as the house sewer line and possibly soil and vent stacks.

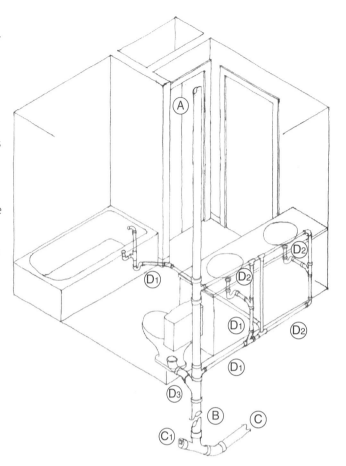

ACCESSIBILITY NOTE

Bathrooms have significant potential to create barriers for people with disabilities. Individuals using wheelchairs or with other mobility issues can be kept from using bathrooms designed with standard fixtures and standard clearances. As noted in Chapter 1, standards such as American National Standards Institute (ANSI) A117.1 and Uniform Federal Accessibility Standards (UFAS), as well as Fair Housing Amendments Act of 1988 (FHAA) legislation, govern privately owned multifamily housing units. In addition, some municipalities are governed by local visitability codes and/or guidelines, which require, at minimum, a ground-floor bathroom consisting of a toilet and sink that can be entered and used by a person using a wheelchair.

Although the Americans with Disabilities Act (ADA) covers public restroom design in detail, this legislation does not create guidelines for private residences. Some designers and students use the ADA guidelines as a default design standard for residential bathroom design, but doing this does not necessarily result in the best solution for a given client or situation. This is because the ADA

guidelines are meant to serve as a standard for a wide range of individuals, whereas the design of private residences often requires special features designed for a particular client. For example, some homeowners require the use of personal aides and/or equipment for toileting and bathing, which will result in the need for clearance space not covered in the ADA guidelines.

Some advocates for the disabled argue that by creating residences that meet basic accessibility requirements for bathrooms (and other areas), designers not only serve the immediate need of wheelchair users in their homes but also serve the future needs of an aging population. In addition to accessibility, designers should be aware of adaptability—those design features that can be changed to serve wheelchair users, such as removable vanity doors and toe kicks that can accommodate wheelchair users.

With these considerations in mind, this chapter includes a discussion of accessibility as it relates to bathroom fixtures, clearances, maneuvering spaces, and grab bar placement.

FIXTURES

Because of the specialized nature of the various bathroom plumbing fixtures, it is important to understand each type of fixture in terms of size, construction, use, and required clearances, as well as issues of accessibility related to each fixture. The following is a review of the most commonly used fixtures.

Sustainability Note

This discussion of toilet systems is important because the type of system selected significantly affects the convenience, noise, and water use of the toilet. The amount of water used by toilets varies a great deal based on the number of gallons consumed for each flush. According to the U.S. Department of Energy, "toilet flushing accounts for 45 percent of indoor water use, or approximately 32,000 gallons (121,133 L) per year for a family of four. . . . By law, replacement or new construction toilets are restricted to flush a maximum of 1.6 gallons [6 L] rather than the 3.5 to 5 [13 to 19 L] or more gallons used by older toilets." In addition to conserving water, this reduction does a great deal toward reducing the amount of energy used to pump and treat water.

Another option in terms of reducing water use is the dual-flush toilet. Dual-flush toilets operate with two water use settings: a full 1.6-gallon (6-L) flush for solids and a reduced-volume flush, often 0.8 to 1.1 gallons (3 to 4 L) for liquids only. Although new to North America, the dual-flush concept has been used in other parts of the world for quite some time. Some dual-flush models use tank-based power assistance, while others employ a gravity tank and "wash-down" bowl type, which washes the waste directly down a larger trapway, pushing it out, instead of using siphonic action. Wash-down-type toilets have not been widely used in North America because they have been seen as requiring more frequent cleaning of the toilet bowl. A few manufacturers now make dual-flush toilets for use in the American market.

Toilets

Toilets are made with flush tanks or flush valves. Those with flush valves are generally used in institutional applications because they require a larger water supply line. Most residential toilets are of the flush tank type, and these are available with integral tanks (one-piece), as well as the more common separate tank (two-piece) type. See Figures 6-6a and 6-6b.

In North America, the most common residential toilets use siphonic action created in the trapway. This "pulls" the waste from the bowl. Reverse-trap toilets introduce water only through the rim, whereas others known as siphon jet types

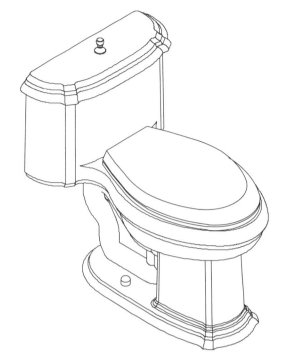

Figure 6-6a An integral (one-piece) toilet.
Image courtesy of Kohler Co.

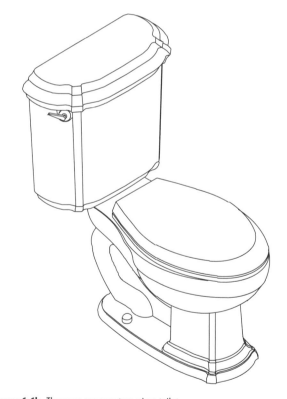

Figure 6-6b The more common two-piece toilet.
Image courtesy of Kohler Co.

employ siphon jets in addition to the rim action. In residences, gravity flush tanks are most commonly used; however, there are also pressure and power-assisted toilets that provide powerful flushing action with less water use.

In addition to the variety of tank types and flushing systems mentioned, toilets are available in a range of finishes, colors, and styles, from old-fashioned to sleek and minimalist in appearance. Toilets are most commonly available in round bowl or elongated bowl styles; many people consider the elongated bowl style to be the most comfortable. Toilet seats are available in a range of shapes to fit the various types of bowls. See Figure 6-7 for typical toilet sizes.

Urinals

While urinals are most commonly found in commercial applications, there are reasons to consider using them in a residential setting. Urinals use less water than toilets and can be quite convenient as well. Used by males, urinals are receptacles attached and plumbed to the wall. Those models used in residential settings are directed to flush using a push button, whereas many commercial models have an automatic sensor that flushes them after a number of uses. Because they are wall mounted, urinal-mounting height can vary. Some urinals are fitted with a sanitary lid, making them more appealing for some residential users. Figure 6-7 includes dimensions for urinals.

STANDARD TOILETS   URINALS   BIDETS

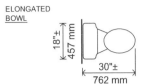

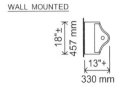

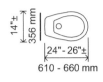

Figure 6-7 Toilet, urinal, and bidet sizes.

Bidets

Bidets are washbasins used for partial bathing more common in Europe than in North America. Typically, the user sits astride the bowl facing the faucets to control water flow. Models are available with vertical or horizontal spray for water flow. Often bidets are manufactured in styles, colors, and finishes that are similar to toilets so that the two can appear to be a matching set. See Figure 6-7 for typical bidet dimensions. There are also bidet functions incorporated into some toilets, as well as add-on kits that outfit standard toilets with a bidet-like water spray.

ACCESSIBILITY NOTE

Standard toilet height is roughly 15 to 16 inches (318 to 406 mm) above the floor. However, there are toilets with higher seats available, allowing for greater ease of movement onto and off of the seat. In addition, devices are available that boost standard seat height by 5 inches (127 mm) or more for those users who have significant difficulty sitting or bending.

It is worth noting that the ADA calls for accessible toilet seats to be 17 to 19 inches (432 to 483 mm) to the top of the seat. However, as noted previously, single-family homes are not required to meet ADA guidelines and meeting the ADA guidelines does not necessarily accommodate a range of users in a way that could be seen as universal. In some rehabilitation settings, a seat as high as 20 inches (508 mm) may be used because it is similar to wheelchair seat height; however, this can cause some people's feet to dangle and can also lead to problems with balance. While 18 inches (457 mm) is seen as a compromise to the 17- to 19-inch (432- to 483-mm) standard set by the ADA, a height of 19 inches (483 mm) can prove better for those who have difficulty bending. Clearly, a bathroom designed for a specific client requires consideration of that particular person's limitations and

stature. In addition, when planning accessible bathrooms, designers must also give careful thought to general floor clearance spaces at the toilet and other fixtures. More information about clearances is provided later in this chapter.

In order to allow for wheelchair transfers and to provide stability, grab bars are required when toilet areas are designed for use by those with physical limitations and disabilities. Grab bars come in a wide variety of shapes and configurations in order to accommodate a range of needs; horizontal, vertical, diagonal, and pivoting (or swing-away) grab bars can all be useful, depending on the needs of the individual. Figures 6-8a to 6-8c show the types of grab bars used at toilet and other locations.

Vertical and diagonal grab bars are useful for pulling from a seated position to a standing position (and in moving into the seated position from the standing position) and therefore can be useful for some ambulatory people. According to the Center for Inclusive Design and Environmental Access (IDEA Center), however, vertical bars are "not as useful for preventing a fall or transferring to a wheelchair. They are also more difficult to use for stabilization. The horizontal bar provides the greatest safety."

Figure 6-8a A range of grab bars made by Hewi, including a swing-away or pivoting grab bar (foreground) as well as a collection of horizontal bars and one rather short vertical bar (not for use at the toilet).

Photograph courtesy of Häfele America.

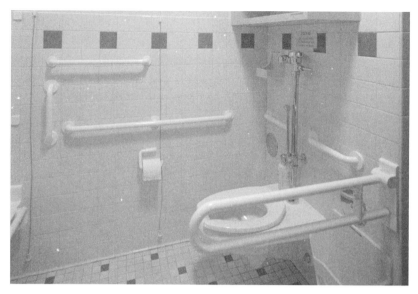

Figure 6-8b A bar similar to that shown in Figure 6-8c in use.

Photograph courtesy of Häfele America.

Pivoting bars can be helpful in assisting semiambulatory people and can be moved out of the way as needed. They are also useful in situations where an assistant aides in transferring, as they move out of the way as needed. However, pivoting bars can prove to be an obstacle to those using wheelchairs, so their use requires careful thought. Bars attached directly to toilets seats can be helpful for some, yet they do not project beyond the toilet seat and are most often mounted too low to easily facilitate a transfer. For additional information about the placement and location of grab bars, see the "Ergonomics and Required Clearances" section of this chapter.

Figure 6-8c A short horizontal bar that serves as an aid in balance; this bar does not meet ANSI standards but works to steady the user and is helpful for some people.

Photograph courtesy of Häfele America.

Sinks (Also Known as Lavatories)

Sinks (also called lavatories) are currently available in a range of shapes, colors, and styles. Porcelain over steel, enameled cast iron, as well as vitreous china, stainless steel, glass, and other materials, are currently used for sink fabrication. Shapes range from oval and round to square, rectilinear, and triangular (used in corner locations).

Lavatories can be wall hung, supported by pedestals, or placed into countertops—often as part of a vanity or storage cabinet. Of the countertop variety, there are several mounting types, in which the sink "mates" to the countertop in a different way. Types include self-rimming, rimless, undermount, counter-over, tile-in, and integral. Often the choice of countertop material and overall design determine the mounting style used.

Self-rimming sinks have a rim or lip that fits over the top surface of the counter. This type works well in countertops made

of plastic laminate, granite, marble, and solid wood and can also be used over tile. Self-rimming sinks are readily available in many styles, colors, and materials. The rim prevents this type of sink from allowing water to be drawn back into the sink bowl, which can cause water and soil to collect at the point where the rim meets the countertop and can be difficult to clean. See Figure 6-9a.

Rimless sink mounting requires the use of a separate mounting rim and clips attached below the countertop, which hold the sink in place. This mounting type works well with plastic laminate countertops. Much like the self-rimming sink, the edges of this type can be difficult to keep clean.

Undercounter sinks attach to the bottom surface of the countertop. They're often used with solid-surface counters and are also used with various stone countertops. Typically, the countertop is cut so that it overhangs the sink, making for easy

Figure 6-9a Self-rimming sink.
Photograph courtesy of Kohler Co.

The mounting styles mentioned previously are all simply methods of mating the sink to the countertop. Other types of sinks are also available, such as pedestal, wall hung, and vessel. Pedestal sinks consist of a sink bowl that sits atop a pedestal base, which conceals supply and drain lines. Because they do not offer the storage found in sinks mounted in countertops or vanities, pedestal sinks are often used in powder rooms or are accompanied by adjacent shelves or some other storage device for holding toiletries and personal items. See Figure 6-10.

Wall-hung (also known as wall-mounted) sinks feature a basin that is hung from the wall at a desired height. The drainpipe and supply lines are usually exposed on wall-mounted fixtures. However, some feature a matching cover placed beneath the basin to conceal the piping and to protect the legs of those using wheelchairs. See Figure 6-11.

Like pedestal sinks, most wall-hung models provide very limited space for storage of toiletries and personal items. Adjacent shelves, built-in wall storage, medicine chests, and other storage devices can help eliminate clutter. In addition, some wall-hung models contain ledges to the side of the sink bowls, which can allow for very limited storage. Console table models are also available. These have legs that help support the unit and create a visual impression different from that of a wall-hung unit.

Vessel sinks are bowl-like basins that generally sit atop a counter or deck, exposing the full body of the bowl form. Vessel sinks often rest atop a counter that appears more like a tabletop than a traditional bathroom vanity countertop. Some vessel

cleanup, as water and debris can be washed directly from the counter surface into the sink bowl. See Figure 6-9b.

Counter-over sinks have a lip that fits under the countertop yet on top of the counter's base material (often plywood, cement board, or particleboard). This type of sink works well when the countertop itself is made of an uneven material such as tile. In such cases, the tile often goes from the countertop surface directly over the sink's rim. The tile setter generally does this after the sink has been mounted.

Various manufacturers and craftspeople produce countertops with integral sinks. Synthetic marble, various solid surfaces, concrete, terrazzo, stainless steel, and stone slabs can be fabricated to create a counter in which the sink is one with the counter surface.

Some manufacturers produce sinks known as tile-in sinks. These sinks allow tile to be taken flush to the edge of the sink. This type of sink does not typically require tile trim pieces to serve as a transition from the tile to the sink edge, allowing for a wide range of tiles to be used on the counter surface, as shown in Figure 6-9c.

Figure 6-9b Undercounter sink.
Photograph courtesy of Kohler Co.

Figure 6-9c Tile-in sink.

Photograph courtesy of Kohler Co

Figure 6-10 Pedestal sink.

Photograph courtesy of Kohler Co.

Figure 6-11 Wall-mounted sink.

Photograph courtesy of Kohler Co.

sinks are placed on a single-layer deck surface made of glass, wood, or stone and attached at the wall. Some vessel sinks can be used as wall mounts supported by rods or brackets. Although beautiful and interesting, such installations are not the most sturdy, easy to maintain, or long-lasting sink selections. See Figure 6-12.

Many vessel sinks are rather tall and require faucets that reach well past the vessel rim. Certain vessel sinks may be used in undercounter applications, while others can be used as self-rimming sinks when inset into the countertop surface. Figures 6-13a and 6-13b illustrate a range of sink types and sizes.

ACCESSIBILITY NOTE

Wall-mounted sinks are a good choice for use by those in wheelchairs, as they allow for chair clearance directly under the sink, easing access to the sink bowl, faucet, and controls. This type of sink is also excellent for use by small children because of the ease of access to the sink bowl and the flexible mounting height. See Figure 6-11. Other types of sinks, such as those shown in Figures 6-9a to 6-9c, can also work well for those in wheelchairs, but the sinks must be set into countertops that allow the chair clear access to roll under the sink.

Figure 6-12 Vessel sink.
Photograph courtesy of Kohler Co.

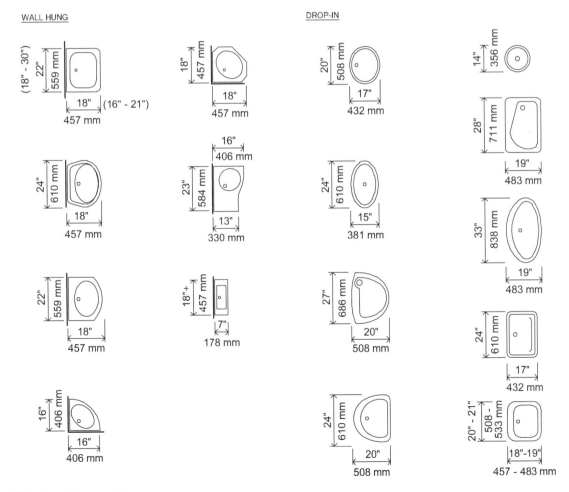

WALL HUNG

DROP-IN

Figure 6-13a Some sink types and sizes.

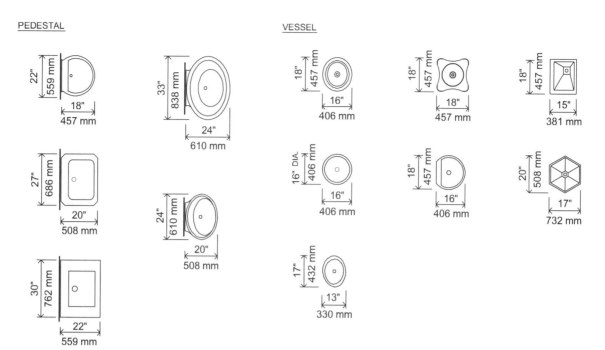

PEDESTAL   VESSEL

Figure 6-13b Some sink types and sizes.

Faucets

Sink selection requires consideration of faucet selection because the two elements must be compatible. Faucets come in a vast range of styles and finishes. Additionally, the types of faucets available include two-handled and single-handled models. Two-handled faucets require sinks with the appropriate number of holes. These are drilled with a distance of 4, 8, or 12 inches (102, 203, or 305 mm) between the hot and cold faucet handles. Single-handled faucets require that the sink be drilled with a single hole as well as possible mounting holes.

Sinks that do not have faucet holes are also available. In this type of sink, the faucet is mounted directly on the countertop or to the wall. Vessel sinks rarely have predrilled holes, thereby requiring that faucets be mounted outside of the vessel, in walls or countertops. Wall-mounted faucet pipes typically must be installed before drywall is installed. Therefore, the decision to use them must occur early.

ACCESSIBILITY NOTE

The designer must seriously consider the selection of lavatory faucets when designing bathrooms for use by individuals with disabilities, the elderly, and small children. According to the Center for Universal Design, faucet options available for universal accessibility include faucets with single-control levers, crosses, or loops (in place of other handle styles); faucets with nonslip textures; faucets with easy-to-control flow rate and/or temperature; pedal-operated options; faucets with motion-sensing activation; and side-mounted options.

The Center for Independent Living describes single-lever faucet handles as the best choice for bathroom use, as does the IDEA Center. These suggestions are in keeping with the ADA, which does not apply to single-family dwellings but which requires that "operable parts shall be operable with one hand and shall not require tight grasping, pinching, or twisting of the wrist. The force required to activate operable parts shall be 5 pounds (22.2N) maximum" (Section 309.4).

Bathtubs

Bathtubs are available in many shapes and installation types and in a range of materials and can be surrounded by various interior finish materials. Tub materials include fiberglass, acrylic, enameled cast iron, and enameled steel. In addition, soft tubs made of polyurethane foam over fiberglass can be used for comfort and safety for individuals with special needs. Installation types include built-in and freestanding tubs.

Built-in units include the alcove-type tub, the most common type of bathtub in the United States. This type is enclosed on three sides, with only the front exposed, as shown in Figure 6-14a. Because there are fewer finished surfaces, these models tend to be more economically priced than other installation types. This type of tub is specified as left-hand or right-hand, terms describing the drain location as one faces the tub. Alcove-type tubs are also the most common installation types used in tub/shower combinations, which are covered in more detail in the "Showers" section later in this chapter. Most alcove units employ wall-mounted faucets with waste and overflow

Figure 6-14a Alcove bathtub. This type of tub is most often set in an alcove of full-height walls, rather than as shown here.

Photograph courtesy of Kohler Co.

framing and decking conceal the plumbing pipes, drop-in tubs may be expensive or difficult to service, especially if access to the plumbing has not been considered by the designer. Undermount installations are also possible.

Freestanding tubs come in a range of styles, from the iconic claw-foot tubs to pedestal-supported models to those that sit on an exposed frame. See Figure 6-14c. These tubs typically sit independently, often with exposed pipes that are easy to service. Most American models come with holes drilled for faucets, drain, and overflow. European models do not have faucet holes drilled into the tub but do have drilled drain and overflow holes. This design allows for deeper filling levels. Such models with no faucet drilling require freestanding water pipes and faucets or wall-mounted faucets.

A pedestal tub is a freestanding type that rests on a base rather than sitting up on feet, giving them a more contemporary,

mounted within the tub. Alcove models can be purchased with matching shower doors. Shower doors may also be purchased separately. More information regarding shower doors can be found later in this chapter.

Another built-in bathtub variety is the drop-in installation type, mounted much like sinks are installed in countertops. The tub is mounted to a deck area that is framed independently. Because of the cost of framing and finishing the deck area, this type of installation is generally more costly than alcove models. In such installations, tubs can be undermounted or self-rimming in a manner similar to sinks. See Figure 6-14b.

Drop-in models may also be installed in walled alcoves similarly to alcove models; however, with drop-in models, a supporting frame and deck must be constructed. Occasionally, drop-in models are installed in a floor-mounted sunken application, which requires space below the floor area and can be very difficult for a bather to get out of. Because the tub

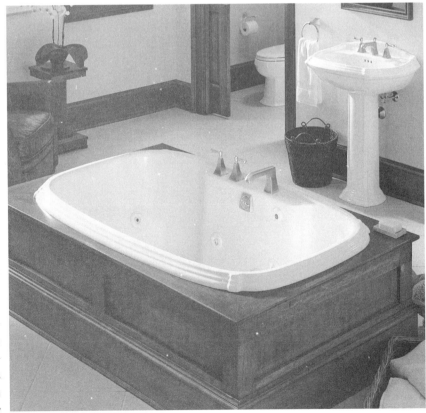

Figure 6-14b Drop-in bathtub.

Photograph courtesy of Kohler Co.

Figure 6-14c Freestanding bathtub; this is an example of an iconic claw-foot tub.

Photograph courtesy of Kohler Co.

sculpted look. Most of these tubs do not have faucet drilling—floor- or wall-mounted faucets are used with these tubs. In some cases, the pedestal tub rests on a base that is custom-made for the client. Wood or another appropriate material can be used for such bases. Some manufacturers are producing freestanding tubs that rest on an exposed framework. In most

cases, these are pedestal-type tubs resting on an exposed wood frame rather than an oval pedestal. It is possible to integrate a shower function using a freestanding tub. This is done through the use of both handheld showerheads and/or freestanding shower-height units, which generally require a shower curtain.

The installation types mentioned are available in various sizes and shapes. The most common bathtub size in American homes is 5 feet (1524 mm) in length. Yet tubs are available that are only 4 feet (1219 mm) long and others more than 6 feet (1829 mm) long. A standard American bathtub height is 14 to 17 inches (356 to 432 mm), with European tubs at 18 inches (457 mm). For a range of bathtub sizes and shapes, see Figure 6-15.

Soaking and Whirlpool Tubs

A soaking tub is typically a bathtub constructed in a manner that allows the bather to sit in an upright position and immerse his or her body more fully than in a standard tub, as illustrated in Figure 6-16a. Japanese and Greek baths both provide an extra-deep basin for soaking and are available in a range of sizes and materials at heights from 22 to 32 inches (559 to 813 mm). These are also available in lengths shorter than standard bathtubs.

A whirlpool is a type of soaking tub fitted with pipes, an electric pump, water jets, and, frequently, a booster and heater. The pump is used to circulate water through the pipes, using several water jets, as shown in Figure 6-16b. Pumps must be installed

Figure 6-15 Bathtub types and sizes.

1. The most common bathtub size (in the United States) is 30 by 60 inches (762 by 1524 mm).

STANDARD ALCOVE AND DROP-IN TUBS

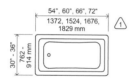

FREESTANDING

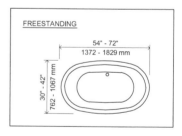

LARGER AND UNUSUAL SHAPED ALCOVE AND DROP-IN TUBS

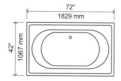
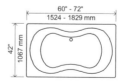
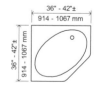

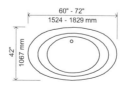

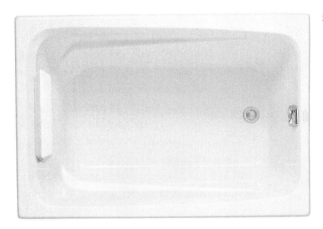

Figure 6-16a A soaking or "Greek" tub meant for an upright sitting position while soaking.
Photograph courtesy of Kohler Co.

Figure 6-16b A whirlpool tub.
Photograph courtesy of Kohler Co.

in a location that allows access. Whirlpool tubs are available in alcove and drop-in models in standard 5-foot (1524-mm) and much larger sizes, as well as in a range of shapes. Five-foot (1524-mm) standard alcove models tend to be less expensive and can work as retrofits in existing rooms (as long as there is appropriate clearance in doorways).

Drop-in whirlpools are generally installed in an elevated deck and placed against a wall or corner or out in the open. Full whirlpools with occupant(s) can weigh as much as 1500 pounds (680 kg), requiring extra floor support. Larger whirlpools can require oversized hot water heaters. Whirlpools can be difficult to enter and exit. For this reason, it is helpful to have

GREEK AND JAPANESE SOAKING TUBS

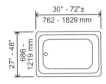

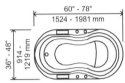

WHIRLPOOLS

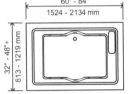

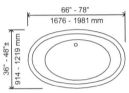

Figure 6-17 Soaking and whirlpool types and sizes.

homeowners sit in the tubs prior to purchase (this can be true of showers as well). See Figure 6-17 for sizes of soaking tubs and whirlpools.

ACCESSIBILITY NOTE

Bathtub accessibility is highly dependent on the specific needs of the individual client. When considering accessibility, the designer must assess current and future needs as well as a client's possible interest in visitability. For example, a particular homeowner may require the assistance of a caregiver in bathing as well as a hydraulic or mechanical lift, resulting in the need for clearance room for the caregiver, the bather, and the lift. Therefore, an understanding of the current and future needs of the given client is essential, rather than simply meeting ADAAG (Americans with Disability Act Accessibility Guidelines) or ANSI standards as a default position for creating an accessible bath.

Generally speaking, standard bathtubs present a series of obstacles to anyone except the average adult in possession of a good range of motion and strength. Entering a tub, bending to recline, and then standing to exit the tub create a situation in which individuals with limited range of motion and flexibility, as well as other mobility issues,

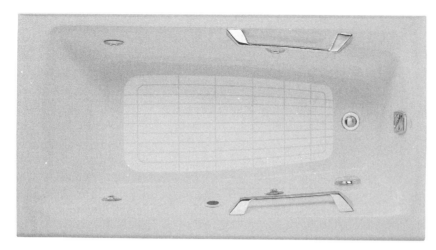

Figure 6-18a Bathtub with integral handles for ease of entry and exit (this type is not ideal for use by wheelchair users).

Photo courtesy of Kohler Co.

but they do provide the experience of soaking in a tub for those that can use them. In addition to walk-in types, soft bathtubs, covered in polyurethane foam, can be useful for individuals with limited mobility and issues with balance, as they provide a cushioned and more comfortable tub area.

Some people with disabilities related to mobility can use standard bathtubs that are fitted with a fixed seat, grab bars, nonslip surfaces, and handheld shower sprays. Use of a tub with these fittings is highly dependent on the nature of the disability, and individual needs should be considered when opting for use of a bathtub. As previously mentioned, for many individuals using a wheelchair, a shower unit is the best choice for bathing. Additional information about accessible showers can be found in subsequent sections of this chapter.

are not well served by a standard tub. Many people benefit from tub designs that include integral handles or rails for entering and exiting the tub (see Figure 6-18a), whereas others require more extensive solutions to problems of balance, strength, and mobility. If wall-mounted grab bars are required, an alcove-type setting is often best, as it offers walls for bar placement.

The IDEA Center has stated that a **shower stall is preferred over a tub**; however, the center does list ways in which a tub can serve a more universal population. These are the inclusion of a "seat; structural reinforcement for grab bars; controls mounted near the entry side of head wall; 30-in. by 60-in. (762- by 1524-mm) minimum clear floor space; hand-held shower spray." If grab bars are required, they should be provided at both ends of the tub together with two bars of different heights along the side of the tub. It is worth noting that there are various color and material options available to the designer when selecting and specifying grab bars. Homeowners are not limited to stainless steel or chrome. For homeowners with limited vision, grab bars of contrasting colors may prove helpful. Figure 6-18b shows a production, one-piece bathtub/shower module with a transfer seat and grab bars. Additional information about clearances and grab bar placement can be found in the next section.

Some manufacturers produce *walk-in* bathtubs with an actual door that opens into the tub and then seals upon closing, allowing the bather to enter without climbing into the tub. Such models are often equipped with whirlpools and are most often available as alcove models. Walk-in tubs are not ideal for all individuals using a wheelchair,

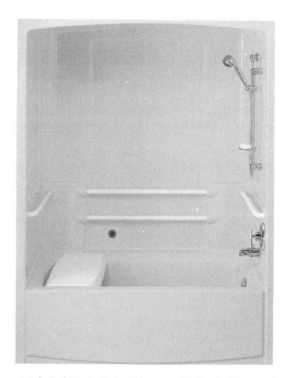

Figure 6-18b Prefabricated bathtub/shower module for wheelchair transfer with a seat, multiple grab bars, handheld shower spray, and controls mounted near the entry side of head wall. Many users prefer the addition of a vertical grab bar at the control side of tub. *Note:* Showers are generally the best option for wheelchair users.

Photograph courtesy of Kohler Co.

Sustainability Note

Baths versus Showers, Faucets, and Water Use

The conventional wisdom holds that taking a shower uses less water than taking a tub bath. However, variation in tub size and type/quantity of showerhead used affects water use greatly. Larger bathtubs hold more than 70 gallons (265 L), while standard tubs hold about 50 gallons (189 L).

Water flow in showerheads is rated in gallons per minute (gpm); flow is also affected by water pressure, which is measured in pounds per square inch (psi). Standards for low-flow showerheads are set at 2.5 gpm at 80 psi; some showerheads deliver as little as 1.5 gpm.

Federal regulations mandate that showerhead flow rates cannot exceed 2.5 gpm at 80 psi. Furthermore, new faucet flow rates can't exceed 2.5 gpm at 80 psi or 2.2 gpm at 60 psi. This means it is illegal to sell products that exceed these flow rates. However, some showerheads are available that have removable restrictors, and multiple low-flow showerheads use much more water, as discussed in the next section. Therefore, taking long showers using noncompliant showerheads may not use less water than baths.

This discussion of water use is important in terms of water conservation as well as the conservation of energy required to heat bath and shower water.

Showers

Showers continue to be an item of interest for today's new homeowners and remodelers. There remains strong interest in large, open showers and showers for two. Other design trends include luxurious showers with multiple showerheads or shower towers. Multiple-head showers require appropriate water pressure and use a significant amount of hot water. According to Keidel's Planning Guide (an online guide), larger multiple-head showers require a dedicated water heater for the shower alone: "A dedicated 50-gallon hot water heater will supply a four-outlet custom shower for approximately 8 minutes (assuming showerheads are restricted and all are turned on for the entire duration). For best performance, one manufacturer (GROHE) recommends a 100-gallon water heater as a minimum." Because of the water used, drain capacity must also be considered with this type of shower.

While these luxury showers are popular, they use significant natural resources, including large amounts of water as well as energy to heat the water, and they impact municipal water systems. Many of the multiple-head showers go against recent trends in water conservation and are not of interest to homeowners with a commitment to water conservation or for use in locations with water use restrictions. However, there are some recirculation systems available that conserve water and some multiple-head showers that have conservation settings, such as the one shown in Figure 6-19.

Showers are available in two distinct types: prefabricated (also known as modular) and site-built. The prefabricated types are available as complete modules, which include the shower base and surrounding wall finishes. Of this type, some are multipiece units, in which the base, walls, and, in some cases, ceilings are separate entities, which are installed together to achieve a watertight seal and the visual appearance of one unified element. This type is ideal for remodeling, as the various components can be easily maneuvered and installed. See Figure 6-20a.

Other prefabricated units are manufactured as one piece, with walls, base, and sometimes a ceiling constructed as a single element, as shown in Figure 6-20b. These units are used in new construction more often than in remodeling. Both the multipiece and the one-piece units come with a range of options such as built-in seats, grab bars, and colors, and are available in fiberglass and acrylic. Both types are available in various sizes and shapes, with most designs fitting into an alcove configuration much like an alcove bathtub. The advantages of prefabricated

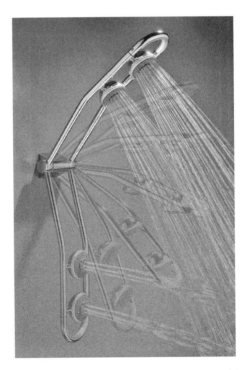

Figure 6-19 The Freehander Shower System by Grohe. This is one of the new shower systems that offer flexibility in the quantity of water used, allowing for water conservation when desired. The Freehander combines showerhead and body spread capabilities through the use of a pivoting arm and rotating showerheads and allows one head to be turned off in order to conserve water and energy.

Photograph courtesy of Grohe America.

Figure 6-20a Multipiece shower module. This type of shower module consists of separate pieces that are installed together. These work very well in remodeling situations, as they easily move through existing doors and other obstacles. This type is available in a range of sizes and styles. The version shown is a combination tub and shower module.

Photograph courtesy of Kohler Co.

as ceramic tile, and a glass shower enclosure and door are included to complete the shower. See Figures 6-21a to 6-21c.

Depending on size and design, most prefabricated shower units require a shower door, a curtain, or some form of screen, which works to keep adjacent areas dry. Glass shower doors are readily available in sliding or swing-type designs. Manufacturers make them in standard sizes for tub/shower combinations, as well as for prefabricated shower modules and receptors, and they are also commonly custom-designed for site-built showers. Shower manufacturers, glass suppliers, and art glass creators all supply glass shower enclosures. Shower screening devices need not be limited to glass. Metal, stone, some plastics, and acrylic can be put to use as interesting and innovative shower screen devices.

Site-built showers are those that are constructed without the use of prefabricated modules or receptors. This type of shower is not restricted by the size or shape limitations of prefabricated units, which results in the creation of highly customized designs such as walk-in showers and

showers can include lower installation costs and, in some cases, ease of maintenance.

Bathtub/shower combinations are available in both one-piece and multipiece units. Bathtub/shower combinations are more economical in terms of space and cost, yet they are being replaced in popularity by single baths or shower units as homes continue to increase in square footage.

Prefabricated shower bases (called receptors) are also available. This type of unit consists of the shower base only, with the surrounding walls and doors often treated in a manner similar to a site-built shower. These units are available in square, rectangular, and angled corner units (often called neo-angle units) in a range of sizes, with 3 by 3 feet (914 by 914 mm) being common. With this type of unit, the surrounding walls are often finished with an appropriate material such

Figure 6-20b A prefabricated shower/tub module. This type is also available in a range of sizes and finishes.

Photograph courtesy of Kohler Co.

Figure 6-22 Example of site-built shower.
Photograph courtesy of Kohler Co.

Figure 6-21a, 6-21b, and 6-21c. A range of receptor bases.
Photographs courtesy of Kohler Co.

shower rooms. Walk-in showers are those without a door and therefore must contain enough space so that splashing onto adjacent surfaces is not a problem. See Figure 6-22.

In most site-built showers, the shower floor is sloped $1/8$ inch per foot minimum (1 percent) and ¼ inch per foot maximum (2 percent). So, for example, in a shower stall measuring 5 by 5 feet (1524 by 1524 mm), a ¼ of an inch (6 mm) drop would fall in that range (example given assumes a center drain).

Creating such a slope requires a depressed area in the construction below the stall, or that the shower itself be raised above floor level and then sloped down to the drain. It also requires some form of step or ramped transition threshold at the entry to the shower.

In order to accommodate a perfectly flush transition (with no raised threshold) in homes with a wood floor structure, the area directly under the shower must contain a lower portion with shallower joists. Homes built on concrete slabs require a depressed area in the slab directly beneath the shower to accommodate the drain slope. This type of sloping shower floor is also used to create roll-in showers for use with wheelchairs. In such cases, a flush transition from bathroom floor to shower floor is desirable, as illustrated in Figure 6-22. In those cases where a flush transition is not possible, a ramped threshold or rubber threshold can be employed to allow wheelchair access. Figures 6-23a and 6-23b illustrate a range of shower types and sizes.

Water shutoff valves are required for all plumbing fixtures to facilitate the repair and maintenance of items such as faucets, showerheads, and toilet tanks, and access to the valves must be provided. Toilet shutoff valves are generally exposed under the tank. For tubs and showers, the valves are generally concealed, often by being placed in an adjacent closet or cabinet. In some cases, an access panel in a wall or floor may be required to access the valves.

Figure 6-23a Modular shower types and sizes.

1. 2-foot, 8-inch (813-mm) showers are under the recommended minimum; while available, they are not comfortable. The recommended minimum, 3 by 3 feet (914 by 914 mm), is the most common American shower size.

2. The most common American tub size is 2 feet, 6 inches by 5 feet (762 by 1524 mm).

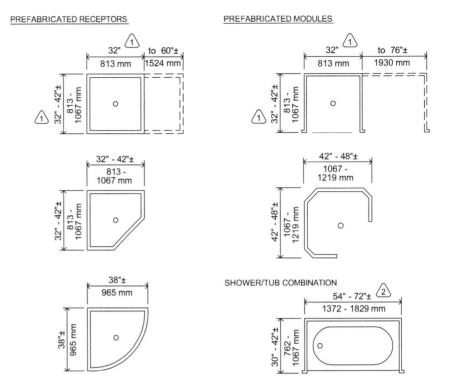

PREFABRICATED RECEPTORS

PREFABRICATED MODULES

SHOWER/TUB COMBINATION

SITE BUILT SHOWERS

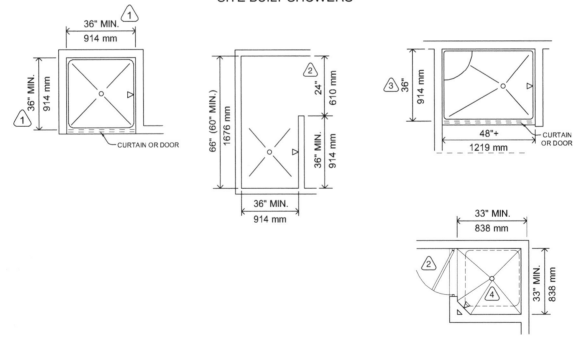

CURTAIN OR DOOR

CURTAIN OR DOOR

Figure 6-23b Site-built shower sizes. Note that sizes shown are minimums, and actual site-built showers can vary in terms of size and shape but should not be smaller than those shown.

1. Recommended minimum is 36 by 36 inches (914 by 914 mm), but 30 by 30 inches (762 by 762 mm) is a code minimum size for residential showers (IRC P2708.1).
2. Code door minimum door/doorway size for residential showers (IRC P2708.1) is 22 inches (559 mm); a larger door is recommended.
3. Code allows this dimension to be reduced to 25 inches (635 mm) if the total stall size is not less than 1300 square inches [0.84 m²] (IRC P2708.1). For example, a shower 25 by 52 inches (635 by 1320 mm) is larger than the minimum of 1300 square inches [.084 m²].
4. A small but useful shower design, providing elbow room inside the shower; well-placed controls, and spray is aimed away from door. Dashed line indicates code minimum of 30 by 30 inches (762 by 762 mm). While this design does not offer the ideal of having shower doors swing in to limit door dripping, it does offer a viable shower with a small footprint.

ACCESSIBILITY NOTE

As stated previously, the IDEA Center has described showers as preferable to tubs for wheelchair accessibility. The center describes two types of useful accessible shower stalls. A smaller stall, 3 by 3 feet (914 by 914 mm), called a *transfer stall*, allows for transfer to a shower seat from a wheelchair. The relatively small size can help users maintain balance and allows them to catch themselves should they fall. This type of shower requires a folding seat because a fixed seat can make the shower difficult for ambulatory users.

A larger 5-foot-long (1524-mm) type known as a *roll-in shower* has enough space to allow a wheelchair to roll directly into the stall, thus eliminating the need for a transfer seat (see Figure 6-36). The "Ergonomics and Required Clearances" section contains detailed information about the dimensional requirements and clearances required for wheelchair-accessible showers.

Although they take up more room, roll-in showers also create additional maneuvering space (within the shower) for people using wheelchairs, which can be helpful. In order to be fully accessible, roll-in showers must have a flush or very limited threshold, as mentioned previously in the discussion on site-built showers. Most prefabricated base and modular shower units have at least a slightly raised threshold; however, some manufacturers, such as Americh, produce a modular shower base with no raised threshold.

In some cases the ideal showers described above cannot be incorporated into a space; in those cases, the following minimums should be followed: showers intended for wheelchair use should have no wall on one side, or an opening of at least 32 inches (813 mm). They should also have a seat and grab bars located as indicated in the "Ergonomics and Required Clearances" section of this chapter.

Grab bars in showers are a necessity for those with mobility issues. In a smaller transfer stall, bars should be located on all sides except the seat side, as that would interfere with using the seat. In roll-in showers, grab bars on all sides are useful. Depending on the needs of the homeowner or the desire of the builder for adaptability, wall reinforcement placed during the initial construction or major remodeling at potential future grab bar locations is worth considering, as it may allow homeowners to stay in their homes if limited mobility becomes an issue in the future. More information on control locations and grab bar placement can be found in the next section.

It is also helpful to allow maneuvering room or additional clear space adjacent to the shower controls so that a wheelchair user can access the controls. This is illustrated in the following section.

In terms of accessibility, as mentioned, controls in tubs and showers should be single-lever types in order to be universally accessible. Pressure-balanced valves and hot water limiters or anti-scalding valves are necessary for users who are not able to move out of the way should the water become too hot.

When designing both tubs and showers for people with disabilities, the designer must carefully consider the controls. According to Marc Mendelsohn, a designer specializing in universal home design who founded the Bomarc Barrier Free Foundation, standard shower controls—those directly above a drain location—can present serious problems. Mendelsohn has stated:

If a person's in a wheelchair, they need to be able to turn the shower on and let it warm up before they get in. You can plumb a shower valve anywhere. We normally install it close to the edge of the shower so if the person is either left-handed or right-handed, they can turn it on and let it warm up.

STORAGE AND CABINETRY

Bathrooms require varied storage areas to house items that support the specialized activities taking place in the room. In planning bathroom storage, the designer should consider the various bathroom fixtures and activities related to their use and plan storage related to these activity areas. The sink, toilet, and shower/bathtub areas each require the use of specialized items, and housing these items requires a careful consideration of the use of each area.

The sink area requires storage for the following placed within close proximity to the sink when possible:

- Items used for washing hands and faces
- Items for shaving, brushing teeth, and brushing hair
- Items required for applying makeup
- First aid kit
- In some instances, items for washing infants or delicate garments
- Hand towels and washcloths

This is usually accomplished through the use of a vanity or some form of shelving directly adjacent to the sink and/or through the use of a medicine cabinet or some similar storage element. Other items, including medicines and toiletries that are used infrequently, may be housed in a storage area such as a linen closet, where an inventory of towels and washcloths may also be located.

Vanities are bathroom cabinets that most often contain sinks and faucets. The vanity is generally a smaller variation of the kitchen cabinet, available from many of the same manufacturers that produce kitchen cabinets. The design and fabrication of many vanities is similar to that of kitchen cabinets. Cabinet frames, doors, and drawers are available in the same styles, with the same methods of construction and generally the same materials, as kitchen cabinets. For further information on materials, construction, and detailing of stock cabinets, see Chapter 4.

While in many cases vanity construction is similar to that of kitchen cabinets, some of the heights and overall sizes vary, with bathroom vanities often being smaller and lower than kitchen cabinets. Standard vanity base dimensions range from 18 to 21 inches (457 to 533 mm) deep. Widths range from 12 to 72 inches (305 to 1829 mm). Those at 15 inches (381 mm) or less are not recommended for actual sink locations. This range in size is made available in 3-inch (76-mm) increments for units under 3 feet (914 mm) and 6-inch (152-mm) increments for units over 3 feet (914 mm).

Some vanities, which are currently popular, vary in terms of depth, with the sink located at the deepest portion of the vanity and storage areas located in narrow portions of the vanity. A vanity base that is a minimum of 24 inches (610 mm) wide is recommended for sink locations, as this size will accommodate most drop-in sinks. Figures 6-24a and 6-24b illustrate vanity construction and dimensions.

Standard vanity heights vary from 29 to 34 inches (737 to 864 mm)—with countertops adding to that height—with 32 inches (813 mm) perhaps the most common height. Interestingly, there is a current trend toward higher vanities. In addition, some clients benefit from a two-tiered vanity system, with one counter higher for the taller partner. These cases generally employ two sinks at the two heights. More common are two sink bowls provided at a consistent single height.

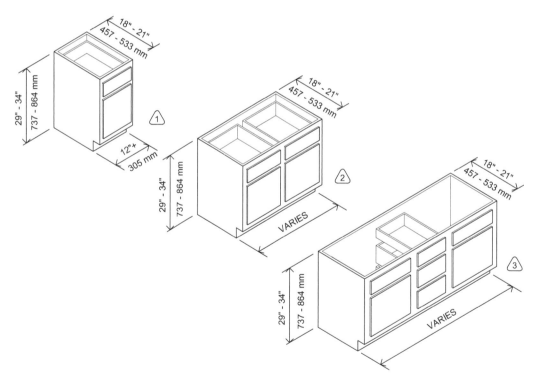

Figure 6-24a Standard vanity bases. These are available in depths of 18 to 21 inches (457 to 533 mm) and in widths of 12 to 72 inches (305 to 1829 mm). Corresponding counter depths are shown in Figure 6-26b. Standard base heights vary from 29 to 34 inches (737 to 864 mm), with the countertop material adding to this height. Additionally, some vanities with more than one sink range in height to accommodate users of varying heights (not shown).

1. While 12-inch (305-mm) cabinets are available, these are not wide enough to allow space for a sink. This single-door type is available in 3-inch (76-mm) increments from 12 to 24 inches (305 to 610 mm) and larger; however, single doors on units larger than 24 inches (610 mm) can become unwieldy.
2. Cabinets should be a minimum of 24 inches (610 mm) to allow for sink installation, which requires that top drawers be eliminated for at least a 24-inch (610-mm) width.
3. Drawer locations (as shown in the middle of this cabinet) do not allow space for a sink; sinks would be installed at either side of this cabinet. Sink mounting locations are illustrated in Figure 6-26b.

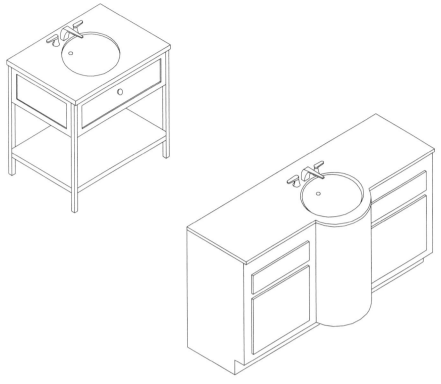

Figure 6-24b Additional vanity options include types like those shown at the left, which are more console-like and may rest on feet or legs rather than a traditional toe kick. Some vanity bases range in depth within the vanity; the areas containing sinks are deeper and storage locations are shallower, as shown at right. Sink mounting locations are illustrated in Figure 6-26b.

Regardless of height, a vanity with two sink bowls requires appropriate clearance for two sink users, which will be discussed further in the next section. It is worth noting that because sinks and their related plumbing lines occupy the space a drawer might use, sinks are not mounted directly over an operable drawer. Instead, doors or false drawer fronts are often mounted to the front of the bowl. Using furniture such as an antique dresser or chest and outfitting it with a sink and related plumbing is becoming a popular alternative to a standard vanity. Some manufacturers of furnishings and cabinetry are now producing vanities that appear more like antique, vintage, or contemporary home furniture pieces.

The toilet area requires far less storage than the sink area—at minimum a roll of toilet paper and one to serve as backup. Additional toilet paper and other similar items, as well as cleaning supplies, may be kept in the immediate toilet area, elsewhere in the room, or in a location outside the bathroom, such as a linen closet or supply pantry.

Storage for toilet area items may be located in a base cabinet, shelving unit, or some storage unit appropriate to the design of the space. Some homeowners prefer storage

for reading materials immediately adjacent to the toilet. When a bidet is included in a toilet area, storage should be provided for soap and towels immediately nearby at a convenient height for the user.

The shower and/or tub area requires conveniently placed towel storage as well as areas provided to hang clothing or robes for use as one dresses and undresses. Storage for shampoo, conditioners, and lotions should be provided as well. Many homeowners find a laundry hamper placed in this area useful.

According to the survey "What 21st Century Home Buyers Want," conducted by the NAHB, "A linen closet topped the list of desired bathroom features, with 88% of the respondents categorizing it as essential or desirable. Other desirable features included an exhaust fan (86%), separate shower enclosure (69%), water temperature control (67%), a whirlpool tub (58%), ceramic tile walls (55%), and a dressing room/make-up area (52%)."

The listing of a linen closet as essential by many homeowners points to the necessity of adequate storage; a related question that could be posed would involve the actual necessity of placing linen storage within the bathroom or merely adjacent to it.

In the design of storage areas for wheelchair users or with visitability in mind, some rules of thumb are helpful. According to the National Kitchen and Bath Association's *Bathroom Basics,* storage for toiletry items, linens, and bathroom supplies should be placed 15 to 48 inches (381 to 1219 mm) above the floor. This allows wheelchair users access to the items and creates less need for bending in those with mobility issues. In the same publication, the National Kitchen and Bath Association states that soap, towels, and other related items should be installed within seated reach and 15 to 48 inches (381 to 1219 mm) above the floor.

Towel bars, soap and tissue holders, and other bathroom storage items are available in a number of finishes to match most faucets and are often available from the faucet manufacturers (and others). Homeowners in certain geographic areas often desire towel warmers, which resemble standard towel bars but with heat circulated through them by an electric current or by a recirculating hot-water system. Such units can be quite costly to purchase and install but are prized by some homeowners.

ACCESSIBILITY NOTE

Burns and scrapes may be caused when individuals with limited feeling in their legs come in contact with supply pipes and drainpipes. For this reason, the pipes must be wrapped with insulating material, or be concealed by an angled panel or apron. According to the IDEA Center, ambulatory users prefer a lavatory height of 34 inches (864 mm), whereas a "32 inch (813 mm) height is better for wheelchair users." The center also advocates using tilted mirrors above vanities used by individuals in wheelchairs so that they are accessible to view. In cases where the mirror is to be shared by ambulatory and wheelchair users, an adjustable mirror allows both types of users to view the mirror.

Lavatory design and sink mounting height and location require careful consideration when bathrooms are designed for individuals with disabilities. The Center for Universal Design describes a preference for lavatories "with bowl mounted as close to front edge as possible." Knee space directly under the sink (29 inches [737 mm] high for most adults) allows someone to use the lavatory from a seated position, as shown in Figure 6-25. This space may be open knee space or accomplished through the use of fold-back or self-storing doors.

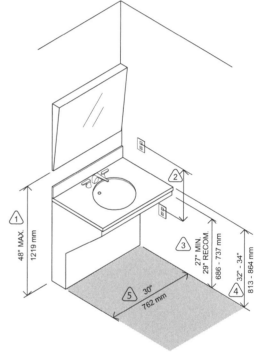

Figure 6-25 Wheelchair-accessible vanity design requires a clear area under the sink that is a minimum of 27 inches (686 mm) above the floor; 29 inches (737 mm) is recommended for most adults, along with 30 inches (762 mm) minimum of clear approach space. For additional information on required clear space, see Figure 6-27b.

1. 40 inches (1016 mm) is the maximum mirror height when mirror is not tilted (tilted mirrors are preferred by many wheelchair users). When tilted as shown, mirror mounting height is 48 inches (1219 mm) maximum.
2. Controls and outlets should be 15 to 48 inches (381 to 1219 mm) above the floor. Note that this measurement is from the top outlet in each receptacle. GFCI protected receptacles must be located within 36 inches (914 mm) of the lavatory; this is true of non-accessible bathrooms as well. (See the "Electrical and Mechanical" section of this chapter for additional information.)
3. Required clear area under the sink is a minimum of 27 inches (686 mm) above the floor; 29 inches (737 mm) is recommended.
4. Top of sink/counter surface: 32 to 34 inches (813 to 864 mm).
5. 30 inches (762 mm) minimum of clear approach space required under sink; when possible, provide 32 inches (813 mm) or more. Accessible wall-hung sink mounting information is shown in Figure 6-26c.

ERGONOMICS AND REQUIRED CLEARANCES

Important dimensional information about toilet clearances includes the space to each side of the toilet as well as clearance in front of the toilet. See Figures 6-26a and 6-27a. Toilets designed for use by those in wheelchairs have distinct clearance and grab bar requirements, which can be found in Figures 6-27a and 6-28a. Like toilets, bidets require appropriate clearance to each side and in front of the fixture. Those dimensions are shown in Figure 6-26a.

When planning sink areas, the designer should consider the space required to approach and use the sink. These dimensions are shown in Figures 6-26a, 6-26b, and 6-26c.

Bathtubs require space in which to enter and exit the tub comfortably. This is often an issue of distance from nearby fixtures. For standard tub clearance dimensions, see Figure 6-26c (whirlpool and soaking tubs require clearances similar to standard tubs).

Much like bathtubs, showers require a clear area for entering and exiting the shower. In addition, showers often include a door, in which case the space for the door swing must be considered. Showerheads and curtain rods are often mounted at 72 inches (1829 mm), although mounting heights will vary based on individual needs. See Figure 6-26c for shower clearance information.

Figure 6-26a Toilet, bidet, and sink fixture mounting locations; fixtures require clearance and placement as noted.

1. Various models require 3 to 9 inches (76 to 229 mm) of clearance between fixture and wall.
2. Dimensions given are rules of thumb for sinks up to 2 feet (610 mm) wide. For oversized or unusual shapes and sizes, consult manufacturer's recommendations.

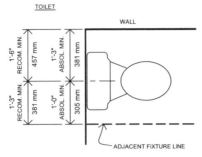

TOILET

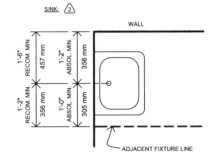

SINK: /2\

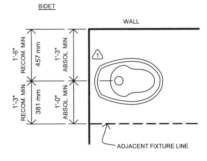

BIDET

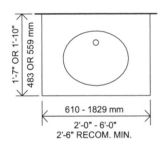

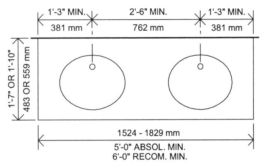

Figure 6-26b Vanity/sink fixture mounting locations; sinks placed in vanities require clearances and placement as noted.

Figure 6-26c Standard bathroom fixture clearances required for comfortable use.

1. Minimum dimension for round bowl models not elongated type.
2. In a 3 by 3 foot (914 x 914 mm) shower as shown, a door must swing out to allow space for occupant. In larger showers, doors can swing in, allowing for a more watertight installation.

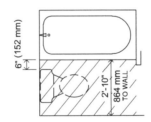

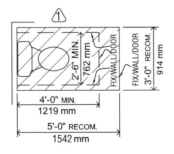

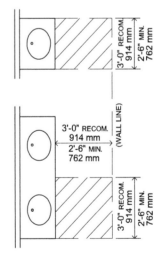

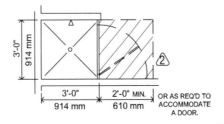

Showerheads

Showerheads are often installed at between 72 and 81 inches (1829 and 2057 mm) above finished floor or to meet the user's specific requirements. For showers with users of varying heights, a slide bar can be installed that allows the shower head height to be adjusted. Most often rods for shower curtains are installed at 72 inches (1829 mm) high; however, this may vary based on curtain and curb design.

ACCESSIBILITY NOTE

Sinks intended for use by those in wheelchairs require specific clearances in approach as well as the ability to access the sink bowl by wheeling under the lavatory. Toilets and bidets also require specific clearances for wheelchair access, as indicated in Figures 6-27a and 6-27b. Toilets and bidets require grab bars, as illustrated in Figures 6-27a, 6-27b, and 6-28a. See Appendix D for information about wheelchair transfer at toilet.

Wheelchair-accessible tubs require a clear space a minimum of 30 by 60 inches (762 by 1524 mm) for a parallel approach and 48 by 60 inches (1219 by 1524 mm) for a forward approach for transferring into the tub. Wheelchair-accessible tubs also require grab bars and a bench or seat. Dimensions for these are shown in Figures 6-27c and 6-28b, although clear space may overlap, as shown in Figures 6-29a and 6-29b.

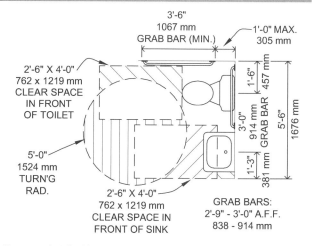

Figure 6-27b Wheelchair-accessible toilet and sink clearances. Up to 1 foot (305 mm) of the 4 feet (1219 mm) required for forward approach can extend under a lavatory with clear access to knee space. While 4 by 4 feet (1219 by 1219 mm) of clear space is recommended, in some cases a clear space of 4 feet by 2 feet, 6 inches (1219 by 762 mm) is used. See Appendix D for information about wheelchair transfer.

Figure 6-27a Wheelchair-accessible toilet, bidet, and sink fixture mounting locations; fixtures require clearance and placement as noted.

1. Various models require 3 to 9 inches (76 to 229 mm) of clearance between fixture and wall.
2. For information on clear space for sink access, see Figure 6-27b.
3. For information about grab bar placement, see Figure 6-28a.
4. Could conflict with vanity.

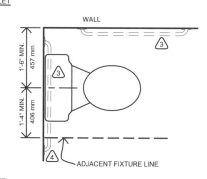

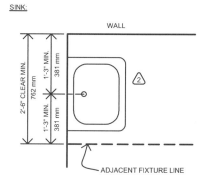

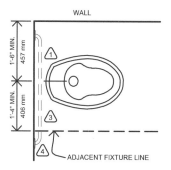

(Continued)

Figure 6-27c Wheelchair-accessible transfer tub approach clearances and grab bar information. Up to 1 foot (305 mm) of the 4 feet (1219 mm) required for forward approach can extend under a lavatory with clear access to knee space.

1. Access area for controls: required by some codes; easier to operate controls before entry because extra maneuvering room allows for ease of reach of controls.

For additional information about vertical and horizontal grab bar placement, see Figure 6-28b.

TRANSFER TUB: SIDE APPROACH

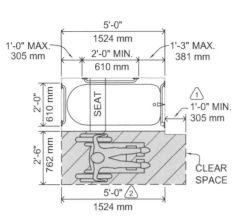

TRANSFER TUB: FORWARD APPROACH

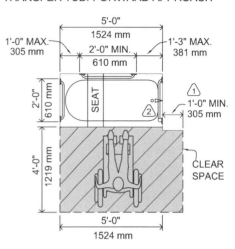

Figure 6-27d Transfer and roll-in shower requirements and clearance information. Up to 1 foot (305 mm) of the 4 feet (1219 mm) required for forward approach can extend under a lavatory with clear access to knee space. While these are both ADA compliant showers, they are also ideal for private residences. The 36 by 36 inch (914 x 914 mm) transfer shower with a folding seat (A) is a versatile and useful bathing fixture for people who use wheelchairs or have mobility/balance issues. The placement of grab bars and controls close to seat support the movement required for transfer. Increasing the size of this shower actually makes it more difficult to transfer due to distance of grab bars. The larger roll-in shower (B) requires that the user enter the shower in the wheelchair; a seat is optional for roll-in showers (see 5 below).

1. Space required by some codes; this extra maneuvering room allows for ease of reach of controls.
2. Clear space flush with the control wall required for entry access.
3. In transfer stalls, the user moves from wheelchair to seat, making use of grab bars as necessary.
4. Provide an 18-inch (457-mm) vertical grab bar placed 3 to 6 inches (76 to 152 mm) above the horizontal grab bar, and 4 inches (102 mm) maximum inward from the front edge of the control wall.
5. Optional seat in roll-in shower requires removal of the horizontal grab bar on the length of wall behind the seat. In showers with no seats, horizontal grab bars are required on all three walls.

TRANSFER SHOWER (A)

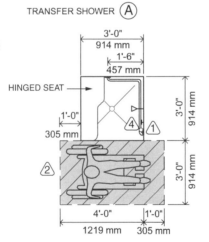

ROLL-IN SHOWER (B)

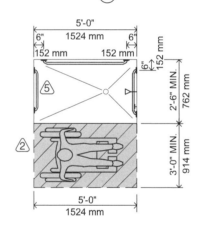

Wheelchair-accessible showers require a clear space of 30 by 48 inches (762 by 1219 mm) adjacent to the shower entry for approach and transfer as well as grab bars. See Figures 6-27d and 6-28b for these dimensions. As stated previously, the required clear spaces may overlap, as shown in Figure 6-29.

As discussed earlier in this chapter, there are two good options for wheelchair accessible residential showers. One option is the smaller 3 by 3 foot (914 by 914 mm) *transfer stall* with grab bars placed opposite a folding shower seat, and the other is a larger 5-foot-long (1524-mm) *roll-in type*, which requires that the user wheel the chair directly into the stall. Both shower types are illustrated in Figure 6-27d. As indicated previously, wheelchair-accessible, roll-in showers must have a flush or very limited threshold, as a curb will impede chair movement.

Figure 6-28a Wheelchair-accessible toilet and lavatory elevations. Note that lavatory height is listed as 34 inches (864 mm) maximum; however, the IDEA Center recommends 32 inches (813 mm) for residences. See also Figure 6-25.

1. Where space does not allow a 36-inch (914-mm) grab bar, a 24-inch (610-mm) bar may be used.
2. Vertical grab bar height is 18 inches (457 mm) minimum.

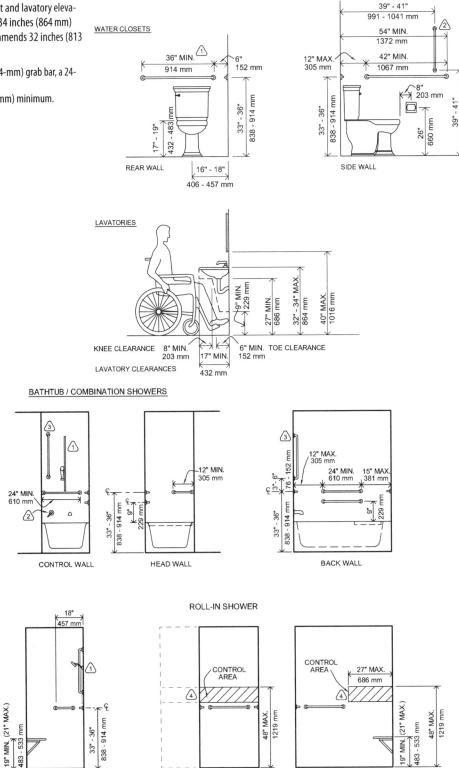

BATHTUB / COMBINATION SHOWERS

Figure 6-28b Wheelchair-accessible bathtub and shower elevations

1. Handheld shower spray (adjustable shown).
2. Controls should be accessible from outside and inside the fixture (controls may be turned on from outside the fixture and off from inside the fixture). In transfer shower, handheld showerhead should be located within control area or adjust to that location.
3. Provide an 18-inch (457-mm) vertical grab bar placed 3 to 6 inches (76 to 152 mm) above the horizontal grab bar, and 4 inches (102 mm) maximum inward from the front edge of the control wall.
4. Controls and handheld showerheads may be located in the hatched locations due to the nature of roll-in showers. (Controls may be located on any wall in roll-in showers without seats.)

When planning a wheelchair-accessible bathroom, the designer should include a full 60-inch (1524-mm) turning radius area inside the room. This often requires more space than is available and in some cases requires taking space over from adjacent rooms or including a roll-in shower area as part of the radius. A T-shaped circulation route can serve as an alternative to the full 60-inch (1524-mm) turning radius. As stated, portions of clear spaces required for wheelchair access can overlap, as indicated in Figures 6-29a and 6-29b. It is also important to provide clear space to the latch/pull side of the door so that the wheelchair user can reach the door pull.

Figure 6-29a and 6-29b Wheelchair-accessible residential full bathrooms. Wheelchair clearances may overlap and may include clear areas under fixtures, as shown in these diagrams. These are the smallest footprints possible for truly wheelchair-accessible bathrooms; space savings have come from overlapping clearances and from efficient placement. Figure 6-29a is the most universally useful design because it uses a shower rather than a tub (see note 3 below).

1. Use of a pocket door allows for a smaller door to create a 2 foot, 8 inch (813-mm) open space. If a standard door is used, it must be 3 feet (914-mm) wide to create a 2, feet, 8 inch (813-mm) inside of stop and frame.
2. Controls should be accessible from outside and inside the fixture (controls may be turned on from outside the fixture and off from inside the fixture). Note that a seat and vertical grab bar are provided; see Figure 6-27d.
3. 36 by 36 inch (914 by 914 mm) transfer shower. While a tub may use less space overall, showers are most useful as a bathing fixture for many wheelchair users.
4 Transfer tub (with seat, as shown), while not ideal for all wheelchair users, can be accessible; see Figures 6-27c and 6-29b.

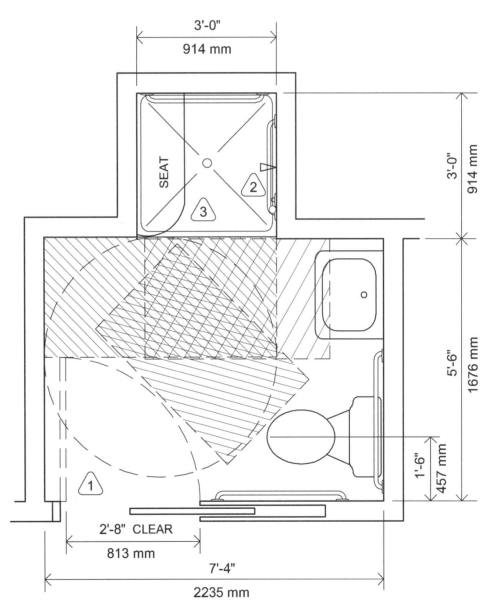

Figure 6-29b

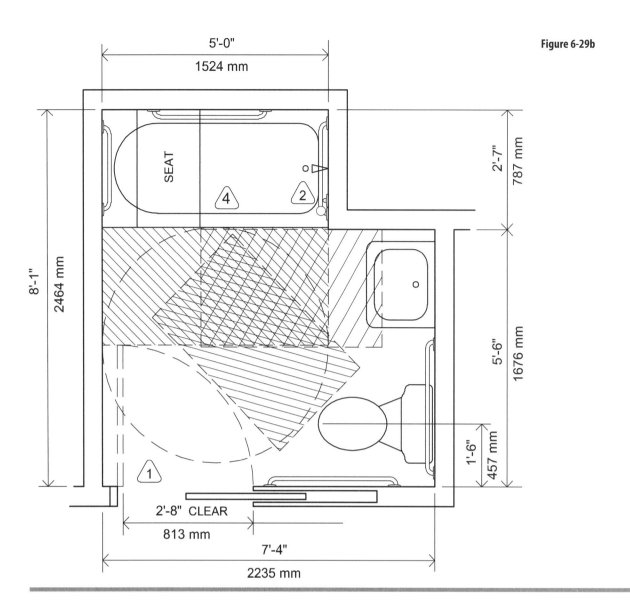

5'-0"
1524 mm

2'-7"
787 mm

SEAT

4

2

8'-1"
2464 mm

5'-6"
1676 mm

1'-6"
457 mm

1

2'-8" CLEAR
813 mm

7'-4"
2235 mm

ORGANIZATIONAL FLOW

A *full bathroom* can be thought of as having three activity areas: a sink/grooming area, a toileting area, and a bathing/showering area. Effective organization of the space requires the successful linking and/or overlapping of the three activity areas, providing the appropriate clearance and access space needed for each fixture as well as adequate circulation space and consideration of plumbing supply and drain lines.

Circulation space within the room requires 30 to 36 inches (762 to 914 mm) of clear space, with a minimum of 32 inches (813 mm) of clear space for wheelchair passage.

The following list contains some rules of thumb for designing a full bathroom.

In terms of fixture use or room organization, common rules of thumb for room organization are:

- Place fixtures or areas used most often *first* (or closest to an entry).

- Place the largest and/or least-used fixtures *last* (or to the rear of the room).

- This rule puts the sink(s) in the location closest to the door and the bath or shower near the rear of the room, as shown in Figure 6-30, thus creating a compact, economical room.

Additional considerations include:

- The number of users, spatial restrictions (or lack thereof)

- The local climate (cold climates limit plumbed wall locations)

- Any specific fixture requirements

- The general ease of use of the totality of space

Figure 6-30 item **a** depicts a full bathroom with a single plumbed wall. Item **b** depicts a full bathroom with two plumbed walls and with the fixtures used most often placed in locations convenient to room entry.

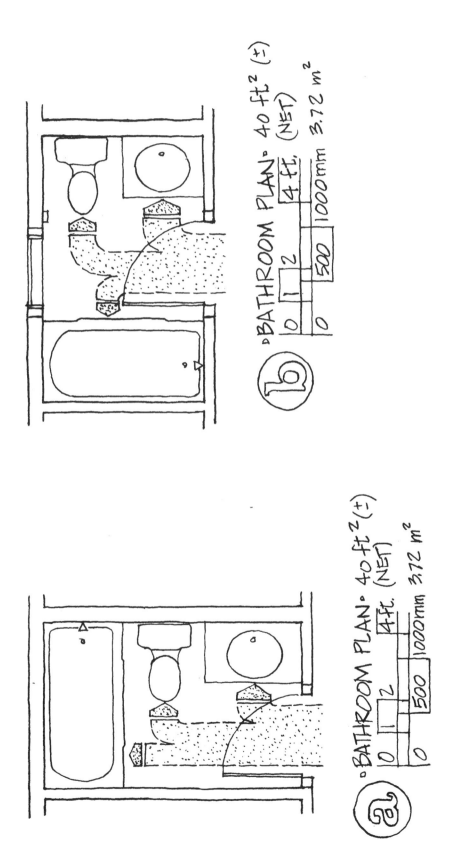

Figure 6-30 Fixture placement overview.

a. A single-wall bathroom plan with fixtures used most often placed closest to the entry and larger fixtures or those used more seldom placed at rear.

Advantages of this plan: It provides a compact and economical use of space and plumbing lines.

Disadvantages: Awkward access to tub/shower controls and the primary possible window area would be in the tub/shower area. In addition, making the room fully accessible would require enlarging the room to allow for greater fixture clearances, a wider doorway, and a wider turning radius (see Figure 6-29).

b. A bathroom plan with two plumbed walls and the fixtures used most often placed conveniently in relation to the entry. This plan uses the same square footage as plan a; however, in this plan, the larger and least often used fixture (the bathtub) is not placed in the farthest position relative to the entry.

Advantages: This plan demonstrates the fact that two plumbed walls can provide good access to everything in a room of limited square footage and also can provide a good window location. In addition, while the door is shown as hinged and at 2 feet, 8 inches (813 mm), it could easily be replaced by a pocket door of the same size or a standard 3-foot (914-mm) door to allow for accessibility/visitability; this room arrangement could also be expanded in terms of width if desired.

Disadvantages: The cost of plumbing two walls and the use of a smaller vanity in order to keep to 40 square feet (3.7 m²), in direct comparison to plan **a.**

Figures 6-31a to 6-31c are negative examples of bathroom plans that contain problems related to organizational flow, fixture placement, ergonomics, and/or clearances.

A *half bath*, also known as a *powder room*, contains toilet and sink areas but no bathing facilities. See Figures 6-32a to 6-32d for illustrations and a discussion of fixture layout and design of this type of room.

Figure 6-31a Negative example.

Problematic bathroom plan.

A. Door swing on linen closet conflicts with entry door because, if left slightly ajar, it can block entry door; changing the hinge location to the left side would alleviate potential door blockage problem.
B. There is space for a 5-foot (1524-mm) vanity. This meets the recommended minimum for each sink of 30 inches (762 mm) per person.
C. Circulation to and clearance at sink is too tight. A minimum clear space of 30 inches (762 mm) and a recommended clear space of 36 inches (914 mm) would be preferable; the code requires a minimum of 21 inches (533 mm).
D. Showerhead location sprays directly on user while he or she is turning standard controls on. Plumbing on an exterior wall is not recommended due to freezing in cold climates, and access for repairs to shower water supply would require an exterior access panel or cutting and subsequent patching.
E. Shower size meets International Residential Code (IRC) minimum of 30 by 30 inches (762 by 762 mm); recommended minimum size is 36 by 36 inches (914 by 914 mm).
F. Not enough clear space between shower and toilet.
G. Center of toilet is not a minimum of 15 inches (381 mm) from the wall, as required by most codes.

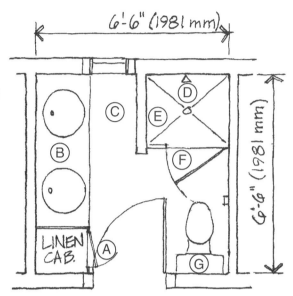

Figure 6-31b Negative example.

Problematic bathroom plan. While this bathroom may seem economical in terms of making use of one plumbing location, it has many serious flaws in terms of clearance and building codes and is rather large, given how poorly the space works functionally.

A. Location of door creates immediate sightline to toilet; this is undesirable to some homeowners.
B. Clearance at sink is too tight. A minimum of 30 inches (762 mm) and a recommended clear space of 36 inches (914 mm) would be preferable; IRC requires a minimum of 21 inches (533 mm). In addition, the long passageway to the tub and linen cabinet is less than ideal; tight for through traffic.
C. Access to window is compromised; more space is required by IRC.
D. Window location is problematic in cold climates due to moisture from the shower.
E. Not enough clear space in front of the toilet.
   E₁. Recommended minimum is 48 inches (1219 mm).

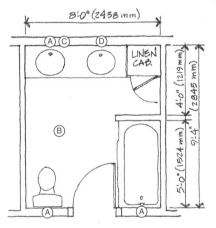

Figure 6-31c Negative example.

Problematic bathroom plan. This bathroom is large with no particular advantage granted by the extra square footage.

A. Plumbing is fragmented into three locations and does not result in any particular functional gains.
B. This area exceeds all clearance requirements to such a degree that there is wasted space; despite the space available around the toilet, it would be difficult to adapt the room for accessibility because the door location conflicts with possible grab bar locations.
C. Plumbing on an exterior wall is not recommended in geographic areas subject to freezing and would need to come from the side wall (though cabinet).
D. Possible window locations on the exterior wall would conflict with mirror locations (this could be solved by clerestory windows).

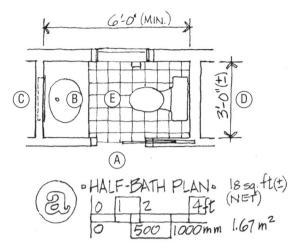

Figure 6-32a Small half-bath/powder room plan.

A. Pocket door is shown at 2 feet (610 mm); door could swing out or in if overall width of room is increased.
B. A 3-foot (914-mm) vanity is shown; a wall-hung or pedestal lavatory, 1 foot, 6 inches (457 mm) deep, could serve as an alternate, and room width could be decreased to some extent.
C. Medicine cabinet with mirror is shown; other options are possible.
D. Absolute minimum IRC dimension is 2 feet, 6 inches (762 mm) (IRC R307.1).
E. Absolute minimum clear space in front of toilet is 21 inches (762 mm).

Note: With the use of a wall-hung lavatory (sink) and round bowl toilet, the room could be reduced to 2 feet, 6 inches (762 mm) by 5 feet (1524 mm) or 13.75 square feet (1.28 m²).

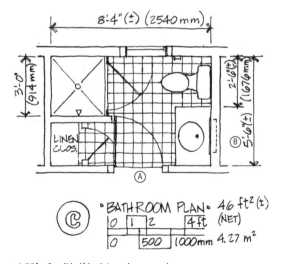

Figure 6-32b Small half-bath/powder room plan.

A. A 2-foot (610-mm) door is shown.
B. A 3-foot (914-mm) vanity is shown; a wall-hung or pedestal lavatory, 1 foot, 6 inches (457 mm) deep, could serve as an alternate, and room width could be decreased.
C. Medicine cabinet with mirror is shown; other options are possible.
D. A minimum space of 4 feet, 2 inches (1270 mm) is required for an elongated toilet bowl; dimension could be reduced to 4 feet (1219 mm) with smaller (round) toilet bowl.
E. A clear space of 1 foot, 9 inches (533 mm) is required by code (IRC).

ACCESSIBILITY NOTE

Creating an accessible half-bath is one means of making a home visitable. While creating a full bath is the ideal, it is not always possible. Doorways that provide an opening of at least 32 inches (813 mm) and a clear turning area within the room must be provided as indicated in Figures 6-32c and 6-32d.

In some bathrooms, the three activity areas are included, but a shower serves as the only bathing fixture (with no tub available). These were formerly referred to as three-quarter baths but are now described as full baths. See Figures 6-33a to 6-33c for illustrations and a discussion of fixture layout and design of this type of room.

The most common option for full baths are rooms that include the three activity areas with bathtub and shower (separate or combined in one unit). Figure 6-34 illustrates various considerations related to the design of full bathrooms.

In cases where there will be multiple users and/or where privacy is desired, multiple rooms or compartments can be used. Figures 6-35a to 6-35c, 6-36, and 6-37 illustrate various design considerations related to multiple-room layouts.

RELATED CODES AND CONSTRAINTS

According to the IRC, bathrooms and toilet rooms are not considered "habitable spaces." They are, however, covered under specified sections of the code. Section R306 covers sanitation and requires that dwelling units be provided with "a water closet, lavatory and a bathtub or shower" (Section R306.1). Section R306.4 requires that all plumbing fixtures be connected to an "approved water supply" and that all "kitchen sinks, lavatories,

ACCESSIBILITY NOTE

Figures 6-33a to 6-35c are not intended to illustrate bathrooms designed for wheelchair accessibility, adaptability, or visitability. However, using a 3-foot (914-mm) door, which would create, at minimum, a 32-inch (813-mm) clear passage through the doorway, would add greatly to the visitability of these rooms. In addition, locating a bathroom on the ground floor is considered a requirement for visitability. For specific accessibility information, see Figures 6-27a through 6-27d, 6-28a, 6-28b, and 6-29, 6-32c, 6-32d, and 6-36. In addition, for information about bathroom design requirements for FHAA, ANSI, and ADA, refer to the overview presented in Chapter 1 and Appendix B.

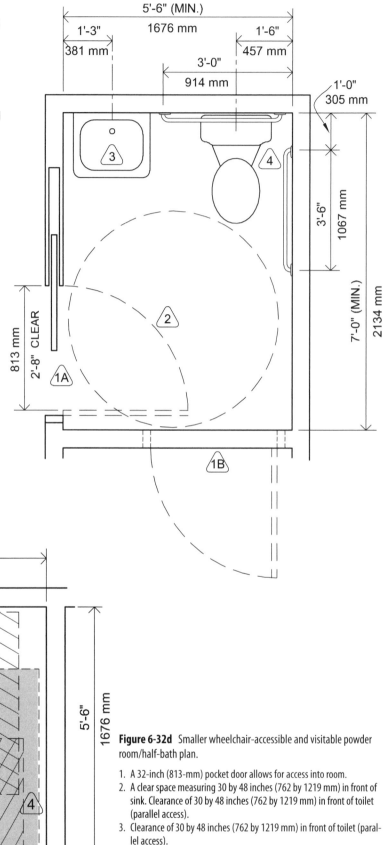

Figure 6-32c Wheelchair-accessible powder room/half-bath plan. Includes a clear turning area with a diameter of 5 feet (1524 mm) and a clear doorway of 32 inches (813 mm). This requires a 3-foot (914-mm) swinging door or a smaller pocket door with 32-inch (813-mm) clear space, so the room must be 60 percent larger than the example shown in Figure 6-32b.

1A. A 2-foot, 8-inch (813-mm) pocket door is shown, which creates a 2-foot, 8-inch (813-mm) opening for wheelchair passage. Dashed line shows a standard door of the same size, which due to jamb/hinges makes the opening smaller than the door size.

1B. Alternate 3-foot (914-mm) door location; when door swings out, it allows the turning radius to exist free of door.

2. Clear turning area measuring 5 feet (1524 mm) in diameter.

3. Wall-hung lavatory, 18 by 22 inches (457 by 559 mm).

4. 36-inch (914-mm) and 42-inch (1067-mm) grab bars mounted 33 to 36 inches (838 to 914 mm) above floor.

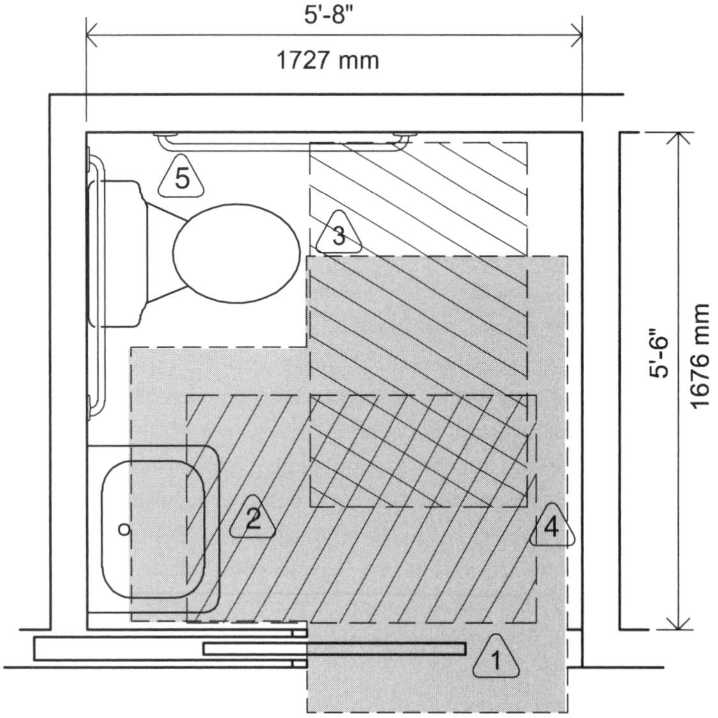

Figure 6-32d Smaller wheelchair-accessible and visitable powder room/half-bath plan.

1. A 32-inch (813-mm) pocket door allows for access into room.

2. A clear space measuring 30 by 48 inches (762 by 1219 mm) in front of sink. Clearance of 30 by 48 inches (762 by 1219 mm) in front of toilet (parallel access).

3. Clearance of 30 by 48 inches (762 by 1219 mm) in front of toilet (parallel access).

4. A T-shaped turning area (shaded) is used to save space (see Figure 2-4c for information about T-turns).

5. 36-inch (914-mm) and 42-inch (1067-mm) grab bars mounted 33 to 36 inches (838 to 914 mm) above floor.

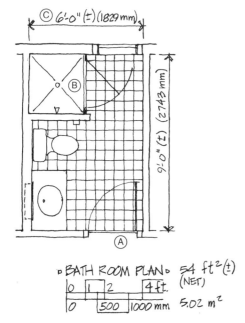

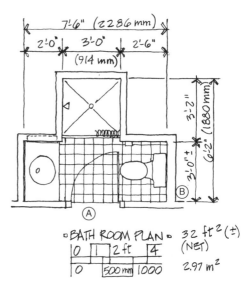

Figure 6-33a Full bath with shower.

A. A 2-foot, 6-inch (762-mm) door is shown; a 2-foot, 4-inch (711-mm) or 2-foot, 6-inch (813-mm) door will also work.
B. Using a 3 by 3 foot (914 by 914 mm) shower module rather than a standard 5-foot-long (1524 mm) tub does not save space. In this example, the bathroom is as large as the full bath with a shower/tub combination shown in Figure 6-34a, but this option may be preferable to some owners. In addition, a longer site-built shower could be placed in this space.
C. The 6-foot (1829-mm) width could be decreased by 10-plus inches (254 mm) if the shower door is held to 24 inches (610 mm) maximum.

Figure 6-33c Full bath with shower. This is a very efficient shape (using minimal square footage), but the room form would not easily be integrated into a configuration of surrounding rooms, and the plumbing is scattered.

A. A 2-foot, 6-inch (762-mm) door is shown.
B. This dimension could be reduced to 2 feet, 6 inches (762 mm) if a smaller lavatory and smaller door or pocket door were used.

bathtubs, showers, bidets, laundry tubs, and washing machines shall be provided with hot water"; this only excludes toilets from requiring a hot-water supply.

Section R305 of the IRC covers ceiling height and requires that bathrooms have ceiling heights of not less than 7 feet (2134 mm). This section contains several exceptions, which are discussed in the "Related Codes and Constraints" section of Chapter 1, with the requirements illustrated in Figure 1-5. There is an exception that is specific to bathrooms, which requires that bathrooms have a minimum ceiling height of 6 feet, 8 inches (2036 mm) over fixtures and their related clearance areas and in shower stalls.

Section R303 covers light, ventilation, and heating and requires bathrooms and similar rooms to be provided with "aggregate glazing area in windows of not less than 3 square feet (0.279 m²), one-half of which must be openable," with an exception for artificial light and a mechanical ventilation to serve in place of the required glazing; ventilation systems must be exhausted directly to the exterior. Clearly, use of this exception is commonplace.

Section R307 covers toilet, bath, and shower spaces, as well as fixture placement, with most of the code fixture placement requirements reflected in the "Ergonomics and Required Clearances" section of this chapter. Section R307.2 requires that bathtub and shower floors, as well as walls above shower compartments and combination tub/shower units, be finished with a nonabsorbent surface to a height of not less than 6 feet (1829 mm) above the floor. Clearly, prefabricated modular

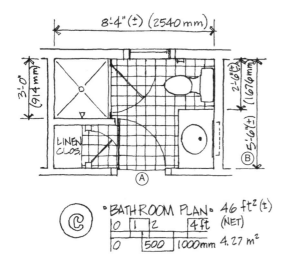

Figure 6-33b Full bath plan. This plan contains the same elements as shown in Figure 6-33a, with the addition of a linen closet. Also, the room is significantly smaller than that shown in Figure 6-33a, illustrating that by employing two plumbed walls, certain spatial economies can be gained.

A. A 2-foot, 6-inch (762-mm) door is shown.
B. This dimension could be reduced if a smaller lavatory and smaller door or pocket door were used.

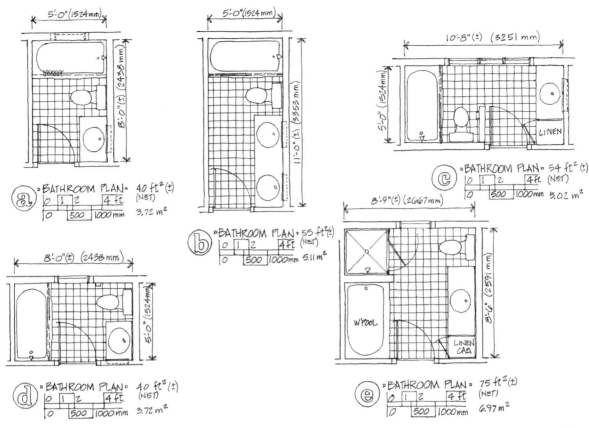

Figure 6-34 Full-bath plans with bathtub/showers. All plans show a 5-foot (1524-mm) combination shower/tub with shower curtain or sliding doors, with the exception of plans **c** and **e**, which contain separate tubs and showers, requiring a sizable increase in square footage. All entry doors are shown at 2 feet, 6 inches (762 mm) but could be reduced to 2 feet, 4 inches (711 mm) or increased to 2 feet, 8 inches (813 mm), with some adjustment in size to plans a and b, and by limiting door trim size in other plans. All plans show the sink at the first position relative to the entry door, which is convenient; however, the door location allows the door to swing into the area where a person would stand to use the sink (with plan e being the exception). Adding a second sink as shown (the difference between plan a and plan b) increases the overall space of the room by 35 percent, which increases the construction costs proportionally. Shown are some typical suburban American post–World War II single-wall bathrooms. In many climates, a window placed in the shower area as shown in plan **a** can cause rotting in the window or within the window wall; glass block can be used in place of a standard window to alleviate this problem or the window could be located elsewhere.

Figure 6-35a Multiple-room plan; commonly used in motel/hotel bathrooms as well as residences.

A. A 2-foot, 6-inch (762-mm) door is shown; could be reduced to 2 feet, 4 inches (711 mm). Door/wall location will vary depending on the size of the vanity and number of sinks.

  A₁. Alternative door/wall location for single-sink bathroom (as indicated with dashed lines). See note above for door size.

B. A 2-foot, 4-inch (711-mm) door is shown.

C. Standard window not recommended in this location; standard windows are designed to resist water intrusion from the exterior, not the interior. Glass block or another suitable material could be used at such locations.

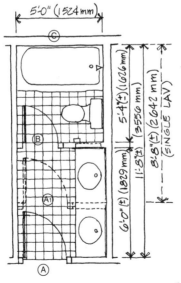

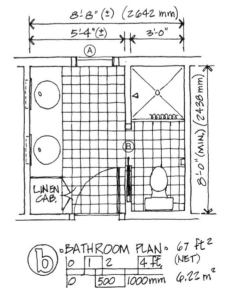

Figure 6-35b Multiple-room plan.

A. Using three plumbed walls creates an area appropriate for a window at this location.
B. A 2-foot (610-mm) pocket door is shown.

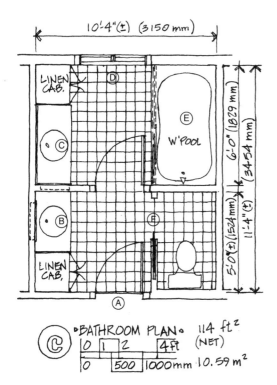

BATHROOM PLAN 114 ft² (NET)
0 1 2 4 ft
0 500 1000mm 10.59 m²

Figure 6-35c Multiple-room plan.

A. 2-foot, 6-inch (762-mm) doors (shown); could easily be reduced to 2 feet, 4 inches (711 mm) or increased to 2 feet, 8 inches (813 mm).
B. A 3-foot (914-mm) vanity is shown.
C. A 4-foot (1219-mm) vanity is shown.
D. Larger room size and use of three plumbed walls creates a large area appropriate for windows at this location. The larger room as shown allows for a good deal of linen and other storage.
E. A 6-foot (1829-mm) whirlpool tub/shower combination is shown; these are available in a range of sizes. Using a 5-foot (1524-mm) tub/shower could decrease room size by 10 percent.
F. A 2-foot (610-mm) pocket door is shown.

Figure 6-36 Bathroom with wheelchair-accessible shower (not a transfer shower).

A. A 2-foot, 8-inch (813-mm) opening with no or very low accessible threshold.
B. Site-built shower accommodating a 5-foot (1524-mm) diameter turning space.
C. A 2-foot, 8-inch (813-mm) pocket door.
D. Medicine cabinet to side with mirror above sink is shown; other options are possible.

shower units made of fiberglass or acrylic meet the code requirements, as they are nonabsorbent surfaces. For showers using receptor bases and for site-built showers, a range of non-absorbent wall surface materials can be used, including tile, stone, acrylics and other plastics, and, in some installations, metals or glass.

The general plumbing chapter of the IRC (Chapter 26) covers the locations of waste pipes and requires that areas with a "winter design temperature of 32°F (0°C) or lower" not have water, soil, or waste pipes installed outside of a building or in exterior walls, attics, crawl spaces, or any other areas subjected to freezing temperatures unless provisions are made to insulate the area from freezing or heat or both (Section P2603.6). This directly influences placement of plumbing lines (and fixtures) in buildings in colder climates.

Chapter 27 of the IRC covers plumbing fixtures and requires that the centerline of water closets or bidets not be less than 15 inches (381 mm) from adjacent walls, and that bidets not be less than 15 inches (381 mm) from the centerline to the outermost rim of an adjacent water closet (Section P2705). This section also requires at least 21 inches (533 mm) of clearance in front of the water closet, bidet, or lavatory.

Section P2708.1.1 covers access and requires that the opening to the shower compartment be a minimum of 22 inches (559 mm) "clear and unobstructed" (this is a reference to the shower access or doorway size).

Item 6 in this same section requires that piping, fixtures, and/or equipment location not interfere with the operation of

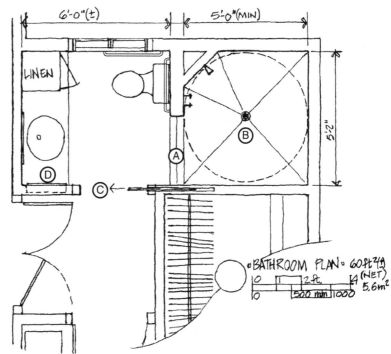

BATHROOM PLAN 60 ft² (NET) 5.6 m²
0 2 ft
0 500 mm 1000

Figure 6-37 Very large multiple-room plan. It is as large as a bedroom and would be the most costly of all the examples shown.

A. A 2-foot, 8-inch (813-mm) door is shown.
B. Medicine cabinet to side with mirror above sink is shown; other options are possible.
C. A 6 by 3 foot (1905-mm) whirlpool tub combination is shown. A larger tub requires that the width of the room be increased accordingly.
D. Window seat.
E. Site-built shower with seat and multiple showerheads. A 2-foot, 4-inch (813-mm) door is shown but is not required unless shower serves as a steam room.
F. A 2-foot (610-mm) door is shown.
G. Potential partition area.
H. Bidet or urinal location (urinal would be enhanced by a separating partition or wall at G).

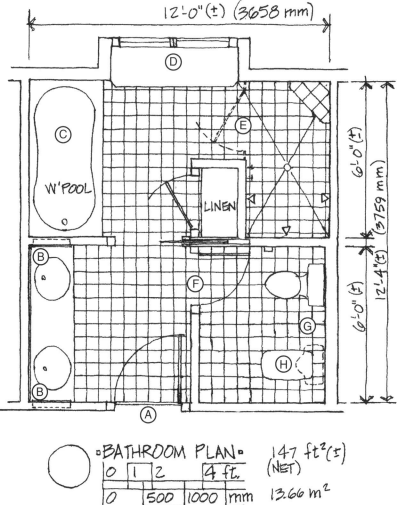

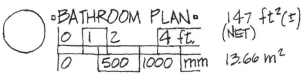

windows or doors. This chapter goes on to state that shower compartments are required to be at least 900 square inches (0.6 m²), "30 inches (762 mm) in minimum dimension," and have an access opening of not less than 22 inches (559 mm). These requirements are reflected in the clearances information provided in this chapter.

The fixture locations and clearances illustrated earlier in this chapter meet the code as described in the previous paragraphs

In terms of shower construction, Section P2709.1 requires that shower receptors have a finished curb threshold of not less than 1 inch (25.4 mm) and a uniform slope toward the drain of "not less than one-fourth unit vertical in 12 units horizontal (2 percent slope) nor more than one-half unit vertical per 12 units horizontal (4 percent unit vertical per 12 units horizontal (4 percent slope) and floor drains shall be flanged to provide a water-tight joint in the floor."

The plumbing portion of the code also covers site-built shower construction, requiring that they be "lined with sheet lead, copper or a plastic liner material" compliant with ASTM D 4068—or "hot mopping" as outlined in Section P2709.2.3.

Additional areas of the IRC that relate to bathroom fixtures state that water closet seats shall be of a "smooth, nonabsorbent material and shall be properly sized." This portion also stipulates that hot water faucets belong on the left.

ELECTRICAL AND MECHANICAL

As mentioned, because the IRC (Section R303.9) calls for heating to a minimum of 68°F (20°C) when the winter design temperature is below 60°F (15.5°C), most bathrooms in the United States (with the possible exception of portions of Hawaii and Florida) require some form of heat source. The location of the heat source or its registers or diffusers, as well as those used by any air-cooling source, must be considered by the interior designer as lighting, furnishings, window, and door locations are planned. The actual engineering of the heating and cooling system is, of course, done by professionals other than the interior designer.

National and local electrical codes call for ground fault interrupters (GFIs) to be used for electrical outlets in bathrooms and other wet locations. These are designed to protect from electrical shock by detecting currents as minor as a few milliamperes and tripping a breaker at the receptacle or at the breaker panel to remove the shock hazard. The IRC (Section E3902.1) requires that "all 125-volt, single-phase, 15-and 20-ampere receptacles installed in bathrooms shall have ground-fault circuit-interrupter protection." Section E3703.4 requires that a minimum of one 20-amp branch circuit be provided to supply the bathroom receptacle outlets.

Bathroom outlet (duplex receptacle) placement is based on the organization of the room and the placement of countertops and vanities. Generally, outlets are located above countertop height, where they are needed for grooming and convenient use of small appliances, and yet away from direct contact with water. The IRC (Section E3901.6) requires that one wall receptacle outlet be installed in bathrooms and located within 36 inches (914 mm) of the lavatory, and that the receptacle not be installed in a face-up position on the countertop. Figure 6-38 shows a simple bathroom electrical and lighting plan, which includes outlet and switching locations.

The on/off switches for general lights are best located close to the room entry door on the latch side of the doorway when possible. In addition to lighting and power outlets, some clients request various communication lines for telephone, cable, and stereo/audio for use in bathroom or dressing areas.

As stated previously, exhaust fans are required in rooms with no glazing and are used in many bathrooms in addition to windows to aid in removing steam and odors. Some local codes may require that the fan be switched with the light; however, when that is not the case, separate switching allows someone to enter the room and turn on only the light when the fan is not needed.

In those situations where there is no window and the fan is meant to do all of the ventilation, central placement is advisable. However, in rooms with windows and fans, locating the fan requires consideration of its purpose. For example, if the fan is required to remove steam created by the shower, then placement near the shower is appropriate. When possible, it is helpful to place the fan switch near the place of use. For example, when the fan is meant to exhaust the toilet area, a switch convenient to the toilet can be helpful.

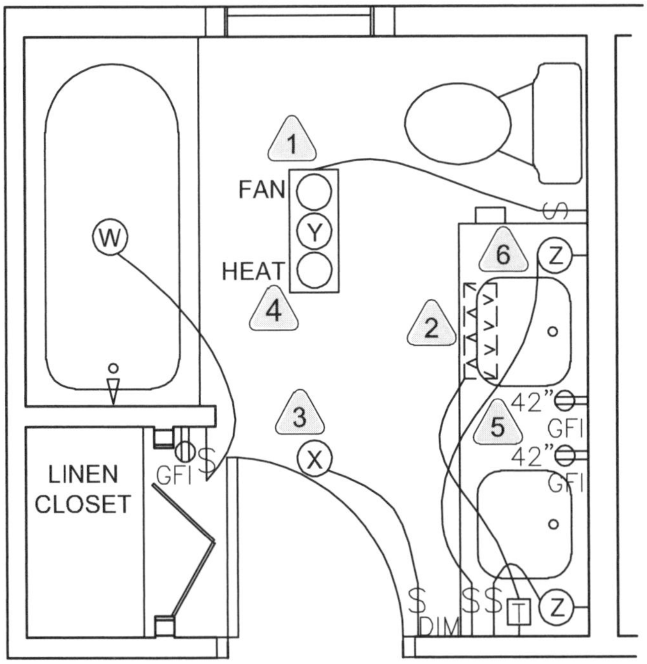

FIXTURE SCHEDULE	
TYPE	DESCRIPTION
W	RECESSED INCAN. WATERPROOF CLG. FIXT.
X	RECESSED LED CLG. FIXTURE
Y	HEAT LAMP/FAN/LT. COMBIN. FIXT.; 3 FUNC. SWITCH
Z	WALL MTD. LINEAR SCONCE FIXTURE

Figure 6-38 A simple bathroom electrical and lighting plan.

1. Ceiling fan (60 cfm minimum) exhausts to exterior with a nearby switch; not required by code where there is an operable window.
2. Undercounter/toe space electric heater for extremely cold climates; thermostat on a separate wall.
3. Ceiling light; not necessarily required with adequate light at other locations, shown on a dimmer switch (also not a requirement).
4. Heat lamp shown; can be combined with a fan in some locations; not required by code.
5. GFIs for all outlets in order to protect from electrical shock at potentially wet locations are required by the IRC (Section E3802.1), and one must be located within 36 inches (914 mm) of the outside edge of each lavatory basin.
6. Mirror area luminaires on separate switches.

LIGHTING

Lighting for bathrooms must provide general illumination as well as task or focal lighting at mirrors, lavatories, and other locations where grooming tasks are performed. Generally, most grooming is done at the sink location in front of a mirror. Therefore, lighting this area well is crucial. Although many such areas have a single light source (or a row of lights) mounted above the mirror, this is not the ideal, as this luminaire location provides inconsistent light on only portions of the face and creates shadows.

Providing two wall-mounted luminaires on each side of the mirror (or at each sink location in larger bathrooms) of 75 watts each and mounted at roughly eye level provides cross-illumination and reduces shadows. According to Randall Whitehead in *Residential Lighting: A Practical Guide,* this manner of lighting a mirror originated in the theater, where actors applied makeup in front of mirrors surrounded by lamps. Traditional wall sconces can be used at such locations, as can more linear vertical luminaires, with such vertical fixtures providing the advantage of cross-illumination for a variety of user heights. See Figure 6-39.

Some bathroom mirrors and grooming areas do not allow for positioning of luminaires to the side of the mirror. If the sink area is located in a small alcove, the fixtures can be mounted on adjacent walls, as illustrated in Figure 6-39. When installed in the locations described, which have the potential to become wet, the fixtures should be installed with an instantaneous cir-

cuit shutoff or GFI, as described in the preceding section. In situations where two wall-mounted fixtures are not possible, an overhead luminaire may be the only choice. In these situations, the fixture should be mounted at roughly 75 to 80 inches (1905 to 2032 mm) above the floor and should contain 150 watts, spread over at least 24 inches (510 mm), to illuminate the user as fully as possible. In such situations, a glossy or light-colored countertop can be used to reflect some of the light upward.

Other areas of the bathroom require general lighting, which is often provided by overhead lights. Recessed downlights can work in bathing areas. However, these may not provide adequate ambient light and can be supplemented by wall sconces or rope lighting (or another form of concealed lighting) at counters, toe kicks, soffits, and ledges. While unusual, locating a concealed luminaire at the toe kick space of a vanity can create pleasant, although rather low, ambient lighting. Pendant

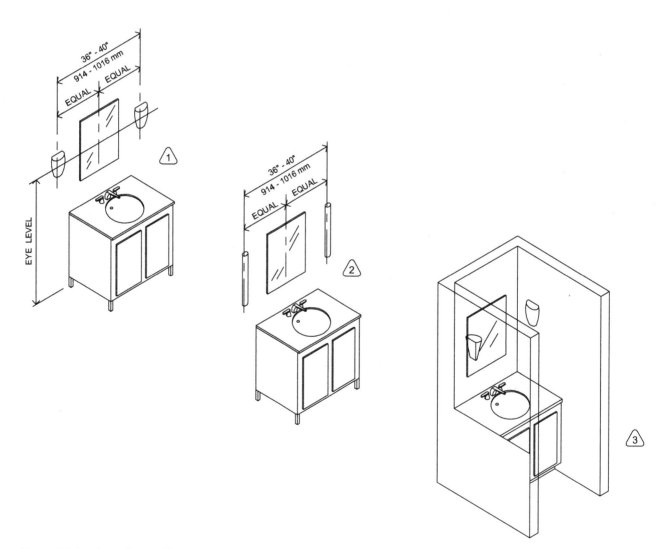

Figure 6-39 Providing wall-mounted luminaires to each side of the mirror can create attractive light for grooming.

1. Sconces placed roughly at adult eye level and spaced equally create balanced, attractive light.
2. Linear luminaires can accommodate a range of user heights.
3. In cases where there is no room for wall-mounted luminaires at the mirror, they may be placed on adjacent walls.

fixtures and chandeliers can also be used depending on bathroom size, ceiling height, and overall design.

Whether recessed or surface mounted, luminaires located in showers, directly above tubs, and in steam rooms should be listed as acceptable for use in wet locations by an approved testing agency such as Underwriters Laboratories (UL). Recently, recessed, adjustable, low-voltage fixtures have become available for use in wet areas.

Some local and state codes limit energy use by requiring particular fixtures in bathrooms. For example, California's Title 24 requires lighting in bathrooms to be "high efficacy" or controlled by a vacancy sensor. The title also states "for safety in bathrooms, it is recommended that at least one high-efficacy luminaire should be installed so that it is not controlled by the vacancy sensor circuit. This will help to ensure that all of the luminaires don't switch off while someone is in the bath." Additional information about Title 24 requirements can be found in Chapter 4.

REFERENCES

Contains both works cited and recommended reading.

Arnold, Susan. 2004. "The Right Light." *This Old House Magazine: Kitchen and Bath Guide*. Winter.

California Energy Commission. 2013. "2013 Residential Compliance Manual." http://www.energy.ca.gov/title24/2013standards/residential_manual.html.

Ching, Francis. 1983. *Home Renovation*. New York: Van Nostrand Reinhold.

———. 2008. *Building Construction Illustrated*. 4th ed. Hoboken, NJ: John Wiley & Sons.

Dickinson, Mary Ann. 2003. *The Water Logue* 2 (5). Sponsored by the California Urban Water Conservation Council.

Frechette, Leon. 2004. *Remodeling a Bathroom*. Newtown, CT: Taunton Press.

International Code Council. 2015. "2015 International Residential Code for One- and Two-Family Dwellings." Country Club Hills, IL: International Code Council.

Nagyszalanczy, Sandor. "Installing a Kitchen Sink." CornerHardware.com. www.cornerhardware.com/howto/ht069.html.

RISMedia. 2010. "Home Size Continues to Decline; Buyers Increasingly Opt for Single-Story Homes." June 14. http://rismedia.com/2010-06-15/home-size-continues-to-decline-buyers-increasingly-opt-for-single-story-homes/.

Steinfeld, Edward. 1996. "A Primer on Accessible Design." v. 1.0. Buffalo: Center for Inclusive Design and Environmental Access, SUNY at Buffalo.

Susanka, Sarah. 1998. *The Not So Big House: A Blueprint for the Way We Really Live*. Newtown, CT: Taunton Press.

U.S. Department of Energy. 2004. "Energy Savers: Virtual Home." www.eere.energy.gov/consumerinfo/energy_savers/virtualhome/508/toilet.html.

Whitehead, Randall. 2004. *Residential Lighting: A Practical Guide*. Hoboken, NJ: John Wiley & Sons.

CHAPTER 7
Utility and Work Spaces

INTRODUCTION: TYPES OF UTILITY AND WORK SPACES

The term *utility space* can be used to describe a range of areas with practical uses. This chapter details a number of such work-oriented spaces as well as the related items that may be found in them. Unlike other chapters, this chapter is not devoted to a specific room type but more broadly includes areas with practical uses, those that do not fit neatly into any single room type.

Garages, Equipment Rooms, and Hobby Spaces

Garages and carports are used to store cars and other vehicles as well as lawn and garden equipment. They may also provide general household storage and work/hobby areas. Garages and carports have a direct relationship to streets and/or alleys as well as to an entry door or doors (and in many cases a mudroom). They may be attached to the home or be freestanding. As with many of the rooms discussed previously, garages (and garage doors) in North America have evolved to be larger over time.

Some homes have equipment rooms/spaces that contain items such as the furnace, one or more hot water heaters (some large homes require more than one), electrical panel(s), and water treatment equipment. These may be located in a basement, on a ground floor, or, in the case of a furnace, perhaps in an attic space (in single-story homes with no basement).

Hobby/craft/sewing rooms may be found in homes where people are involved with specific hobbies. Hobby spaces are often former bedrooms that have been fitted with appropriate work counters and storage elements to support the work being done. In the case of custom homes, such rooms may be designed and located to specifically support some important hobby or activity. In some cases, such rooms are combined within a larger laundry room, in which case the issues mentioned in the following paragraphs may apply.

Laundry Spaces

Laundry rooms/spaces contain laundry equipment and related storage and, when possible, spaces for related activities such as sorting, folding, and possibly ironing (and, much less frequently, sewing). In contrast to other types of utility spaces, laundry rooms/areas are used very frequently by occupants, particularly in large households and those with young children. Given the daily use of these spaces and the varying lifestyles of homeowners, laundry room/area placement varies greatly.

Placement of laundry rooms near bedrooms allows clothes to be kept in the area where they are removed for cleaning, sorted, and put away. For many homeowners, placement on a second floor near bedrooms (rather than on a ground floor many steps from where clothes are removed and stored) is the most desirable laundry room location. Another common location for laundry rooms is near a second entrance, often a service entry or mudroom. Often such areas are adjacent to a garage and serve as a buffer between public and private realms of a home (such placement is discussed as it relates to circulation in Chapter 2).

Location of laundry spaces within a kitchen, or just off a kitchen, is also common. This adjacency allows the person doing work in the kitchen to have easy access to the laundry. In older homes with basements, laundry areas are often located in the basement, although there is currently a remodeling trend that moves laundry areas to a top floor (near bedrooms) in such homes. In new custom home design, the location of laundry rooms is often based on homeowner preferences, whereas in existing homes or tract housing, options for laundry room placement may be quite limited by existing plumbing locations and space availability.

Another major limitation to the design and location of laundry areas is restricted space. Smaller homes, apartments, condominiums, and town houses may simply not offer the space required to create a separate room for laundry-related activities. In such cases, laundry areas may be combined with kitchens, bathrooms, hallways, and mudrooms or second entrances. Often when part of other rooms, laundry areas are neatly hidden behind some type of door or visual screen, nicely shielding untidy items from view. Stacking appliances, which have greatly improved in performance in recent years, allow for stacked washers and dryers to take up a limited footprint, making space available for storage and folding counters or reducing the spatial requirements for the room.

There is a range in terms of homeowners' preferences for the location of the clothes washer and dryer, with many favoring a location near bedrooms, and an equal number favoring a location near the kitchen; some prefer a basement location, and others find a garage preferable. This range of preferences most probably has to do with the owners' lifestyle preferences, whether there are children in the home, and the age and level of mobility of the respondents, as well as simply what people are accustomed to.

ACCESSIBILITY NOTE

Generally, designing utility spaces for wheelchair users requires providing adequate circulation space to the various areas, with no steps (changes in floor level) along the way, and providing enough wheelchair turning space and clear space for wheelchair access in front of appliances and work areas. In designing accessible garages, thought must be given to creating no steps between the garage and the most immediate entrance, as well as to allowing 32 inches (813 mm) of clear circulation space for all portions of the path of travel.

For laundry areas, front-loading appliances work very well for wheelchair users. Controls must also be within reach limitations. In addition, all appliances require clear access space. While some front-loading washers and dryers are stackable, a side-by-side arrangement allows much easier seated use and facilitates transferring laundry. In cases where front-loading versions are not used, assistive devices are available for wheelchair users and those who have mobility limitations; however, this is not an ideal design solution. Accessible laundry room shelves and counters must be located within the comfortable reach range of seated users. For more information on actual clear space requirements and mounting heights, see the "Ergonomics and Required Clearances" section of this chapter.

Clearly, deciding on the best location and room design requires careful consultation regarding homeowners' preferences and a careful review of the overall building design. Location of the laundry room relative to other areas of the home is also discussed in the "Organizational Flow" section of this chapter.

Mudrooms

The concept of a mudroom originated in areas with cold climates, where items such as boots and outer clothes were deposited at the rear entrance to the house as inhabitants came in from outside. This type of utility space has grown in popularity in recent years and is seen as a useful option by many homeowners. The term *mudroom* may be used for an actual room as well as for a hall or simply a transitional area. The space is generally adjacent to the entry used most often by family members and therefore tends to be a high-traffic area.

The mudroom is best located at the rear or side entry of the house and may therefore be adjacent to the garage. The room can serve as a place to drop such items as purses/backpacks/briefcases/laptop cases, shoes, electronic devices, shopping bags, outerwear, and sporting items. Storage of such items in this location keeps them from piling up in the kitchen or other nearby rooms. In some cases the mudroom can serve as a small version of a warehouse or "shipping and receiving" facility. Some of the items mentioned earlier may be better stored elsewhere, depending on the frequency of use and the amount of available space. When possible, the mudroom should contain items for everyday use rather than those items used infrequently.

In some cases, the mudroom is combined with the laundry facilities to form a laundry/mudroom. In other situations, the mudroom is completely separate from the laundry facilities and in some cases may include a home office or hobby area. The "Organizational Flow" section of this chapter includes plans for laundry areas combined with mudrooms, as well as one mudroom without laundry facilities. Larger homes are most likely to have the mudroom separate from the laundry facilities, as are those with laundry areas adjacent to upstairs bedroom areas.

In designing mudrooms, one must consider the lifestyle of the homeowner(s) and the ages of the inhabitants, needs for accessibility, and requirements for any special items. Mudrooms meant to house children's items must have coat hooks and storage areas set at heights that can be reached by children, whereas mudrooms meant for sports enthusiasts require adequate spaces for sporting equipment and clothing storage. Some homeowners prefer the mudroom as a location for a charging station for electronic devices, whereas others prefer an area with no exposure to damp and wet items for a charging station location.

Depending on the situation (and budget), mudrooms may include sinks and/or be adjacent to bathrooms or showers. Given that mudrooms are meant as transitional areas where shoes and clothing are changed or removed, including a bench or seat and shoe storage is worth pursuing. The following is a list of items that may be included in mudrooms or similar transitional areas within a home.

Mudroom Options Checklist

☐ Clothing hooks, rods, pegs, shelves, or lockers—cold-weather items require more space than warm-weather items, as they are bulkier. Closed storage such as closets or storage cabinets help to keep the area looking tidy, although space and budgets do not always allow for this.

☐ Shoe storage with a waterproof or water-resistant base. This may be provided with portable waterproof trays or through the use of flooring finishes that can withstand water, dirt, and mud.

☐ Storage for wet items, such as mittens and umbrellas, is helpful at or near air diffuser(s).

- ☐ Seating, with or without storage underneath (make every inch count).

- ☐ A range of storage options depending on lifestyle: bins, trays, open cubbies, baskets, key racks, specialized sporting goods storage (bins, lockers, or shelves may be included).

- ☐ A "staging area" for the life of the home that might include any of the following:

  - ☐ Electronic device charging and storage area.

  - ☐ Recycling/rubbish bins.

  - ☐ Hooks or storage for pet-related items.

  - ☐ Pantry-type storage for nonperishable food.

  - ☐ Secondary refrigerator, freezer, or beverage storage (rare but worth considering if space is limited in other areas of the home).

  - ☐ Mirror and related grooming items.

  - ☐ Cork board, whiteboard, or chalkboard.

  - ☐ Boot/shoe scraper.

  - ☐ Sink. This includes the option of utility-type sinks at counter height as well as floor sinks for washing off boots or pets.

  - ☐ Drinking water fountain.

  - ☐ Shower.

Because mudrooms tend to be similar to closets or may incorporate closets, a review of the discussion of closets in Chapter 5 may be helpful. Due to their location in heavy-traffic areas, it is important to provide enough space for both circulation and use of storage areas, as discussed later in this chapter in the "Organizational Flow" section.

Home Office/Work Spaces

Homeowners' requirements for home offices and related work spaces vary greatly. Some home offices function much like formal, private offices, with a standard desk, credenza, file cabinets, and conference table, while others are not much more than a small work surface with room for a laptop computer. Creating a useful home office or work area requires very careful assessment of the actual needs of the homeowner, the budget, and the limitations of space (in both new construction and remodeling situations).

In cases where the home office is meant to serve as the primary office (or serves as a professional office a few days a week), a needs assessment much like those done for commercial office projects should be conducted. Such an assessment would uncover answers to the following questions.

Home Office/Work Space Requirements List

- Is this the primary office?

- What level of privacy is desired? Is a separate room required? If so, is there space available and money in the budget to allow for this?

The need for privacy may mean the need for a separate room or small building on the home site. If so, research should be conducted about zoning restrictions applicable to secondary building(s) on the property.

In some cases, the need for privacy is not as much an issue as is keeping work and work surfaces protected from children and pets—this is worth investigating.

- Does the public visit the space?*

  This may mean an adjacency to an exterior entrance is required.

- Will there be additional employees who require a work space/desk?*

  In addition to needs for space and furnishings, this means the room should be adjacent to an exterior entrance.

- What type of equipment is needed: printer/fax machine?

  Desk or work surface space should be provided as necessary. Additional horizontal surfaces may be required for a monitor, copier, and other equipment.

- Is space required for reference materials such as books, large sheets of paper, and notebooks?

  Desk or work surface space should be provided as necessary. This means literally measuring the necessary items and providing appropriately located space for them.

- Are additional areas required for drawing, painting, working with art or craft-related items, or sewing, as well as for storage of such items and/or related supplies?

  Desk or work surface space should be provided as necessary.

- Is a visual or spatial connection to family members or other rooms/areas within the house desired?

  A need for visual or spatial connection creates a need for adjacency to specific rooms or areas and may mean that the work space is set within a larger room rather than separated. Or perhaps the space can be divided using transparent partitions.

- Is equipment needed for paper storage and/or filing? Is any additional storage required?

  Filing cabinets, shelves, and additional storage furnishings may be required as well as space to access these.

- Is any other special equipment required?

  These items may require additional electrical or plumbing. In addition, special furnishings and additional circulation space may be required.

- Is a bulletin board, pin-up board, chalkboard, or whiteboard required?

- Can any existing furnishings be used to furnish the space?

   An inventory (including each item's dimensions) should be completed.

- Is wheelchair accessibility required?*

In some cases, the home office is used for "homework," that is, work done after the homeowner leaves the primary office. Needs for this type of space vary widely, in that some people do not want to be isolated from family members or entertainment while doing this work, so that privacy may not be desired. However, for other individuals privacy is necessary.

Using the preceding list can point to the level of privacy/quiet required in the space as well as its placement relative to an exterior entrance or rooms within the house.

Some homeowners desire work areas where they can use a computer and have access to household or personal files but do not require a traditional work space. For this type of work, the space may be best located where family members are present or in or near the kitchen so that multiple tasks related to family responsibilities may be performed while working.

In cases where the home office/work space is not needed as the primary office space or in cases where significant paper storage is not required, a rather simple desk, a desk-like built-in, or a version of an old-fashioned secretary desk may work well to serve as a casual, nonprivate home office.

As technology evolves to allow us to work with ever smaller electronic devices, the area required for home offices may actually shrink. However, less room for certain types of hardware must be balanced with the needs for secondary (or more) computer monitors for work and gaming as well as work areas for non-computer-related activities.

As indicated in the preceding paragraphs, the design of home offices and work spaces must relate directly to the type of work being done, the level of privacy required, the needs for nonfamily members to visit the space, and other constraints. These needs must be identified so that the space works well for the intended purposes.

In planning for furniture sizing and placement, a careful review of the home office/work space requirements will lead to an understanding of specific requirements. Significant requirements for computer hardware or monitor space may require larger work surfaces or desks. Requirements for access to reference materials may lead to larger work surfaces or a credenza-type piece of furniture located adjacent to the main work surface.

---

*If goods or services are provided that make this a public space, it may need to meet ADAAG and/or there may be zoning and parking issues that fall outside the realm of this book; this is true in the case of having employees working within a residence as well.

Planning for art, crafts, and specialized types of work requires a careful inventory of the required materials, tools, and equipment as well as an understanding of basic ergonomics of work areas. Information on basic work surface/desk ergonomics can be found in Appendix G.

Managing Electronic Devices

Charging stations used for storing and charging electronic devices are a useful addition to home work areas or other utility areas. These can be seen as "drop-off stations" or as a "home base" for electronics, where items are dropped as one comes home. This means a charging station may be located within home work areas or at the entry (front or rear) or in any other location (such as a closet or dressing area) that makes sense given the lifestyle of the homeowner.

Options for charging stations include manufactured versions that come ready to plug in and accept a number of devices, those that may be ordered with furniture (such as those for desks and mudroom-type storage furniture), versions of power strips that are well located within utility spaces, and custom versions designed for specific locations. Wireless charging stations are evolving for home use and offer the benefit of fewer power cords.

The key to creating a well-designed home base or charging station is to identify the needs of the homeowner and any spatial or budgetary constraints. An important aspect of understanding the needs of the homeowner is to clearly identify the best location for the station or stations. Possible locations include a home office or work area, a mudroom at the rear of the house, or the kitchen. The "Organizational Flow" section of this chapter has some examples of utility rooms with charging stations. Increasingly, charging stations may be housed in a number of locations.

Managing Household Paperwork and Activities

Some households deal with large quantities of paperwork in the form of mail and papers generated by schools, clubs, and organizations. One approach to dealing with this is to team a mail/paperwork station with the drop-off or charging station described previously.

As with other rooms and areas mentioned, the design of a mail/paper station requires an understanding of the homeowner's lifestyle and available space. Shelves, cubbies, file cabinets, and standard cabinets with drawers and/or doors are some options for storage and management of the various types of paperwork found within a home.

A paperwork/mail station is best located in an area/space where mail and/or people come in and out of the house or in another central location where items are easily deposited and retrieved. Some homeowners find it helpful to locate bulletin boards and chalkboards/whiteboards in this location so that paperwork, calendars, schedules, and notes are all in a single location. Others find that keeping calendars and schedules in (or near) the kitchen or another spot that is often visited is most helpful.

Home Gyms and Exercise Equipment

Home gyms range in size and complexity. In some cases, there is no dedicated space (just some equipment tucked away), while other home gyms are large, luxurious spaces with rows of expensive equipment that would rival any club. Designing home gyms (or areas for exercise equipment) requires an understanding of a client's lifestyle, budget, available space, and motivation.

Relative to lifestyle, it is important to understand a client's motivation and objectives for creating a home gym. A client who is interested in simply losing weight may be well served by a single piece of cardiovascular equipment (such as a treadmill, stationary bike, or elliptical machine) that is located within a family room or within a bedroom. A client who is motivated to lift weights, do cardiovascular work, and stretch or do yoga often may require a room dedicated to these activities and equipped with audiovisual equipment.

Even those homeowners who are highly motivated to work out and maintain a home gym may benefit from starting with a few pieces of equipment and buying additional items progressively as they deem new items necessary. This is worth considering from constraints of both budget and space, because high-quality machines are expensive and take up significant space. It is also worth noting that some serious athletes find it perfectly acceptable to place a treadmill directly in front of a television in a great room. In this scenario, the athlete treats the treadmill much like others treat a comfortable recliner chair, but this may be the exception rather than standard practice.

In many cases, homeowners have the desire, funds, and space to create a room dedicated to service as a home gym. Such rooms must be large enough to contain the desired equipment as well as circulation space to access the equipment. In some cases, areas intended for mats for stretching and yoga or dance activities may do double duty as circulation space (if only one person at a time uses the space). Consideration of cooling and ventilation is necessary in rooms dedicated to exercise in order to cool the participant and to exhaust the space. According to the American Council on Exercise (2009), exercisers may be better off with a multi-gym, which is safer to use unsupervised than free weights. In cases where a multi-gym does not fit the budget or space, the council indicates that "a set of free-weights is an affordable alternative, as is resistance tubing." One caution: free weights may be quite heavy and can be dropped,

so they therefore are best housed on a floor designed for that increased load.

One way to approach the planning of home gyms is to consider each type of equipment as existing within a zone, as indicated in the following list.

Home Gym Zones or Areas

- Cardio

  Should include at least one cardiovascular-type machine such as a cross-trainer, elliptical trainer, treadmill, or stationary bicycle. Some homeowners opt for two cardio-type machines.

- Stretching/aerobics/pilates

  Must be at least the size of a full-body-length mat and provide circulation space as required. This may be roughly 25 to 50 percent of the total floor area of the room.

  Possible additions include an incline bench, resistance bands, foam blocks, and large inflatable balls.

- Weights and resistance equipment

  May include free weights, dumbbells, and/or a multi-gym machine.

  May include a weight bench with or without a bar.

  May include additional machines, including seated types and pull-up bars.

Due to the wide variation in quality, cost, and equipment size, providing standard dimensions is problematic, so no dimensions are given here. However, the American Council on Exercise has created guidelines for planning home gyms that are listed in Table 7-1. Note that the actual space required will vary greatly and that these are meant for preliminary planning only.

Table 7-1 Planning Estimates for Exercise Equipment

Item	Area Needed	
	Square feet	**m²**
Treadmill	30	2.79
Single-station gym	35	3.25
Free weights	20–50	1.86–4.645
Stationary bike	10	0.92
Rowing machine	20	1.86
Stair climber	10–20	0.92–1.86
Ski machine	25	2.32
Multi-station gym	50–200	4.645–18.6

APPLIANCES

Both front-loading and top-loading washers are available in full-sized models that are roughly 27 inches (686 mm) wide. Considering size is critical for fitting into cabinetry, closets, and small rooms. Compact models are typically 24 inches (610 mm) wide and can be stacked with compact dryers of the same width. Information on appliance sizes can be found in Figure 7-1. In considering the size of the machine and its relationship to built-in cabinetry, one must consider adequate space at the rear and sides of the machines in order to allow for venting and for ease of removal for maintenance. Note that the height of equipment varies greatly. Check with manufacturer's specifications and verify against existing ceiling heights.

Clothes dryers may use gas or electricity to heat the air. Additionally, dryers vary in how sensors are programmed to shut off, which can be done by way of a thermostat or moisture sensors. Full-sized models measure between 27 and 29 inches (686 and 737 mm) wide, and, as with washers, size is critical. Front-mounted controls on some models allow stacking the dryer atop a front-loading washer.

Gas dryers are more costly to purchase but may result in lower energy costs in the long run (this will vary based on world energy costs).

Compact models are generally electric and are roughly 24 inches (610 mm) wide, with a drum capacity roughly half that of full-sized models. Compact dryers can be stacked on top of a companion washer. Some compact dryers operate on 120 volts, while others require a 240-volt outlet (as do full-sized electric dryers).

A combination washer and dryer, a single appliance similar to stacked units, is another space-saving option. These are available with gas or electric dryers in full-sized and compact sizes. Space saving is also supplied by units that combine washing and drying in a single unit. Such models use the same drum for washing and drying.

One additional consideration in washer/dryer utility spaces is noise. In small living spaces, or those where the utility space is in close proximity to leisure or sleeping spaces, quiet models should be selected. Front-loading washers are generally considered less noisy than top-loading models, but this varies with the model selected. Appliance noise is less of an issue when appliances are located in a separate room with a door.

Storage provided by cabinetry can be much like that discussed for kitchens and baths. Laundry rooms/areas are made much more useful with the inclusion of work counters for folding and sorting clothing. In addition, storage for laundry products and other household items can be provided with built-in cabinetry. Generally speaking, cabinets designed for kitchen use can be used in laundry and hobby/craft/sewing rooms. Manufacturers of kitchen cabinets make fittings and specialty units for use in utility rooms; these include hampers, ironing boards, and special height/depth wall cabinets that accommodate front-loading washers/dryers on pedestals (see Figure 7-2). Compact washer and dryer models are typically available in heights that allow them to sit under a standard counter.

Figure 7-1 Washer and dryer sizes—plan views.

1. Front-loading models are typically 34 to 38 inches (864 to 965 mm) high, with matching pedestals available that raise the door height to prevent stooping and bending; pedestals often offer storage and are roughly 12 inches (305 mm) high. Top-loading models are typically higher than front-loading models, at roughly 36 to 42 inches (914 to 1067 mm) high. There are full-sized combination units that combine a washer and dryer in the same single machine.
2. Compact models are roughly 33 inches (838 mm) high and can fit under standard countertops. There are compact units that combine a washer and dryer in the same single unit (not stacked).
3. Heights vary from 71 to 75 inches (1803 to 1905 mm), plus or minus.
4. Heights vary from 36 to 42 inches (914 to 1067 mm), plus or minus.

WASHERS: PLAN VIEWS

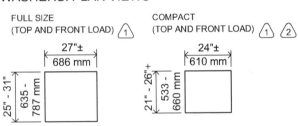

DRYERS: PLAN VIEWS

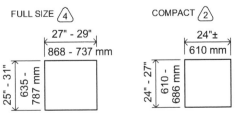

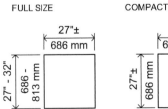

Figure 7-2 Kitchen cabinet manufacturers make laundry room cabinets that are similar to kitchen cabinets in size and construction. In addition, cabinets in special sizes and with special laundry-related fittings such as hampers and foldout ironing boards are available. The wall cabinets shown are deeper and taller than standard kitchen wall cabinets, to accommodate a front-loading washer and dryer on a pedestal.

Photograph courtesy of KraftMaid Cabinetry.

Sustainability Note

Energy-efficient washers can lower energy costs, and can also help reduce greenhouse gas emissions. In addition to conserving energy, an efficient washing machine can conserve water resources and lighten the burden on municipal sewer systems. Some states offer financial incentives related to the purchase of highly efficient washers and dryers, and some municipalities and states limit water use.

Washing machines come in a variety of loading types, including front-loading and top-loading models. Front-loading models are gaining in popularity because of their good washing performance, large capacity, and efficient use of energy and water. In response to this, manufacturers have developed top-loading models that offer some of the advantages of the front loaders. All types of washing machines and clothes dryers have become more efficient as a result of consumer demand and stricter U.S. Department of Energy standards regulating water and energy use. Both washers and dryers are regulated under the mandatory EnergyGuide and the voluntary Energy Star programs. According to the Energy Star website, a full sized Energy Star–certified washer uses 13 gallons of water per load compared to the 23 gallons used by a standard machine."

ERGONOMICS AND REQUIRED CLEARANCES

Generally, laundry rooms require appropriate space for the desired appliances as well as clear space in front of appliances to access them. Figure 7-3a illustrates "good practice" standard clearances for washers, dryers, and ironing board.

ACCESSIBILITY NOTE

Laundry rooms designed for use by those in wheelchairs must grant clear space for access in front of the washer and dryer. In addition, seated reach height and appliance control locations must be considered—in most cases stacked washer/dryer combinations are not a good choice for wheelchair users. See Figure 7-3b for wheelchair clearance information.

Figure 7-3a Standard clearances for laundry rooms.

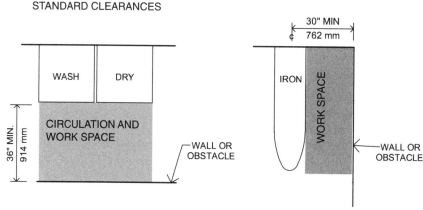

STANDARD CLEARANCES

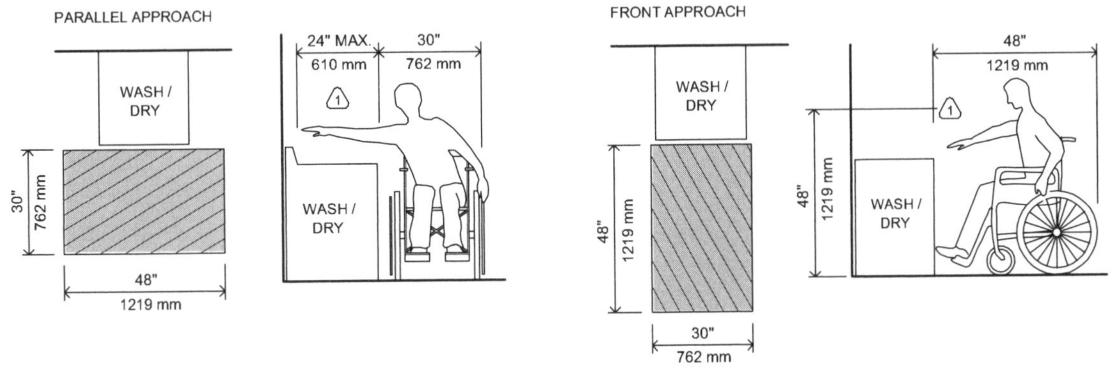

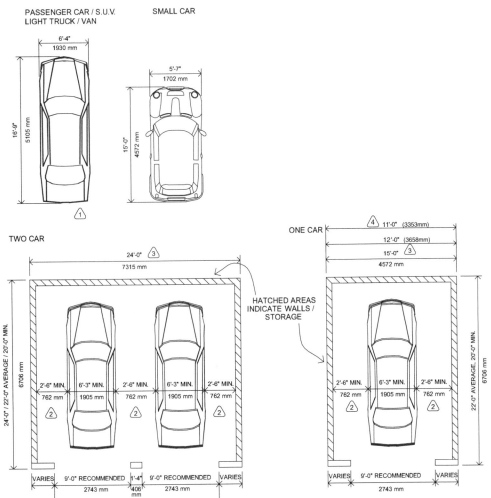

Figure 7-3b Wheelchair clearances for laundry room/space items.

1. Equipment controls must be within this zone (controls must be within reach height of a wheelchair user). Front-load models with controls on the front are ideal as the controls are well within this range.

Garages and carports require space for circulation around the car as well as room for door clearance and, of course, room enough for the car itself. These spaces should allow a range of car sizes. Carports may be designed to include storage spaces, and these may provide secure storage (when locked) for items often stored in garages, such as sporting and lawn equipment. Figure 7-4 illustrates a range of car sizes and minimum clearance spaces recommended for garages and carports. Figure 7-5 illus-

Figure 7-4 Car sizes and garage/carport clearances.

1. Some SUVs and pickup trucks may be up to 19 feet (5842 mm) long.
2. To allow wheelchair access would require 5 feet (1524 mm) of clearance space in at least one of these locations.
3. Wheelchair access will require minimum garage width: 15 feet (4572 mm) for a single garage; 24 feet (7313 mm) for a double garage.
4. This dimension requires that passengers be let out of the vehicle before it pulls into garage

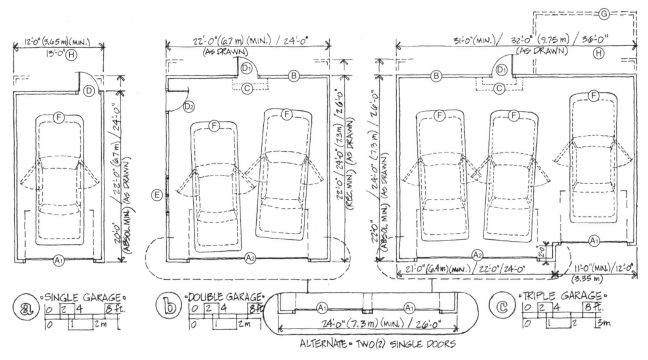

Figure 7-5 Dimensional requirements for one-, two-, and three-car garages.

A₁. Single: 9 feet (2743 mm) wide minimum by 7 feet/8 feet (2134/2438 mm) high.

A₂. Double: 16 feet (4877 mm) wide minimum by 7 feet/8 feet (2134/2438 mm) high. Alternative: larger doors; as large SUVs have become more common, homeowners may desire taller doors. Wider doors have also become more common:
  Single: 10 feet (3048 mm) wide by 8 feet (2438 mm) high.
  Double: 18 feet (5486 mm) wide by 8 feet (2438 mm) high.

B. As noted in the "Related Codes and Constraints" section, in attached garages, fire-rated walls and doors are required between the house and garage, as is a fire-rated ceiling if there is habitable space above the garage.

C. Houses that are built over basements or crawl spaces will require steps up from the garage (floor) level to the house floor level; this is generally provided by a minimum of two steps that are 7 inches (178 mm), plus or minus, each.

D. Passage door widths: 2 feet, 6 inches to 3 feet (762 to 914 mm).
  D₁. Although not a requirement, garage-to-house door will generally swing into the house.
  D₂. Garage-to-exterior door can swing in or out, but commonly swings in. There is no requirement for this door except in code jurisdictions where a second exit out of the house can be through the garage; in such cases the overhead garage door would not be a legal exit.

E. Windows. None required, but if provided, select windows that relate visually to those used in the house.

F. Vehicle icons show a small car (dashed line) and a larger car (solid line); the solid line represents the footprint of a vehicle such as an average SUV or van.

G. Ancillary space for storage can be achieved by adding depth (front to back) to the garage, or in some cases, the footprint of the attached house may allow space for an alcove (this can be used for shop or storage).

H. Use of larger doors, such as 10 feet (3048 mm) wide for single and 18 feet (5486 mm) for double, will typically require the larger building width shown.

trates additional issues related to garage sizes, clearances, and design.

ORGANIZATIONAL FLOW

As stated previously, laundry room placement varies greatly and relates to adjacent spaces and their uses as well as to overall spatial limitations and constraints. Laundry room design also varies greatly in items included and overall space used. Clearly, there is quite a range of workable possibilities. Some reasonable options are illustrated here to convey various possible room and space sizes. Figure 7-6 shows some small utility rooms and closets.

Figures 7-7 and 7-8 illustrate larger utility rooms, some of which serve combined purposes. These larger rooms are shown with a bubble diagram of adjacent spaces in order to convey spatial relationships within the residence.

RELATED CODES AND CONSTRAINTS

According to the International Residential Code (IRC), laundry rooms and utility spaces are not considered habitable rooms and therefore need not meet previously mentioned requirements such as minimum room dimensions and window requirements. Most codes related to laundry areas concern

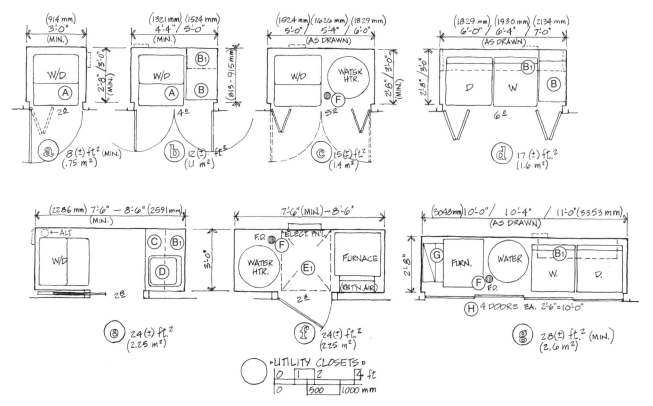

Figure 7-6 Utility closets with washer/dryers.

A. Stacking washer and dryer, drawn 27 inches (686 mm) wide by 30 inches (762 mm) deep (see Figure 7-1).
B. Small base cabinet with door; counter at 36 inches (915 mm) high with back shelf.
 B_1. Wall cabinet for laundry supplies.
C. Counter at 36 inches (915 mm) high with clothes hamper below.
D. Utility sink.
E. Electrical service panel requires (per the IRC) a clear space (E_1), 3 feet by 2 feet, 6 inches wide (915 by 762 mm) by 6 feet, 6 inches (1981 mm) high, in front of the electrical panel for service access.
F. Floor drain for water heater and condensate from furnace/air conditioner. A floor drain (F_1) at washing machine locations is a good idea, when possible.
G. Return air to furnace; ideally mixing with some outside, tempered, fresh air.
H. Sliding doors on three tracks.

Note: Water heater and furnace equipment vary greatly in terms of size; items shown are average sizes.

electrical and plumbing and are covered in the section that follows. Local codes may require second-floor (or higher) clothes washers to sit on an overflow pan (laundry tray) to prevent water overflow from pouring onto the floor and intruding into the ceiling below.

Section R302.6 of the IRC requires that garages be separated from the residence and its attic area by "not less than ½ inch (127 mm) gypsum board applied to the garage side." This section also calls for garages beneath habitable rooms to be separated from habitable rooms above "by not less than ⅝ inch (15.9 mm) Type X gypsum board or equivalent." Section R309 of the IRC governs garages and carports and requires that the floor surface in garages and carports be of "approved noncombustible material" and that they be sloped to facilitate draining. Carports are required to be open on a minimum of two sides (Section R309.2).

ELECTRICAL AND MECHANICAL

Section E3703.3 of the IRC requires a minimum of "one 20 ampere-rated branch circuit" for receptacles in the laundry area and states that these " shall serve only receptacle outlets located in the laundry area." In addition to these items required by code, an electric dryer may require a 240-volt circuit.

Section E3901.5 of the IRC requires appliance receptacle outlets for specific appliances, for instance, laundry equipment, be installed within 6 feet (1829 mm) of the appliance location. Section E3901.9 requires that each basement and garage have at least one receptacle outlet in addition to any provided for laundry equipment (Section E3901.8), and garages must have one receptacle outlet for each motor vehicle space.

Regarding storage and equipment spaces, Section E3903.4 requires that in "attics, under-floor spaces, utility rooms, basements,

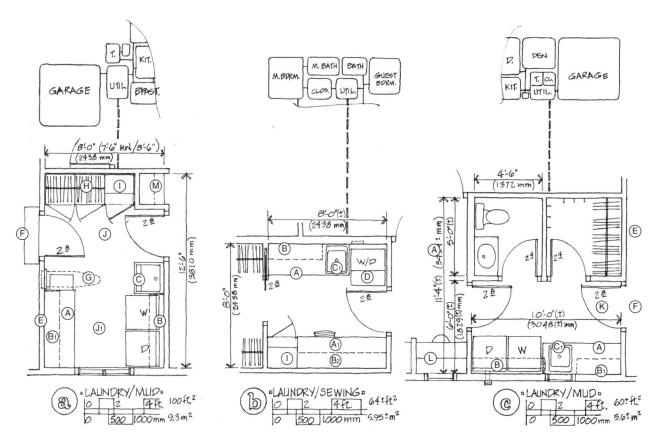

Figure 7-7 Laundry rooms.

A. Work counter for sorting and folding clothes with hamper below.

  A_1 Lower work counter required for sewing (28-inch [711-mm] height). A_1 could also be adapted for use as a charging/mail station with a change in counter height (see Appendix G for work surface height information).

B. Wall cabinet for laundry/cleaning supplies.

  B_1. General storage.

  B_2. Sewing supplies.

C. Utility sink.

  C_1. Deep utility sink in base cabinet.

D. Stacking washer/dryer.

E. In attached garages, fire-rated walls and doors are required between the house and garage, as is a fire-rated ceiling if there is habitable space above the garage. See the "Related Codes and Constraints" section for additional information.

F. Steps to garage, as required.

G. Semi-recessed fold-down ironing board, with fixed bench below.

H. Wardrobe cabinet.

I. Pantry-style cabinet for laundry/cleaning supplies and equipment and/or remote food storage.

J. Through circulation; this is a short distance and the circulation avoids laundry work areas (J_1).

K. Door leads to the garage as shown; an alternate design would allow exit directly to the exterior (exterior or garage steps may be required).

L. Desk with charging and mail station and two shelves (below window).

M. Small work surface and charging station.

and garages at least one lighting outlet shall be installed," where these areas are used for servicing of equipment or storage. The section continues by stating that the required lighting outlet should be controlled by a wall switch or "an integral switch."

Dryers vent heat and water vapor, including some lint, through a duct that must attach to the machine and carry exhaust to the building exterior. Flexible dryer ducts made of foil or plastic can prove problematic because they can sag and allow lint buildup at low points. For this reason, it is best to select rigid metal or flexible metal ducts.

LIGHTING

Because they are rooms in which a range of visual tasks is performed, laundry rooms are made more pleasant, useful, and comfortable with well-designed lighting features. Laundry room and hobby/craft/sewing room cabinetry and work

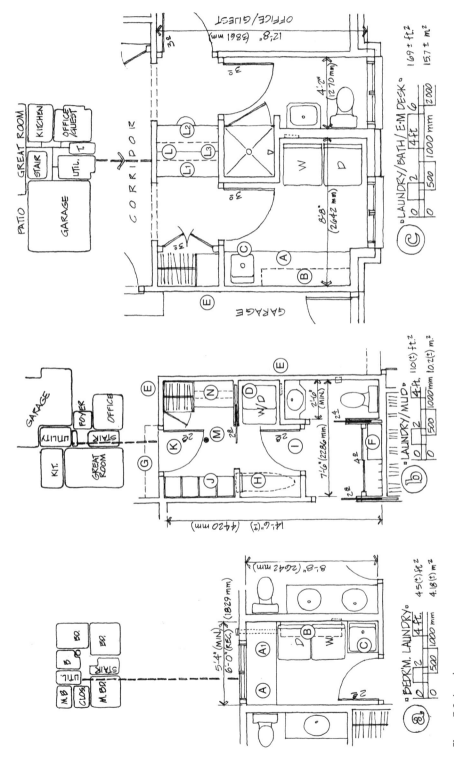

Figure 7-8 Laundry rooms.

A. Work counter for sorting and folding clothes with hamper below. (In **example a**, the disadvantage of this arrangement is a dead corner at A_1.)

B. Wall cabinet for laundry/cleaning supplies.

C. Utility sink.

D. Stacking washer/dryer.

E. In attached garages, fire-rated walls and doors are required between the house and garage, as is a fire-rated ceiling if there is habitable space above the garage. See the "Related Codes and Constraints" section for additional information.

F. Closet (12 inches [305 mm] deep, with sliding doors) for laundry/cleaning supplies and equipment.

G. Steps to garage, as required.

H. Semi-recessed fold-down ironing board, with fixed bench below.

I. A door can be useful at this location; serves as an acoustic, visual, and/or thermal barrier when door at K is open.

J. Cubbyholes/open storage for outerwear, boots, and so on.

K. Door leads to the garage as shown; an alternate design would allow exit directly to the exterior (exterior steps may be required).

L. Charging/mail station at desk with access from both sides. Standing height (42 inches [1067 mm]) (L_1) and sitting (at stool) desk/work center (L_2) is just outside adjacent guest room/office. With overhead cabinets (L_3). See Appendix G for information on sitting and standing desk heights.

M. Floor drain. Floor must slope to drain in order for it to be effective.

N. Bench with cabinet above.

counters are similar to those in kitchens, and therefore room lighting for these is much like that in kitchens. Undercabinet lighting can provide helpful task lighting, while top-of-cabinet lighting as well as pendant luminaires can create pleasant ambient lighting, making the many hours spent doing laundry more agreeable. Reviewing the information in Chapter 4 about kitchen area lighting can aid in planning laundry and hobby/craft/sewing rooms. Mudrooms and other rooms that include desks and charging and/or mail stations may require good task lighting as well as ambient lighting.

Figure 7-9 is an electrical/lighting plan included to illustrate fixture locations and switching.

California Title 24

California's Energy California's Title 24 regulates lighting in laundry and utility rooms and requires the following:

1. **High efficacy and controls:** High-efficacy luminaires are required in garages, laundry rooms, and utility rooms. These must be controlled by a vacancy sensor.

2. **Garage door openers:** Lighting integral to garage door openers does not have to be high efficacy when there are no more than two screw-base sockets integrated by the manufacturer and the lights automatically turn on and off.

The following are additional Title 24 recommended practices; these are not requirements but offer helpful guidelines for energy efficiency:

1. **Ensure light levels are up to the task:** Ensure that general light levels are sufficient for navigation from the garage to the house, but provide much more light in areas where auto repairs take place or power tools may be used, etc. IESNA recommends light levels up to 20 times higher for these types of task areas.

2. **Switch task lighting separately:** Task lighting, such as undercabinet lighting, helps make work areas safer, more comfortable, and more energy efficient. Place task lighting on a separate switch from general lighting.

3. **Choose ultrasonic or dual-technology vacancy sensors:** Compared to standard passive infrared (PIR) vacancy sensors, ultrasonic and dual-technology sensors are less likely to turn off while occupants are behind cars or other objects.

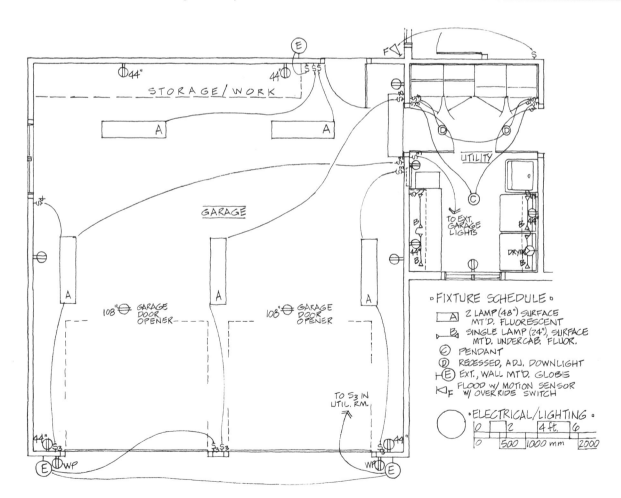

Figure 7-9 An electrical/lighting plan illustrating some options for utility area lighting.

REFERENCES

Contains both works cited and recommended reading.

American Council on Exercise. 2009. "How to Design Your Own Home Gym." http://www.acefitness.org/acefit/ fitness-fact-article/2588/how-to-design-your-own-home-gym/.

California Lighting Technology Center. 2014. "2013 Title 24 Part 6: Building Energy Efficiency Standards." http://cltc.ucdavis.edu/title24.

Clagette, Leslie. 2010. "Plumber. Making a Mudroom." This Old House. http://www.thisoldhouse.com/toh/article/0,,195148,00.html.

Curtis, Sophie. 2015. "Wireless Charging: Everything You Need to Know."

http://www.telegraph.co.uk/technology/news/11434736/Wireless-charging-everything-you-need-to-know.html#disqus_thread.

International Code Council. 2003. *International Residential Code 2003*. Florence, KY: Thomson Delmar Learning.

Keidel.com. 2010. "Mudrooms." http://www.keidel.com/design/mud.htm.

National Association of Home Builders. 2004. "*Housing Facts, Figures, and Trends 2004: What 21st Century Home Buyers Want.*" Washington, DC: NAHB Advocacy/Public Affairs and the NAHB Economics Group.

———. 2010. "Home Size Continues to Decline; Buyers Increasingly Opt for Single Story Homes." http://www.nahb.org/news_details.aspx?newsID510898.

Rumbarger, Janet, and Richard Vitullo, eds. 2003. *Architectural Graphic Standards for Residential Construction*. Hoboken, NJ: John Wiley & Sons.

U.S. Department of Energy. 2015. Energy Star: Clothes Washers for Consumers. https://www.energystar.gov/products/certified-products/detail/clothes-washers.

CHAPTER 8

Sample Project and Related Drawings

Because this book has a fragmented, room-by-room approach, this chapter is provided as a means of illustrating a synthesis of the first seven chapters. This chapter outlines a sample project, with the related scenario and program and the related project drawings, so that readers may see an illustration of the synthesis of all of the elements that are called for in the first chapter. As noted in Chapter 1, successful design requires careful consideration of the needs of the client measured against budgetary, code, climate, and site restrictions—all of which require careful development of a project program prior to the beginning of the actual design of the project. Those issues brought together with elements covered in each previous chapter form the basis of this chapter.

Additional information about building construction and structure is provided in Chapter 9 and may prove helpful as a reference as one reviews the information provided here.

SAMPLE PROJECT SCENARIO/ PROBLEM STATEMENT

The owners are a man (aged 52) and woman (aged 55), who wish to downsize and move from their current home located on the outskirts of a city (population 72,000) to a location closer to the core of the city. One of them works in the city, while the other works at home.

They wish to build a home that does not exceed 1000 square feet (92.9 m²) in the initial construction and that is designed with future expansion capabilities. Plans for future expansion are based on recognition of the fact that future owners may need more space—especially more bedrooms (these are among the items they are seeking in the expansion). Ideally, the need for a home office would be met by a separate structure built on the property in the near future.

The homeowners share an interest in gardening and would like an outdoor living space with as much privacy as possible. Given the local climate, the outdoor space would be used about five months out of the year. Both of the homeowners have spent considerable time at family cottages in Upper Michigan during summers and have requested a "cottage feel" for their new home (they have mentioned they would erect a log cabin, but realize that it would not be appropriate to the urban setting where they will build).

The following are additional requirements, constraints, and budgetary and site information.

Project Programming Information

Construction budget:

$225,000 for Phase 1, not including site purchase, landscaping, or fees

Phase 1 to Include:

Basement:

They want a basement for the following functions (all unfinished in Phase 1):

> A future guest room with full bath
>
> Mechanical/electrical equipment
>
> Storage
>
> Storm safety
>
> Multipurpose activity room

First floor:

They need to have all essential living functions on the main floor level so they can, reasonably, age in place (with adaptations).

> Great room:
>
> An open living area with kitchen, dining, and a sitting area with a small (gas) fireplace and television; as much natural light as possible
>
> Owner's bedroom suite:
>
> A bedroom to accommodate a queen-size bed (accommodate a king size for future owners, if possible); adjacent bathroom with shower—no tub; walk-in closet preferred
>
> Visitors' half bath
>
> Utility/mudroom with a washer and dryer

Expansion capabilities:

A minimum of two more bedrooms and full bath for future owner(s)

Phase 2 to Include:

A future building with one garage stall, a writer's studio, and a small gardening/potting room

Outdoor space:

Patio; plumbing for future kitchen: sink, gas grill

Deck: optional

Site Considerations

The site is half of a larger site that contained three Quonset hut residences (post–World War II), each on a 40-foot-wide (12,192-mm) lot. A builder/developer bought all three, demolished the buildings, and divided the site in half, yielding two lots, each 60 feet (18,288 mm) wide. She built one house prior to the recession of 2008; however, the remaining parcel, measuring 60 feet by 120 feet (18,288 by 36,576 mm), was purchased by the client for this project.

The lot is zoned R-1; most of the houses in the neighborhood were built late in the 1920s and immediately following World War II. Neighborhood houses are a mix of 1-story and 1½-story, with the occasional 2-story.

There is an alley at the rear of the property; the street runs for 10 blocks but is not heavily traveled. The nearest through street runs perpendicular—2½ blocks away—and has bus service. The edge of the historical/commercial center is about 1.8 miles (2.9 km) away. Roughly a quarter of the houses in the neighborhood have a front porch, and the owners would like a front porch (if the budget allows). The neighborhood has sidewalks and appears pedestrian friendly.

Space, furniture, and equipment requirements are indicated in Table 8-1.

SAMPLE PROJECT DESIGN DRAWINGS

Diagrams

As stated in Chapter 1, diagrams can serve as a bridge between programming and preliminary project design. Figure 8-1 illustrates preliminary site diagrams for the sample project.

As previously discussed, designers generally create many bubble and other schematic diagrams. Figure 8-2 shows bubble diagram studies for the project. Another type of diagram, known as a blocking diagram, shows rooms/spaces in rough approximation of their final proportions with accurate adjacencies and room orientation, as shown in Figure 8-2, item **e**.

Preliminary Orthographic Projection Drawings

Figures 8-3 to 8-7 were drawn manually (freehand, without drafting tools other than a pencil, on ⅛-inch fade-out grid paper). For many designers, drawing manually prior

Table 8-1 Sample Project Space, Furniture, and Equipment Requirements, with Notes (Phase 1)

Net Square Footage	Room/Area Comments
480 (44.6 m²)	Great room: Capture daylight. Kitchen: Open to the room, two cooks, an island with counter seating for 2 (min.), large refrigerator/freezer, 30-inch dual range (gas cooktop/electric convection oven), dishwasher, no garbage disposer (owners will compost). Dining: Guests (three to four visits, on average, a month) as well as occasional larger gatherings and buffets.
240 (22.3 m²)	Owner's bedroom suite: Bedroom: Accommodate a queen-size bed, good lighting for evening reading. Bath: Water closet (toilet), lavatory (sink), walk-in shower, no bathtub. Closet: Walk-in or reach-in clothes storage; requirements are modest.
65 (6.0 m²)	Utility and mudroom with washing machine and dryer, with door to exterior.
20 (1.9 m²)	Guest half bath: Water closet (toilet), lavatory (sink).
15 (1.4 m²)	Miscellaneous (closets, charging station, etc.).
820 (76.2 m²)	Net programmed space (80–85% of total gross).
180 (16.7 m²)	Estimated unprogrammed space (wall thicknesses, circulation, etc.).
1000 (92.9 m²)	Target square footage (gross).

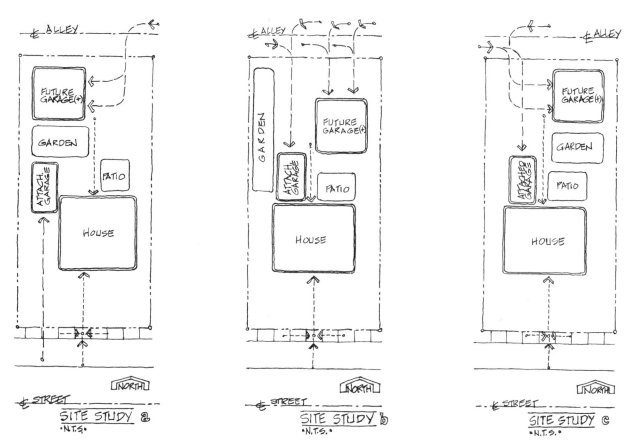

Figure 8-1 Schematic site diagrams showing access to the attached garage from the street.

a. This option creates problems due to duplication of driveways and creates potential massing problems with the house (roofs).
b. This option puts most of the garden and future garage out of view of the house and is too accessible to the alley.
c. This option achieves most of what the owner wants in terms of house, garden, and future garage locations.

to putting projects in CAD (computer-aided design) helps them develop ideas more fully. Some designers create manual drawings on tracing paper first, while others use vellum (grid or plain).

Figures 8-3 to 8-7 are preliminary design drawings used to work through design solutions with the client. These drawings are meant to communicate design intent and to raise and solve issues prior to explicit delineation in the construction documents/contract documents. These preliminary drawings are not intended to provide information for obtaining permits, bidding, and/or construction (that is the purpose of the contract documents).

While these drawings are preliminary and reflect the early design process, they must necessarily follow basic drafting conventions such as the inclusion of titles and north arrows and the use of an accurate scale on all site and floor plans. Drawing scale should also be indicated either in written form or by use of a graphic scaling device.

Chapter 1 contains some basic additional information about design drawings, including commonly used symbols and abbreviations.

Site Plans

A site plan often includes a roof plan of the building as well as the surrounding property and site boundaries, along with adjacent street information and topographic information as required. Site plans require the use of a north arrow and are generally drawn in a scale that permits including the necessary information. In some cases, site plans are drawn at engineer's scales of 1 inch = 20 feet or 1 inch = 30 feet; in other instances, a standard architectural scale such as $1/16$ inch = 1 foot, 0 inches may be used.

When reviewing the site plan shown in Figure 8-3, it might be helpful to consider site-related issues involved in building design. There are, of course, myriad issues to consider related to any building site. The following list provides only an introductory overview of some site-planning issues:

- Local ordinances govern site design and building occupancy; check local zoning prior to beginning the design of any project. Frequently, those areas zoned for single-family occupancy will allow for duplexes. Increasingly, prescriptive standards that are instituted by the municipality, neighborhood, or developer discourage houses

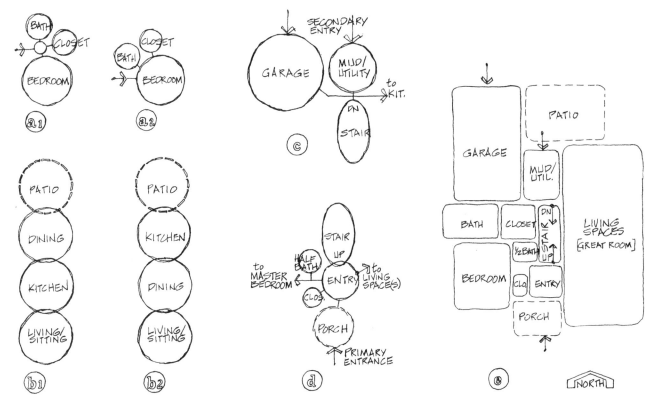

Figure 8-2 Sample bubble diagram studies, with blocking diagram for the project.

a. Owner's suite; these meet or exceed the owner's needs (a_1 and a_2).
b. Great room; these show a shift in kitchen and dining locations—the owners prefer b_2.
c. Secondary entry/exit; approved by owner.
d. Primary entry/exit; approved by owner; while they want a front porch, a large one is not necessary, as they intend to spend most of their time in the backyard garden.
e. This is a blocking diagram with the rooms shown approximately proportional and oriented as they would be placed relative to the site.

that are out of scale and/or out of character with the neighborhood.

- Setbacks are key issues in residential site design. Front setbacks can vary widely, with 20 to 40 feet (6096 to 12,192 mm) the most common. Side setbacks are often 6 feet (1829 m). Rear setbacks can be a percentage of lot depth or a percentage of green space. See Chapter 10 for an additional discussion of setbacks.

- Site design should encourage drainage of water away from building structures, and water should be viewed as an enemy of construction materials. Therefore, positive drainage away from buildings is required, and no standing water should be allowed to collect immediately adjacent to buildings.

- Orientation to the elements is a significant issue in building/site design. Sunlight and protection from the elements vary widely with geography and region, but should be considered and reviewed with clients.

- The location of utilities is another important consideration in site design. When possible, electrical service should be buried. Water service is buried, and the depth is a function of climate. Sewer depth is also deeper in cold climates. The lowest drain in the house should be sufficiently above the sanitary sewer main in the street to allow gravity flow to carry away the house waste. This avoids having to pump the waste up to the sewer main.

- Site design involves planning for the movement of vehicles onto the property in most cases. Local ordinances may require on-site/off-street vehicle parking and/or storage.

- The site should be a major consideration in the design of the building from the very first moment work begins on the project. Site design is about context; the next larger context must be considered. For example, in the design of a building, not only should the immediate site (owner's property) be considered but the larger neighborhood as well.

Floor Plans

As noted previously, floor plans are drawn as though a horizontal cut has been made in the building—typically between

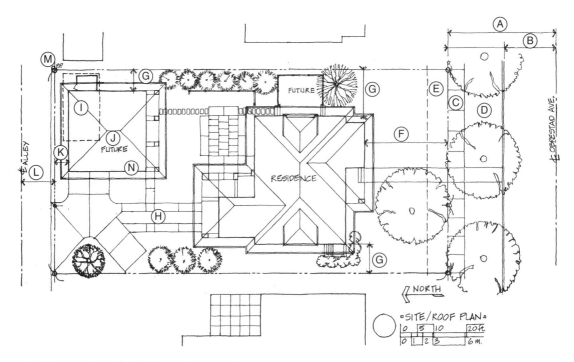

Figure 8-3 A hand-drawn site (and roof) plan for the sample project. The lot size for this project is 60 by 120 feet = 72,000 square feet (18,288 by 36,576 mm = 668.9 m²). The percentage of green space (uncovered ground that will absorb rainfall) is 55 percent, with the proposed building on the lot (local ordinance is 50 percent minimum).

A. Street right-of-way width (R.O.W.) is up to local jurisdiction; very frequently it is 66 feet (20,117 mm); therefore, the centerline of the street is 33 feet (10,058 mm) from the property line.

B. Street width (curb to curb) is a local jurisdictional matter dependent on whether or not it is a through street and whether or not there is parking on one side or two sides, or no parking.

C. Public sidewalk, generally located within the public right-of-way. The width is up to local jurisdiction, but is frequently 4 to 6 feet (1219 to 1829 mm).

D. "Boulevard" strip, generally landscaped with grass or other ground cover and maintained by the property owner, even though it is within the public right-of-way (R.O.W.). Municipality often maintains trees.

E. A 6-foot (1829-mm) utility easement (in this case for communication utilities).

F. Front setback. It is frequently permissible to set the residence farther back (more than the minimum) on the lots—but never closer to the street without a *variance*. This type of variance is generally difficult to obtain (neighbors tend to fight these).

G. Side yard setbacks. Minimum setback is very often 6 feet (1819 mm). Different jurisdictions will have different rules regarding exactly what is measured to determine setback (e.g., from the building face or the edge of any overhanging roof).

H. Two paved tracks with ground cover in between to fractionally reduce storm runoff.

I. Existing wood frame garage with concrete block foundations and a brick paver floor; to be removed just prior to construction of a new garage building. It is important to remove all existing below-grade construction (including footings and foundation walls) and to compact granular backfill.

J. "Future" garage/office/potting shed in this case is intended to be within three years. The buildings will require water, sewer, electrical service, and communication lines; these should be stubbed in during Phase 1.

K. Setback from the alley is often zero; there is a risk of buildings placed at that setback to be struck and damaged by vehicle traffic. Strategically placed bollards can ameliorate that risk.

L. Alley—in this case, a public right-of-way measuring 20 feet (6096 mm), of which roughly 18 feet (5486 mm) is paved. In this case, the storm drainage is down the center of the alley; this is the opposite of most streets, which are *crowned*, with the storm water moving to the gutter at the curb on both sides of the street.

M. The alley serves as an easement for overhead power lines (denoted P.P., for power pole, on the diagram).

N. A knock-out panel will be framed for a future second garage door opening (for possible future owner).

3 feet, 6 inches and 5 feet, 6 inches (1067 and 1676 mm) above the floor. The floor plan is generated as though the portion above the cut has been removed, allowing the viewer to see the thickness of walls, understand door and window locations, and see additional elements such as cabinetry and flooring materials as required.

Preliminary floor plans like the one shown in Figure 8-4 are used to indicate the locations of architectural elements, rooms, equipment, fixtures, and, in some cases, furniture placement. Figure 8-4 is a main-level floor plan for the sample project.

When drawing floor plans, the designer must convey significant spatial relationships with consistent graphic conven-

tions. In standard floor plans, various line weights are used to convey depths and qualities of form. Additionally, architectural elements and other items are shown using conventions as covered in the following list.

Drafting Conventions for Floor Plans

Lines

- The boldest line weight is used to outline those elements that have been cut through and are closest to the viewer (such as full-height wall lines).

- An intermediate line weight is employed to outline objects that lie below the plane of the cut but above the floor plane, such as fixtures, cabinetry/built-ins, half walls, railings, and furnishings.

- A finer line weight is used to outline surface treatment of the floors and other horizontal planes such as tile and wood grain.
- Objects that are hidden, such as shelves, or above the plane of the cut are dashed or ghosted in; this must be done in a manner that is consistent throughout the drawing or set of drawings.

Doors and Windows

- Standard doors are generally drawn open at 90 degrees to the wall and are most often shown with the arc of their swing.
- The doorframe and the space it requires must be considered in the drawing of the door system—this means the dimensions (width) of the frame trim must be considered (see Figures 5-11 and 9-4b for additional reference).

- Windowsills are typically outlined, often with a lighter line weight at the sill only.
- Window frames and sheets of glass are shown in various detail as scale allows.

Stairs

- Stairs are generally shown as broken off past the height of the plane of the cut; this is signified with a special break line (more information about stairs can be found in Chapter 2). An arrow should be included indicating the direction of the stairs from the level of the floor plan being shown, with the word up (UP) or down (DN) adjacent to the directional arrow.

Additional Standards

- A title, a north arrow, and some type of scale notation should be included on all floor plans. Scale notation can be stated numerically, for example: ¼'-0". Current practice often requires the use of a graphic scaling device, which

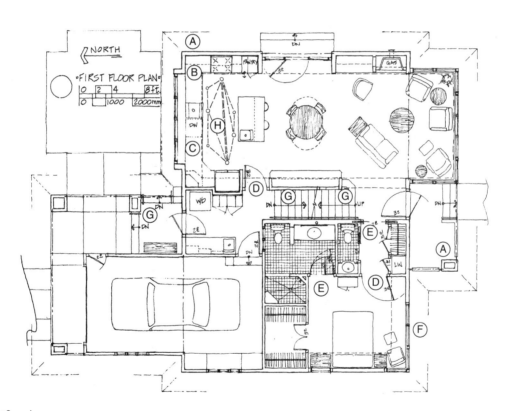

Figure 8-4 First floor plan.

A hand-drawn preliminary main-level floor plan for the sample project.

A. The boldest lines indicate the location of a cut, meaning that full-height walls are bold.
B. Fixtures, cabinetry, and finish materials are drawn with progressively lighter lines as they recede from the cut location.
C. Elements that are above or below the cut line, such as cabinets and soffits, or hidden, such as dishwashers, are indicated with dashed lines.
D. Standard doors are drawn open at 90 degrees with the arc of the swing shown. The full swing can be shown to ensure that nothing impedes the full swing of the door.
E. Specialized doors, such as smaller closet doors (shown), bifold doors, sliding doors, and pocket doors, are drawn in a way that indicates size and construction.
F. Window glass and sill lines are shown, often with lighter-weight lines than walls.
G. Stair designation: an up (UP) or down (DN) with directional arrow must be shown at any stairs or step(s) and at any change in floor level.
H. Kitchen work triangle(s) are shown to assist the client in understanding and assessing the rationale of major fixture placement.

A title, north arrow, and scale notation are required on all plans. Because this drawing was reduced, a standard written scale was omitted. Instead, a graphic scale device is included. Typically, the title and related information is located below the plan; it has been moved in this instance for publication.

Figure 8-5 Basement floor plan.

A hand-drawn preliminary basement floor plan for the sample project. The entire basement is intended to, initially, be unfinished except at the stairwell.

A. Location of a future 175-square-foot [16.25-m²] guest bedroom with required window for natural light (daylight) and egress into an exterior *area well*.
B. Plumbing is to be "roughed in" for a future bathroom, including a drain and sloped floor for a future shower.
C. The area under the garage and the front porch is unexcavated.
D. Mechanical/electrical equipment will be clustered in one location—under the utility room above.
E. A 395-square-foot [36.5-m²] space is available for future development.

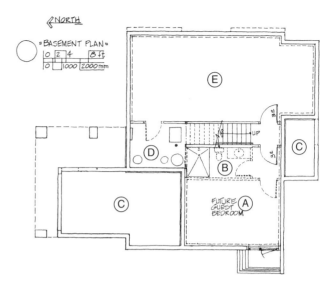

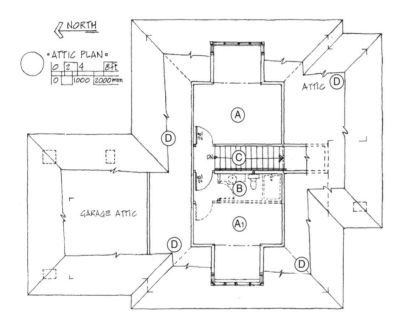

Figure 8-6 Attic floor plan.

A hand-drawn preliminary attic floor plan for the sample project. The attic level is intended to be unfinished initially, except at the stairwell.

A. Future possible bedroom with dormer windows for required natural light and egress. A similar space (for future bedroom or office) is at A_1.
B. Plumbing is to be roughed in for future bathroom.
C. Stair. Because this is the top floor, all steps are visible down to the main floor, and therefore, there is no break line.
D. The "plan cut" is made part of the way up the roof slope; the roof terminates in a break line. Between the roof and the attic walls is attic space that is not usable, in this case because it is full of structural framing such as roof trusses (see also Figure 8-14).

facilitates reduction, enlargement, and electronic transmission of the drawings.

Additional floor plans can be found in the following sections of this chapter, including dimensioned floor plans (see Figures 8-10 to 8-13). The remaining figures in this chapter illustrate many of the drafting conventions described in the previous list.

Exterior Elevations

As described in Chapter 1, exterior elevations depict only what is visible when viewed directly through the imaginary picture plane on a single side of a building (or portion of a building), as shown in Figure 8-7.

Additional floor plans can be found in the following sections of this chapter, including dimensioned floor plans (see Figures 8-10 to 8-13). The remaining figures in this chapter illustrate many of the drafting conventions described in the previous list.

Final Sample Project Drawings

Figures 8-8 to 8-17 are drawings that are suitable for use in obtaining permits, bidding, and construction. This type of drawing is frequently referred to as "working drawings" or as part of the "contract documents" (due to their use in owner/contractor agreements). Subsequent, postbidding changes to these drawings would require a "change order," which can be

Figure 8-7 South exterior elevation.

Hand-drawn preliminary exterior elevation for the sample project. The south elevation is shown for reference purposes. Exterior elevations are labeled by identifying the "face" of the building that is being viewed. In this case, looking north—the south face of the house is seen.

A. Asphalt-shingled roof.
   A_1. All roof surfaces are at 12/12 pitch.
   A_2. Roof ridge vents, coupled with soffit vents, maintain attic temperatures as close as possible to outdoor temperature.
B. Cedar shingle siding.
C. "Chimney" housing for the myriad vents and/or flues required, such as plumbing, dryer, and bathroom vents.
D. Double-hung windows.

costly. Figures 8-8 to 8-17 are either AutoCAD-generated or freehand drawings.

The following drawings are meant to provide a sample of the types of drawings used on a residential project (for the purposes of this book), rather than to serve as the definitive final set of working drawings. The drawings and related notes also provide illustrations of code-related requirements as well as elements and terms that can aid in an understanding of residential building construction. At the same time, the drawings illustrate one design solution for the sample program.

Dimensions

Dimensions are included in a wide range of drawings at various points in the design process (such as in both preliminary and design development drawings) and in construction drawings (as shown in Figure 8-10).

When included in drawings, dimensions are always listed in feet and inches, for example, 2'–4" rather than 28", except for those dimensions that are less than a foot, for example, 11" or 0'–11". Dimensions should be placed on top of the dimension line, so that they are underlined by the dimension line, and they should be placed so they don't have to be read by rotating the

sheet counterclockwise (reading from left to right) or turning it upside down.

Generally, for standard construction, dimensions and dimension lines are placed outside of the object (such as the building), as shown in Figure 8-10. In terms of organizing a series of dimensions, specific dimensions are placed close to the particular object they are related to, while the overall distances are placed in the position farthest from the construction.

Dimensions typically run from the outside of exterior walls to the centerline of interior walls. Where interior tolerances are critical, dimensions can be run from the face of the finished wall to the face of the other finished wall (paint to paint, so to speak), as shown in Figure 8-11. This type of dimension is often used for interior design projects created within existing architecture. For example, when dimensioning walls for an interior renovation of an existing office or retail space, designers commonly dimension only the paint-to-paint dimensions rather than the exterior-to-center dimensions.

Openings such as windows and doors are dimensioned to centerlines or to rough frame openings. Masonry openings are drawn to the nominal face of masonry. Another rule of thumb is to dimension things once and only once; attempts at repetition from one drawing to another can lead to discrepancies.

Sections

As described earlier, a building section is a view of a building that has been created as though a vertical plane has cut through the building and the portion behind the cut has been removed. Unlike interior elevations, which depict only what occurs in the interior, sections can expose the structure of the building. In drawing sections, the designer must include the outline of the structural elements as well as the configuration of the interior space.

Sections require varied line weights as a means of describing depths and spatial relationships. It is typical to show what is cut through, and therefore closest to the viewer, in the boldest line weight. Receding features and details are drawn using progressively lighter line weights. A section for the project is illustrated in Figure 8-14 and referenced in Figure 8-9.

Interior Elevations

Interior elevations are used extensively in professional practice. Successful elevations must clearly depict all interior

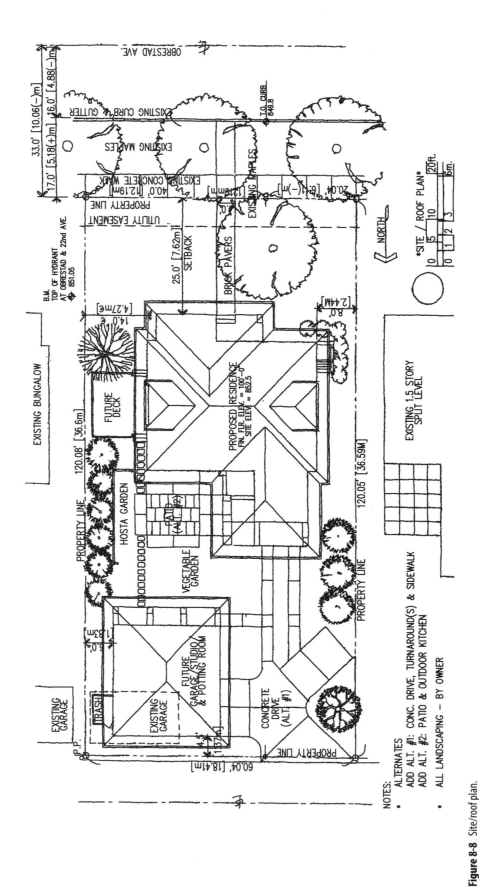

Figure 8-8 Site/roof plan.

A hand-drawn site plan, with labels and dimensions added digitally. The lot size for this project is 60-plus feet (18,288 mm) by 120-plus feet (36,576 mm). On-site storm-water retention may be required when the "future garage" is built. Note that site dimensions are in decimal feet as opposed to feet and inches, largely because land surveying and site engineering are executed in decimal feet. The most important function of a site plan is to locate the building(s) horizontally and vertically on the property.

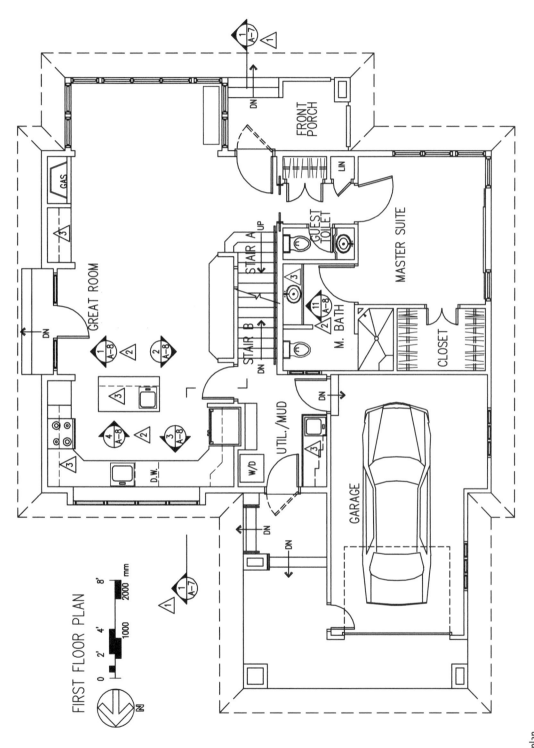

Figure 8-9 Floor plan.

An AutoCAD-generated main-level floor plan for the sample project, with appropriate reference symbols and labels shown here as a separate drawing for clarity; labels and reference symbols are most frequently combined with dimensioned drawings (see Figure 8-10). Note that some furniture locations included here vary from those shown in Figure 8-4.

1. This is a section reference symbol. The arrow indicates the direction of the view of the section. The top number within the symbol indicates the individual drawing number, while the bottom number indicates the sheet number the drawing is on, in this case, sheet A-7.

2. These are elevation reference symbols. The arrow indicates the direction of the view of the elevation. The top number within the symbol indicates the individual drawing number, while the bottom number indicates the sheet number the drawing is on, in this case, sheet A-8.

3. Built-in/fixed furniture and equipment are always shown.

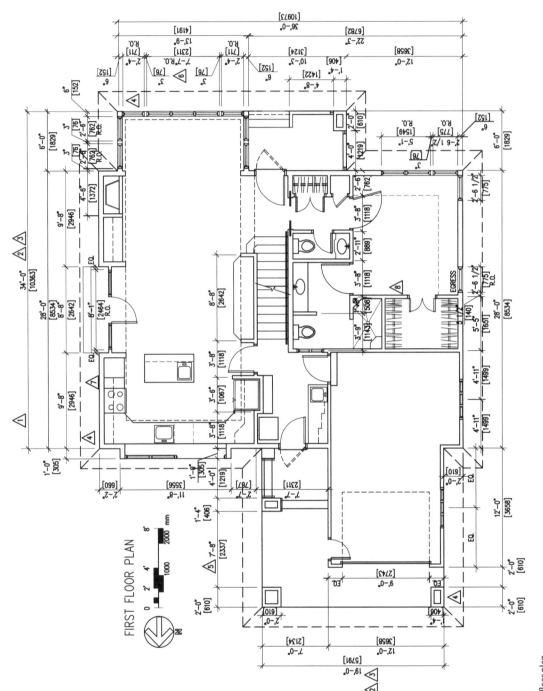

Figure 8-10 Dimensioned floor plan.
An AutoCAD-generated main-level floor plan for the sample project, with dimensions.

1. Dimension lines and leader lines should be lighter than wall lines or objects measured.
2. Horizontal written dimensions sit above the dimension lines so they are underlined by the dimension line as shown, or they are written in a break in the dimension line.
3. Note the location of dimensions. They should not have to be read by rotating the sheet counterclockwise (as in reading from the left side of the sheet), and one absolutely should not have to turn the sheet upside down to read these dimensions.
4. Leader lines run from the building location being dimensioned to the dimension lines. Leader lines should not touch the building; instead, they should be drawn slightly away.
5. Dimensions are written in feet and inches unless they are less than 1 foot. Here metric equivalencies are noted in millimeters within brackets.
6. Dimensions measured from centerlines must be clearly indicated. Windows are commonly measured to centerlines or rough openings (R.O.), as shown.
7. Exterior walls (and plumbing walls) are shown as nominal 6 inches (152 mm) thick (actual: 6½ to 7½ inches [165 to 190.5 mm]), depending on the exact composition of the exterior wall "sandwich."
8. Interior walls are shown as nominal 4 inches (102 mm) thick (actual: 4½ inches [114 mm], typically).

FIRST FLOOR PLAN

212

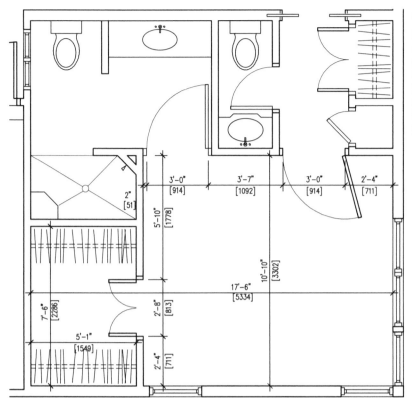

Figure 8-11 Partial floor plan.

In some cases, dimensions are shown from interior wall finish to interior wall finish (called paint-to-paint dimensions by some), as shown. This is most common in interior renovation/remodeling projects. Generally, rules for dimension lines, leader lines, and text are consistent with those listed in Figure 8-10, with only the location of leader and dimension lines different from exterior or centerline dimensions. Metric equivalencies are noted in millimeters within brackets.

architectural elements in a consistent scale. Interior elevations are typically drawn in a scale ranging from ¼" = 1'–0" to 1" = 1'–0". Using metric measurements, a scale of 1:50 is relatively common; it is somewhat similar to the 1¼" = 1'–0" scale (that would be 1:48 to be exact), with 1:20 roughly equivalent to ⅜" = 1'–0". Elevations drawn to depict accessories, equipment, cabinetry, fixtures, and design details are often drawn at ⅜" = 1'–0" or ½" = 1'–0". Millwork and other highly complicated elevations are often drawn at ½" = 1'–0" or larger.

All elevations require the use of differing line weights to clearly communicate spatial relationships. Typically, any portions of walls cut through and those closest to the viewer are drawn using a bold line weight. Receding elements become progressively lighter in line weight as they move farther from the picture plane. Some designers draw the line representing the floor line as the boldest line, with the lines representing the top and sides of the wall drawn just slightly lighter in weight. Figure 8-15a shows elevations for the sample project that were drawn manually (freehand) and then reduced considerably for publication. Figures 8-16b and 8-17c are AutoCAD-generated interior elevations for the sample project.

Interior elevations can be difficult for beginning students to master. However, they deserve a student's full attention because accurate elevations are necessary to successfully communicate key elements of a design. Like floor plans and sections, elevations used for design presentations vary greatly from those used for construction. Elevations used for construction drawings must necessarily contain significant dimensions as well as appropriate technical information. Elevations used for presentations can be drawn more freely and often contain less technical information, but they must be drawn accurately and in a consistent scale.

Regardless of how preliminary, or final, the interior elevations may be in relation to the design process, specific drawing conventions should be followed in their creation, as noted in the following list.

Interior Elevation Drawing Conventions

The following must be included for all interior elevations:

Titles.

Reference symbols.

Scale notation (written or using a graphic device).

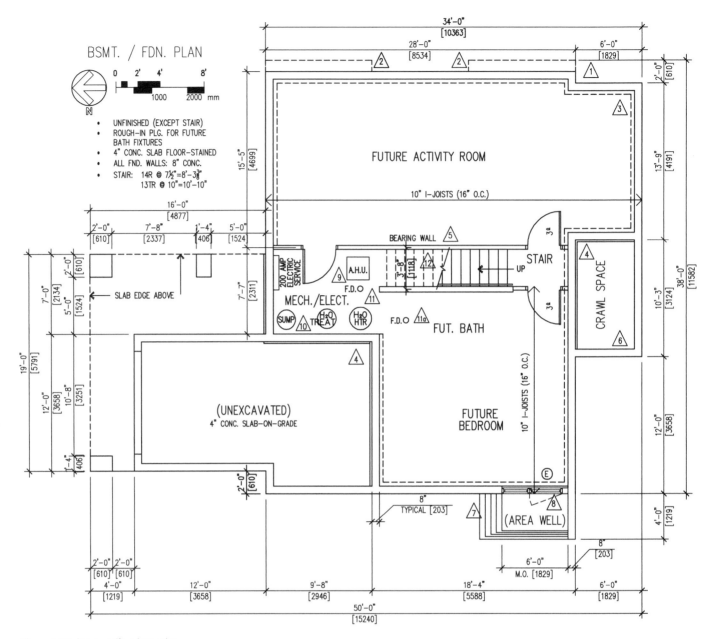

Figure 8-12 Basement/foundation plan.

An AutoCAD-generated basement floor plan for the sample project, with dimensions. Conventions for drafting line weights and symbols are consistent with those listed in Figure 8-10.

1. The thickness of a poured-concrete foundation wall 8 feet (2438 mm) in height is 8 inches (203 mm). Walls that are higher are commensurately thicker.
2. Line of overhanging first floor above.
3. Future finished, insulated frame walls. Some codes—especially in northern climates—may require that this be completed before a certificate of occupancy can be issued.
4. Rigid (extruded polystyrene) insulated foundation walls. 1½ inches (38 mm) or thicker.
5. A wood frame bearing wall; nominal 4 inches (102 mm) thick.
6. Ground level should be a minimum of 18 inches (457 mm) below the wood frame porch floor (see Figure 8-14).
7. Concrete masonry units or treated timbers form an area well with a drain connected to the drain tile (see Figure 8-14).
8. Windows are required in any future bedroom, including an operable window for fresh outside air and emergency egress as well as natural light (daylight).
9. Air-handling unit (denoted A.H.U. on the diagram) to move filtered air that can be heated, cooled, or both.
10. A sump pit and pump that receives groundwater from the perimeter foundation wall drain tile. The pump will discharge the water to the exterior at grade. It is a virtual necessity for a basement that will be occupied. Some soil conditions will require far more infrastructure to relieve the groundwater pressure.
11. Floor drains, slope floor to drain; future shower drain.
12. A wood frame stair. The "up" run terminates in a break line; steps above the break line are shown with a dashed line in this case.

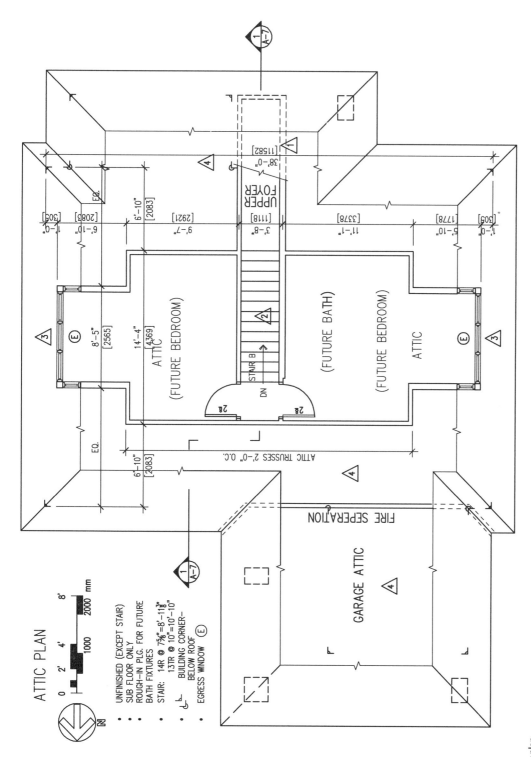

Figure 8-13 Attic plan.

An AutoCAD-generated attic floor plan for the sample project, with dimensions. Conventions for drafting line weights and symbols are consistent with those listed in Figure 8-10. See Figure 8-14 for the location of the cut used to create this floor plan.

1. Dashed lines can show future possible construction; dashed lines are also used to show the walls hidden below the roof.
2. Stair: all steps are visible and therefore shown with no break line.
3. Dormer windows required for natural light (daylight) as well as ventilation and emergency egress: E.
4. This is virtually unusable attic space due to the fact that there will be attic truss structure every 2 feet (610 mm).

215

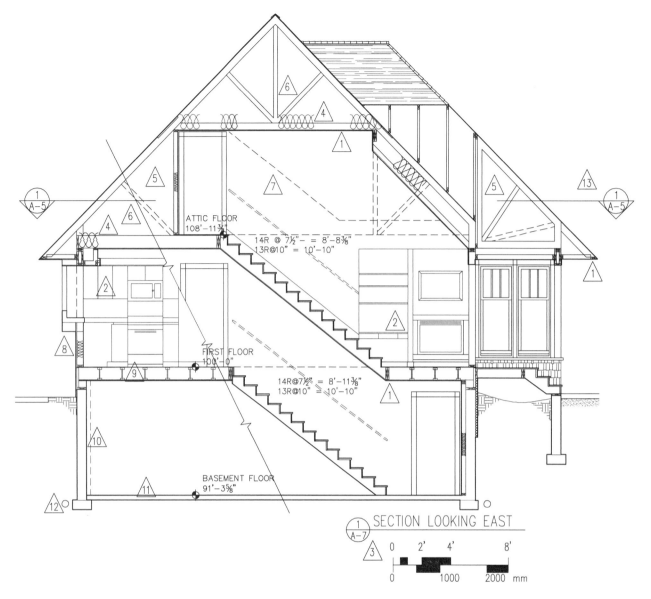

Figure 8-14 Section looking east.
An AutoCAD-generated section for the sample project.

1. The boldest lines indicate the relative location of the cut.
2. Receding elements are drawn with progressively lighter lines; important hidden elements are shown as dashed lines.
3. Sections require titles, reference symbols keyed to a floor plan (names or numbers), and scale notation.
4. Attic insulation.
5. Dead attic space.
6. Structural members (wood frame) that comprise attic trusses, which are 2 feet (610 mm) O.C.
7. Alternate ceiling profile at stair (dashed line).
8. Exterior wood frame wall.
9. Wood floor joist (I-joist in this example). Commonly 16 inches (406 mm) O.C.; alternative spacing, when appropriate, is 19.2 inches (487.7 mm) O.C. or 24 inches (610 mm) O.C.
10. 8-inch-thick (204-mm) concrete foundation wall with 2-inch-thick (51-mm) furred finish wall in the mechanical room.
11. 4-inch-thick (102-mm) concrete slab (basement floor).
12. Drain tile, where required by the presence of groundwater; slope to drain to the sump.
13. A section symbol is not typically drawn to reference floor plans; however, in this case, one is shown to depict the location of the cut for the attic/loft floor plan shown in Figure 8-13.

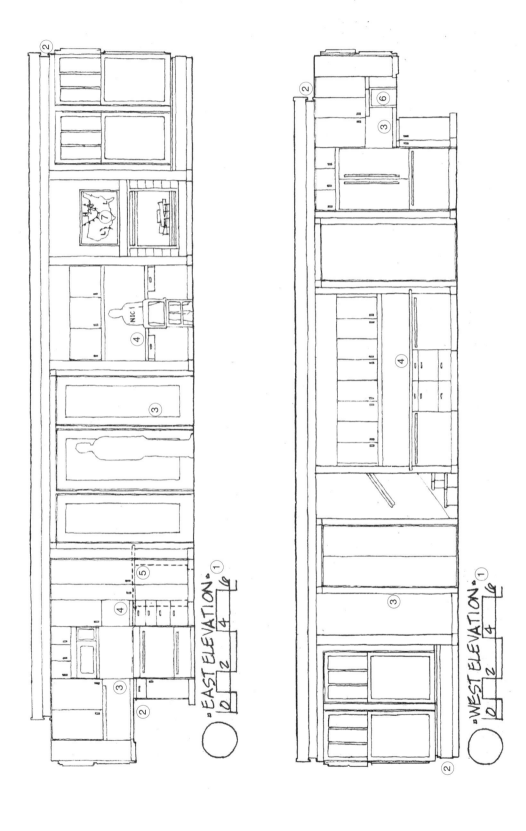

Figure 8-15a Interior elevations.

Selected interior elevations for the sample project. (These were drawn by hand and are meant as a companion to the plan shown in Figure 8-4).

1. Interior elevations require titles, reference symbols (names and numbers), and scale notations—similar to plans and sections.
2. Portions of walls cut into or closest to the viewer are bold.
3. Receding elements are drawn with progressively lighter lines.
4. Elevations showing items such as cabinetry and other millwork should include sufficient detail to show countertops, doorframes, and hardware.
5. Profile of island shown with dashed line.
6. Appliance garage.
7. Wall-mounted flat-screen television.

Figure 8-15b Interior elevation.
Selected interior elevation for the sample project. (This was drawn using AutoCAD and is meant as a companion to the plan shown in Figure 8-9).

1. Interior elevations require titles, reference symbols (names and numbers), and scale notations—similar to plans and sections. Note that there is a direct reference to the elevation symbol (3/ A-8) shown in the floor plan in Figure 8-9.
2. Portions of walls cut into or closest to the viewer are bold.
3. Receding elements are drawn with progressively lighter lines.
4. Undercabinet lighting with light baffle.
5. Elevations showing items such as cabinetry and other millwork should include sufficient detail to show countertops, doorframes, and hardware.
6. Sink is shown dashed.
7. Dishwasher.
8. Appliance garage.

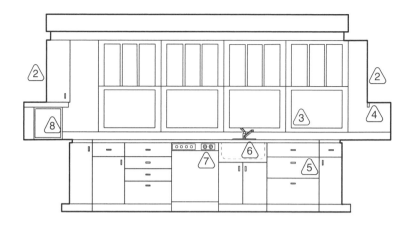

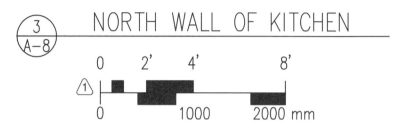

Figure 8-15c Interior elevation.
Interior elevation for the sample project. (This elevation of the bathroom was drawn using AutoCAD and is meant as a companion to the plan shown in Figure 8-9).

1. Interior elevations require titles, reference symbols (names and numbers), and scale notations—similar to plans and sections. Note that there is a direct reference to the elevation symbol (11/ A-8) shown in the floor plan in Figure 8-9.
2. Portions of walls cut into or closest to the viewer are bold.
3. Receding elements are drawn with progressively lighter lines.
4. Elevations showing items such as cabinetry and other millwork should include sufficient detail to show countertops, doorframes, and hardware.
5. Mirror with wall-mounted light fixtures on each side.
6. Shallow wall cabinet.
7. Wall-hung vanity cabinet (requires additional wall bracing).

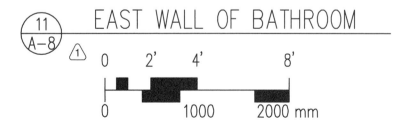

Table 8-2 Finish Schedule for the Sample Project

ROOM	FLOOR	BASE	WALLS MAT'L.	WALLS FINISH	CEILING MAT'L.	CEILING FINISH	HT.	REMARKS
GREAT ROOM:								
KITCHEN	HDW'D.	HDW'D.	½ GYP. BD.	TEXT./PAINT	1X4 HARDWD.✱	OIL	8'-0"/✱	✱7'-0" GYP. BD. SOFFITS
DINING	✱							✱ W/ AREA RUG (N.I.C.)
LIVING	✱				↓	↓	↓	↓ ↓
ENTRY	↓				⅝" GYP. BD.	TEXT./PAINT	VARIES✱	✱ SEE SECTION
STAIR (UP)	CARPET						↓	↓
HALL	HDW'D.	↓					7'-0"	
HALF-BATH	C.T.	C.T.	↓	↓	↓	↓		
OWNER'S SUITE								
BEDROOM	CARPET	HDW'D.	½ GYP. BD.	TEXT./PAINT	HARDWD.✱	OIL	8'-0"/✱	✱7'-0" GYP. BD. SOFFITS
CLOSET	↓	↓			EASTERN CEDAR	—	/	
BATH	C.T.	C.T	C.T.✱ ↓	↓	WP. GYP. BD.	PAINT	↓/	✱ 40" C.T. WAINSCOT
SHOWER	↓	↓	/		↓	↓	7'-0"	
UTILITY/MUD	SHEET RUBBER	SHEET RUBBER	½ GYP. BD.	TEXT./PAINT	⅝" GYP. BD.	TEXT./PAINT	8'-0"	
STAIR (DN)	CARPET	NONE	↓	↓			VARIES✱	✱ SEE SECTION
GARAGE	CONC.	4" C.M.U.	½" M.D.O. PLYW'D.\✱	UN FIN.	⅝" FIRE RATED GYP.	↓	9'-1"±	✱ ⅝" FIRE RATED GYP. BD. AT REQ'D. FIRE SEP.
BASEMENT	CONC.	U N F I N I S H E D						
ATTIC	PLYW'D. SUBFL.	U N F I N I S H E D						

NOTE: DOOR & WDO. CASINGS & MISC. EXPOSED WOOD TRIM: HARDWOOD THROUGHOUT

LEGEND:
C.T. - CERAMIC TILE (2"x2" x 5/16") ON 3/8" CEM. BD.
HDWD. - HARDWOOD - TO BE SELECTED
C.M.U. - CONC. MASONRY UNIT
M.D.O. PLYWOOD - MED. DENSITY OVERLAID PLYWOOD

Line weight conventions:

Portions of walls cut into or closest to the viewer are bold.

Receding elements are drawn with progressively lighter lines.

Items such as cabinetry and other millwork should include sufficient detail to show countertops, doorframes, and hardware in most cases.

Finish Schedules

A finish schedule is used to communicate the materials and finishes to be applied to walls, floors, and ceilings in the various rooms of a building. Typically, a finish schedule includes a column that lists the various rooms by name or number, as well as column headings for floors, walls, bases, and ceilings. Also included are remarks or notes for any comments necessary to clarify information or details. Finish schedules vary greatly in terms of complexity and in the information conveyed, depending on the complexity of the project or situation. Table 8-2 is a simple finish schedule for the sample project.

Reflected Ceiling Plans

Reflected ceiling plans are often used in conjunction with floor plans, elevations, and sections to communicate interior design. Reflected ceiling plans communicate important information about the design of the ceiling, such as materials, layout and locations of fixtures, and ceiling heights. A reflected ceiling plan is drawn as though a giant mirror were on the floor, reflecting the elements located on the ceiling. These are used commonly for commercial interior design projects and are used infrequently for residential projects, although one is included in Figure 8-16 for the sample project as a means of communicating the concepts covered.

Reflected ceiling plans are typically drawn in the same scale as the corresponding floor plan, although, for complex designs, larger-scale partial reflected ceiling plans are prepared. More complex ceiling designs also may require that dimensions be included, which is not the case with simple ceiling plans. In addition to ceiling heights, finish materials, light fixtures (those located on the ceiling), and diffusers/registers (those located on the ceiling) are included; switching information may also be included.

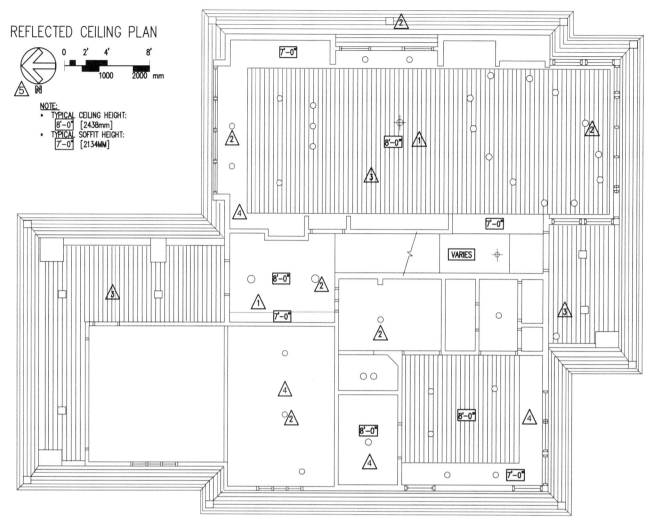

REFLECTED CEILING PLAN

N

NOTE:
- TYPICAL CEILING HEIGHT:
  8'-0" [2438mm]
- TYPICAL SOFFIT HEIGHT:
  7'-0" [2134MM]

Figure 8-16 Reflected ceiling plan.

A simple reflected ceiling plan for the sample project.

1. Ceiling and soffit heights are noted (dimensioned above the finished floor—A.F.F.) and enclosed in a symbol, or covered in a general note. In this example both types of notations are included to illustrate concepts.
2. Light fixture locations at ceiling are shown. Here some of them are noted with a 2 in order to illustrate the concept.
3. Finish materials such as wood are indicated in scale; in this case, the wood is indicated in scale, whereas other ceiling locations are shown as gypsum board (also called drywall or Sheetrock). In this example, interior wood ceiling finishes are shown as well as exterior wood ceiling areas. Often reflected ceiling plans include only interior areas.
4. Gypsum board locations are shown with no texture or pattern; here some of them are noted with a 4 to illustrate the concept.
5. Reflected ceiling plans require titles, north arrows, and scale notation, similar to the other types of plan views discussed.

Electrical and Lighting Plans/Power and Lighting Plans

Often for residential projects, light fixtures, electrical outlets, and switching information are all included directly on a standard plan—not a reflected plan. These are referred to as *electrical and lighting plans* or *power and lighting plans*. Figure 8-17 is an example of an electrical and lighting plan for the sample project. Throughout this book, electrical and lighting plans are included to convey information about lighting, switching, and outlet locations. Electrical symbols are discussed and illustrated in Chapter 1.

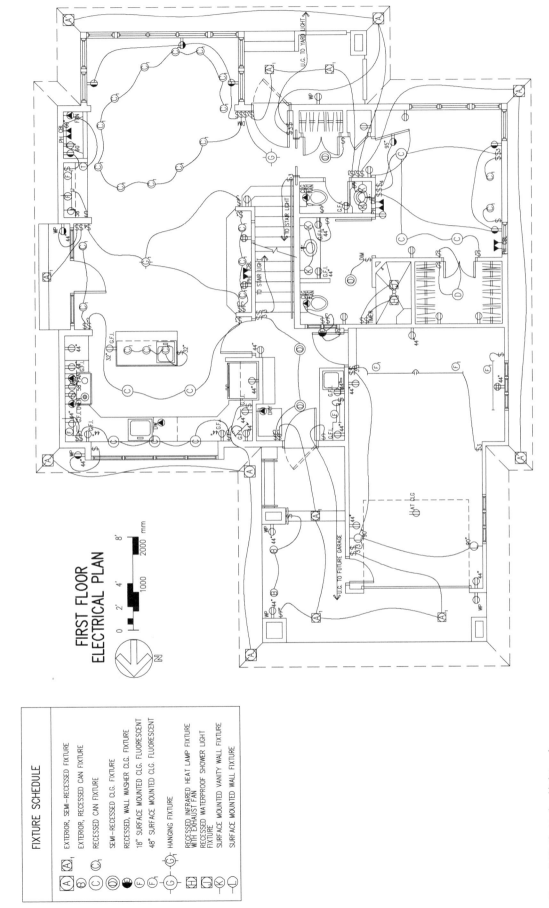

FIXTURE SCHEDULE

Ⓐ₁	EXTERIOR, SEMI-RECESSED FIXTURE
Ⓑ₁	EXTERIOR, RECESSED CAN FIXTURE
Ⓒ₁	RECESSED CAN FIXTURE
Ⓓ	SEMI-RECESSED CLG. FIXTURE
Ⓔ	RECESSED, WALL WASHER CLG. FIXTURE
Ⓕ₁	18" SURFACE MOUNTED CLG. FLUORESCENT
Ⓕ₂	48" SURFACE MOUNTED CLG. FLUORESCENT
Ⓖ₁	HANGING FIXTURE
Ⓗ₁	RECESSED INFRARED HEAT LAMP FIXTURE WITH EXHAUST FAN
Ⓙ	RECESSED WATERPROOF SHOWER LIGHT FIXTURE
Ⓚ₁	SURFACE MOUNTED VANITY WALL FIXTURE
Ⓛ₁	SURFACE MOUNTED WALL FIXTURE

FIRST FLOOR
ELECTRICAL PLAN

0 2' 4'   8'
1000   2000 mm

N

Figure 8-17 Electrical and lighting plan.

An AutoCAD-generated electrical and lighting plan for the first floor of the sample project. Electrical plans and lighting plans are scaled floor plans containing electrical components represented by various symbols with an accompanying legend. The legend references the symbols shown in plan and provides related details about switching, fixtures, receptacles, and items such as smoke detectors and power. Sweeping lines (often shown dashed, but solid in this example) depict connection lines between switches and fixtures or outlets. Heights of items may also be noted.

While the reflected ceiling plan (see Figure 8-16) shows only components installed on ceilings, the electrical and/or lighting plan shows all electrical components, including those on walls, floors, and ceilings. Electrical/power and lighting plans require titles, north arrows, and scale notation as shown. Detailed information about lighting can be found in Chapter 1 and at the end of each chapter.

REFERENCES

Contains both works cited and recommended reading, with occasional annotation.

International Code Council. 2015. "2015 International Residential Code for One- and Two-Family Dwellings." Country Club Hills, IL: International Code Council.

Kilmer, W. Otie, and Rosemary Kilmer. 2009. *Construction Drawings and Details for Interiors*. 2nd ed. Hoboken, NJ: John Wiley & Sons. A good, basic guide to construction drawings for interior design/interior architecture.

Rumberger, Janet, ed. 2003. *Architectural Graphic Standards for Residential Construction*. Hoboken, NJ: John Wiley & Sons.

CHAPTER 9

Basic Light Frame Residential Construction

Interior designers are not responsible for the design of structural or mechanical systems; however, practicing interior designers must understand the basic structural and mechanical building systems in order to work well within them. Our discussion here is limited to common standards of current light wood-frame residential construction and is a brief overview of the basic components of construction intended to supply the reader with the knowledge required to begin to gain an understanding of this topic. It is important to know local conditions and construction practices related to local wind, flooding, and fire conditions.

This book does not examine any of the myriad alternative, less common modes of construction that are used in residential construction, such as straw bale, adobe, timber frame, rammed earth, geodesic domes, and others. These and others have a place in the construction of homes in special circumstances and may be more sustainable than traditional construction, but they fall outside the scope of this book. These are covered in detail in specialty publications.

STANDARD RESIDENTIAL BUILDING PLATFORM TYPES

Houses sit on some type of concrete or wood platform, which, together with the foundation, supports the portions of the house that rise above it. These include the following:

Standard Residential Building Platform Types

1. *A concrete slab platform that sits directly on the ground.* Concrete can resist termites, moisture, and rot; these can serve as a suitable substrate for a wide variety of finish floor materials. The platform (slab) is most typically on a single plane, but it can be designed as a multilevel platform—a more complicated and more expensive option. In some cases, a very slight indentation in the slab is created to accommodate floor finishing materials of varying thicknesses, such as wood flooring, or to provide slopes for drainage (e.g., a roll-in shower).

   In geographic areas subject to frost upheaval due to low temperatures and/or soil conditions (such as water-retaining clays), it is necessary to augment the concrete slab platform with a perimeter foundation wall that extends deep enough into the ground to reach stable soil. Figure 9-1 illustrates slab foundations.

2. *A wood platform that sits off the ground to avoid rot and/or termite infestation.* This type can sit above the ground far enough to form a crawl space or a basement. Figure 9-2 illustrates wood frame floors over crawl spaces and basements, and Figure 9-3b also shows a basement foundation.

There are methods of support for the wood platform apart from foundation walls. These include piers (posts) of wood, steel, or concrete supporting beams that, in turn, support the platform. While this method is less common, it is useful on hillsides or sites that are prone to flooding. Deference to local building practices with a history of success is recommended.

BASIC WOOD FRAME CONSTRUCTION

Major construction elements of a wood frame building system are illustrated in Figure 9-3a, 9-3b, and 9-3c. These include elements that combine to form the roof and walls, such as structural and insulating elements and related finish materials, as shown in Figure 9-3a and 9-3b. Electrical, plumbing, heating, and air-conditioning elements are shown in Figure 9-3c, with detailed notes.

DIMENSIONAL LUMBER

Wood frame construction makes use of *dimensional lumber*, a term used to describe wood that is cut to standard sizes. Generally, the name used for such lumber relates to the size of the particular stock being referred to, such as "2 × 4." However, over time, the size of dimensional lumber has changed, but that change has not been reflected in a corresponding name change and, for that reason, a 2 × 4 is not actually 2 by 4 inches. Table 9-1 lists dimensional lumber sizes and actual dimensions.

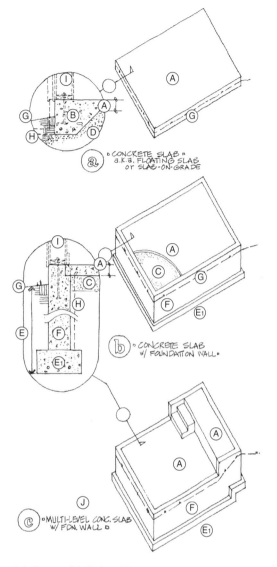

Table 9-1 Dimensional Lumber

Nominal Size	Actual Size	Actual Size (millimeters)
2" × 4"	1½" × 3½"	38 × 89
2" × 6"	1½" × 5½"	38 × 140
2" × 10"	1½" × 9¼"	38 × 235
4' × 8' Structural and Nonstructural Sheets	48" × 96" Common thicknesses ¼"–1"	1219 × 2438 Common thicknesses 6.35–24.5 mm

DOORS AND WINDOWS

Doors

Doors provide access and connections between the interior and exterior and within interior spaces. Therefore, their placement, design, and physical qualities directly impact how we move through, use, and experience space. The door and doorway must be of such a size as to allow for comfortable movement of people and furnishings. Standard residential door height is 6 feet, 8 inches (2032 mm), with sliding glass doors and French doors as high as 8 feet (2438 mm). Exterior doors are available in standard widths up to 3 feet (914 mm); interior passage doors are available in widths of 2 feet (610 mm) to 3 feet (914 mm). At least one exterior door at 3 feet (914 mm) is required by most codes for emergency egress (e.g., IRC, Section R311.2) and is recommended for ease of movement and visitability (see Figure 9-5a). Interior doors are available in a range of widths as indicated in Figure 9-5a.

In addition, the placement of doors provides circulation within spaces and therefore requires careful consideration. For example, placement of a door in the middle of a room or hallway tends to divide the room in half, whereas door placement at a room's corners tends to open up the interior by encouraging movement along the sides. This is discussed in detail in relationship to many of the types of rooms covered in each chapter. Review the "Organizational Flow" section of each chapter for additional information on door placement.

In terms of interior placement, when possible, doors should swing against a blank wall and not impede movement or conflict with nearby door swings. Doors in rooms where privacy is required, such as bathrooms, should be placed in such a way that they do not interfere with room privacy. The examples provided in Chapters 5 and 6 show examples of good practice in this regard. In those cases where the swing of a door interferes with movement, privacy, or the swing of nearby doors, pocket doors may be a useful alternative to swinging doors. Figure 9-6b illustrates some common door types and styles.

Door design, style, placement, and ease of operation must be considered in the context of the larger building and the

Figure 9-1 Concrete slab platform. Note: Metric equivalencies for dimensional lumber are given in Table 9-1.
  A. Slab is typically 4-inch-thick (102-mm) reinforced concrete and serves as suitable substrate for a full range of floor materials.
  B. Perimeter of slab is thickened and reinforced.
  C. Compacted granular fill (6 inches [152 mm] plus or minus).
  D. Well-drained compacted substrate under floating slab.
  E. Depth of footings (E₁) (below grade) is a function of climate (frost depth) and soil conditions (some layers of different soil types may be more stable under load than others).
  F. Foundation wall(s) are commonly 8-inch-thick (203-mm) concrete or concrete masonry units (CMUs); less commonly brick or stone (for example, these may be found in historic or period houses).
  G. Ground line surface, also known as "grade."
  H. Rigid insulation (dashed line) required in cold climates.
  I. Walls of the building envelope (walls and roof) are anchored to the concrete slab or foundation wall.
  J. This is an uncommon multilevel slab, which can be costly but can provide for an interesting ground floor.

PLUMBING

For purposes of clarity, we have included basic plumbing system information in Chapter 6 as it relates to bathroom design.

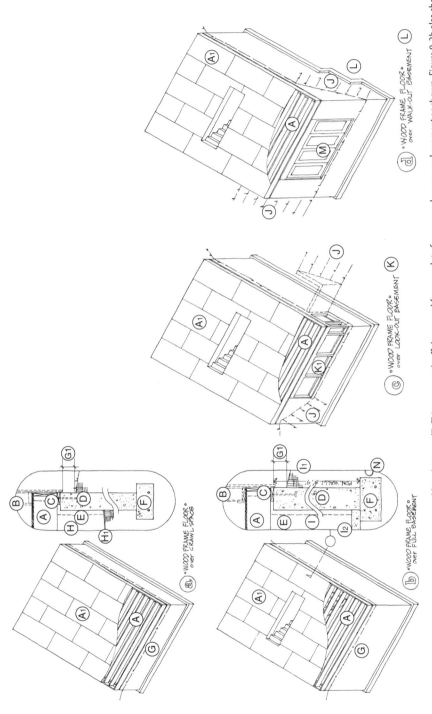

Figure 9-2 Wood platform options. These sit above the ground (on some type of foundation wall). This type can sit off the ground far enough to form a crawl space or a basement as shown. Figure 9-3b also shows a basement foundation. *Note:* Metric equivalencies for dimensional lumber are given in Table 9-1.

A. Floor joists. Floor structure is typically constructed of wood joists and structural sheets (A_1) (4 by 8 feet) of plywood or oriented strand board (OSB) that is ¾ inch (19 mm), plus or minus, thick. Z or I joists are most commonly spaced 16 inches (406 mm) O.C. (less commonly, 19. 2 inches (488 mm), often requiring a thicker subfloor; the longer the span, the deeper the joist).

B. Frame walls. The floor serves as the platform for the construction of the building envelope (walls and roof) above.

C. Sill plate. Floor joists rest on this "plate" (typically 2 by 6 inches [51 by 152 mm]) that rests on and is anchored to the foundation and treated to resist rot and/or termites.

D. Foundation wall. Typically, reinforced concrete (8 to 10 inches [38 by 140 mm]) or CMUs (10 to 12 inches [254 to 305 mm]). The higher the foundation wall, the thicker the wall must be. Typical foundation heights are 8 or 9 feet (2438 or 2743 mm).

E. Insulation (shown with a dashed line). Required in colder climates.

F. Footing. Reinforced concrete. Typically, the width is twice the thickness of the foundation wall and the thickness (depth) is half the width of the footing. This may vary; be aware of local soil conditions and practices.

G. Grade. Ground line, 8 inches (203 mm) (minimum) below the wood structure:(G_1).

H. Crawl space. 18-inch (457-mm) height (minimum) with vapor barrier (H_1).

I. Full basement. 8-foot-high (2438-mm) foundation wall (minimum) (I_1) with a 3- to 4-inch-thick (76- to 102-mm) concrete slab floor (I_2).

J. Look-out and walk-out basements require a site that slopes sufficiently to accommodate the required change in grade and yet drain properly—away from the building.

K. Look-out basement can provide legal egress windows (K_1), allowing bedroom(s) without requiring changing the footing depth.

L. Walk-out basement requires stepping down the footings and associated foundation walls in colder climates.

M. Door(s).

N. Drain tile to carry away excess groundwater and reduce the pressure of groundwater against the foundation wall.

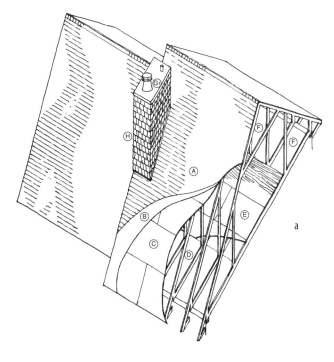

a

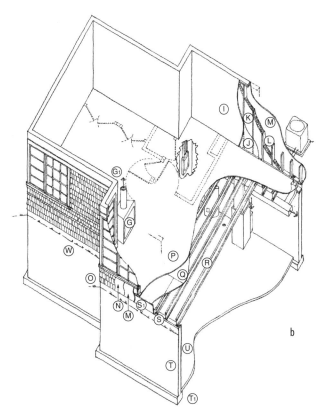

b

Figure 9-3a and 9-3b "Peel-away" exploded views of a wood frame house meant to illustrate some of the most common residential construction techniques currently used in the United States. (For common metric equivalencies, refer to Table 9-1.)

A. Roofing. Commonly asphalt shingles; less commonly clay tile, wood (cedar shingles), sheet metal (includes copper, steel, and other metals), fiber-reinforced cement, and slate; roofing materials are variable by region.

B. Roofing felt. Commonly #15 asphalt-impregnated paper; however, in climates prone to ice formation, a modified bitumen layer (sometimes referred to as "ice shield") is also used.

C. Roof sheathing (also known as the roof deck). Typically sheets of plywood or oriented strand board (OSB) measuring 4 feet by 8 feet by ⅝ inch thick (plus or minus, depending on snow loads).

D. Roof trusses. Commonly 2 feet (610 mm) on center; shown in this case as attic trusses. Most commonly prefabricated off-site using dimensional lumber (such as 2 × 4, 2 × 6, etc.); less frequently fabricated of light-gauge steel.

E. Subfloor. Structural plywood or OSB measuring 4 feet by 8 feet by ¾ inch thick (plus or minus); provides a walkable surface in the unfinished attic (as shown); serves as the structural base (support) for the finished flooring materials (see also Q).

F. Attic insulation. Commonly fiberglass (batts, blankets, or blown-in); see also Figure 8-14.

G. Gas fireplace. Requires venting to the outdoors (G_1); shown here venting to the roof.

H. Chimney. In this case, a gas vent; the chimney housing can be of light frame construction, as shown, or masonry, such as brick or stone.

I. Interior wall material. Commonly gypsum board, ½ inch (12.7 mm) thick (this is also called drywall), serves as a suitable surface for application of paint or wall covering. Less used alternatives include wood or composite paneling (boards or sheets); composite options include Homasote and medium-density fiberboard (MDF).

J. Vapor barrier. Polyethylene sheet, placed on the room side of the insulation in cold climates in order to prevent water vapor from entering (from the interior) and condensing within the insulation. In hot, humid climates, the vapor may enter from the exterior; check local codes and construction practices.

K. Wall insulation. Commonly fiberglass blanket (batts), or sprayed foam fills the entire wall stud cavity.

L. Studs. Commonly 2 × 4s or 2 × 6s, 1 foot, 4 inches (406 mm) on center. An alternative is steel (C-studs). These carry roof loads to the floor and/or foundation and serve as a structural entity to attach interior and exterior sheeting/sheathing materials. Exterior studs shown here are 2 × 6s; interior studs are commonly 2 × 4s.

M. Wall sheathing. Structural sheets, commonly 4 feet by 8 feet by ½ inch (12.7 mm) thick—plus or minus—fastened securely to the studs (L) to resist lateral forces (such as wind or earthquake) and serve as a substrate for fastening finish exterior materials such as siding.

N. Infiltration barrier (also known as building wrap). Resists air (wind) penetration; does not (and should not) impede water vapor transmission.

O. Exterior finish (also known as siding). Cedar shingles are shown; wood, fiber-reinforced cement, vinyl, and metal products are used for lap or vertical siding. Alternatives to items mentioned are stucco (and stucco-like products), brick, stone veneers, etc.

P. Underlayment. Sheets of wood fiber material measuring 4 by 8 feet and ranging in thickness from ¼ to ⅝ inch (6.4 to 16 mm); used to level substrate under finish floor materials such as carpet; plywood is used under vinyl; cement-based products are used under ceramic tile.

Q. Subfloor. Sheets of structural plywood or OSB, ¾ inch (19.05 mm) thick (plus or minus).

R. Floor joist. I-joist is shown; dimensional framing lumber such as 2 × 10 can also be used. Allowing 12 inches (305 mm) for the total thickness of a structural wood floor system is a good preliminary rule of thumb.

S. Sill. Floor joists sit on a sill plate (commonly a treated 2 × 6), which is anchored to the foundation wall. A rim joist (S_1) caps the ends of the floor joist and serves as edge support for the subfloor.

T. Foundation wall. Commonly concrete, 8 inches (203 mm), 10 inches (254 mm), or 12 inches (305 mm) thick and 8 feet (2438 mm), 9 feet (2743 mm), or 10 feet (3048 mm) high (the higher the wall, the thicker the concrete required). Common alternatives include 10- or 12-inch-thick (254- or 305-mm) concrete masonry unit (CMU). Treated wood is used far less frequently. Liquid or sheet dampproofing is applied to the exterior prior to backfilling with soil. Footing (T_1) is almost always poured concrete, minimally twice as wide as the thickness of the wall it supports, and spreads building loads over more ground surface for support.

U. Concrete slab (also known as basement slab). Commonly concrete with a thickness of 4 inches (102 mm) over a membrane vapor barrier (polyethylene).

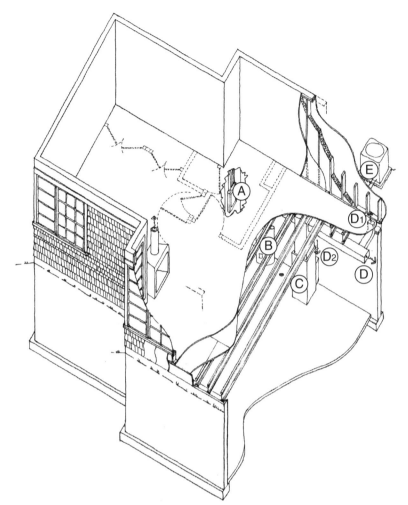

Figure 9-3c A "peel-away" exploded view of a house meant as an illustration of building systems.

A. Electrical service panel. 100-amp service is minimum; a 200-amp panel is common. Service is brought to the house by underground or overhead wire, through a meter mounted at an exterior location (typically the exterior wall of the house), and then to the service panel; branch circuits feed from the service panel to a variety of outlets (also known as receptacles), light fixtures, switches, and appliances throughout the house. The International Residential Code (IRC) requires a clear space, 3 feet by 2 feet, 6 inches (914 by 762 mm) wide and 6 feet, 6 inches (1981 mm) high, in front of the service panel.

B. Water heater. Should be located near a floor drain. Ideally, minimize the length of the hot water lines that serve sinks and appliances. Heaters that burn a fuel (as compared to electric models) require a vent to the exterior.

C. Furnace/air-handling unit. Designed to heat, clean air (filter), move air (blower), and mix indoor with outdoor (fresh) air— and, with the addition of refrigeration coils and condensing unit, cool and dehumidify air. Located in this example in the basement. For houses without basements, this equipment can be located on any floor or in an accessible attic. Forced-air furnace systems, as shown, are very common because of the ability to integrate the variety of functions listed above. However, other heating unit types are available, such as radiant in-floor heating systems and baseboard convectors. Both can be accomplished with either electricity or hot water heat systems.

D. Supply air. The furnace blower moves air through ducts to diffusers (D_1) located throughout the house. Return air is ducted from the rooms back to the furnace, ideally mixing with ducted outside (fresh) air before it arrives back at the furnace to be recirculated (D_2).

E. Compressor/condensing unit. Supplies cold refrigerant to the evaporator coils at the furnace. Unit is commonly located on a concrete slab near the house and requires adequate air circulation space around the unit.

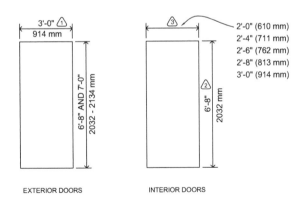

EXTERIOR DOORS   INTERIOR DOORS

Figure 9-4a Standard door sizes.

1. Also available in widths of 2 feet, 8 inches (813 mm) and wider than 3 feet. A 2-foot, 8-inch (813-mm) door will not meet the code or guideline requirement for a 2-foot, 8-inch (813-mm) clear opening.
2. Standard residential doors are 6 feet, 8 inches (2032 mm) high, but taller versions are available.
3. Narrow widths noted below are used for reach-in closets:
   1'- 0" (305 mm)
   1'- 4" (407 mm)
   1'- 6" (457 mm)
   1'- 8" (508 mm)

DOOR OPERATION

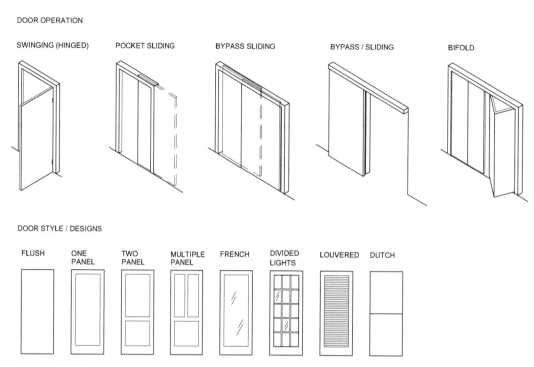

SWINGING (HINGED)   POCKET SLIDING   BYPASS SLIDING   BYPASS / SLIDING   BIFOLD

DOOR STYLE / DESIGNS

FLUSH   ONE PANEL   TWO PANEL   MULTIPLE PANEL   FRENCH   DIVIDED LIGHTS   LOUVERED   DUTCH

Figure 9-4b Door types and styles. Door types can be classified by operation and include swinging (these swing on hinges or pivots and are the most common), bypass sliding, pocket sliding, surface sliding (not commonly used in residences), and bifold. Door style designs include flush, panel, French, and louvered. Flush types may be solid core, 1¾ inch (44.5 mm) thick; or hollow core, 1⅜ inch (34.9 mm) thick. Panel doors have one or multiple panels and are available with a range of trim and panel designs. French types include single glass panels or panes divided by muntins (called divided lights).

Figure 9-4c Doorframe construction diagram showing jamb condition(s). The door head will be similar, with the addition of a structural header in load-bearing wall(s).

A. Door frame. Generally hardwood or hardwood veneer, sized to match the wall thickness; doors are often purchased pre-hung (hinged) in the frame.
B. Applied stop. This will stop the door swing but will also stop the passage of light and air. An exterior door will have an integral stop and be more weathertight (B_1) than interior types.
C. Wall. An interior 2 × 4 stud wall is shown with ½-inch (12.7-mm) gypsum board on both sides and double studs at the rough door opening. A metal-stud wall would be similar. The wall cavity is frequently filled with blanket insulation—in better construction—to dampen sound.
D. Door casing (trim) at jamb and head at both sides of wall. Generally, hardwood with a wide variety of sizes and configurations available from standard to custom, wide to narrow, to none at all. Shown factory installed on a pre-hung door at D and field installed at D_1.
E. Butt hinges:
    1 pair per door for light interior residential construction, 1⅜-inch (35-mm) hollow core doors.
    1½ pairs per door for heavier solid core doors, 1¾ inches (44.5 mm).
F. Shim space to allow setting doorframe perfectly plumb.
G. Any floor material change should occur directly under the door in its closed position.

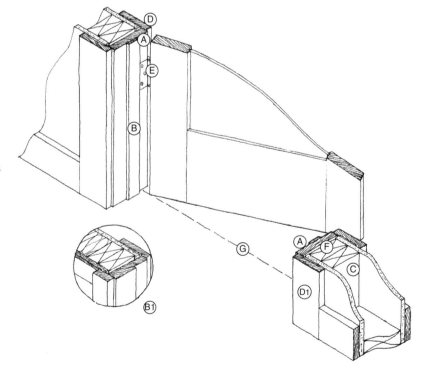

room; in addition, frequency and type of use must be considered. Exterior doors must provide watertight seals along with thermal insulation. Exterior door design and placement have a significant impact upon the appearance of the building and therefore should be carefully considered in terms of appearance and impact upon the building composition. Additional information about the design and placement of exterior doors can be found in Chapter 2.

Door types can be classified by operation and include swinging (these swing on hinges or pivots and are the most common), bypass sliding, pocket sliding, surface sliding (not used commonly in residences), and bifold, as illustrated in Figure 9-4b. Doorframe construction is illustrated in Figure 9-4c.

Door construction for residential doors includes flush and wood panel types. Flush doors may be hollow core or solid core. Hollow core types are much lighter and are suitable for interior use only. Hollow core types may be hinged or used in pocket sliding applications. Glass and louver inserts are available for flush doors. Solid core types are primarily used as exterior doors, as are insulated metal doors.

Wood panel doors have an exposed framework that holds solid wood or plywood panels; these panels may also be glazed. Panel doors may have one or multiple panels and are available with a range of trim and panel designs.

Windows

According to the National Trust for Historic Preservation, "While they vary in size, shape, materials, and proportion, windows give scale to a home and provide a sense of depth. The proportion, divisions, and materials of a window are essential elements of design." The trust also states that a home's windows "typically comprise about a quarter of the surface area of its exterior walls." Therefore, window choice is a significant design element and should be carefully considered. In addition to contributing to the overall aesthetic qualities of the home's exterior, windows provide light, views, and natural ventilation for interior spaces. Thus, their placement, design, and construction are significant factors in creating an appealing and healthful environment.

Windows also impart a building's interior–exterior connection. Those areas that are meant to "connect" to the exterior require some expanse of windows to do so, while those that are intended not to "connect," such as areas that require privacy, tend to have fewer windows or have windows placed in such a way that they do not allow for views from the exterior to the interior. See Figure 9-5a for illustrations of window placement considerations.

In considering window placement, orientation, and design, the following items should be analyzed.

Window Placement, Orientation, and Design Considerations

- Need for connection to the out-of-doors. Windows should be placed in relationship to standing and seated eye level and in a manner that frames the view.
- Need for privacy. Placing windows above eye level or using translucent glazing allows for daylighting but does not limit privacy.
- Flexibility for furniture placement. Window placement should not be based on a single furniture layout but rather related to multiple options when possible.
- Possible desirable views (these should be enhanced).
- Possible undesirable views (these should be screened).
- Desire for daylighting. Windows near corners wash walls with light; windows on more than one wall create more balanced light. Note that, depending on the climate and window construction, windows are sources of heat gain and loss; placement of windows relative to the location and angle of the sun requires careful thought.

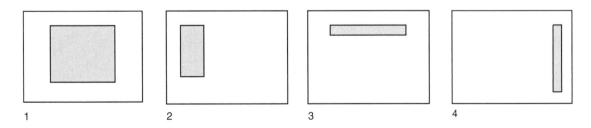

1   2   3   4

Figure 9-5a Some options for window placement, orientation, and design considerations.

1. 1 and 2. Window locations that can create a connection to the outdoors (windows placed in relationship to standing and seated eye level and in a manner that frames the view).
2. A window location that can create flexibility for furniture placement (window placement should not be based on a single furniture layout but rather related to multiple options when possible). This option can also take advantage of views and daylight.
3. Window placement for privacy or screening (placing windows above eye level allows for daylighting and can create privacy and screen interior activities).
4. Window placement creating possible screening of undesirable views. This option allows for daylighting but does not afford privacy. This location also allows for flexibility in furniture placement.

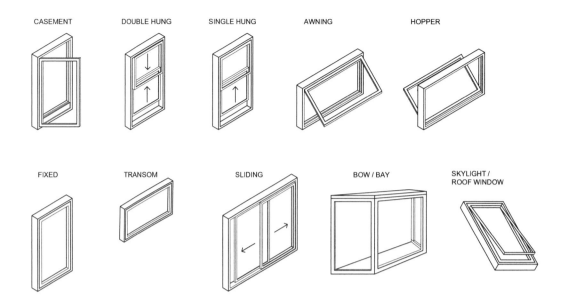

CASEMENT DOUBLE HUNG SINGLE HUNG AWNING HOPPER

FIXED TRANSOM SLIDING BOW / BAY SKYLIGHT / ROOF WINDOW

Figure 9-5b Window types and styles include the following:

Casement windows are hinged at the side and open outward.
Double-hung windows open by sliding vertically—both sashes slide vertically.
Single-hung windows open by sliding vertically—only the bottom sash slides vertically, hence the term *single hung*.
Awning windows are hinged at the top and open outward. This type is often paired with fixed windows.
Hopper windows are hinged at the bottom and open inward (very limited applications)—must be well protected from weather. This type is often paired with fixed windows.
Fixed windows are stationary and can be used in combination with other types—particularly double-hung and casement types.
Transom (fixed) used in combination, in top position, with other types such as double hung and casement.
Sliding windows open by sliding horizontally.
Bow and bay windows use other types in combination and project outward from the building.
Skylights and roof windows are designed for installation on sloped surfaces; options include operable or fixed.
There are also a variety of specially shaped windows that employ curved shapes or angles other than 90 degrees; also known as trapezoidal.

Figure 9-5c Exterior wood window construction diagram.

A. Wood window frame and sash (A_1) with an exterior low-maintenance skin of aluminum (often available in a broad color palette) or vinyl (A_2).
B. Sash is shown double glazed; window manufacturers will frequently offer a third layer of glass (a triple-glazed option) (B_1).
C. The finish outside material (aluminum, vinyl) can be continuous to form a weather seal flange on all four sides, secured with nails/screws and weatherproof tape to the substrate.
D. Studs (in this case 2 × 6s) are doubled at the rough (window) opening (jambs); the head condition is similar with the addition of a structural load-bearing header (see Figure 9-5d item A_1).
E. Typical (2 × 6) stud wall "sandwich" (from inside to outside) includes the following:
   Gypsum board (drywall), ½ inch thick.
   Vapor barrier (with climate exceptions).
   Wall cavity filled with insulation.
   Exterior structural sheathing.
   Air filtration barrier sheet.
   Exterior finish: siding, stucco, brick, etc.
F. Interior extension jambs (F_1) and casing/trim (F_2) are generally hardwood; size and configuration are designer's choice. Alternative option: drywall returns to the window frame with no casing and no extension jamb.
G. Window frame and sill (trim); size and configuration are designer's choice. Alternative option: no frame trim; the exterior finish material abuts the window frame (A_1).

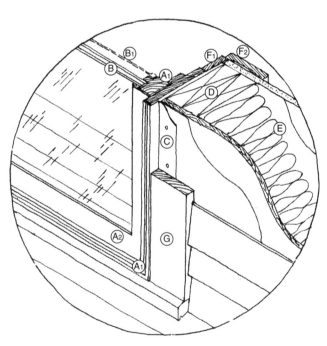

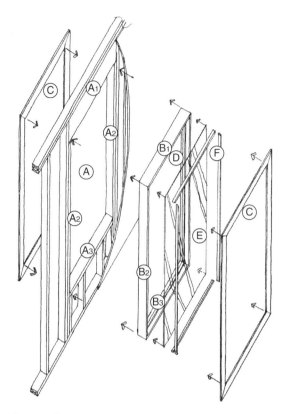

Figure 9-5d Window construction and terminology (applicable to fixed windows).

A. Rough opening.
  A_1. Header.
  A_2. Double stud at jamb(s).
  A_3. Sill.
B. Frame.
  B_1. Head.
  B_2. Jamb(s).
  B_3. Sill (sloped for exterior conditions).
C. Trim (casing).
D. Fixed stop.
E. Glass (single or double).
F. Removable stop.

Note: Door rough opening is similar but would contain no wall at the sill. Additional information on doors and door framing can be found in Figure 9-4c.

- Scale and proportion of window relative to the scale of the room and larger dwelling.

Note: All of the above should be balanced in relationship to the composition of the exterior of the dwelling and the larger architectural context of the structure.

When adding windows in a renovation, special care must be taken to consider the exterior appearance and context of the dwelling. In addition, window locations require consideration based on the local climate, site issues, and solar orientation of the building. Providing adequate natural ventilation is a major component of sustainable design practice and is often achieved through the thoughtful placement of operable windows.

Windows are categorized by how they open, as indicated in Figure 9-5b. Windows may open by sliding vertically (double and single hung), sliding horizontally (known as sliding), and hinged to open outward (casement, hopper, and awning types). Fixed windows, as the name implies, are fixed; they do not open to allow for ventilation or cleaning. Fixed windows are available in a variety of specialty shapes and sizes and are often used in combination with other types of operable windows.

It is important to understand window construction (illustrated in Figure 9-5c and 9-5d).

Materials used in window frame construction include metal (aluminum and steel) and wood. Aluminum types are lightweight and are available in baked anodized finishes and other factory finishes. Steel windows are not common for residential use but may be found in some modernist buildings. Steel is stronger than aluminum. It is often painted but is also available in other factory-applied finishes. Aluminum and steel tend to be poor thermal insulators and should have a nonmetal thermal break. Metal windows tend to be more common in mild climates.

Wood is a very common material for residential window construction. Wood frames are most often thicker than metal and are more effective thermal insulators. There are also composite windows that are made from more than one type of material. This type includes wood windows that are clad in vinyl. Other types include those that are wood on the interior and aluminum on the outside (shown in Figure 9-10c), allowing for paintable/stainable wood interior surfaces and more weather-resistant exterior surfaces.

All-vinyl and all-fiberglass windows are also available. Vinyl types tend to be inexpensive and durable but may have the unmistakable look of plastic and also tend to be a bit chunky looking. Fiberglass types are less common and more costly than vinyl. Neither vinyl nor fiberglass types are meant to be painted and are therefore limited to manufacturers' color selections.

In discussing windows, the term *glazing* refers to the glass portion of windows. Glazing options for windows include insulating glass, consisting of two or more sheets of glass with a sealed air space, which provides an increased thermal barrier and inhibits condensation. There are double-pane (double-glazed) and triple-pane (triple-glazed) types of insulated glass. In addition, some insulated types are filled with low-conductance gas such as argon or krypton, which boosts energy efficiency significantly.

Low-e glass is another option available for energy conservation. This type of glass reduces the passage of radiant heat due to the coating that is applied to the insulated glass. The coating tends to reflect infrared energy while letting visible light pass. (As a point of reference, the "e" in low-e glass stands for *emissivity,* which is defined as the power of a surface to emit heat by radiation.)

ROOF TYPES AND STYLES

Roof design and form have a significant impact upon the visual characteristics of the exterior and can also impact how the interior spaces are formed. The primary functions of a roof are to shed water, to shade and insulate the interior, and to protect walls and windows from the ravages of the elements. Much the same way an umbrella shields a person from the weather, a roof serves to shield and protect a building. In addition, the roof of a house contributes a great deal toward the visual qualities of the building. Complex plan shapes generally require complex roof forms, which can be wonderful but typically add to the building cost. Figure 9-6 is a review of simple roof styles and forms.

Roofing materials and configurations for residential construction include shingles, tiles, and sheets. Shingles rely on the redundancy of at least two layers, as well as lapped joints, whereas sheets and tiles are laid as single layers with lapped joints. Asphalt is the most commonly used material for shingles; wood (commonly western red cedar), metal (steel, aluminum, and copper), and slate are also used. Materials used for roofing tiles include clay, cement fiber, metal, and concrete.

Sheet materials used for roofing include sheet metal with standing seams (including galvanized steel, aluminum, and copper). This type of roof is constructed of interlocking panels that run vertically from the roof's ridge to the eaves. Two materials used for very flat roofs include built-up types (made from multiple layers) and single-ply roofing membranes (ethylene propylene diene monomer, or EPDM).

FIREPLACES AND STOVES

Many homeowners continue to desire some type of fireplace, as a fireplace seems to provide a symbol of warmth and "home and hearth" rather than supplying necessary heating. A fireplace can also provide a focal point, support a gathering space, and add architectural interest.

Fireplaces and stoves use the following fuels: wood, wood by-products, natural gas and propane, and corn pellets. There are also purely decorative types of fireplaces that do not require venting and burn alcohol gel.

With the exception of wood- or pellet-burning stoves, fireplaces are not efficient sources of heat. Such inefficiency can be ameliorated by enclosing the fire—most commonly with glass—and making the fireplace function more like a stove, or by controlling the introduction of combustion air. In addition, introducing convection, with a double-walled firebox and fan, can extract and move the warm air into the room.

There are two types of fireplaces: masonry and prefabricated. Masonry types are built on-site and, as the name implies, are constructed of brick, with firebrick used in the firebox and standard brick or stone for other areas. Masonry fireplaces require a chimney. According to *Fireplaces Magazine,* "Masonry fireplaces can weigh as much as 6 or even 7 tons. This means they need an extensive footing to support them." Figure 9-7a and 9-7b illustrate the components of masonry fireplaces.

Prefabricated fireplaces, as the name implies, have components that are manufactured off-site. Prefabricated types have a firebox lined with cast refractory panels and a round metal chimney that rises through the roof. These chimneys may be left as is or may be encased in some manner. Figure 9-8 illustrates the components of prefabricated fireplaces.

Another item that offers fireplace-like properties is the wood-burning or pellet-burning stove. These can offer efficient heating and can provide some of the aesthetic and symbolic pleasures of a fireplace. In 2015 the U.S.

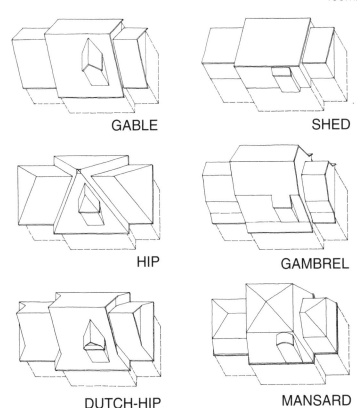

GABLE

SHED

HIP

GAMBREL

DUTCH-HIP

MANSARD

Figure 9-6 Basic roof styles and forms.

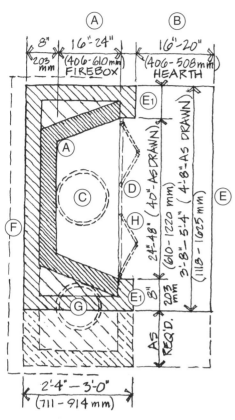

Figure 9-7a Plan of a built-in-place masonry fireplace capable of burning wood (or housing a gas "log" fire). The basic configuration and range of size(s) of the firebox is similar for prefabricated wood-burning or prefabricated gas-fired fireplaces (see Figure 9-8). The principal difference (in plan view): the firebrick (A) will be replaced by a double-walled metal housing, which will be approximately half the thickness of the firebrick.

A. Firebox should be lined with firebrick (never concrete, concrete block, or face brick; sides should be splayed to radiate more heat into the room. The IRC requires a minimum depth of 20 inches (508 mm).
B. Hearth outside the firebox requires a noncombustible finish such as stone, brick ceramic, slate, or concrete.
C. Flue size (clear cross section): 1/10 of fireplace opening. For example:
    36 inches (914 mm) wide by 28 inches (711 mm) high = 1008 square inches (0.65 m²)
    $\frac{1}{10}$ x 1008 = 100.8 square inches (0.65 m²) (flue area)
    This means a 12-inch (305-mm) diameter flue area would be required.
    Flues for prefabricated gas fireplaces are somewhat smaller and can be vented out the top of the firebox to the roof (see Figure 9-3a) or vented out the back of the firebox through an exterior wall.
D. Enclose with operable (bifold) glass doors for better burn control and more heat efficiency.
E. Overall width: anything over selected firebox width must be a minimum of 8 inches (203 mm) at each side (a 12-inch [305-mm] minimum opening at each side is required at larger fireplaces with on opening exceeding 6 square feet [0.56 m²]).
F. Hold combustible structural building components 4 inches (102 mm) away from the back and 2 inches (51 mm) away from the sides of the fireplace masonry mass.
G. Flue from a lower-floor fireplace can be buried within the expanded masonry mass if required.
H. 48 inches (1220 mm) is a large opening width; it is possible to go larger. For example, a fireplace with a width of 72 inches (1829 mm) and a 40-inch (1016-mm) opening would require a flue with an inside diameter of 20 inches (508 mm), which is quite large.

ADDITIONAL FIREPLACE NOTES

■ The size of the fireplace opening and surrounding masonry mass is highly variable. This must be scaled for the space it is within, as well as for how much heat it is intended to produce.

■ A masonry fireplace mass heats up very slowly and releases its heat slowly.

■ Codes require a noncombustible separation of structural wood components from the masonry mass.

■ It has been said that the least efficient way to heat your home is with an open fireplace—glass enclosures or inserts increase efficiency.

■ Wood-burning fireplaces may be illegal in some localities. In addition, in some locations, there may be burn bans for certain periods of time based on air pollution levels.

■ There are regional differences in masonry fireplace construction; finding a highly skilled mason with a good track record is the key to a successful masonry fireplace.

Environmental Protection Agency (EPA) updated its clean air standards for residential wood heaters (woodstoves and pellet stoves) to make new heaters burn significantly cleaner and to improve air quality in areas where people burn wood for heat. The new standards apply to new stoves (those installed in 2015 or later) and do not apply to wood heaters installed prior to 2015. See the references section of this chapter for a link to information about the new standards.

Wood-burning stoves have evolved to become quite efficient and emit far less pollution than older types and, for these reasons, have become popular with consumers. Like prefabricated fireplaces, wood-burning stoves have a metal flue pipe that rises through the roof (with a straight and direct approach). Since they are intended to provide heat, such stoves must be properly sized so that they do not overheat or underheat spaces.

Like prefabricated fireplaces, wood-burning stoves are regulated by Underwriters Laboratories (UL) requirements and by the manufacturer's recommendations in terms of materials used nearby and in the hearth area.

Increasingly, homeowners are opting to place wood-burning inserts into masonry fireplaces. Many manufacturers of wood-burning stoves produce inserts that fit directly into the firebox and make use of existing chimneys, creating a more efficient heat source for the dwelling. Figure 9-9a and 9-9b show design drawings for a fireplace with a wood-burning stove insert.

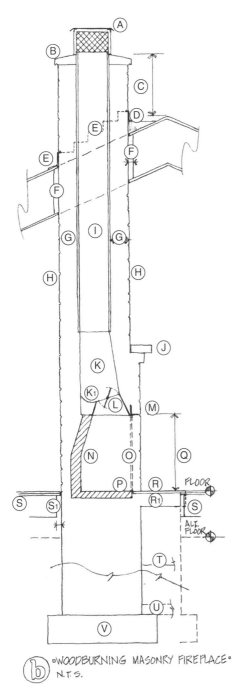

Figure 9-7b Wood-burning masonry fireplace section.

A. Metal spark arrestor with hood; can also serve to keep out squirrels and other vermin.
B. Stone, concrete, or sheet metal cap; sloped to shed water.
C. General rule of thumb: 2 feet (610 mm) to prevent downdrafts from prevailing winds.
D. Sheet metal saddle (also known as a cricket) to divert rainwater around the chimney.
E. Sheet metal roof flashing; stepped up the sloping sides; sheet metal needs to be set into the masonry joints as they step up the roof.
F. Structural (combustible) framing needs to be held away from the chimney; 2 inches (51 mm) minimum.
G. It is good practice to have 8 inches (203 mm) or more (finish and backup) of masonry surrounding the flue.
H. Exposed portion(s) of the chimney mass could be brick, stone, CMUs, or ceramic tile. These are used for purposes of appearance as well as because these materials hold heat and disperse it slowly.
I. Fired-clay flue line; this needs to withstand high temperatures and be cleanable. A round (in cross section) flue is best. This area must be cleaned due to soot and creosote buildup, which can be a source of fuel for a chimney fire. A rule of thumb for the clear size of flue is $\frac{1}{10}$ the size of fireplace opening.
J. Mantel; optional. The height and configuration are design decisions. See also Figure 9-9.
K. Smoke chamber and smoke shelf (K_1).
L. Steel operable damper.
M. Structural steel lintel angle is required to support masonry above the fireplace opening.
N. Firebox must be lined on all sides with firebrick. Standard concrete and masonry products do not perform and may prove to be dangerous.
O. An operable heat-treated glass enclosure (preferably two layers that are vented between the layers). This is done to mitigate heated room air from going up the chimney.
P. Combustion air should be introduced at a low point in the firebox, either at the sides or at the bottom via a ducted passage to the outside. A less preferable, less efficient option is a damper-controlled opening at the glass (see O) to draw in room air.
Q. The height of the fireplace opening is a function of the size of the fire desired and the scale of the room; 28 to 32 inches (711 to 813 mm) are common heights. The opening height is generally less than the width, although this is not a code requirement.
R. Floor or raised hearth, the height of which is the choice of the designer. Materials for this area must be noncombustible, such as stone, brick, slate, or ceramic tile (R_1 structure is cantilevered).
S. A structural wood floor over crawl space or basement. Where appropriate, a concrete slab on grade is often easier in terms of hearth construction (2-inch [51-mm] separation at S_1).
T. Grade at crawl space condition.
U. Floor slab in basement condition.
V. Masonry fireplaces and chimneys are very heavy; therefore, footing requirements should be well engineered and not underestimated.

Figure 9-8a A prefabricated fireplace. Gas (as shown) and wood-burning types generally have the following in common.

A. Construction with a double wall (on all sides), allowing air to circulate within the cavity (heavy-grade sheet metal for gas versions; structural-grade sheet steel for wood-burning types).
B. Cooler room air is pulled in by natural convection at the bottom.
C. Heated air is discharged at the top.
D. Glass enclosure; this is highly recommended. Glass doors in wood-burning versions must be operable.
E. Methods vary, but combustion air must find its way to the fire chamber—this is preferably not room air but rather ducted to a nonheated source of air, such as from the attic, basement, or exterior.
F. A gas fireplace flue connection is out the top (vertically) or the upper back (for horizontal discharge). In wood-burning fireplaces, the flue will always be out the top and will look different from that shown here.

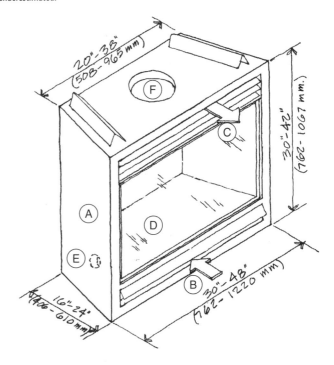

PREFABRICATED FIREPLACE
N.T.S.

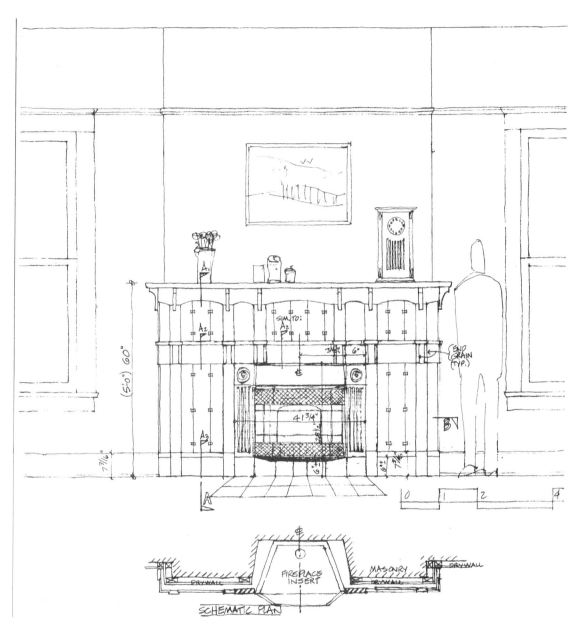

Figure 9-9a and 9-9b Design drawings for a custom walnut surround for a fireplace with a wood-burning stove insert. The surround was constructed to conceal a deteriorating brick fireplace.

Regardless of the type of fireplace used, its placement within the room—and within the larger context of the building—requires significant thought. The fireplace should be located in such a manner that it enhances the room and does not impede traffic flow or create a situation in which the room is difficult to furnish. A range of placement and configuration options are available, as shown in Figure 9-10. Of course, the general location of the fireplace and its chim-ney must be considered in relationship to the larger context of the building.

In addition, the inclusion of a hearth, the design of the hearth, and the material qualities of the hearth and sur-rounding areas require careful consideration. The location and size of the hearth area are governed by the IRC (Section R1001.10). Clearances of combustibles at fireplace are cov-ered in Section 1001.11.

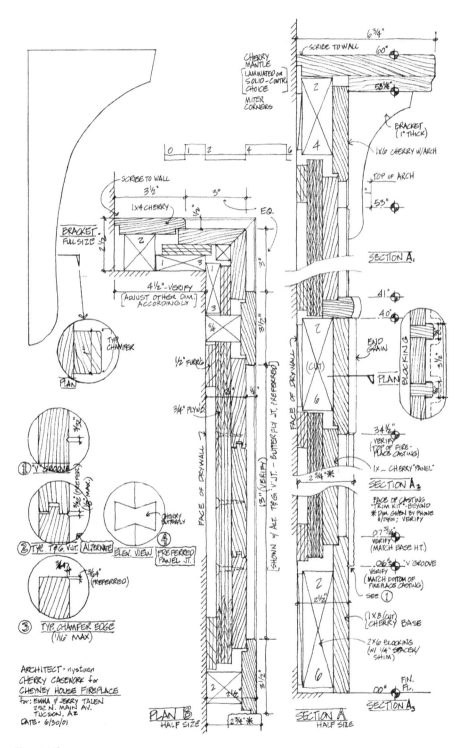

Figure 9-9b

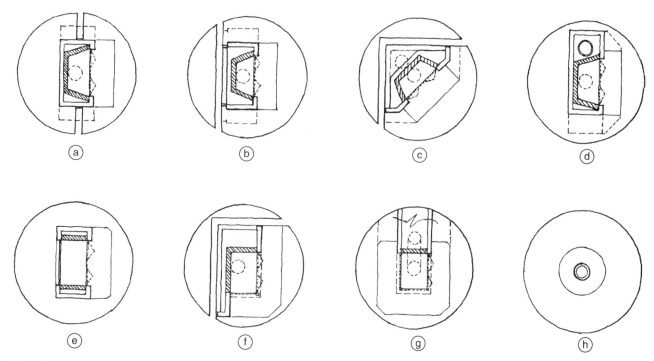

Figure 9-10 Masonry wood-burning fireplace design and configuration options.

a. One-side-open masonry fireplace in an exterior frame wall; this inside-outside type of fireplace produces very little net heat gain because a great deal is lost by conduction and radiation directly to the exterior.

b. One-side-open masonry fireplace against an exterior or interior wall. This configuration will lose less heat to the exterior than type a.

c. One-side-open masonry fireplace set at a 45-degree angle into a corner works well in certain spaces. This configuration has a loss of heat similar to type b.

d. One-side-open freestanding masonry fireplace radiates heat to all directions of the interior space; this type can be used as a room divider.

e. Two-side-open freestanding masonry fireplace. This type disperses radiant heat similarly to type d. It is preferable to have glass in the fireplace opening on both sides, with one side fixed and the other operable, as a means of building and tending the fire. Without the glass, this type is very vulnerable to allowing smoke into the rooms with the least cross-draft.

f. Two-side-open masonry fireplace. This type can work in a corner with either closed side against a wall or freestanding. Without a glass enclosure, this type is prone to the smoking problem described in type e.

g. Three-side-open masonry fireplace. This requires a large masonry mass if it is necessary to cantilever a masonry "hood" over the firebox. This type is very prone to smoking if there is no glass enclosure.

h. An open fire pit with a hood, generally made of sheet metal. This type is not recommended for indoor residential applications and is very prone to smoke drifting horizontally into adjacent interior space.

Notes on fireplaces a to g (above):
In fireplaces a to g, the firebox is always constructed of firebrick, including the floor portion (even fireplace h requires a firebrick floor).
Exposed surfaces are made of brick, stone, or ceramic; sheet metal hoods are often used in types f and g.
A round flue is shown; this is required by some codes. Square or rectangular flue(s) may be allowed.

REFERENCES

Contains both works cited and recommended reading, with occasional annotation.

Carter, Tim. 2010. "Low E Glass-Types and Benefits." Ask the Builder. http://www.askthebuilder.com/B97_Low_E_Glass_-_Types_and_Benefits.shtml.

Ching, Francis. 2008. *Building Construction Illustrated*. 4th ed. Hoboken, NJ: John Wiley & Sons.

Fisette, Paul. "Understanding Energy-Efficient Windows." Fine Homebuilding. http://www.finehomebuilding.com/how-to/articles/understanding-energy-efficient-windows.aspx.

Jacobson, Max, Murray Silverstein, and Barbara Winslow. 1990. *The Good House: Contrast as a Design Tool*. Newtown, CT: Taunton Press. This publication contains wonderful sketches and drawings and follows up on some issues raised in *A Pattern Language*. What the authors refer to as "studies of contrast" provides some guidance to hierarchy of experience and plan balance.

International Code Council. 2015. "2015 International Residential Code for One- and Two-Family Dwellings." Country Club Hills, IL: International Code Council.

National Trust for Historic Preservation. "Residential Field Guide." http://www.preservationnation.org/information-center/sustainable-communities/buildings/weatherization/windows/additional-resources/nthp_windows_field_guide.pdf.

U.S. Environmental Protection Agency. 2015. "Fact Sheet: Summary of requirements of Woodstoves and Pellet Stoves." http://www2.epa.gov/residential-wood-heaters/fact-sheet-summary-requirements-woodstoves-and-pellet-stoves.

CHAPTER 10

Notes on Remodeling

INTRODUCTION

While current episodes of television home improvement shows may give the impression that home remodeling and renovation can be done in a few weeks leading to a fabulous, happy, surprise ending, the reality is that home renovation and remodeling can be physically and emotionally stressful, and can often take longer and be more costly than anticipated.

Keys to a successful remodeling or renovation project include hard work related to planning, rational thinking, and often, a having a long view. This chapter is intended to provide an overview of ways to understand and plan a home remodeling project. The previous chapters covered individual spaces within a home, and that room-specific information can form the basis of the design direction for the project.

This chapter is intended to fill in some specifics about remodeling that did not fit neatly into previous chapters. Given the scope of this book, this chapter is not an exhaustive overview of renovation; instead, it is intended to provide some limited information about the process.

First, it is important to understand that the terms *remodel*, *renovation*, and *restoration* have specific definitions. Understanding these terms and using them correctly can help clarify the nature of the project. Note that these terms are also used by real estate professionals.

The term *remodel* refers to projects that change the structure, shape, or appearance of something. Remodeling may be used to describe a change to the character of a building, or a change to a portion of a house or building. It can include combining rooms and removing walls. Creating an addition to the existing structure is also considered remodeling (see Figure 10-1).

Figure 10-1 This residence was remodeled with a two-story rear addition providing a new bathroom, family room, and home office.

Renovate means to make new again, or to make repairs to a building that bring it back to a good condition. *Renovate* may also refer to making a space new without changing its use, for example by replacing windows or updating finishes in an older kitchen.

Figure 10-2 This period home was restored, bringing it back to its original condition.

Restore refers to returning something to an earlier condition by repairing, cleaning, or refinishing. For example, bringing an old building back to its original condition is considered historic restoration rather than renovation (see Figure 10-2).

According to Harvard University's Joint Center for Housing Studies, the United States "home improvement market has largely recovered from the Great Recession" and "the aging of the US population brings several opportunities for further growth," this including a growing demand for accessibility improvements. Also noted by the Center is an upswing in discretionary home improvement projects, particularly kitchen and bath remodeling.

Remodeling projects can be seen as a multistage process. As stated previously, successful projects require careful thought and planning; these are key components of that multistage process. This process can be thought of as having four distinct phases, with numerous steps in each:

Remodeling, Renovation, Restoration Project Phases:

1. Assessment Phase:

- Consider long-range plans.
- Assess and document existing conditions.
- Determine wants and needs.

- Review resources and constraints (these include budgetary constraints as well as zoning, code, and physical constraints of the property/existing structure).
- Develop a project timeline.

2. Design Phase:

- Explore design solutions.

3. Selection Phase:

- Make decisions about design direction.
- Refine design direction/solution; this includes all elements of the design, such as materials and design details. (Typically the design is delineated in drawings and specifications as it is refined).

4. Construction Phase:

- Prepare design drawings for bidding and construction.
- Prepare for construction with bid review, obtaining required permits, and possible construction financing.
- Begin construction, and complete construction.

Note that Chapter 8 contains a sample project that provides an overview of the design process, and Chapter 9 contains basic construction and framing information. In addition, as the project moves into the design phase, individual chapters may be consulted regarding specific room types and needs. The following sections contain additional information about each of the four phases.

ASSESSMENT PHASE

The assessment phase requires assessment of the homeowners' long- and short-range plans, functional needs, and desires as well as an assessment of the property in question.

The following is a checklist of items to consider during the various stages of the assessment phase:

ASSESSMENT
Consider long-range plans:

☐ How much time do you plan to stay in the home?

The answer to this question relates directly to two components: 1, quality of life, and 2, return on investment (ROI). For example, a family may have a one-bathroom home with several young children, and a desire to remain in the home for twenty years. Given this, the addition of a second bathroom would improve the quality of life over many years and would not be greatly affected by a desire to sell the home. In contrast, another homeowner may desire a larger bathroom with a walk-in shower and spa-like fixtures, and have a plan to move within five years. In this case, the return on investment for resale should be considered.

☐ Might there be upcoming changes in lifestyle or living patterns?

This requires the homeowner to make a personal assessment about changes in living patterns, stage of life, and lifestyle. For example, will some of the occupants be leaving the home soon, or might elderly parents be joining the family? Do the occupants wish to age in place, and will the home require changes to support this?

☐ List the major problems that the project is intended to solve.

☐ List the minor problems that the project is intended to solve.

☐ Is there a change in appearance desired for the residence?

In some cases, no change in the appearance of the home is desired, and in fact the homeowners may want additional space with no changes to the appearance or style.

In other cases a new and very different physical appearance is desired. Appearance also relates to the lifestyle of the client, as they may wish to have the residence feel more secluded, or be better suited to outdoor entertaining.

Assess and document existing conditions:

☐ Measure exterior and interior existing elements.

It is often best to measure individual room interiors first, starting with the overall dimensions (interior wall surface to wall surface) and ceiling; include key elements such as window and door dimensions, including heights, and room elements such as alcoves and columns.

In addition to individual room dimensions, exterior dimensions should be taken, including all necessary site measurements.

Identify and measure plumbing fixtures, light switches and outlets, heating and air vents, and gas hookups.

Using graph paper can help make shorter work of measuring, as one can rough-sketch the floor plan as measurements are taken.

☐ Photograph exterior and interior elements.

Photograph rooms at the time of measurement, and make notes about plumbing, outlets, columns, alcoves, etc.

If possible, note problematic areas at the time of measurement, as well as any areas that should be retained. Also note circulation patterns that should be retained.

☐ Draw "as built" or "existing conditions" floor plans and additional drawings that may be needed (these may include exterior and interior elevations, building sections, and a site plan). See Chapter 8 for detailed information on working with design drawings.

Determine wants and needs:

☐ What items are required?

Develop a well-considered list of all required items; this should include any new rooms and room functions, as well as furniture and/or fixtures to be contained in the new room or area.

☐ List existing items/elements that should be retained.

☐ List problematic areas in terms of structure, materials, mechanical systems, safety issues, conservation, or code violations.

☐ List any changes in appearance desired for the residence.

What should be retained and/or is there any clear visual direction for the new work? This includes interior and exterior aesthetic.

Review resources and constraints (these include budgetary constraints as well as zoning, code, and physical constraints of the property/existing structure):

☐ Available funds and sources (funds on hand, equity in home, additional sources of funding).

In addition to construction costs, there may be costs from fees for building permits, filing fees, and consulting fees (for design/architectural/engineering, etc.).

☐ Working with an existing structure combined with possible unforeseen project complications will often create project costs that are not anticipated.

☐ There are some rules of thumb that can help to keep costs lower:

- Projects requiring relocation of ductwork, gas lines, electrical, or plumbing tend to be more expensive than similar projects not involving these changes.

- Replacing items with those of similar dimensions tends to be less expensive than installing elements of very different dimensions.

- Projects requiring that existing elements be removed rather than allowing existing elements to remain tend to be more expensive (removing load-bearing walls is almost always more expensive).

- Moving exterior doors and windows tends to be costly.

- Refurbishing and refinishing is far more cost effective than remodeling, removing, and replacing.

  See also the "Budgeting and Return on Investment" section.

☐ Research local zoning and code restrictions (see the "Zoning and Building Codes" section of this chapter).

☐ Lot size constraints (including setback requirements and easements).

☐ Constraints related to current building structure or style.

Develop a project timeline:

☐ The timeline should include time for planning, design, decision-making, any plan approval that might be necessary, and construction.

Generally speaking, remodeling and renovation projects take longer than homeowners tend to imagine; creating a realistic timeline is essential. If the project is built around an upcoming event, the process should *begin* eight to twelve months prior to that event (this varies greatly based on project scope and availability of design and construction professionals).

Weather, climate and construction timing should be considered when creating the timeline.

Many of the items mentioned under rules of thumb related to reducing the costs can be time savers as well.

The nature of working with an existing structure combined with the various project constraints and possible unforeseen project complications can bring to mind the adage, "Hope for the best, plan for the worst."

DESIGN PHASE

The design phase involves engaging in the design process discussed in Chapter 8 and creating a range of possible options. Those options are best understood when referenced against the needs and requirements uncovered in the project assessment phase described in the previous section. Upon completion of the assessment phase, the following items can be combined into a list that identifies the project scope:

Remodeling Assessment List:

☐ Required repairs such as:

Structural

Improvement of watertightness

Materials and finishes

Electrical/mechanical

Building code violations

☐ Functional problems such as:

Need for additional space and/or rooms

Room location and layout

Circulation

Need for accessibility or aging-in-place updates

☐ Aesthetic problems such as:

Updating of interior appearance

Updating of exterior appearance

Restoration of previous condition

Removal of unnecessary items

Responses to this list combined with the other details uncovered in the assessment phase can be used to generate a design solution that is *affordable* (fits within the budget), *realistic* (meets timeline, scope, and constraints), and *efficient* (solves as many problems as possible).

With a single complete list of required items and an eye on affordable, realistic, and efficient solutions, the following options can be considered. These are presented roughly in order from lowest to highest in cost:

Possible Design Options

- Make repairs and refurbish rather than remodeling.

  As noted previously, a cost-effective way to add to the appeal (and in some cases function) of a home is to correct deficits and make needed repairs.

  Enhancing existing space with fresh finishes such as paint, new countertops, built-in casework, or wall finishes can add greatly to the beauty and usefulness of a home.

  Upgrades in lighting and color can create quite an impact.

Interestingly, a new entrance door is considered a top residential investment in terms of cost replacement according to several sources. Additionally, new siding is also considered a top item for return on investment. For more information, see the "Budgeting and Return on Investment" section.

Replacement windows are also worth considering in terms of refurbishment. They can offer energy savings, visual appeal, and ease of use.

- Rearrange existing space, including moving walls, and add or remove windows and doors.

Rearranging space can cost very little to quite a bit, with the variation based on the complexity of new construction and the related demolition. Adding new walls and/or removing older ones can be a cost-effective way to create more usable space.

As stated previously, adding doors and windows can be costly but may be a good choice if doing so creates a more livable, useful environment.

- Convert unused spaces.

Attic spaces: Attics may have the space for the required minimum ceiling height. In cases where there is not enough headroom, the roof can be raised or dormers can be added.

Basements: With humidity controlled, basements can be used for hobby areas, workshops, and entertainment spaces. With appropriate egress and ventilation, these spaces can be converted to bedrooms (see Chapter 5: Related Codes and Constraints).

Garages: In many cases, the structure is complete and may have utilities nearby if attached to a house. When unattached to house, a new entry or connection to a house can be added if desired.

Porches: Small porches may be converted into a sunroom or alcove within a larger room, while large porches may be suitable for a new leisure space or study. Some porches require extensive work for the conversion, while others require much less; porch conversions may require upgrades to the foundation.

Roofs: When planning an addition to an existing building, careful thought should be given to how the new roof ties in to the existing roof. This is an aesthetic concern in that the old and new should relate well visually. Additionally, this is a functional concern in that the two should be brought together so as not to leak.

- Adding new space can range from moving a wall a few feet to enlarge a room, to adding substantial square footage in a second story or wing addition.

Options include the following:

Small extension.

Adding to the entire width or length of structure.

Creation of a wing.

Addition to main structure with a linked connection.

Ideally, to move forward with the design, the process outlined in Chapter 8 should be followed. This includes reviewing the items mentioned above and generating a range of options as a brainstorming exercise. Creating a number of very different design solutions is useful, as these can be reviewed and refined in the next phase.

SELECTION AND CONSTRUCTION

Several varying solutions should be created and reviewed. Ideally, after reviewing several very different approaches, one or a combination emerge as meeting most of the requirements. This best solution or approach should be judged carefully against the items uncovered in the assessment phase. In moving forward with a final design solution, it is exceptionally important to aim for a solution that is affordable, reasonable, and efficient, and not to succumb to falling for a design that neglects to solve problems or is not in line with the budget or timeline.

Often a design that meets most of the project requirements needs additional refinement or a careful review of specific details before the design, and therefore the project, is ready to move into the construction phase.

In order to prepare the project fully for construction, drafted working drawings must be developed. Larger projects may require plans, elevations, sections, and specifications. For smaller projects, simple plans and elevations may suffice. Working drawings are used for two very important purposes: 1, to obtain required approvals of building officials; and 2, for use by contractors in creating a bid or estimate and to serve as the basis for the project construction. See the "Zoning and Building Codes" section for more information about building permits.

BUDGETING AND RETURN ON INVESTMENT

Budgetary constraints play a key role in the direction and scope of a project. A project budget should be based upon issues related to funds on hand and other funding sources:

The amount of cash or liquid savings the homeowner has.

The value of the home and the owner's equity in the home.

The monthly payment the homeowner can afford, in the case of a new or additional loan.

The owner's comfort level with added debt or use of savings.

The appraisal of the property by the loan issuer, typically a bank or credit union.

The financial resources available for the project budget should be seen in connection with the potential costs of the project. There are several websites that list average project costs. In some cases, these sites clarify specific costs for items such as walls, windows, and finishes, and in other cases, this information is simply lumped into groups such as "major kitchen remodel." The percentage of the construction budget devoted to different elements of a project such as building an addition are as follows:

Foundation and concrete slabs: 8–12%

Framing (floor systems, walls, windows, roof): 45–55%

Finishes: 10–15%

Mechanical and electrical: 15–22%

Cabinets and equipment: 8–12%

Site work, landscaping, and financing costs are not included. It is very difficult to create a clear set of construction costs within the context of this book. For example, a major kitchen remodel that requires all-new finishes, appliances, a building addition, and the moving of gas lines and ducting is going to be far more expensive per square foot than creating a small bedroom within an existing structure.

In planning the budget one must use the information gained in the assessment phase to help make decisions. Of prime importance is the amount of time the homeowner plans to stay in the home, because if it is a short time span, the return on investment (ROI) must be considered. For many years *Remodeling Magazine* has compared the average costs for popular remodeling projects with the value the projects may retain at resale to develop a report focused on ROI. Interestingly, the percentage returned on certain projects varies greatly from one year to the next. For example, according to the Remodeling 2015 Cost vs. Value Report, the biggest drop in 2015 value was for a backup power generator, which also had the biggest gain in 2014.

The 2015 report indicates that overall, on average, the increase a remodeling or replacement project would bring to a home's value was up only 0.29 percent from the previous year, although individual items rose as much as 11.6 percent. The report also notes that costs for projects rose by 4.22 percent on average for projects completed by construction professionals. Table 10-1 shows some popular remodeling and replacement projects and the projected return on investment, or cost vs. value, according to the report. Table 10-2 shows the return on investment for a replacement-type project, and Table 10-3 shows the estimated return on bathroom and kitchen remodeling and addition projects.

Based on this study of value, in the current economy major kitchen remodeling is not seen as providing as much resale value as it had in the "hot" resale markets of the past. This points to what *Consumer Reports* magazine has called "live-in value," which refers to remodeling projects done for the homeowner's enjoyment rather than as a means of boosting the home's value. A related online poll conducted by *Consumer Reports* showed that 40 percent of respondents would remodel to update kitchen styling, while 36 percent would remodel to make the kitchen more functional for cooking, and only 8 percent would remodel to boost the home's value.

It is also worth noting that while statistics related to remodeling projects are helpful, many remodeling projects combine

Table 10-1 2015 National Average Cost vs. Value Report: Remodel/Addition

Project	Job Cost ($)	Value Added at Resale ($)	2015 Cost Recouped (%)
Attic bedroom	51,696	39,908	77.2
Basement remodel	64,442	47,637	72.8
Family room addition	84,201	53,955	64.1
Sunroom addition	75,726	36,704	72.8
Master suite addition	111,245	68,596	61.7
Two-story addition	161,925	103, 848	64.1

Source: Remodeling 2015 Cost vs. Value Report

Table 10-2 2015 National Average Cost vs. Value Report: Replacement Items

Project	Job Cost ($)	Value Added at Resale ($)	2015 Cost Recouped (%)
Entry door (steel)	1,230	1,522	101.8
Garage door	1,595	1,410	88.4
Roofing	19,528	13,975	71.6
Siding (vinyl)	12,013	9,694	80.7
Siding (fiber-cement)	14,014	9,694	84.3
Windows (vinyl)	13,837	10,365	74.9
Windows (wood)	17,422	12,533	71.9

Source: Remodeling 2015 Cost vs. Value Report

Table 10-3 2015 National Averages Cost vs. Value Report: Kitchens and Baths

Project	Job Cost ($)	Value Added at Resale ($)	2015 Cost Recouped (%)
Bathroom addition (midrange)	39, 578	22,875	57.8
Bathroom addition (upscale)	76,429	44,750	58.6
Bathroom remodel (midrange)	16,724	11,707	70.0
Bathroom remodel (upscale)	54,115	32,385	59.8
Kitchen remodel, minor* (midrange)	19,226	15,255	79.3
Kitchen remodel, major** (midrange)	56,768	38,485	67.8
Kitchen remodel, major** (upscale)	113,097	66,747	59.0

*Minor remodel is primarily cosmetic, with new cabinet fronts/drawers, new countertops, midpriced sink and faucets, and new wall finishes.
**Major remodel includes new layout, new wood cabinets, new appliances, and new ventilation system. Upscale version has higher-end appliances and cabinets, etc.

Source: Remodeling 2015 Cost vs. Value Report

improved function with aesthetic updates and therefore do not fit neatly into the minor/major remodeling parameters found in the study. In addition, it is careful programming, good communication, and an understanding of design that allow a designer to uncover what a client most needs in a project—and provide it.

ORGANIZATIONAL FLOW, ERGONOMICS, AND REQUIRED CLEARANCES

Whether adding new rooms and spaces or rearranging space, a careful consideration of circulation, organizational flow, and clearances is important. See Chapter 2 for information on circulation. In addition, each room-related chapter can serve as a design reference for that room type relative to organization, ergonomics, and required clearances.

For those planning a project that centers on aging in place, a review of each chapter's Accessibility Notes will help provide an understanding of how to plan for creating accessible and visitable spaces. Additionally, Chapter 1 can serve as an introduction to basic concepts such as sustainability and accessibility, so that they may be incorporated into the design.

ZONING AND BUILDING CODES

As stated in Chapter 1, zoning regulations control building size, height, location, setbacks, and occupancy type, and are adopted by local municipalities. Many of the changes undertaken in a

remodeling project are subject to local zoning regulations, and therefore research of local zoning regulations is imperative. The following is a list of the type of zoning regulations that might impact the project.

Zoning Regulations

Maximum or minimum area density

This may require a minimum lot size or control the type of occupancy (for example, not allow rental residences). This may also control the minimum or maximum allowable floor area.

Required setbacks

Minimum setback dimensions may be required for the front, back, and sides of a residence and can greatly constrain the size and shape of additions. Front setbacks can vary widely, with 20 to 40 feet (6096 to 12,192 mm) the most common. Side setbacks are often 6 feet (1829 m). Rear setbacks can be a percentage of lot depth or a percentage of green space.

Easements

Other parties may have a right of access (such as a utility easement), which would control the shape and location of an addition.

Parking requirements

Required parking spaces may limit a garage conversion project.

Lot coverage

Limits on the maximum percentage of a lot area that can be covered by the house may affect the size of an addition; these limits are sometimes more restrictive than setbacks.

Maximum height

Maximum height limits may control the height of a story addition. In some cases, portions of a structure such as pitched roofs can extend beyond the allowable height.

Design restrictions

Some communities have design review boards, and projects are subject to review. When a project is part of a homeowner's association, there may be covenants or design restrictions.

Variances

A variance request claiming hardship or special exceptions can be made to local officials.

Note: Setbacks and easements are illustrated in Chapter 8, Figure 8-3.

Building codes are discussed throughout this book, with an introduction in Chapter 1 and room-specific information covered in later chapters; consulting appropriate chapters will be useful in planning and designing a remodeling project.

It is important to note that building permits are required for most home remodeling projects, from simple decks to room additions. Some smaller projects, when done by the homeowner, may be allowable without a permit. However, it is well worth consulting local code officials to determine if a permit is required for the project in question. Typically, cosmetic fixes and refurbishing do not require a permit; new light fixtures installed per manufacturer's directions do not require a permit, but must comply with the codes.

A building permit insures that the project in question meets local zoning and building codes (this includes electrical and plumbing), and environmental restrictions (waste and water systems, etc.). If a project requires a permit and one is not obtained, fines can be imposed. In some cases, the lack of a permit for a remodeling project creates issues in the future with reselling the home.

Obtaining a building permit requires that forms and fees be filed. For projects involving additions and reuse of existing space (attic conversions, for example), drawings such as floor plans and sections are required. A description of the work to be done, estimate of the project cost, square footage added, lot number, and other pertinent information is required on forms filed for a building permit. A major project may require separate electrical and plumbing permits. General contractors often include the permit filing in their fees; in other cases a plumber or electrician obtains the permit required for their individual work on the project.

Once the permit is approved (called "pulling a permit" by some), the project construction can begin, and generally a building code official will make various inspections as the project commences.

REFERENCES

Contains both works cited and recommended reading, with occasional annotation.

Ching, Francis. 1983. *Home Renovation*. New York: Van Nostrand Reinhold. As stated in Chapter 1, this is a good general guide to residential design as it relates to renovation. The list of project phases for renovation is adapted from this book.

Consumer Reports Online. 2010. "Has 'Live-in Value' Replaced ROI When It Comes to Kitchen Remodeling?" http://www.consumerreports.org/cro/news/2010/04/has-live-in-value-replaced-roi-when-it-comes-to-kitchen-remodeling/index.htm.

Joint Center for Housing Studies of Harvard University. 2015a. "Emerging Trends in the Remodeling Market."

———. 2015b. "Pick-Up Projected in Home Improvement Activity Moving into 2016."

Remodeling. 2015a. "Remodeling Spending Could Hit Record This Year." http://www.remodeling.hw.net/benchmarks/economic-outlook-rri/remodeling-spending-could-hit-record-this-year-jchs_o.

———. 2015b. "2015 Cost vs. Value Report." http://www.remodeling.hw.net/cost-vs-value/2015. Complete data from the Remodeling 2015 Cost vs. Value Report can be downloaded free at www.costvsvalue.com.

Taylor, Richard. 2015. "Zillow Blog: Remodel, Renovate or Restore? Start with Clear Definition of Terms." http://www.zillow.com/blog/remodel-renovate-or-restore-start-with-clear-definition-of-terms-59710.

IGCC, LEED, and Sustainability/Green Design Certifying Programs, Agencies, and Associations

IGCC

IGCC is the International Green Construction Code, which is also referred to as "the green code." This model code was developed by the American Institute of Architects and ASTM International in consultation with the American Society of Heating, Refrigerating and Air-Conditioning Engineers (ASHRAE), the U.S. Green Building Council (USGCB), and the Illuminating Engineering Society (IES).

According to the International Code Council website, the code "creates a regulatory framework for new and existing buildings, establishing minimum green requirements for buildings and complementing voluntary rating systems, which may extend beyond baseline of the IGCC. The code acts as an overlay to the existing set of *International Codes*."

The following is a list of chapters found in the draft version of the 2015 IGCC; these reflect the code's scope and coverage. Information provided under "Intent" is meant to clarify chapter intent:

2015 International Green Construction Code (IGCC) Chapters

Chapter 1: Scope and Administration

Chapter 2: Definitions

Chapter 3 Compliance Method

Chapter 4: Site Design and Development

Intent: This section applies to land development for the eventual construction of buildings or additions thereto that contain dwelling units.

Chapter 5: Lot Design, Preparation, and Development

Intent: This section applies to lot development for the eventual construction of residential buildings, multi-unit buildings, or additions thereto that contain dwelling units.

Chapter 6: Resource Efficiency

Intent: Design and construction practices that minimize the environmental impact of the building materials are incorporated, environmentally efficient building systems and materials are incorporated, and waste generated during construction is reduced.

Chapter 7: Energy Efficiency

Chapter 8: Water Efficiency

Intent: Measures that reduce indoor and outdoor water usage are implemented.

Chapter 9: Indoor Environmental Quality

Intent: Pollutant sources are controlled.

Chapter 10: Operation, Maintenance, and Building Owner Education

Intent: Information on the building's use, maintenance, and green components is provided.

Chapter 11: Remodeling

Intent: Relates to the lot and changes to the lot due to remodeling of an existing building.

Chapter 12: Remodeling of Functional areas

Intent: To address the most common residential remodeling projects such as kitchens, baths, basements, etc.

LEED

The term *LEED* refers to the U.S. Green Building Council's (USGBC) Leadership in Energy and Environmental Design (LEED) Green Building Rating System. LEED v4 was approved in 2013 and replaces LEED 2009 (however, projects may be registered under LEED 2009 until Oct. 2016). One major change in the newer version is a focus on materials that requires an understanding of products' composition and origin. Rating system types were also modified to include specific building types, as was a focus on the team of project designers (under "Integrative Design Process"). The following are the rating systems for specific project types in LEED v4:

LEED v4 Rating Systems

Building Design and Construction (BD+C)

BD+C: New Construction

BD+C: Core and Shell

BD+C: Data Centers

BD+C: Healthcare

BD+C: Hospitality

BD+C: Retail

BD+C: Schools

BD+C: Warehouses and Distribution Centers

Operations and Maintenance (O+M)

O+M: Existing Buildings

O+M: Data Centers

O+M: Hospitality

O+M: Retail

O+M: Schools

O+M: Warehouses and Distribution Centers

Interior Design and Construction (ID+C)

ID+C: Commercial Interiors

ID+C: Hospitality

ID+C: Retail

Homes: Building Design (Residential BD+C:)

BD+C: Homes

BD+C: Multifamily Midrise

Neighborhood Development (ND)

ND: Plan

ND: Built Project

Clearly, the LEED residential project types that relate most directly to the content of this book area BD+C: Homes and BD+C: Multifamily Midrise. For these project types, the following are required:

BD+C: Homes and BD+C: Multifamily Midrise Credit Categories:

Applies to single-family homes and low-rise multifamily projects (one to three stories)

Integrative Design Process

Location and Transportation

Sustainable Sites

Water Efficiency

Energy and Atmosphere

Materials and Resources

Indoor Environmental Quality

Innovation

Regional Priority

SUSTAINABILITY/GREEN DESIGN CERTIFYING PROGRAMS, AGENCIES, AND ASSOCIATIONS

There are a number of programs that provide certification and standards for green products and materials, some of which are included in the following list:

Collaborative for High Performance Schools (www.chps.net)

Cool Roof Rating Council (www.coolroofs.org)

Energy Star, U.S. Environmental Protection Agency (www.energystar.gov)

Environmentally Preferable Purchasing, U.S. Environmental Protection Agency (www.epa.gov/opptintr/epp/)

Floor Score, Resilient Floor Covering Institute (www.rfci.com)

Forest Stewardship Council (www.fsc.org)

Green Globes (www.greenglobes.com)

Greenguard, Greenguard Environmental Institute (www.greenguard.org)

Green Guide for Health Care (www.gghc.org)

Green Label Testing Program, Carpet and Rug Institute (www.carpet-rug.com)

Green Seal (www.greenseal.org)

GreenSpec, Building Green Inc. (www.buildinggreen.com)

Institute for Market Transformation to Sustainability (www.mts.sustainableproducts.com)

International Code Council. "International Green Construction Code" (http://www.iccsafe.org/international-green-construction-code/)

LEED, U.S. Green Building Council (www.usgbc.org/leed)

National Institute of Standards and Technology. NIST Engineering Laboratory (www.nist.gov/el/)

Scientific Certification Systems: Green Products Certification (www.scscertified.com/gbc/index.php)

U.S. Green Building Council's Green Homes Guide (http://greenhomeguide.com/)

APPENDIX B

ANSI/Fair Housing Bathrooms and Kitchens

BATHROOMS

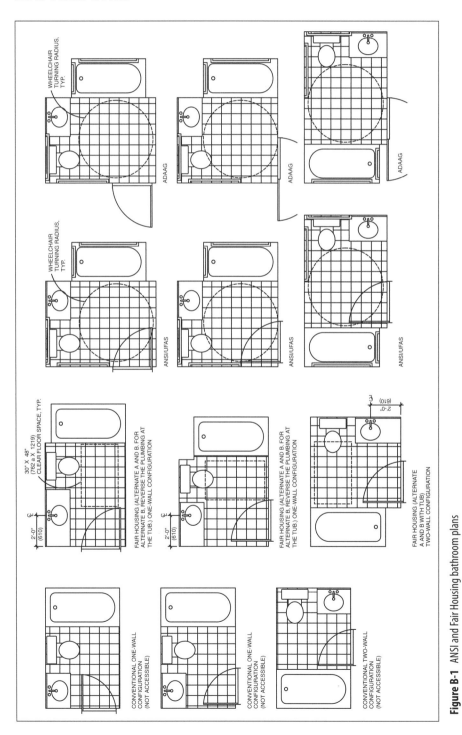

Figure B-1 ANSI and Fair Housing bathroom plans

From Ramsey/Sleeper, *Architectural Graphic Standards*, Tenth Edition, John Wiley & Sons, Hoboken, NJ, 2000; American Institute of Architects, *Architectural Graphic Standards for Residential Construction*, John Wiley & Sons, Hoboken, NJ, 2003.

KITCHENS

Figure B-2 A U-shaped counter arrangement must include a 5-foot (1524-mm) clearance between the opposing counters (or appliances or walls) in order to comply with American National Standards Institute (ANSI) standards or Uniform Federal Accessibility Standards (UFAS). The Fair Housing Amendments Act of 1988 (FHAA) guidelines require a 5-foot (1524-mm) clearance if a sink, range, or cooktop is installed in the base leg of the U. If the base leg fixture includes a knee space or removable base cabinets, the 5-foot (1524-mm) clearance is not required.

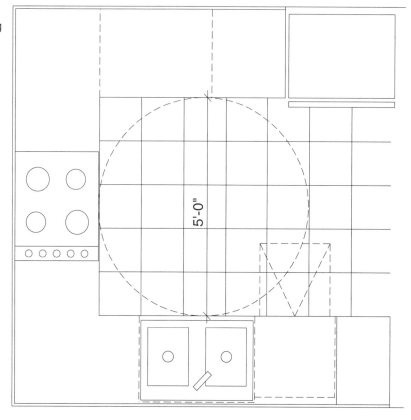

U-SHAPED KITCHEN PLAN

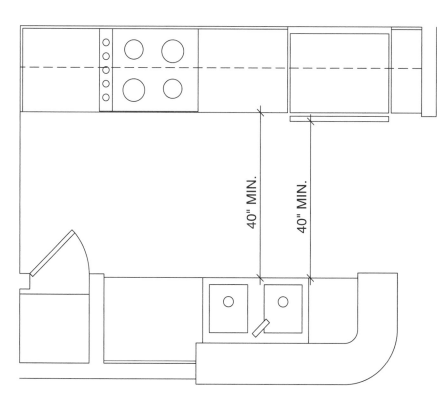

Figure B-3 ANSI and UFAS require 40 inches (1016 mm) of clearance between kitchen cabinets and opposing walls, cabinets, or appliances where the counters provide knee space. In other instances, an accessible route is required. The FHAA guidelines, however, require a 40-inch (1916-mm) clearance in all cases. Passage widths between opposing counter sides or walls and counter sides are not specifically addressed in the FHAA guidelines. If this passage's length does not exceed 24 inches (610 mm), ANSI and UFAS permit the width to be a minimum of 32 inches (813 mm).

GALLEY KITCHEN PLAN

Table B.1 Floor Space and Knee Space Requirements for Fixtures and Appliances

Appliance	Requirement	Fair Housing	ANSI/UFAS
Sink	Approach	Parallel	Parallel or front
	Knee space	No	Yes
Range/cooktop	Approach	Parallel	Parallel or front
	Knee space	No	Optional
Work space	Approach	Not required	Front
	Knee space	No	Yes
Refrigerator	Approach	Parallel or front	Parallel or front
	Knee space	No	No
Dishwasher	Approach	Parallel or front	Parallel or front
	Knee space	No	No
Oven (self-cleaning)	Approach	Parallel or front	Front
	Knee space	No	No
Oven (non-self-cleaning)	Approach	Parallel or front	Front
	Knee space	No	Yes (offset)
Trash compactor	Approach	Parallel or front	Parallel or front
	Knee space	No	No

Figure B-4 Fair Housing guidelines and most building codes require a clear floor space at most kitchen fixtures and appliances. This space can permit a parallel or a perpendicular (front) wheelchair approach, depending on the fixture or appliance selected or the decision of the designer. The U.S. Department of Housing and Urban Development (HUD) has interpreted its FHAA guidelines to require centering of the clear floor space on the appliance or fixture. This is not a requirement of the building codes, however, and may exceed the 1986 ANSI "safe harbor" for FHAA.

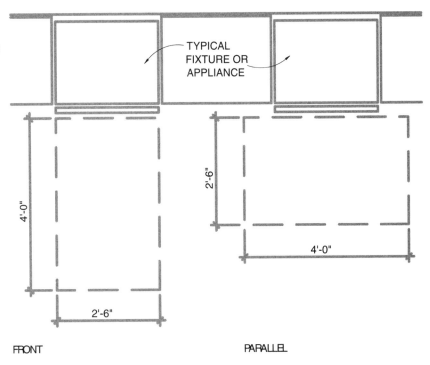

APPROACH DIAGRAM FOR FIXTURES OR APPLIANCES

Figure B-5 Locating the kitchen sink next to the dishwasher has accessibility benefits as well as functional advantages. The sink knee space provides convenient access for a wheelchair user to the adjacent dishwasher. The sink itself should be a shallow unit with easy-to-operate faucets. A tall spout and a pullout spray attachment are also recommended. Garbage disposals must be offset in order to provide full knee space under the sink.

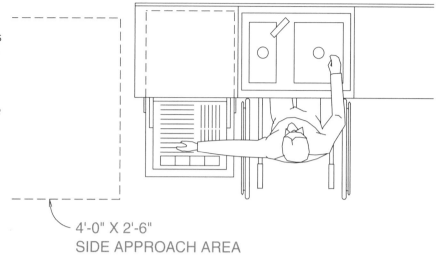

4'-0" X 2'-6"
SIDE APPROACH AREA

KITCHEN SINK AND DISHWASHER

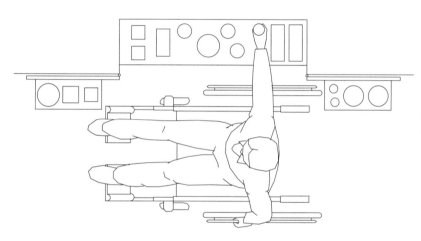

Figure B-6 The design of kitchen storage space for wheelchair users should provide both visual and physical access to wall and base cabinets, drawers, and pantries. Base cabinets, for example, can be specified to include pullout shelves or drawers that will provide easy access to items stored in the back of the cabinets. Similarly, shelf racks on pantry doors make it easier for the user to find and reach stored items.

KITCHEN STORAGE

Figure B-7 A range or cooktop should have front- or side-mounted controls so the seated user does not need to reach over the heated surfaces. A smooth cooktop surface allows pots to be slid rather than lifted on and off the burners. Separate cooktop and oven units allow the alternative of providing knee space below the cooking surface, although this arrangement can also create safety issues.

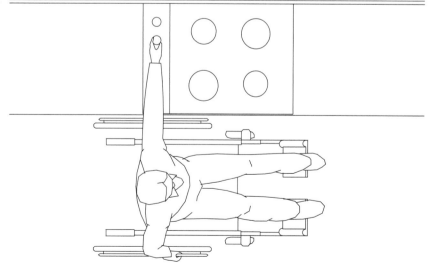

STOVES AND COOKTOPS

Figure B-8 Side-by-side models offer the user both freezer and refrigerator storage at all height levels from the floor to the top shelf. Over-and-under models can also be a satisfactory choice for many wheelchair users. Models with narrower doors are easier to operate, and the desired parallel access is easier to provide if the refrigerator doors swing back a full 180 degrees.

Figures B-5 through B-8 from Ramsey/Sleeper, **Architectural Graphic Standards**, *10th ed., John Wiley & Sons, Hoboken, NJ, 2000.*

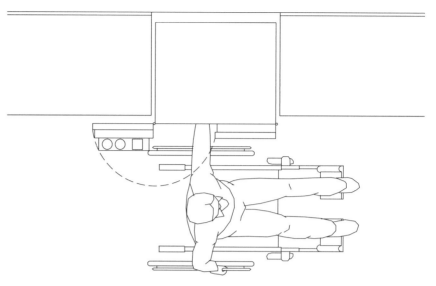

REFRIGERATORS

APPENDIX C
Seated Wheelchair Dimensions

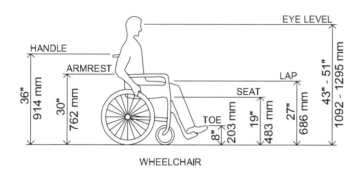

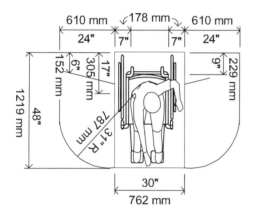
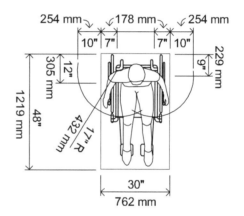
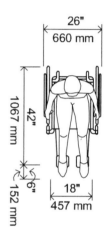

Figure C-1 Dimensional information for wheelchairs and users.

Wheelchair Transfer and Clear Floor Space at Toilet Fixtures

The clear floor space at toilets is larger than required clear space for other fixtures and varies based on the direction of approach. Many people using wheelchairs are not able to stand to transfer from the chair to the toilet, and some can transfer to and from the toilet on one side only. Some people can complete right, left, and/or front transfers. The technique used depends on which is easiest, most familiar, and safest. The transfer techniques most commonly used are the forward, perpendicular, diagonal, reverse diagonal, and parallel.

In public settings, designing for a range of users, or planning for aging in place, it is ideal to position the toilet to allow forward, perpendicular, and diagonal approaches, as shown in Figure D-1a. It is also important to understand how reverse diagonal and parallel transfers occur, as shown in Figure D-1b.

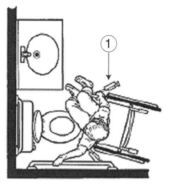

FRONT APPROACH
(Front Transfer)

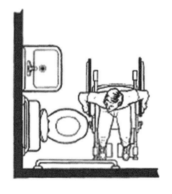

PERPENDICULAR APPROACH
(Side Transfer)

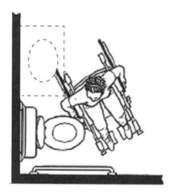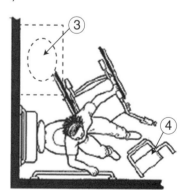

DIAGONAL APPROACH
(Probably the Most Frequently Used Unassisted
Transfer Technique)

Figure D-1a Forward perpendicular, and diagonal toilet transfer approaches.

1. User swings footrest to side and pulls chair close to toilet to transfer.
2. Armrest is removed from wheelchair so user can make a sliding side transfer more easily.
3. Vanity cabinet could prevent this type of common transfer; with the cabinet removed, 6 to 8 inches (152 to 203 mm) of the rear wheels may fit under lavatory.
4. Armrest (removed).

Figure D-1b Reverse diagonal and parallel toilet transfer approaches.

1. Sliding board.

Figures D-1a and D-1b are adapted from the Fair Housing Act Design Manual, *chapter 7, "Usable Kitchens and Bathrooms," http://www.huduser.org/portal/publications/destech/fairhousing.html.*

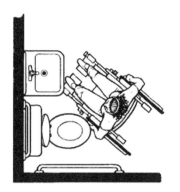

REVERSE DIAGONAL APPROACH
(DiagonalTransfer)

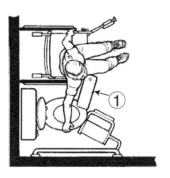

PARALLEL APPROACH
(SideTransfer Using
Sliding Board)

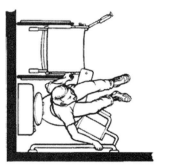

Outdoor, Secondary, and Compact Kitchens

Secondary and outdoor kitchens are of interest to some home-owners. Secondary kitchens may be full kitchens, or they may simply be kitchen components. They are typically located some distance from the primary kitchen.

Outdoor kitchens vary from little more than a well-located grill with adjacent counters to a fully equipped kitchen with a fireplace and dining area. An understanding of fixture clearance requirements and the issues mentioned in the "Organizational Flow" section of Chapter 4 is necessary when designing outdoor kitchens that go beyond the basic grill and counter setup.

In most cases, the grill or cooking area is the most important feature of the kitchen layout, with a possible outdoor sink and refrigerator completing the standard single work triangle, as shown in Figure E-1. It may be helpful to consider the outdoor kitchen as being designed around the grill, with the other elements and fixtures serving a secondary role.

The outdoor kitchen is usually located close to the house to take advantage of gas, electrical, and plumbing lines in the house. In addition, an adjacency to the indoor kitchen is typically necessary because even the most elaborate outdoor kitchens do not have the storage and preparation capacities of the indoor kitchen. Therefore, food, drinks, and dishes may need to be carried back and forth from the outdoor kitchen to the indoor kitchen.

Outdoor kitchens require lighting that is appropriate to the tasks at hand, as well as appliances and finish materials that are meant for outdoor use. When possible, outdoor kitchens should include some type of overhead shelter for protection from sun and inclement weather. Some homeowners desire outdoor fireplaces and/or wood-burning ovens (for baking) as part of the outdoor living experience.

Secondary kitchens may be desired in areas away from the main kitchen, such as recreation areas, home bar areas, home offices, or guest accommodations. The term *outpost kitchen* is used to describe mini-kitchens that exist away from the primary kitchen. In some cases, these are simply areas for brewing morning coffee, while others may provide refrigerated drinks, a microwave, and a sink. In planning a secondary or outpost kitchen, local zoning and other codes must be consulted to determine whether the secondary kitchen is permitted.

Because the secondary kitchen is generally used for less complex cooking duties than a primary kitchen, some of the required clear counter areas described in Chapter 4 may be minimized.

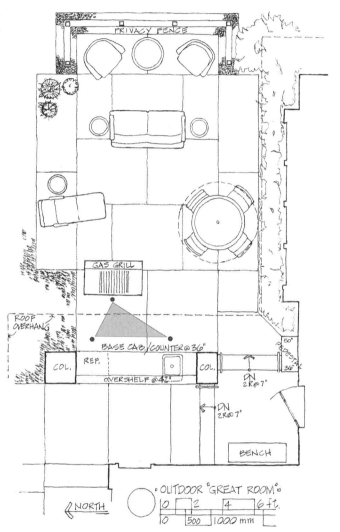

Figure E-1 An outdoor kitchen with grill, sink, and refrigerator (forming a standard single work triangle); with adjacent dining and seating areas, this becomes an outdoor great room.

Additionally, appliances and fixture sizes may be scaled down, with compact versions used. In many cases, a compact or undercounter refrigerator is used rather than a full-sized model. Cooktops are not required by many homeowners in secondary or outpost kitchens, but a microwave is used in some. Small residential projects may make use of strategies employed in designing secondary kitchens. Figure E-2 illustrates options and considerations for secondary and compact kitchens.

Figure E-2 Counter depth is typically similar to standard kitchens at 24 inches (610 mm). A range of dimensions of widths is given, with smaller compact versions listed first.

A. Prefabricated modular kitchen units are available in a range of sizes. Small versions, 48 inches (1219 mm) wide, may include a small sink, undercounter refrigerator, and cooktop. Larger versions may include a small oven and/or dishwasher and may contain base and wall cabinets.

B. Compact kitchens as shown do not provide the clear counter space required for daily cooking needs.

1. A dishwasher or undercounter refrigerator could be placed here. Compact dishwashers are 18 inches (457 mm) wide; undercounter refrigerators are 21 to 27 inches (533 to 686 mm) wide.

2. Two-burner cooktops are sometimes only 12 inches (305 mm) wide, compact ranges may be just 20 inches (508 mm) wide and sometimes contain an oven. A microwave oven could be substituted for the cooktop (some compact versions are only 18 inches (457 mm) wide; alternatively, the microwave could be placed in wall cabinets or nearby.

C. A range of dimensions for secondary kitchens, including those for required clear counter spaces described in Chapter 4. Dimensions given for appliances and sink reflect compact and full-size options, with compact sizes listed first. The clearances could be minimized, as noted below, and smaller appliances could be used. Because this is a secondary kitchen, no 36-inch (914 mm) preparation area is provided, and the single-wall layout is less problematic than in a busy primary kitchen. Some secondary kitchens are part of bar/island areas, and in some cases the sink is moved to the island or bar (shown dashed).

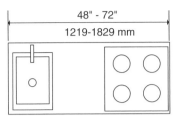

A MODULAR KITCHEN UNIT

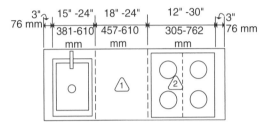

B COMPACT KITCHEN OPTIONS

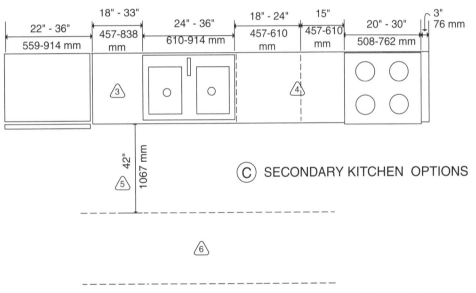

C SECONDARY KITCHEN OPTIONS

3. The 33-inch (838-mm) dimension reflects the required clear counter space for refrigerator and sink. If those are not required, providing 18 inches (457 mm) is helpful.

4. Dashed lines indicate dishwasher location and the full clear counter space required for primary kitchens as well as clear counter space required at primary cooktop. If those are not required, providing 24 inches (457 mm) between sink and cooktop is helpful.

5. A clear space of 42 inches (1067 mm) for circulation and operation of appliances should be provided.

6. Possible island or bar location; sink could move to this location.

European Cabinets

Base cabinet - carcase height 78.0 cm

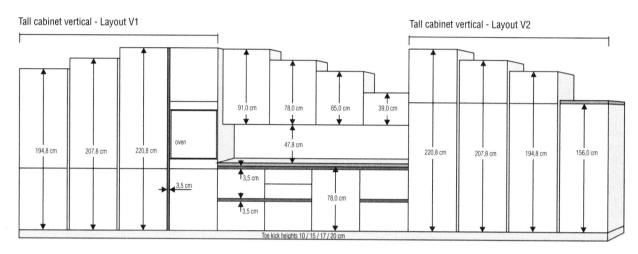

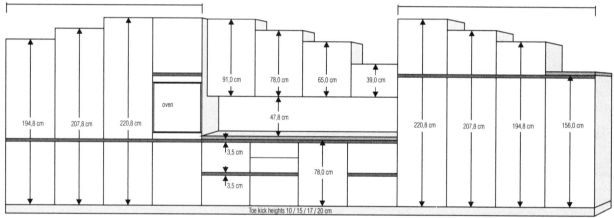

Toe kick height	Base cabinet - carcase height	Countertop height*	Tall cabinet - carcase height	Tall cabinet height
10 cm	78,0 cm	92,0 cm	156,0 cm 194,8 cm 207,8 cm 220,8 cm	166,0 cm 204,8 cm 217,8 cm 230,8 cm
15 cm	78,0 cm	97,0 cm	156,0 cm 194,8 cm 207,8 cm 220,8 cm	171,0 cm 209,8 cm 222,8 cm 235,8 cm
17 cm	78,0 cm	99,0 cm	156,0 cm 194,8 cm 207,8 cm 220,8 cm	173,0 cm 211,8 cm 224,8 cm 237,8 cm
20 cm	78,0 cm	102,0 cm	156,0 cm 194,8 cm 207,8 cm 220,8 cm	176,0 cm 214,8 cm 227,8 cm 240,8 cm
Carcase depths				
Base cabinets	35,4 cm	46 cm	61 cm	71 cm
Tall cabinets	35,4 cm	46 cm	61 cm	
Wall cabinets	35,4 cm			

Figure F-1 Sampling of dimensional information for European cabinets.

Courtesy of SieMatic.

* by 4 cm countertop thickness.

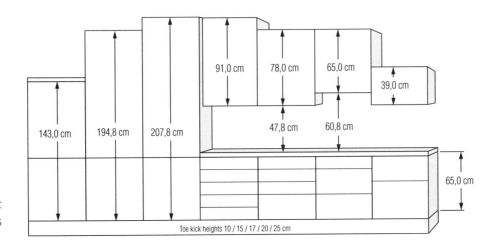

ED: Place this text in toe kick area, as on p 258 ?

Toe kick height	Base cabinet - carcase height	Countertop height*	Tall cabinet - carcase height	Tall cabinet height
10 cm	65,0 cm	79,0 cm	143,0 cm 194,8 cm 207,8 cm	153,0 cm 204,8 cm 217,8 cm
15 cm	65,0 cm	84,0 cm	143,0 cm 194,8 cm 207,8 cm	158,0 cm 209,8 cm 222,8 cm
17 cm	65,0 cm	86,0 cm	143,0 cm 194,8 cm 207,8 cm	160,0 cm 211,8 cm 224,8 cm
20 cm	65,0 cm	89,0 cm	143,0 cm 194,8 cm 207,8 cm	163,0 cm 214,8 cm 227,8 cm
25 cm	65,0 cm	94,0 cm	143,0 cm 194,8 cm 207,8 cm	168,0 cm 219,8 cm 232,8 cm

Carcase depth**				
Base cabinets	35,4 cm	46 cm	56 cm*	71 cm
Tall cabinets	35,4 cm	46 cm	56 cm*	
Wall cabinets	35,4 cm			

**Carcase depth 61 cm available without surcharge.

Figure F-1 *(continued)*

APPENDIX G

Seated and Standing Work Surfaces and Desks

In terms of size, the ideal work surface (or desk) will, at a minimum, accommodate the work to be done. However, frequently used items must be within the functional arm reach (i.e., that area within comfortable reach of the user's arm).

The functional arm reach creates an area called the work space envelope, and the items used most frequently for the tasks at hand should be located within this envelope. For typical office activities, this includes, at a minimum, room for a monitor (or laptop), keyboard, and mouse, as well as the necessary reference items. Combined, these items typically take up at least 30 inches (762 mm). For specialized workstations such as those for art or sewing, the items used most frequently, such as a sewing machine or art surface, should be located within the work space envelope.

Additional considerations involve designing the visual work space, which involves planning the location of items that are viewed frequently. Items such as computer monitors should be placed within 18 to 24 inches (457 to 610 mm) of the user. See Figure G-1 for an illustration of the functional arm reach and visual work space.

Desk and work surface heights vary depending on the height of users. When planning a *seated* desk height for a specific user, the height of that user should be considered. When planning a desk for a range of users, a height in the range of 25 to 30 inches (635 to 762 mm) can be used. Freestanding desks are often 29 inches (737 mm) high.

In some cases, a *standing* work surface or desk is best. This is true in cases where users have work or reference items spread out over several surfaces (allowing them to walk between the items), where users need to move their bodies along with their arms for certain hobbies or tasks, and where items used may require a reach longer than the standard seated reach. For planning purposes, a height of 38 to 44 inches (965 to 1118 mm) is reasonable, with adults on either side of that range.

Some individuals find that a standing work surface can relieve the fatigue and pain associated with being seated for long periods of time. Standing desk heights are also advocated for some as more healthful than seated postures, and there are advocates for walking on a treadmill while working on a standing height work surface.

See Figure G-1 for an illustration of work surface heights.

WORK SURFACE AND DESK
DIMENSIONS
NOT WHEELCHAIR ACCESSIBLE

SEATED AND STANDING
WORK HEIGHTS

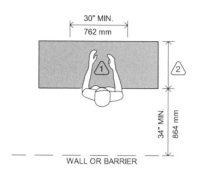

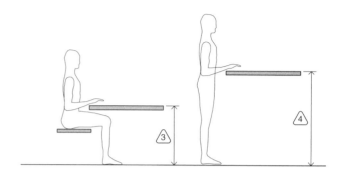

FREESTANDING FURNITURE DIMENSIONS ⑤

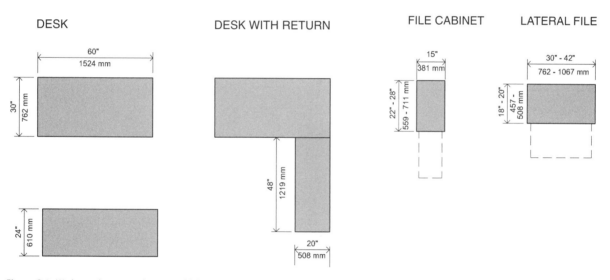

Figure G-1 Work area dimensions (not accessible).

1. Items used frequently must be placed within the user's functional arm reach, which, for adults, is between 15 and 18 inches (381 and 457 mm). This image does not include a keyboard tray, which may be preferred by some. A minimum knee space 24 inches (610 mm) wide by 22 inches (559 mm) deep must be provided; more space is recommended. The visual work area is also located here. Computer monitors should be placed within comfortable viewing distance, which varies widely depending on the individual; guidelines vary from 20 to 30 inches (500 to 762 mm). Books and papers are more comfortably read at a closer range.

2. Required depth is dependent on the type of work done and the functional arm reach; 24 inches (610 mm) is a minimum depth (in most situations); 30 inches (762 mm) is a common choice.

3. Optimum seated work surface height varies widely, with 27 to 30 inches (635 to 762 mm) being common options, with some adults on either side of that range. Freestanding desks are commonly 29 inches (737 mm) high from floor to top of desk. Computer monitors should be placed so that they are 20 to 50 percent below horizontal eye level and do not create back or neck strain.

4. Standing work surface height varies widely from 38 to 42 inches (635 to 762 mm), with some adults on either side of that range. Computer monitors should be placed so that they are 20 to 50 percent below horizontal eye level and do not create back or neck strain.

5. These dimensions are based on widely available furnishing sizes; individual models may vary, and the examples given are for preliminary planning purposes only. For example, desks and credenzas may be 72 inches (1829 mm) wide or wider and in varying depths.

INDEX

A

B

Luminaires, 17–19, 57, 59, 63–65, 111–114, 147, 185–187, 200. *See also* Lighting (light fixtures)
    defined, 17

M

Mace, Ron, 6
Mansard roof, 232
Major preparation area (kitchen), 70, 71, 72, 115, 117, 257
Material symbols (architecture), 25
Maximum height (zoning), 245
McDonough Braungart Chemistry (MBCD), 9
McDonough, William, 9, 10
Mechanical systems, 223, 227, 240. *See also* Electrical and mechanical
Media rooms, 51, 52, 55. *See also* Leisure spaces
    screen viewing, 55
Mendelsohn, Marc, 167
Metal frame sinks, 76, 77
Microwave ovens, 70–72, 79–81, 83, 84, 95–98, 103, 104, 115–122, 256, 257
Millwork (on drawings), 213, 217, 218, 219
Minimum room areas, 14, 62, 140
Minnesota Sustainable Building Guidelines, 10
"Miracles" (Walt Whitman), 1
M.O. (masonry openings), 26
Model codes, 9, 10, 13, 246
Modular showers, 163, 166, 167, 181, 183
Mudrooms, 29, 30, 32, 33, 59–61, 188, 189–191, 201–203
    options (checklist), 189, 190
Multiple-panel doors, 228, 229

N

National Association of Home Builders (NAHB), 2, 11, 12, 149, 169
National Average Cost vs. Value Report, 243, 244
National Electrical Code, 110
National Kitchen and Bath Association (NKBA), 70, 74, 99
Net Zero Energy Buildings (NZEB), 9, 12
Newman, Oscar, 3–5
NKBA, *see* National Kitchen and Bath Association
Nosings, stairs, 34, 35, 40, 41, 47, 48
The Not So Big House (Sarah Susanka), 2, 149

O

One-panel doors, 228
Organizational flow, 1, 5, 12, 29
    bathrooms, 176–179
    bedrooms, 133–140

circulation spaces, 42–46
    kitchens, 142–157
    leisure spaces, 56–62
    utility spaces, 196
Orthographic projections, 22, 23, 203–221
Outdoor kitchens, 66, 67, 109, 256, 257
    Outpost kitchens, 109, 256, 257
Outlets, electric (duplex receptacle), 14, 15, 49, 63, 221, 227, 240
    accessible, 15, 111
    for bathrooms 15, 170, 185, 187
    for bedrooms, 146, 147
    on electrical and lighting plans, 25, 221
    for kitchens, 110–112, 114
    for leisure spaces, 63
    for utility spaces, 193, 197, 225, 226
Ovens, 72, 79–84, 95–98, 100, 101, 104, 107, 113–114, 117, 118, 122, 123, 203, 250, 251, 256–258
    accessibility for, 84, 98
    kitchen counter clearances, 97, 98
    microwave, 70–72, 79–81, 83, 84, 95–98, 103, 104, 115–122, 256, 257

P

Paint-to-paint dimensions, 209
Panero, Julius, 12
Pantry, 42, 60, 61, 66, 69, 91, 99, 100, 108, 109, 116–118, 124, 126, 133, 135, 139–142, 169, 190, 198, 202, 203, 251
Parlors, 51. *See also* Leisure spaces
A Pattern Language (Christopher Alexander), 3, 29
Pedestal sink, 155, 156
Pendant lighting, 18, 50, 59, 63–65, 112, 146, 186, 200
Personal distance, 4, 5
Personal space, 4, 5
A Philosophy of Interior Design (Stanley Abercrombie), 29
Piers, 223
Pivoting grab bars, 154,
Placement of furnishings, *see* Organizational flow
Plante, Ellen M., 66
Platforms, 223–226
    concrete slab, 223, 224
    wood, 223, 225
Plumbing, 15. *See also* Electrical and mechanical
    in bathrooms, 150, 151, 159, 165, 169, 176, 177–179, 181, 183, 184
    in laundry rooms (utility rooms), 188, 190, 197
    IRC code for, 206
Pocket sliding doors, 23, 134, 135, 140, 145, 175, 177, 179–183, 207, 224, 228, 229
Pollutants, 10, 11

V

W

Z